Countries &
Continents

QUESTIONS & ANSWERS

Countries & Continents

THE COUNTRIES AND CONTINENTS ON EARTH

Herbert Genzmer • Christian Schütz

Bath · New York · Singapore · Hong Kong · Cologne · Delhi · Melbourne

Introduction

Since time immemorial, humankind has displayed a burning desire to learn about the world's countries and continents. This book, which proposes a guided tour of planet Earth through a succession of stimulating questions and answers, is designed to help readers do just that. Succinct questions and clear, memorable explanations make for an extremely interesting and entertaining read for the whole family. As well as providing a vast amount of enjoyment, the chosen format will also help readers retain a wealth of facts and background information.

Arranged by continent, this book paints a picture of each of the Earth's nations in words and photographs. A summary of the key data relating to a particular country is followed by a series of interesting questions and straightforward answers concerning that country's history, geography, politics, economy, and culture. Our aim was to create a useful and fascinating reference work, and, despite the necessary concision, we believe the book succeeds in painting a fact-based portrait of each country that provides the reader with a reliable overview and reveals many unusual aspects at the same time.

The word "continent" (from the Latin *terra continens*, meaning "connected land") is generally understood to mean a large, self-contained landmass separated by water from other such landmasses. As long ago as antiquity, attempts were made to divide the world and its landmasses into continents. Greek historian and geographer Herodotus (484–424 BC) split the world into three continents: Europe, Asia, and Libya (Africa).

Today the world can be subdivided according to a number of different geographical models (five, six, and seven-continent versions) depending on whether a topographical, geological or historico-political approach is being adopted. From a geological perspective, for example, Europe and Asia form a single continent (Eurasia) because they are part of the same, connected, landmass, most of which rests on the same tectonic plate. From a historico-political viewpoint, however, they display such significant

Background: Brooklyn Bridge against the impressive skyline of New York City on the East Coast of the United States of America.

differences in terms of development and cultural manifestations that they are generally regarded as two different continents. We have adopted the seven-continent model because it gives the most differentiated picture. Taking the Greenwich Meridian as its starting point, the book begins by examining the continents of the Northern Hemisphere (in the order Europe, Asia, North America) before moving to the Southern Hemisphere (South America, Africa, Australia). The final chapter is devoted to the Earth's polar regions: the Arctic and Antarctica.

Each chapter starts with physical and political maps of the relevant continent. These maps give an overview of the position of the individual countries and their spatial relationships with each other. The order in which the countries are presented is based on their geographical position within the continent—from north to south and west to east. Each continent has also been divided into geographical "subgroups." Europe, for example, has been split into northern, western, central, eastern, southern, and southeastern regions.

Neuschwanstein Castle in Germany is just one of countless European castles that have survived to the present day.

The chapter on South America takes the reader on a quest for lost civilizations and their special sites, such as the legendary Inca city Machu Picchu in modern-day Peru.

National parks such as the Amboseli National Park in Kenya are extremely important for tourism in Africa. A significant proportion of the populations of many countries in what is the second-largest continent live below the poverty line.

A total of 194 countries is described—all 193 states currently recognized by the United Nations (UN), plus Taiwan, which, although not yet recognized by all the nations of the world, has been conducting its own affairs since 1952. Under international law, states are deemed to have been recognized once the population (national people) of a geographically defined area (national territory) is governed by a sovereign administration (state authority) and the country is free to establish diplomatic relations with other states.

The most recent country to join the UN is Montenegro, which achieved independence in June 2006. Autonomous areas represented by their parent states in foreign affairs only (e.g. Greenland or the Faroe Islands, which belong politically to Denmark) have been dealt with under the country by which they are represented.

The panel at the head of each entry displays the national flag and provides information on the country's currency, political system, capital city, languages (official language as well as any others widely spoken in the country), surface area, population, religion (religious faiths observed by more than five per cent of the population and

the percentage of those not belonging to any denomination where this figure is particularly high), and any unusual geographical or geological features. These information panels are designed to help readers compare the individual countries with one another. The country pages also feature special topic boxes that look at a particular issue in depth.

The final section of the book provides a summary of all these facts and figures and more, and compares the different countries in terms of size, population, economy, distribution of religions, climate, geographical and political peculiarities, colonial history, and crisis regions.

The book's authors and editors have made every effort to collate the most up-to-date facts and figures from reliable sources, including the publications of national and international organizations, but sometimes (in the case of many developing countries,

for example) it is only possible to get hold of out-of-date statistics. Other countries (e.g. socialist North Korea) hold information back for political reasons and the same is often true of warring nations or nations recently hit by natural catastrophes. But it is not only statistical data such as population figures and religious affiliation that occasionally have to be based on estimates or older surveys. Surface area measurements can also fluctuate. This may be because new land surveys have been undertaken (something industrialized nations do far more frequently than less developed nations). In the case of significant discrepancies, however, it may also be because disputed territories have been attributed to different claimants.

We wish all our readers a pleasant journey to destinations near and far and an exciting time learning more about lands both familiar and unfamiliar.

The continent of Australia comprises far more countries than simply the country of the same name (shown here is Sydney's famous skyline). It also includes the many island nations of Micronesia and Polynesia.

Sweden

Czech Republic

France

Netherlands

EUROPE

From a strictly geographical point of view, Europe is not a continent but a subcontinent of the vast landmass known as Eurasia. The reasons for classifying it as a continent in its own right—at 4.05 million sq miles (10.5 million sq km) the second smallest after Australia— are cultural and historical. These cultural and historical factors have been and still are powerful enough for 46 different countries speaking 120 languages to be regarded as a single unit. Europe's most powerful political structure is the European Union (EU).

Germany

Ireland

Greece

PHYSICAL MAP

Greenland

▲12,139 ft
Gunnbjørn Fjeld

Greenland Sea

Spitzbergen

Novaya Zemlya

Kara Sea

Yamal Peninsula

Arctic Ocean

Barents Sea

Ural Mountains

Ob

Reykjavik
Iceland

Norwegian Sea

Lake Inari

Kola Peninsula

▲6,214 ft
Mount Narodnaya

Pechora

Scandinavian Mountains

Torne

Ume

Atlantic Ocean

Ireland
Dublin

United Kingdom

North Sea

Glama

Oslo

Lake Vänern

Lake Ladoga

Lake Onega

Helsinki

Rybinsk Reservoir

Volga

Moscow

Pega

Stockholm

Tallinn

Lake Peipus

Lake Vättern

Riga

Baltic Sea

Jutland

Copenhagen

Vilnius

Minsk

London
Thames

Amsterdam

Berlin

Weser

Elbe

Oder

Warsaw

Rhine

Vistula

Kiev

Don

Dnieper

Volga

Ural

Azores

Brussels

Luxembourg

Paris

Seine

Loire

Prague

8,711 ft
Bratislava

Carpathians

Chișinău

Sea of Azov

Caspian Sea

Danube

Bern

6187 ft
Mont Dore

15,771 ft
Mont Blanc

Grossglockner
Vienna
12,461 ft

A L P S

Budapest

Lake Balaton

Moldoveanu
8,346 ft

Crimea

Caucasus

Elbrus
Tbilisi

Po

Ljubljana

Zagreb

Bucharest

Rhône

Pyrenees

11,168 ft
Pico de Aneto

Appenines

Adriatic Ocean

Sarajevo Belgrade

Danube

Black Sea

Pontic Mountains

Yerevan

14,864 ft
Ararat

Madrid

Ebro

Tagus

Corsica

Rome

Podgorica

Sofia

Rhodope Mountain Range

Ankara

Lake Van

Lake Urmia

Lisbon

Balearic Islands

Tyrrhenian Sea

Sardinia

Tirana

Skopje

9,570 ft
Mt. Olympus

Aegean Sea

Taurus

Euphrates

Tigris

Mulhacén
▲11,421 ft

Mediterranean

Algiers

Tunisia

10,902 ft
Etna Sicily

Ionian Sea

Pindus Mountains

Athens
Peloponnese

Nicosia
Cyprus

Beirut

Baghdad

Rabat

High Atlas

Saharan Atlas

Malta

Crète

Sea

Damascus

Amman

Jerusalem

Tripoli

1:28 000 000

Greenland
(associated with Denmark)

Spitzbergen
(Norway)

Longyearbyen

Greenland Sea

Arctic Ocean

Novaya Zemlya

Kara Sea

Barents Sea

Vorkuta

Hammerfest

Murmansk

Norwegian Sea

Reykjavik
Iceland

Atlantic Ocean

Lake
Inari

Narvik

Torne

Arkhangel'sk

Ob

Pechora

Luleå

Faroes
(Denmark)

Ume

Finland

Shetland Islands
(UK)

Sweden

Tampere

Lake
Onega

Perm

Norway

Bergen

Glama

Oslo

Turku

Helsinki

St. Petersburg

R u s s i a

Ufa

Lake Vänern

Stockholm

Tallinn

Rybinsk
Reservoir

Kazan

Glasgow

Gothenburg

Estonia

Lake
Peipus

Nizhniy
Novgorod

**Northern
Ireland**

Edinburgh

Belfast

Lake
Vättern

Denmark

Malmö

Riga

Latvia

Volga

Moscow

Samara

**United
Kingdom**

Ireland

Copenhagen

Lithuania

Vilnius

Cork

Dublin

Liverpool

Odense

Leeds

Kaliningrad

Manchester

Sheffield

Gdańsk

Minsk

Kazakhstan

Cardiff

Birmingham

Netherlands
Amsterdam

Bremen

Hamburg

Poznań

Belarus

Ural

North Sea

London

Thames

Hanover

Berlin

Warsaw

Belgium

Rotterdam

Germany

Łódź

Rhine

Leipzig

Don

Le Havre

Brussels

Bonn

Cologne

Dresden

Poland

Kraków

Lviv

Kiev

Kharkiv

Volgograd

Volga

Lux.

Frankfurt

Elbe

**Czech
Republic**

Prague

Wrocław

Vistula

Luxembourg

Paris

Strasbourg

Stuttgart

Brno

Slovakia

Ukraine

Dnieper

Astrakhan

Nantes

Seine

Munich

Bratislava

Dnipropetrovs'k

Rostov

Danube

Linz

Loire

**Liechten-
stein**

Austria

Vienna

Hungary

Moldova

Chişinău

Sea of
Azov

Caspian Sea

France

Lyon

Bern

Switzerland

Graz

Budapest

Cluj-Napoca

Odessa

40° N

Bordeaux

Turin

Milan

Slovenia

Ljubljana

Lake
Balaton

Romania

Timişoara

Braşov

Bilbao

Andorra

Venice

Croatia

Zagreb

Bucharest

Black Sea

Varna

Toulouse

Genoa

**San
Marino**

**Bosnia and
Herzegovina**

Serbia

Belgrade

Danube

Porto

Florence

Monaco

Marseille

Sarajevo

Montenegro

Sofia

Portugal

Zaragoza

Ebro

Corsica

Italy

Podgorica

Priština

Bulgaria

Tagus

Madrid

Barcelona

Vatican
City

Rome

*Ionian
Sea*

Tirana

Skopje

Macedonia

Istanbul

Lisbon

Tyrrhenian Sea

Albania

Thessaloniki

T u r k e y

Lake Van

Spain

Naples

Palermo

Greece

*Aegean
Sea*

Lake Tuz

Lake
Urmia

Seville

Valencia

Patrai

Athens

Euphrates

Tigris

Gibraltar
(UK)

M e d i t e r r a n e a n   S e a

Nicosia

Malta

1:28 000 000

Introduction

What are the so-called gateways to Europe?
The traditional points of access to Europe are Gibraltar in the west, the Bosporus in the east, and the Suez Canal in the south. Europe is bounded to the north and northwest by the Arctic, the Atlantic Ocean, and the North and Baltic seas.

Where is Europe's eastern extremity?
The Urals are generally considered to be Europe's eastern boundary. This mountain range and its foothills extend from the Arctic Circle in the north through Russia and Kazakhstan to the Caspian Sea in the south.

Why do most European countries benefit from a good climate?
Western Europe owes its mild climate to the warm Gulf Stream. The Alps and Pyrenees form a natural east-west barrier that prevents cold air from the north penetrating further south. Another factor is the warm Mediterranean Sea, which influences the whole of southern Europe, giving it a warm and

Background: The imposing, ice-capped Wetterhorn, which rises to 12,113 ft (3,692 m) and towers above Grindelwald in the Bernese Alps (Switzerland).
Below: Portugal's Algarve coast is a popular destination for holidaymakers. Once an idyllic fishing village, Albufeira is now a much-loved holiday resort.

> **The Alps**
>
> The curve of the Alps is dominated by the Mont Blanc Massif. At 15,768 ft (4,806 m), Mont Blanc is Europe's highest peak. The region's countless mountain rivers are used to generate electricity for industry and the Alpine landscapes attract over 100 million visitors a year from all over the world in winter and summer alike. The downside of this constant stream of visitors is the adverse impact of construction (e.g. new skiing areas, building complexes, and roads) on the area's delicate ecology. Slovenia, Italy, Austria, Liechtenstein, Germany, Switzerland, and France are well aware of the enormous economic and ecological significance of the mountain range (Europe's highest) they share. Environmentalists warn of the dangers of excessive exploitation and overdevelopment of the Alps, but, as so often, mankind's greed regularly prevails.

pleasant climate. Only to the east does a cooler, continental climate prevail.

Which geological forces were responsible for shaping Europe's landscape?
Europe's landscape was formed by colliding tectonic plates and the retreating glaciers of the last Ice Age. The rugged Alps were formed 65 million years ago when the African plate began to collide with the Eurasian plate. Repeated earthquakes and eruptions

occurred as the tectonic plates moved apart again. Although the Ice Age ended 10,000 years ago, the Alpine glaciers have not yet completely melted away.

Are there any volcanoes in Europe?
Volcanoes have also played an important part in shaping the landscape and are to be found in many European countries. Iceland alone has over 2,000. At 10,991 ft (3,350 m), Mount Etna, on the island of Sicily, is Europe's highest and best known. It covers a surface area of 580 sq miles (1,500 sq km), and, since its creation around 2.5 million years ago, has erupted on average 15 times a year. Over the last 100 years, five major eruptions have devastated the surrounding villages and farmland.

What feeds Europe's largest rivers?
Europe's major rivers, such as the Danube, the Rhine, the Rhône, and the Po, are fed mainly by Alpine glaciers.

Why has Europe played such an important role in world exploration over the centuries?
Viewed on a map, the continent of Europe looks like an agglomeration of bays and peninsulas. The European coastline, formed by four seas and two oceans, provides numerous countries with direct access to the sea. This explains Europe's long history of seafarers, explorers, and merchants and, in turn, its wealth and influence over the rest of the world.

The deep, narrow inlets of the fjords bring seawater far into Norway's interior as here in Finnmark, the country's least populated county.

Interesting facts

- The original vegetation of Europe's temperate and Mediterranean zones has all but disappeared.

- Around a third of all Europeans describe themselves as non-religious and approximately five per cent are atheists.

- In 1950, four European cities (London, Paris, Milan and Naples) were among the 20 largest in the world. This is no longer the case. Most European cities have stopped growing and many are actually declining due to a general reduction in population.

- Moscow is now Europe's largest city.

- A period of major cultural and economic achievement began in the Mediterranean region (and slightly later in northern and eastern Europe) during the Neolithic and Bronze Ages.

of Europe (above all Germany and Slovakia), the EU as a whole has recently started to see a degree of natural growth once more. The reason for this modest increase is that life expectancy is steadily rising, thereby counterbalancing the general reduction in the birth rate observable in particular since the 1950s. Specialists in European demographics are predicting that between now and 2050 the population of the 27 EU states will fall from around 460 million to an estimated 450 million.

Stonehenge (circa 3100–2000 BC), in the county of Wiltshire in England, has not yet given up all its secrets. It is still not known for certain why the stone circle was erected.

Background: St Basil's Cathedral in Moscow is a breathtaking example of Russian 16th-century architecture.

What is the population of Europe?
With over 680 million inhabitants, the world's second-smallest continent has a larger population than Australia, North America, and South America combined. The average population density is 168 people per sq mile (65 people per sq km), although the northern and eastern parts of the continent are significantly more sparsely populated than its western and central areas.

How is Europe's population likely to develop in the 21st century?
Despite very low birth rates in certain parts

Why is unemployment steadily rising in some European countries?

Europe has deposits of raw materials that it extracts and exploits, but ever since the industrial revolution the key to its prosperity has been its manufacturing and consumer goods industry. In the 1960s Europe's industrial nations started to satisfy the demand for additional labor by importing workers from southern Europe. As affluence increased, so too did wages, while at the same time the world economy was becoming ever more globalized. As a result, many industries decided to shift production to low-wage countries abroad. This in turn has caused unemployment to rise in many European countries over the last few years.

What ecological problems does Europe face?

Ever since the beginning of the industrial revolution around 200 years ago, atmospheric pollution has been steadily increasing. Because of its high population density, advanced state of development, prosperity (large numbers of automobiles), and industrial density, Europe is one of the world's worst polluters. Smog is making people sick and acid rain is destroying the forests. There is also a discrepancy in attitudes between western and eastern Europe. While the west is making considerable efforts to tackle the problems, outdated industrial plants are still operating in many parts of the east. These are polluting not just the entire continent but the entire world.

The 177-ft-high (54-m) St Mathieu lighthouse near Brest (Brittany, France). The 16th-century monastery was plundered and destroyed during the French Revolution.

What is the European Union?

The European Union (EU) came into being with the Maastricht Treaty of 1993 but its history goes back considerably further. The first union between European countries was the European Coal and Steel Community (ECSC), formed in 1951 by Germany, Italy, France, Luxembourg, Belgium, and the Netherlands. This was followed by Euratom (the European Atomic Energy Community) and the European Economic Community (EEC) which were established by the Treaty of Rome in 1957 and permitted the free circulation of people, goods, and services across borders. Following expansion eastwards between 2004 and 2007, the EU now has 27 member states.

ICELAND

Flag

Currency
1 Icelandic króna (ISK) = 100 aurar

System of government
Republic since 1944

Capital
Reykjavík

Languages
Icelandic (official language)

Surface area
39,769 sq miles (103,000 sq km)

Population 297,000

Religion 93% Protestant (Lutheran)

Notable features
Iceland is the world's largest volcanic island.

How thick is the ice sheet that covers Iceland?

Some 11 per cent of Iceland's surface area is still covered by plateau glaciers. Unlike Greenland's ice sheet, they are not remnants of the last Ice Age but were formed during the Holocene period, which began around 11,700 years ago. Iceland's glaciers are approximately 3,300 ft (1,000 m) thick—entire mountains lie buried within them. Measuring 3,200 sq miles (8,300 sq km), the Vatnajökull in the southeast of the country is Iceland's largest glacier.

What are geysers?

Geysers are hot springs that shoot water and steam into the air like fountains. The phenomenon takes its name from one geyser in particular, Iceland's Geysir. The island is often referred to as the "Land of Geysers" although it has only two major examples. A large number of geysers can also be found in the Yellowstone National Park in the United States.

How densely is Iceland populated?

The interior is almost devoid of people; only a narrow strip around the coast is inhabited. About 93 per cent of the population live in the towns and cities and almost two thirds of all Icelanders live in the capital (greater Reykjavík area), where most of the service-sector jobs are based. This sector now accounts for 72 per cent of all employment.

When did Iceland become an independent state?

Having belonged to Denmark since the 14th century, Iceland was granted a degree of autonomy in 1904 but the independent Republic of Iceland was not founded until 1944. It joined the UN in 1946.

The aurora borealis above the port of Njardvik. This wonderful natural phenomenon occurs when electrically charged particles collide with the upper layers of the Earth's atmosphere. In the Northern Hemisphere it is only observable north of 60 degrees latitude.

Elves

For most people, elves are mythical creatures who live in Fairyland. In Iceland, it is not generally doubted that they really exist. Their habitat is protected by a special Elves Representative whose job is to ensure that the shy elves are not frightened away by clumsy human intrusion into the natural environment. A road near Reykjavík, for example, makes a detour in order to avoid a hill believed to be the home of elves.

NORWAY

Flag	**Population** 4.7 million
	Religion 86% Protestant (Lutheran)
Currency	**Notable features**
1 Norwegian krone (NOK) = 100 øre	In addition to its national territory,
System of government	Norway also possesses the following
Constitutional monarchy since 1905	territories: Svalbard (23,561 sq miles/
Capital Oslo	61,022 sq km), Jan Mayen Island
Languages	(146 sq miles/377 sq km), and the
Norwegian (Bokmål and Nynorsk)	Bilandet (dependencies) of Bouvet Island
(official languages)	(19 sq miles/49 sq km), Peter I Island
Surface area	(60 sq miles/156 sq km), and Queen
125,003 sq miles (323,758 sq km)	Maud Land in the Antarctic
	(1.08 million sq miles/2.8 million sq km).

What are Bokmål and Nynorsk?

Bokmål and Nynorsk are Norway's two official written languages. Bokmål ("book language") is the most widespread form. It is based on Dano-Norwegian and was developed from standard written Danish. It is the main language spoken in Oslo and the larger towns and cities. Nynorsk ("new Norwegian") was codified from Norwegian dialects and is spoken by around 10 to 15 per cent of the population, predominantly on the west coast. It is also used in government documents.

What are fjords?

Fjords are sea inlets that extend a far distance inland. They were originally valleys formed by glaciers during the Ice Age and became flooded with water when the ice melted. In addition to Norway, fjords can be found along the coasts of British Columbia, western Patagonia, New Zealand, and Greenland.

What was the Kalmar Union?

The Kalmar Union was a close alliance (through marriage and inheritance) between the three kingdoms of Norway, Denmark, and Sweden that lasted from 1397 to 1523. It came into being largely at the instigation of Denmark, which wanted to extend its influence in the Baltic region. Present-day Finland, which belonged at that time to Sweden, was also part of the Kalmar Union, as was Iceland and the Faroe Islands (which were then Norwegian). The union fell apart when Sweden gained its independence.

Is Norway in the EU?

No. The people of Norway have voted on whether to join the EU in two plebiscites. The outcome each time was a narrow majority against.

To what does the country owe its prosperity?

Norway is the world's seventh-largest producer and third-largest exporter of petroleum, having started to exploit its reserves in 1969. Large-scale production, high world market prices, and the country's relatively low population are all factors that contribute to Norway's high per capita income.

Bergen, with a population of around 250,000, is Norway's second-largest city.

Interesting facts
• In 2007 Oslo was the world's most expensive city and Norway the country with the highest standard of living.
• Norway has one of the highest birth rates in Europe.
• Norway is one of the few countries that still permits whaling.

SWEDEN

Flag

Currency
1 Swedish krona (SEK) = 100 öre

System of government
Constitutional monarchy since 1809

Capital
Stockholm

Languages
Swedish (official language), Finnish, Sami

Surface area
173,732 sq miles (449,964 sq km)

Population 9 million

Religion 85% Protestant (Lutheran)

Notable features
The country has around 221,800 islands.

A typical country house made of timber in a wintry Södermanland Province.

What is the significance of the Swedish "Principle of Publicity"?

All official government documents are made available to the people through publication in the press. No one is expected to give a reason or present identification in order to view information of this kind. This right has been guaranteed since 1766, when what is effectively the world's oldest freedom of information act came into force.

What is an ombudsman?

The system of ombudsmen was born in Sweden and is an institution designed to protect the rights of the citizen against the state authorities. Anyone who feels he or she has been unfairly treated can seek representation from the appropriate ombudsman. There are now ombudsmen for consumer protection, child protection, equal opportunities, and racial and sexual discrimination.

Is the summer solstice celebrated in Sweden?

The *Midsommarfest* is a lavish celebration held in Sweden on the first Friday night after June 21. At this time of year the sun never sets in the north of the country and even in the south there are only a few hours of darkness. Dancing around a decorated May tree—the Swedish national symbol—plays an important part in the celebrations.

The small, vegetation-free islands that dot the coastline are called skerries. Like the fjords, they were created during the last Ice Age. The Stockholm Archipelago alone comprises 24,000 islands.

Interesting facts: Nature and the environment

- The islands of Gotland and Öland boast a diverse flora including an astonishingly wide variety of orchids.
- Sweden was the first country in Europe to establish nature conservation areas (starting in 1910).
- 52 per cent of the country is covered by forest.

Why is Finland known as the "Land of 1,000 Lakes"?

The last Ice Age, which ended some 10,000 years ago, left a strong mark on the Finnish landscape. Already flat, the country was polished even smoother by the advancing glaciers. When they eventually retreated, they left in their wake an enormous landscape of lakes that filled the hollows. The area known as the Finnish Lakeland, in the southeast of the country, has more than 190,000 lakes larger than 5,400 sq ft (500 sq m).

How is the population distributed?

At 40.1 people per sq mile (15.5 people per sq km), Finland is sparsely inhabited. Furthermore, the population is distributed extremely unevenly throughout the country. Nearly 40 per cent of the population live in the south while the northern province of Lapland is almost uninhabited.

What is unusual about the Finnish education system?

The Finnish education system is one of the best in the world. Illiteracy is almost nonexistent and foreign languages are studied as a matter of course. A great emphasis is placed on personal responsibility and lifelong learning. Comparatively small class sizes (the average number of pupils is 19.5) are an important factor. Psychologists and special needs teachers play an important role in the education system.

FINLAND

Flag

Currency
1 euro (EUR) = 100 cents

System of government
Republic since 1919

Capital
Helsinki

Languages
Finnish, Swedish (official languages)

Surface area
130,559 sq miles (338,145 sq km)

Population 5.2 million

Religion
84% Protestant (Lutheran)

Notable features
The Åland group of islands belongs to Finland but is Swedish-speaking and possesses a large degree of autonomy.

What is "everyman's right"?

Everyman's right is an ancient common-law right that exists in the Nordic states of Finland, Sweden, and Norway. It grants everyone certain rights with respect to the use of nature, regardless of ownership. These rights include pitching a tent for one night and sailing on lakes. Everyman's right also prohibits the leaving behind of trash and the lighting of campfires, however.

Background: The sparse vegetation is due to the short, cool summers and cold, dark winters.

The antlers of the bull elk can achieve a spread of up to 6 ft 6 in (2 m).

Elk

Each year a third of all elk (as moose are known in Europe) are killed during the hunting season, but the population always recovers to over 100,000 head. Elk also pose a certain threat to people; each year there are numerous serious road accidents in Finland involving elk.

DENMARK

Flag

Currency
1 Danish krone (DKK) = 100 øre

System of government
Constitutional monarchy since 1953

Capital
Copenhagen

Languages
Danish (official language), German

Surface area
16,639 sq miles (43,096 sq km)

Population 5.4 million

Religion 84% Protestant (Lutheran)

Notable features
Although self-governing, Greenland and the Faroe Islands also belong to Denmark.

Is Denmark an island state?
No. Although it has around 400 islands, they make up only a third of its surface area. The country is extremely flat, rising to a mere 561 ft (171 m) at its highest point.

How long has Denmark been an independent kingdom?
The Danish monarchy was established well before AD 1000. Its rule has extended at various times to Norway, Sweden, and England. The current royal house has reigned since 1863, when King Christian IX inherited the throne from the childless Frederick VII. The current monarch is Queen Margrethe II.

Is Denmark prosperous?
Yes. Denmark's standard of living is one of the highest in the world and it occupies positions towards the top of the European employment and budget surplus tables. The Danish economy is broadly based, with tourism playing an important though not crucial role.

What is Denmark's most famous export?
The Danish toy manufacturer LEGO enjoys a worldwide reputation. Since 1949 it has manufactured the popular plastic building bricks used to make models of all kinds. LEGO was invented by Ole Kirk Christiansen (1891–1958).

Above: Holiday homes on the Jutland Peninsula. Denmark is a popular holiday destination for Scandinavian and German tourists in particular.

Right: The world-famous Little Mermaid in Copenhagen harbor is one of the Danish capital's best-known landmarks. The statue honors Danish writer Hans Christian Andersen (1805–1875).

Greenland
Greenland is the world's largest island. It is an autonomous part of the Kingdom of Denmark, which means that it is fully independent in the administration of its internal affairs while its foreign policy is handled by Denmark. Covering some 0.88 million sq miles (2.16 million sq km), Greenland is inhabited by a mere 57,000 or so people, predominantly from the Kalaallit (Inuit) ethnic group. All but 15 per cent of the land is covered by ice. Were this ice to melt, the water level of the world's oceans would rise by 20 ft (6 m).

Why is Ireland known as the "Emerald Isle"?

The reason for this name immediately becomes apparent when one views Ireland from the air; it looks like a green gem set in a blue sea. The island is undulating and covered with thick grass.

Who is Ireland's patron saint?

Ireland's patron saint is St Patrick, who arrived in the country as a Christian missionary in the 4th century. He founded monasteries and schools there and died on March 17, 461. The anniversary of his death became the national holiday of St Patrick's Day, and is also celebrated by Irish living abroad.

Why did so many Irish emigrate to the United States?

Between 1845 and 1849 the entire potato crop was destroyed by potato blight and Ireland was afflicted by a great famine. Starving smallholders had no option but to flee the country with their families. Within a few years the population shrank from 8.5 million to 6 million. Many of these emigrants headed for the United States.

When did Ireland become independent?

For centuries, Ireland was ruled by the English. It did not become formally independent until 1937, by which time the country was economically underdeveloped. Only after joining the European Economic Community in 1973 did the country benefit from an economic upturn, which continues today.

Ireland's green meadows are crisscrossed by countless stone walls.

IRELAND		
Flag		**Surface area** 27,135 sq miles (70,280 sq km)
Currency 1 euro (EUR) = 100 cents		**Population** 4 million
		Religion 92% Catholic
System of government Republic since 1937		**Notable features** The island of Ireland comprises not just the Republic but also the province of Northern Ireland, which is part of the United Kingdom.
Capital Dublin		
Languages English, Irish (official languages), Scots		

The Celts

The Celts were a group of tribes that spread during their heyday (5th–1st centuries BC) throughout the whole of central Europe. All the Celtic clans shared cultural and linguistic similarities. Around 600 BC, Celtic tribes arrived in Ireland and interbred with the indigenous people. Around 150 small Celtic kingdoms developed on the island. During peacetime the Druids (priests, sages, and judges) were the most important social group.

UNITED KINGDOM OF GREAT BRITAIN AND NORTHERN IRELAND

Flag

Currency
1 pound sterling (GBP) = 100 pence

System of government
Constitutional monarchy
(Commonwealth member)

Capital
London

Languages
English (de facto official language as none designated), Welsh, Scots, Irish Gaelic, Scottish Gaelic

Surface area
93,788 sq miles (242,910 sq km)

Population 60.4 million

Religion
59% Anglican, 9% Catholic, 3% Muslim, 23% non-denominational

How many constituent parts does the United Kingdom have?

The United Kingdom (UK) is Europe's biggest island state and comprises four parts: England, Scotland, Wales, and Northern Ireland. The Isle of Man and the Channel Islands are also Crown dependencies. In addition to the United Kingdom, Queen Elizabeth II is the head of state of 15 other Commonwealth Realms (see box) around the world.

What is the country's proper name?

"England" is often used as a synonym for the UK but this is mainly because of England's predominance in the union with Scotland, Wales, and Northern Ireland and is politically incorrect. The British themselves call their country the "UK" or "Britain."

Tower Bridge was built in 1876 and is 800 ft (244 m) wide. It spans the River Thames, linking the borough of Southwark to the city center.

What is a pub?

The pub (from "public house") is a peculiarly British institution, a combination of bar and restaurant. Traditionally, pubs consist of two rooms. In the first, patrons stand at the counter or at high tables and drink mainly beer (typical varieties being ale, porter, and stout) freely and informally without any kind of dress code. The second has tables and is where meals are served. The menu usually features rustic-style dishes such as steak and kidney pie or hot pot.

The pub plays a key role in British social life. People often meet up with their friends there straight after work. In fine weather patrons like to sit at outdoor tables or simply spill out onto the street. During the First World War the government introduced compulsory closing times in order to prevent factory workers turning up to work in an unfit state following a late night at the pub. These closing times remained in force until a few years ago and meant that guests were turned out by 11 p.m. The law has now been relaxed although many pubs still stick to the old ways and call "last orders" after 10.45 p.m.

What is the Church of England?

The Church of England is England's established church and the mother church of Anglicanism. The schism with Rome began with the refusal of Pope Clement VII to annul the marriage of King Henry VIII (1491–1547) and Catherine of Aragon (1485–1536). The bishops immediately named the English monarch supreme head of their church in place of the Pope, thereby triggering the English Reformation. Today Queen Elizabeth II is Head of the Church of England, and is followed in the hierarchy by the Archbishops of Canterbury and York. The Church is characterized by loyal adherence to the Christian tradition.

What are the Commonwealth Realms?

The Commonwealth Realms are monarchies or other sovereign Commonwealth member states that have entered into a voluntary union (with the aim of realizing common goals) and recognize the British monarch as their head of state. The Queen is represented in each of these countries by a governor-general.

The 16 Commonwealth Realms are: Antigua and Barbuda, Australia, Bahamas, Barbados, Belize, Canada, Grenada, Jamaica, New Zealand, Papua New Guinea, St Kitts and Nevis, St Lucia, St Vincent and the Grenadines, Solomon Islands, Tuvalu, and the United Kingdom itself.

The 315-ft-high (96-m) clock tower of the Houses of Parliament in London was built by Sir Benjamin Hall (1802–1868) in 1858. The diameter of each of the four clock faces is 26 ft (8 m), making Clock Tower (better known as "Big Ben") the biggest clock in the UK.

Eilean Donan Castle and Loch Duich on Scotland's west coast.

What is Stonehenge?

Stonehenge, near Salisbury, Wiltshire, is a site surrounded by several stone circles. It has been baffling scientists for an eternity as it is still not clear what purpose it served. The name Stonehenge derives from the Old English *stanhen gist*, meaning something like "hanging stones." The earliest part of the site is a circular earthwork dating from around 3100 BC. The pillars, which are up to 13 ft (4 m) tall and linked by horizontal coping stones, were erected at some point between 2500 and 2000 BC. It is thought today that the site was for the observation of the sun and the moon, but its construction presupposes astronomical knowledge that was not available until far later.

Why do road vehicles drive on the left in Britain?

In the UK, it was stipulated in a law of 1835 that traffic should drive on the left. In general, the decision of whether to drive on the left or right in a particular country depended on what type of carriages were used and how the draft animals were driven. In Swindon in the English county of Wiltshire, not far from London, wheel marks made by fully laden Roman vehicles driving away from a quarry (identifiable because they are deeper than those made by vehicles approaching the quarry) are on the left-hand side. This invites the assumption that even in Roman times traffic drove on the left. It is known moreover that the Roman army marched on the left.

Nineteenth-century Penrhyn Castle near the small city of Bangor in North Wales.

NETHERLANDS

Flag

Languages
Dutch, Frisian (regional)
(official languages)

Currency
1 euro (€) = 100 cents

Surface area
16,033 sq miles (41,526 sq km)

System of government
Constitutional monarchy since 1848

Population 16.3 million

Capital Amsterdam
(seat of government: The Hague)

Religion
30% Catholic, 20% Protestant,
6% Muslim, 42% non-denominational

What does Benelux mean?

Benelux is an abbreviation of **Be**lgium, **Ne**therlands, and **Lux**embourg. In 1958 the three countries signed a treaty providing for the creation of an economic union. The agreement came into force in 1960 and did away with virtually all trade restrictions. Many people regard it as the nucleus of the European Community, the predecessor of the European Union.

Was the Netherlands a colonial power?

Yes, a major one. In the 17th century the Netherlands grew into one of the biggest maritime and trading powers in the world. It established colonies all over the globe. What later became New York on the East Coast of the United States was originally founded as Nieuw Amsterdam, present-day Indonesia was an Asian colony of the Netherlands, and Suriname, Aruba, Curaçao, Saba, Sint Eustatis, and Sint Maarten were its American ones. Aruba and the Netherlands Antilles are today autonomous parts of the Koningrijk der Nederlanden (Kingdom of the Netherlands).

How does the country defend itself against flooding?

As almost half the surface area of the Netherlands lies below sea level (50 per cent lies less than 3 ft 3 in/1 m above, 25 per cent lies below, and around 20 per cent lies under water), 1,864 miles (3,000 km) of dikes have been built to protect the country from the sea.

What are *koog* and *polder*?

Koog and *polder* are names given to land reclaimed from the sea by means of diking. Dikes are constructions that drain the reclaimed land and simultaneously protect it from flooding.

Typical Dutch houseboats on a canal in the center of Amsterdam.

Many of Holland's windmills are not grain mills but water or *polder* mills. It is only draining that makes the land usable.

Liberal laws

The Netherlands has a very liberal set of laws. Soft drugs can be purchased legally in so-called coffee shops, and prostitution is a recognized trade whose workers are required to pay social security contributions. The country was one of the first in which abortion and euthanasia were legalized and the first to recognize same-sex marriage. While these freedoms are normal in the big cities, in rural areas the reality often lags some way behind the liberal legislation.

BELGIUM

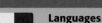

Flag

Currency
1 euro (EUR) = 100 cents

System of government
Parliamentary monarchy since 1831

Capital
Brussels

Languages
Dutch, French,
German (official languages)

Surface area
12,566 sq miles (32,545 sq km)

Population 10.4 million

Religion 80% Catholic

Notable features
85% of the Belgian population live in
the towns and cities.

Right: The
medieval center
of the Belgian city
of Bruges was
named a UNESCO
World Heritage site
in 2000.

One of the
landmarks of
the Belgian capital,
Brussels, is the
Atomium. This
was erected for
the World's Fair of
1958 as a symbol
of the peaceful
exploitation of
nuclear energy.

Why are there three official languages?
Some 63 per cent of Belgians are Dutch-
speaking Flemish and 36 per cent are French-speaking
Walloons. An agreement was drawn up in 1921 on
the division of the country into three linguistic zones.
Dutch is spoken in Flanders, French is spoken in
Wallonia, and German is spoken by a small minority
in eastern Belgium.

How important is the Antwerp diamond trade?
Antwerp is regarded as the world's major diamond
trading center. Some 70 per cent of all uncut
diamonds exchange hands here. The diamond
industry has for a while been in a state of flux,
however, and business is increasingly shifting
to other countries such as
tax-free Dubai. The
Belgian government is

currently considering the introduction of a tax
amnesty to discourage dealers from completely
turning their backs on Antwerp.

Is Brussels the capital of Europe?
No, although because important European Union
(EU) institutions such as the Council of Ministers
and (jointly with Strasbourg) the European
Parliament are based here, the city is often
referred to unofficially as the capital of
Europe. Because other European
cities (Strasbourg, Luxembourg, Frankfurt)
also accommodate important EU
institutions, the title is not generally
recognized.

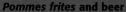

Pommes frites and beer

The Belgians have been credited with the invention of the
now universal *pommes frites* or french fries. It is thought
that the poor people of the region began to fry fish during
the 18th century. When the rivers froze in winter, potatoes
were cut into the shape of fish and fried instead. Belgium
also claims an important place internationally in the brewing
of beer. However, this relates to the enormous number of
different types rather than the volume produced; in Germany,
for example, there are ten times as many breweries.

Who governs Luxembourg?

Who governs Luxembourg? Grand Duke Henri of Luxembourg (born 1955) has been the Head of State of this constitutional monarchy since 2000 and in theory at least has far-reaching powers. In reality he performs an almost entirely symbolic role. The legislative function is carried out by the Chamber of Deputies.

What percentage of the population do foreigners represent?

Almost 40 per cent of Luxembourg's population come from beyond its frontiers, with 14 per cent from Portugal alone. There are even communities in which the Portuguese make up the majority. In addition to this high quotient of foreign residents, the country also attracts large numbers of commuters from neighboring Belgium, Germany, and France, who make up 40 per cent of the workforce.

Does Luxembourg play an important role in Europe?

Yes. The Luxembourgers have been strong supporters of Europe from the outset and have made a major contribution to European unification. Luxembourg was a founding member of the European Economic Community (EEC), a forerunner of the EU, in 1957 and fought for equal status for Europe's small states. Luxembourg City is today the seat of important European institutions such as the European Court of Justice and the European Court of Auditors.

Which branch of the economy predominates in Luxembourg?

Luxembourg's economy is strongly oriented towards the service sector. The capital is an international financial center and nearly 200 banks have offices there. About 11 per cent of the working population are employed by the financial sector. Large numbers of administrative jobs are also provided by the EU.

LUXEMBOURG

Flag

Currency
1 euro (EUR) = 100 cents

System of government
Parliamentary monarchy (grand duchy) since 1866

Capital
Luxembourg

Languages
Luxembourgish, German, French (official languages)

Surface area
999 sq miles (2,586 sq km)

Population 469,000

Religion 90% Catholic

Notable features
Luxembourg is the only country in the world to be governed as a grand duchy.

The town of Vianden, on the border between Luxembourg and Germany, is dominated by its castle, which is mentioned in the 13th-century *Nibelungenlied*.

RTL

RTL is an abbreviation of **R**adio **T**élé **L**uxembourg. The RTL Group is Europe's largest operator of private television and radio stations and is financed by advertising. Although RTL is headquartered in Luxembourg, it runs national broadcasters throughout almost the whole of Europe. The group is 90 per cent owned by German conglomerate Bertelsmann.

FRANCE

Flag		Breton, Alsatian, Flemish, Catalan, Corsican, Occitan
		Surface area
		210,026 sq miles (543,965 sq km)
Currency		**Population** 60.7 million
1 euro (EUR) = 100 cents		**Religion**
System of government		73% Catholic, 8% Muslim
Presidential republic since 1958		**Notable features**
Capital		France also has four overseas
Paris		departments: Guadeloupe, Martinique,
Languages		French Guiana, and Réunion.
French (official language), Basque,		

The Eiffel Tower, named after its architect Gustave Eiffel (1832–1923), was built for the World's Fair of 1889 that commemorated the 100th anniversary of the French Revolution.

Why is France sometimes referred to as the "Hexagon"?

This is roughly the shape it takes. France is bordered to the north and west by the Atlantic Ocean and to the southeast by the Mediterranean Sea. Its border is formed by the Pyrenees to the southwest and a portion of the Alps on the opposite, southeast, side. This is also where Mont Blanc (15,768 ft/4,806 m), Europe's highest mountain, is situated.

Many people associate the name "Le Mans" with motor racing, but the city in western France is also famous for its historic old town.

How long has France existed as a state?

The history of France as a state goes back to the Kingdom of Western Francia, which was created in 843 out of the western part of the divided Frankish empire. The first King of Western Francia was Charles II (823–877), who also entered history as Charles the Bald.

French Guiana

French Guiana is part of the French state. Unlike the motherland, it is located not in Europe but in the northeast corner of South America. As part of France, however, it is also part of the European Union and the euro is its legal tender. Its climate is tropical and 90 per cent of the country is covered by forest. French Guiana was made famous by the film *Papillon* (based on the novel by Henri Charrière), which is set in the penal colony on Devil's Island off its northern coast. In 1968 Europe built a rocket-launching site outside the coastal town of Kourou from which the Ariadne rockets blast into space.

What was the Hundred Years' War?

The Hundred Years' War was a war of succession between England and France that lasted from 1339 to 1453. When the Capetian dynasty died out in 1328, the French throne was claimed by both the French Count of Anjou and the Duke of Aquitaine (King Edward III of England). Battles were fought continually with victory going one way and then the other. During the final phase of the war, Joan of Arc (1412–1431) became a French national heroine. A peasant who claimed to be guided by God, her military successes ultimately forced the English troops to leave France.

What was the storming of the Bastille?

The Bastille prison in Paris was stormed by an angry mob on July 14, 1789. It housed only a small number of prisoners but large stocks of ammunition, which were the rebels' real target. July 14 is generally seen as the start of the French Revolution and is now France's national holiday.

Is France the largest country in Europe?

In terms of surface area, France is the largest country in the European Union. In terms of population, however, it has now been overtaken by Germany, although due to France's higher population growth rate this could change during the course of the 21st century.

Is France a nuclear power?

Yes, in a double sense. Firstly, 80 per cent of France's electricity is generated by nuclear power stations, the highest proportion in the world. Secondly, France is also a nuclear power militarily. It has possessed nuclear weapons since 1960, when it became the fourth nation after the USA, the Soviet Union, and the UK to acquire them.

Mont Saint-Michel, a rocky island situated between Normandy and Brittany, is one of the country's biggest tourist attractions. The fortified Benedictine monastery is still inhabited by monks today.

Tahiti

Another French overseas territory is French Polynesia in the South Pacific, which consists of a total of 130 islands and atolls. The largest of the islands is Tahiti, which was made famous by the mutiny on the *Bounty* and the paintings of Paul Gauguin (1848–1903). Today Tahiti enjoys the highest standard of living of all the South Sea Islands.

and controls that are now monitored by the French National Institute for Quality Wines (INAO).

Is Paris the center of France?

Yes, but not in a geographical sense. Paris is the center of the country politically, economically, and culturally. The national highway network radiates outwards from Paris and so the city has also become the country's main traffic hub. About 12 million people live in the greater Paris region.

Is France a technologically advanced nation?

Yes. France has always striven to be at the forefront of technological development. This is evident not only in its exploitation of nuclear energy but also in ambitious projects such as the supersonic aircraft Concorde and the TGV high-speed train.

"To live like God in France" is a German expression that alludes to the country's exceptional food. Shown here are wine, cheese, fruit, and a baguette.

Why is French wine world famous?

After Italy, France is the biggest wine producer in the world. However, the high status of France's wine-growing regions rests on quality rather than quantity. Wine producers all around the world take their cue from the standards set by the wines of Bordeaux and Burgundy. This high quality has been assured for 100 years by stringent production regulations

A vineyard in the Champagne region. The climate here allows the grapes to ripen slowly, thereby contributing to the wine's wonderful freshness.

Champagne

French cuisine is renowned throughout the world for its refinement and sophistication. France also produces the most festive of all drinks: Champagne. This name can only be used by sparkling wines made from grapes grown and vinified in the Champagne region in accordance with strict rules.

Where does the name Monaco come from?

Where does the name Monaco come from? Greek settlers inhabited the part of the Mediterranean that is now Monaco as long ago as the 5th century BC. They erected a temple to Heracles Monoikos (Heracles "alone") and it was from this epithet that the area took its name.

How is the population made up?

The true locals are called Monégasques but they make up only a small part of the population (some 7,600) as a whole, which is composed of nationals of 125 countries. At 47 per cent, the French make up the largest single group. Among the world's rich, Monaco is a highly sought-after place to live as there are no taxes. There is, however, a tax agreement between Monaco and France so the French residents are an exception to this rule.

What is the difference between Monaco-Ville and Monaco the state?

Monaco is a city-state so to this extent Monaco-Ville is not a city but merely the *quartier* (district) in which the palace and cathedral are located. The city/state also contains other districts: Monte Carlo describes itself as a "luxury resort with casino"; La Condamine is a newly developed area with harbor, banks and businesses; and Fontvieille was created on land reclaimed from the sea and includes residential and industrial buildings, a nature park, sporting facilities and a new yachting harbor.

Monaco's Monte Carlo district is famous for its casinos. However, only visitors are allowed to enter them. Monégasques are not permitted to gamble in what is perhaps the most celebrated casino in the world.

MONACO

Flag

Currency
1 euro (EUR) = 100 cents

System of government
Constitutional monarchy (principality) with limited sovereignty

Capital
Monaco-Ville

Languages French (official language), Monégasque, Italian, English

Surface area
0.75 sq miles (1.95 sq km)

Population 33,000

Religion 91% Catholic

Notable features
Monaco is the second-smallest state in the world, but with 43,831 people per sq mile (16,923 people per sq km), the most densely populated too.

Grace Patricia Kelly, Princess Grace of Monaco

American actress Grace Kelly (1929–1982) was born in Philadelphia as the daughter of a wealthy building contractor. After graduating from stage school, she acted alongside leading stars of the day in countless films. Among her most famous movies are *High Noon* with Gary Cooper and *To Catch a Thief* with Cary Grant. In 1956 she married Prince Rainier III of Monaco (1923–2005). In September 1982 she suffered a stroke while driving a car in which her daughter Stephanie was a passenger. The vehicle plunged 130 ft 40 m) down a mountainside. Stephanie was badly injured while her mother, Princess Grace, died the day after the accident.

GERMANY

Flag

Currency
1 euro (EUR) = 100 cents

System of government
Parliamentary federal republic
since 1949

Capital
Berlin

Languages
German (official language)

Surface area
137,847 sq miles (357,023 sq km)

Population 82.4 million

Religion
31% Catholic, 31% Protestant,
31% non-denominational,
4% Muslim

Notable features
Between 1949 and 1990 Germany
was divided into the Federal Republic
of Germany (FRG) and the German
Democratic Republic (GDR).

Who was the last German emperor?
The German imperial tradition was resumed in 1871 with the proclamation at Versailles of Prussian King Wilhelm I (1797–1888) as German emperor. The new empire lasted until the end of the First World War. Kaiser Wilhelm II (1859–1941) was forced to abdicate in 1918.

Did Germany have colonies?
Yes. Germany had a number of colonies (mainly in Africa) during a short period of its history, between 1884 and 1918. The best-known are German East Africa (present-day Tanzania, Rwanda, and Burundi) and German Southwest Africa (present-day Namibia). After Germany's defeat in the First World War, the victorious powers shared its colonies between themselves in 1918.

Why were there two Germanies for 40 years?
In 1945, at the end of the Second World War, the defeated Germany was divided into four occupation zones. Two German states eventually

The Reichstag (parliament) building in the German capital Berlin. This was the seat of the German parliament from the end of the 19th century until 1933, and again from 1999.

How long has Germany existed?
In AD 962 the king of East Francia, Otto I (912–973), journeyed to Rome to be crowned Holy Roman emperor. This is generally regarded as the beginning of the first German nation. The tradition of Holy Roman emperors continued until 1806. The last ruler of this old empire, Franz II (1768–1835), lost his crown as a result of the reorganization of Europe during Napoleonic times.

The Goethe Institute: a global presence
Named after the writer Johann Wolfgang von Goethe, the Goethe Institute was founded in 1951 in order to promote the learning of German by foreign students and thereby disseminate knowledge of German culture and the German language throughout the world. Today there are branches of the Goethe Institute in around 90 different countries.

emerged from this division: the Federal Republic of Germany (FRG) in the west and the German Democratic Republic (GDR) in the east. The division was effectively overturned in 1989, symbolized by the fall of the Berlin Wall, and ended formally with the reunification of the two states on October 3, 1990.

How is Germany split geographically?
The north of the country is low-lying and forms part of the North German Plain. Farther south the land rises from low mountains to the high peaks of the German Alps. These high mountains include the country's highest peak, the Zugspitze, at 9,718 ft (2,962 m).

Does Germany have a big population?
Germany has more than 82 million inhabitants. This makes it the most highly populated country in the European Union (EU). It is also one of the most densely populated territorial states in the world. However, as the Federal Republic also has one of the lowest birthrates, it is anticipated on the basis

The small town of Freudenberg in the German federal state of North Rhine-Westphalia has retained its ancient half-timbered center and still looks very much as it would have done in the 17th century.

Cologne Cathedral
Cologne Cathedral is Germany's best-known sacred building and a major tourist attraction. Along with those of Seville and Milan, it is one of the three largest Gothic cathedrals in the world. Soaring to 515 ft (157 m), it was the tallest building in the world between 1880 and 1888. Construction started in 1248 and did not officially end until 1880. In 1996 the cathedral was made a UNESCO World Heritage site.

Carnival

Carnival (Karneval or Fastnacht in German) is the festive season immediately before Lent, which lasts from Ash Wednesday until Good Friday. In Germany this season of merrymaking is celebrated most enthusiastically in carnival hotspots Mainz, Cologne, and Düsseldorf, all of which are on the Rhine. Among the main festivities are parades in which the participants dress up in brightly colored fantasy uniforms. These costumes were originally worn as a parody of the unpopular occupying forces during periods of French and Prussian occupation of the Rhineland.

Hegel (1770–1831) are among the most celebrated of German philosophers.

What is the significance of the Rhine?
The Rhine is one of Europe's major waterways. The romantic Middle Rhine, overlooked by numerous medieval castles, is important for tourism. The Rhine is not an exclusively German river, however, as its headstreams rise in Switzerland and it flows into the sea in the Netherlands. For most of its 820-mile (1,320-km) journey, however, the river flows through German territory.

Is Germany a sporting nation?
Sport plays a very important part in German life. Every third German is a member of a sports club. While the most popular sport is soccer (the national team has won the World Cup three times), German athletes have achieved international success in many other disciplines too. The Olympic Games were held in Germany in 1936 (Berlin) and 1972 (Munich).

of current demographic trends that by 2050 the German population will have dropped to 75 million.

What raw materials does Germany possess?
Germany is essentially very badly off in this regard. Coal and salt are the only raw materials it possesses in significant quantities. The economy therefore depends heavily on the import of raw materials. Most of the oil and gas it needs for the provision of energy also needs to be imported.

What does it export?
Despite its shortage of raw materials, Germany is the third-largest industrial nation in the world and the biggest exporter. Among the chief exports of the Exportweltmeister (world export champion) are machines of all kinds, chemical products, and automobiles. Germany's two biggest industrial corporations are auto manufacturers DaimlerChrysler and Volkswagen.

Why is Germany sometimes referred to as the "land of poets and thinkers?"
In addition to the wealth of scientists produced by the country, Germany is also renowned for its numerous writers and philosophers and their works of international significance. Among writers, Johann Wolfgang von Goethe (1749–1832) and Friedrich Schiller (1759–1805) are two of the key names, while Gottfried Wilhelm Freiherr von Leibniz (1646–1716) and Georg Wilhelm Friedrich

Where does the name Poland come from?

The country takes its name from the Polan tribe that settled in the area between the Oder and Vistula rivers in the 5th century around the time of the collapse of the Roman Empire.

What was Polish particularism?

In political science terms, the phenomenon of particularism occurs when the interests of constituent elements within a state acquire such weight that the state becomes difficult to govern. In Poland this happened between 1138 and 1295, when the nation fragmented into six independent duchies: Lesser Poland, Greater Poland, Pomerania, Pomerelia, Silesia, and Masovia. This division was accompanied by significant reduction in the political power of the state.

When did the Second World War begin for Poland?

The invasion of Poland by Nazi Germany on September 1, 1939 marked the beginning of the Second World War. Troops of the Third Reich and its puppet state the First Slovak Republic occupied the western part of the country, and on September 17, Soviet troops invaded and occupied the east of the country. This division of Poland was formalized in the Hitler-Stalin Pact, a non-aggression pact between the two countries signed in Moscow on August 24, 1939. Some 6 million people died in Poland alone during the Second World War, half of them Jews.

What is Solidarność?

Solidarność is a trade union founded in 1980. Having grown out of a strike movement, its work eventually brought about political change in Poland. In 1989 the first free elections in the Eastern Bloc were held in Poland, resulting in the collapse of the communist regime and the ushering in of a democratic government.

POLAND

Flag

Capital Warsaw

Languages
Polish (official language)

Currency
1 złoti (PLN) = 100 groszy

Surface area
120,728 sq miles (312,685 sq km)

System of government
Republic since 1918

Population 38.6 million

Religion
95% Catholic

Background: A typical landscape in Masovia.

Kraków, with a population of over 750,000, lies on the upper Vistula in the south of Poland. Shown here is a group of folk musicians wearing the traditional costume of the region.

Interesting facts

- With more than 10,000 lakes of 2.5 acres (1 ha) or more, Poland has one of the highest numbers of lakes of any country in the world, beaten only by Finland.

- The country's 23 national parks account for one per cent of its surface area, the highest proportion of any European country.

- Poland is home to many creatures that have already died out across large parts of Europe, including the wisent (European bison), brown bear, wolf, lynx, and moose.

CZECH REPUBLIC

Flag

Currency
1 koruna (CZK) = 100 heller

System of government
Republic since 1993

Capital Prague

Languages
Czech (official language)

Surface area
30,450 sq miles (78,866 sq km)

Population 10.2 million

Religion
27% Catholic,
60% non-denominational

What was the Prague Spring?

Following years of authoritarian communism, Alexander Dubček (1921–1992) became first secretary of the Communist Party on January 5, 1968 and immediately inaugurated a series of new freedoms. In early March censorship was lifted, freedom of assembly guaranteed, small-scale free enterprise was legalized and political prisoners were freed. Dubček's aim was to introduce "socialism with a human face."

On August 21, 1968, Soviet troops marched into Prague. Dubček was forced out of office in April 1969 and Gustáv Husák was made general secretary. With this action the dream of freedom made possible by the Prague Spring was well and truly shattered and Czechoslovakia developed into one of the most repressive of Soviet Bloc countries.

Work started on Charles Bridge in Prague under Charles IV in 1357. It is one of the oldest surviving stone bridges in Europe.

When was the Czech Republic founded?

The Czech Republic, with its three historical regions Bohemia, Moravia, and Moravia-Silesia, was founded in 1993, two years after the dissolution of the Warsaw Pact. It joined NATO in 1999.

What are the origins of the word "pilsner"?

The word "pilsner" stems from the style of brewing that originated in Pilsen (Plzeň) in 1842. The resulting brew was a bottom-fermented beer with a strong flavor of hops and a maximum original wort of 12.5 per cent volume.

When did the Thirty Years' War begin?

On May 23, 1618, a group of mainly Protestant Bohemian envoys forced their way into the chancellery of Prague Castle on Hradčany Hill and threw two imperial governors out of the window.

Known as the Prague Defenestrations, this was the trigger though not the cause of the Thirty Years' War. The root causes of the war were power struggles and religio-political conflict between Habsburg Austria and Spain and its German allies on the one hand, and France, the Netherlands, Denmark, and Sweden on the other. Fighting took place mainly on the territory of the Holy Roman Empire and resulted in devastating famine and epidemics which depopulated vast tracts of land.

SWITZERLAND

Flag

Currency
1 Swiss franc (CHF) = 100 centimes

System of government
Parliamentary federal republic
since 1848

Capital Berne
Languages
German, French, Italian,
Romansh (official languages)
Surface area
15,940 sq miles (41,285 sq km)
Population 7.5 million
Religion
42% Catholic, 35% Protestant

Cheese fondue

Fondue is a typical Swiss dish made of melted cheese, white wine, a shot of kirsch, garlic, and pepper. It is served in a *caquelon*, a special earthenware pot, and kept warm over a flame in order to ensure that its contents remain runny. Diners dip bread into the cheese mixture with long forks. Traditionally, anyone who loses their bread in the fondue has to buy wine or schnapps for all those present or else sing a song.

What is a "consensus nation"?

A "consensus nation" is a state whose citizens are unified by a sense of belonging and common identity. Although its population displays a wide variety of different origins, Switzerland is a consensus nation because the state represents a freely chosen community or association of citizens.

What is the meaning of Switzerland's official name, the "Swiss Confederation"?

A confederation is a loose association of states and represents the very opposite of feudalism. The Swiss Confederation came into being in the 13th century and was sealed by an oath sworn by its original members.

Which were the original cantons in the confederation?

Although Switzerland now consists of 23 cantons, at the outset there were just three: Uri, Schwyz (from which the country takes its name), and Unterwalden. In 1291 these three cantons formed an alliance in order to defend their traditional freedoms. The oath by which they were bound is traditionally believed to have been sworn on the Rütli ("small clearing"), a meadow by Lake Lucerne.

What is a watershed?

A watershed is a physical division between the drainage basins of rivers that flow into different seas. Watersheds are usually lines of hills or mountains but can also follow the course of a valley.

Which two major rivers rise in Switzerland?

The sources of the Rhine and Rhône rivers rise in the Gotthard Massif. Switzerland has a number of watersheds, which is why the Rhine flows into the North Sea and the Rhône into the Mediterranean.

Which languages are spoken in Switzerland?

German (in dialect form) is spoken by 64 per cent of the population, French by 20 per cent, Italian by 7 per cent, and Romansh by just 0.5 per cent. As very many immigrants also live and are well established in Switzerland, a variety of other languages is spoken in addition to the "Swiss" ones.

Above: The famous Emmental cheese comes from the Emme Valley in the Bernese Alps.

The Lauterbrunnen Valley (also visible here is the village of Wengen) is famous for its "big three" mountains: the Eiger, the Mönch, and the Jungfrau.

LIECHTENSTEIN

Flag	**Languages** German (official language), Alemannic (dialect)
Currency 1 Swiss franc (CHF) = 100 centimes	**Surface area** 62 sq miles (160 sq km)
System of government Constitutional monarchy since 1921	**Population** 34,000
Capital Vaduz	**Religion** 76% Catholic, 7% Protestant

The reigning prince, Hans Adam II of Liechtenstein, lives in Vaduz Castle. Affairs of state have been looked after by his son Alois since 2004.

Where is Liechtenstein?

Liechtenstein is a small mountainous state in the European Alps. It borders Austria to the east while to the west its border with Switzerland is formed by the Rhine. The principality lies at elevations of between 1,411 and 8,530 ft (430 and 2,600 m).

When did Liechtenstein become an independent state?

Liechtenstein has been independent since the dissolution of the Holy Roman Empire in 1806.

Even after this date, however, it remained closely associated with its neighbors, firstly Austria and subsequently (from 1924) Switzerland, whose currency the principality still shares. It did not join the UN in its own right until 1990.

Why are there so many letter box companies in Liechtenstein?

Liechtenstein's low taxes have attracted thousands of such firms to the extent that the principality now has more letter box companies than inhabitants. Letter box companies are companies whose registered office consists of an address alone, i.e. no management or administrative function is based there. This perfectly legal method of reducing a tax liability is often regarded as a form of tax evasion.

Is tourism Liechtenstein's main source of income?

No. Most of the country's earnings are generated by the trade and services sectors and an industrial sector dominated by the manufacture of high-quality specialist goods.

Vaduz Castle

Vaduz Castle, the oldest parts of which date from the 12th century, overlooks the capital. It has been in the possession of the princely family of Liechtenstein since 1712 and has been the family's permanent residence since 1938. The castle is the country's national emblem but is not open to the public.

AUSTRIA

Flag

Currency
1 euro (EUR) = 100 cents
System of government
Parliamentary democratic federal
republic since 1918
Capital
Vienna

Languages
German (official language), Slovenian,
Croatian, Hungarian (official languages
locally)
Surface area
32,383 sq miles (83,871 sq km)
Population 8.3 million
Religion
73% Catholic, 5% Protestant

South Tyrol

The whole of the Tyrol region, whose main language is German, belonged to Austria until the end of the First World War, when it was split and the southern part ceded to Italy. The Alto Adige, as it is known in Italy, remained the subject of dispute for many years. Austria regards South Tyrol as an exclave of its federal province of Tyrol and took its case to the UN in the 1960s. The outcome was autonomy for the inhabitants of the former Austrian territory and a new official name, the Autonomous Province of Bolzano/Bozen.

Is Austria a country of immigration?

Yes. In tandem with its increasing prosperity, Austria has developed from a country of emigration into a country of immigration since the 1950s. It is now one of the wealthiest countries in the world. This is due not least to the strength of its tourist industry, in which many of its immigrants work. Austria has also repeatedly been the destination of political refugees over the decades, recently welcoming refugees from the countries of the former Yugoslavia. The latest additions to its immigrant population are Germans who come to work in Austria's service sector having been unable to find work at home.

What are the ecological consequences of tourism in Austria?

Tourism is the largest economic sector and every third job depends on it either directly or indirectly. Austria serves both the winter and summer tourist markets but high levels of deforestation and the creation of ever more ski runs are increasing the incidence of natural catastrophes—above all the danger of avalanches—during both winter and summer.

Who is Ötzi?

Ötzi is an approximately 5,300-year-old (Copper Age) mummy of a man found well-preserved in the Ötztal Alps in the vicinity of the Hauslabjoch in 1991.

Above: The Bregenzer Tal is dotted with tiny, idyllic villages that present a picturesque scene against the backdrop of the Alps.

The Ferris wheel in the Prater, Vienna's famous pleasure gardens, was built by English engineer Walter Basset in 1896/7.

SLOVAKIA

Flag

Currency
1 Slovak koruna (SKK) = 100 heller

System of government
Republic since 1918

Capital
Bratislava

Languages
Slovak (official language), Hungarian, Czech

Surface area
18,932 sq miles (49,034 sq km)

Population 5.4 million

Religion
69% Catholic, 11% Protestant

Saints Cyril and Methodius, the Apostles of the Slavs

Brothers Cyril (826–869) and Methodius (815–885), who were born in Thessaloniki, were the most important missionaries to the Slav lands, hence their epithet "Apostles of the Slavs." It is believed that Cyril only adopted this name upon entering a Greek monastery shortly before his death, as his birth name was Constantine. The brothers are celebrated in Slovakia on July 5.

What are the High Tatras?

The High Tatras are a mountain group in the Carpathian Mountains. Two thirds of the group lies in Slovakia and the remaining third in Poland. The High Tatras are the only group of high mountains in the Carpathians and in each country constitute a national park and biosphere reserve under the protection of UNESCO. The highest peak in the High Tatras is Gerlachovský štít at 8,711 ft (2,655 m).

When was Czechoslovakia founded?

Czechoslovakia, covering the territory of present-day Slovakia and the Czech Republic (and until the Second World War a small part of Ukraine), was founded in 1918. Its official name was the Czechoslovak Republic (ČSR) between 1945 and 1960 and the Czechoslovak Socialist Republic (ČSSR) from 1960 to 1990.

When did Slovakia become an independent state?

Slovakia had its first spell of independence between 1939 and 1945 as a puppet state of Nazi Germany but was subsumed into the ČSR/ČSSR after the war. The country has been an independent republic since the collapse of the Eastern Bloc.

Slovakia or the Slovak Republic?

The full and official Slovak designation for the country is Slovenská republika. In English, the official designation is the Slovak Republic and hence both terms refer to the same nation-state. For formal purposes use the official designation. Slovakia borders five countries: Austria, Czech Republic, Hungary, Poland, and Ukraine.

A panoramic view of the High Tatras in all their splendor near the town of Poprad.

Interesting facts

- Slovakia achieved a growth rate of 8.3 per cent in 2006, the highest in the EU.
- It also has the lowest wage level in the EU.

When did Hungary gain its independence?

When did Hungary gain its independence? Hungary withdrew from the union with Austria on October 31, 1918 and recalled its troops from the front, thereby putting an end to the Austro-Hungarian Dual Monarchy.

What is the significance of Lake Balaton?

Lake Balaton in western Hungary is central Europe's largest lake. Thanks to its beaches and thermal springs, it is Hungary's biggest tourist attraction after Budapest.

Who are the Sinti and Roma?

The Sinti and Roma are peoples of northern Indian origin who migrated all over the world. For centuries these Gypsies have been discriminated against across Europe and thousands of Sinti and Roma were killed in concentration camps under National Socialism (1933–1945). Different estimates put the number of Roma living in Hungary today at between 400,000 and 1 million. While many lead a settled existence, others evade the censuses, hence the widely fluctuating figures. It is thought that around five per cent of the Hungarian population speak Sinti or Roma.

What was the Hungarian Uprising?

The Hungarian Uprising was a rebellion against the USSR-supported communist regime which broke out on October 23, 1956. Imre Nagy (1896–1958), who had already been prime minister between 1953 and 1956, called for parliamentary democracy. Soviet troops suppressed the uprising bloodily. Those who could, left Hungary and went into exile in western Europe or North America. Nagy was executed in 1958 for "counter-revolutionary activities" and has been honored as a national hero ever since.

HUNGARY

Flag	**Languages** Hungarian (official language)
	Surface area 35,919 sq miles (93,030 sq km)
Currency 1 forint (HUF) = 100 fillér	**Population** 10.1 million
System of government Republic since 1918	**Religion** 68% Catholic, 20% Calvinist, 5% Lutheran
Capital Budapest	

Goulash or *pörkölt*?

The Hungarian national dish *pörkölt* is often wrongly referred to as *gulyás* or goulash. *Pörkölt* is pork or beef braised with onions and paprika and accompanied by different side dishes according to region. *Gulyás*, on the other hand, is a soup, so the expression "goulash soup" is technically correct. It was traditionally prepared in a large cauldron over an open fire, a style of cooking that dates to the nomads.

Below: With a surface area of 232 sq miles (600 sq km), Lake Balaton in Transdanubia is the largest lake in central Europe.

Above: Postonja Cave is one of the world's most beautiful stalactite caverns. A small train takes visitors through almost 12 miles (20 km) of passages and galleries.

The picturesque town of Piran, with its population of 6,000, lies approximately 22 miles (35 km) south of the Italian city of Trieste on the northwest corner of the Istrian Peninsula.

What are the main features of Slovenia's topography?

Slovenia may be small but its landscape is varied. In addition to high mountains (forming part of the Southern Limestone Alps) with peaks of up to 9,396 ft (2,864 m), Slovenia also has extensive and highly forested low mountain ranges and approximately 29 miles (47 km) of Adriatic coastline (part of the Istrian Peninsula).

What was the Ten-Day War?

On November 29, 1945, a number of Balkan states joined together to form the Democratic Federal People's Republic of Yugoslavia, which changed its name to the Socialist Federal Republic of Yugoslavia (SFRY) in 1963. During the 1980s, dissatisfaction with the federal government in Belgrade grew and Slovenia eventually declared its independence on June 25, 1991. Yugoslavian troops immediately invaded but were successfully resisted during what became known as the Ten-Day War. A democratic constitution was adopted on December 23, 1991.

What is a *bora*?

A *bora* is a cold, dry, gusty katabatic wind (one that blows down an incline) unique to the Dalmatian Coast. It is common during the winter and spring months when an area of low pressure over the Adriatic sucks in the cold air from a continental high pressure area over the Balkans. After crossing Slovenia's high mountains, the wind is warmed slightly as it descends the sheltered side but still feels cold.

Tourism in Slovenia

Slovenia has plenty to offer holidaymakers. In addition to the capital Ljubljana, its most popular tourist destinations include 16 spas and health resorts, which have been attracting visitors for centuries, Alpine regions offering a wide range of winter sports facilities, numerous caverns, most famously the karst systems including Postojna Cave, and the Adriatic coastal resorts.

ESTONIA

Flag

Currency
1 kroon (EEK) = 100 senti

System of government
Republic since 1991

Capital
Tallinn

Languages
Estonian (official language), Russian

Surface area
17,462 sq miles (45,226 sq km)

Population 1.3 million

Religion
14% Protestant (Lutheran),
13% Estonian Orthodox,
33% non-denominational

Was Estonia part of the Soviet Union?

Yes. Estonia was annexed by the Soviet Union during the Second World War. Between 1945 and 1990 the Soviet Union deliberately encouraged an influx of Russians into what was the Estonian Soviet Socialist Republic with the result that Russians still make up a significant proportion (28 per cent) of the population. Estonia gained its independence in 1991 and has been a member of the EU since 2004.

Are there still wolves in Estonia?

Estonia is a flat land fashioned largely by the last Ice Age and 44 per cent of its surface area is still covered by forest. Its unspoiled nature is home to a number of beasts of prey including the lynx, the brown bear, and the wolf.

Is Estonia an undeveloped country?

No. The Estonians have embraced modern communications media. Within just a few years of independence, 93 per cent of the population had acquired cell phones, and Internet access is free to all Estonians by law.

Estonia's west-coast hinterland is dotted with windmills, thatched farmhouses, and sleepy fishing villages.

LATVIA

Flag

Currency
1 lats (LVL) = 100 santīme

System of government
Republic since 1991

Capital
Riga

Languages
Latvian (official language), Russian

Surface area
24,938 sq miles (64,589 sq km)

Population 2.3 million

Religion
55% Protestant (Lutheran),
24% Catholic, 9% Russian Orthodox

One of Riga's main sights is the House of Blackheads. This old merchants' house was destroyed in the Second World War and reconstructed between 1993 and 1999.

Does present-day Latvia cover the same territory as former Livonia?

No. In the Late Middle Ages, Livonia covered the entire area occupied by present-day Estonia and Latvia. Over the centuries, however, the region found itself repeatedly split and re-split between different nations. Livonia was finally divided into Estonia and Latvia in 1919.

What role did the Teutonic Order play?

After the Knights of St John of Jerusalem and the Knights Templar, the Teutonic Knights were the third major order of Christian knights to be founded during the time of the Crusades. After the Crusades, the order turned its attention to the colonization of northeast Europe, the Baltic, where it founded

a monastic state. The area covered by present-day Latvia was part of this state between 1237 and the Late Middle Ages.

When did Latvia gain its independence?

Latvia had already been an independent state from 1921 until the Second World War. During the war it found itself on the front between Germany and the Soviet Union, the ultimate consequence of which was that it was annexed by the Soviet Union as the Latvian Soviet Socialist Republic. It finally gained its independence from Russia in 1991.

What social problems does Latvia have?

After independence a large number of Russians who had been resettled in Latvia found themselves living in a country that was no longer part of the Soviet Union. Most of this substantial minority (34 per cent of the population) were unable to satisfy the conditions for adopting the new Latvian citizenship. Many failed to pass the difficult Latvian language test despite having been born in the country.

Riga

Latvia's capital, which is also the largest city of the three Baltic States, is the old Hanseatic town of Riga. Situated on the Gulf of Riga, it is renowned for its Art Nouveau buildings and well-preserved old town.

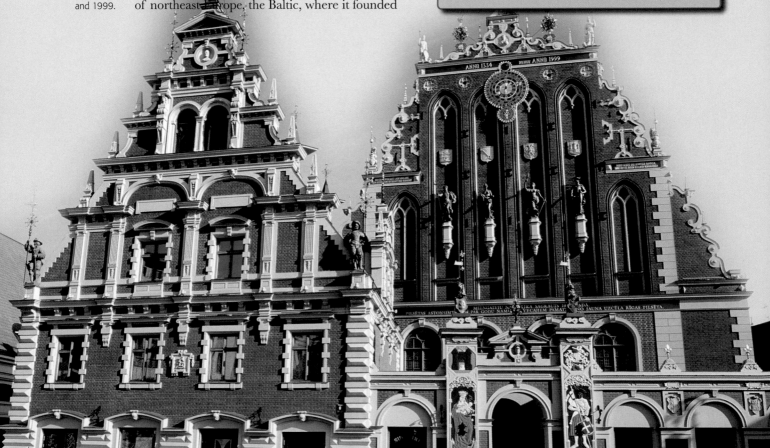

What exactly are the Baltic States?

The Baltic States are the countries bordering the Baltic Sea to the east: Lithuania, Latvia, and Estonia. While the "Balts" were early inhabitants of this region plus what is now the Russian exclave around Kaliningrad (the former German city of Königsberg), the "Baltic Germans" were the ruling classes who arrived from the 12th century onwards with the Teutonic Knights and the Hanseatic League.

Was Lithuania once a powerful country?

Yes. In the Middle Ages the Grand Duchy of Lithuania governed large parts of present-day Belarus, Ukraine and western Russia. It achieved its greatest territorial importance in a union with Poland as the Polish-Lithuanian Commonwealth, which extended to the south almost as far as the Black Sea.

LITHUANIA

Flag

Currency
1 litas (LTL) = 100 centų

System of government
Republic since 1991

Capital
Vilnius

Languages
Lithuanian (official language), Russian, Polish

Surface area
25,174 sq miles (65,200 sq km)

Population 3.6 million

Religion 79% Catholic

Notable features
Part of Courland Spit belongs to Lithuania.

When did modern Lithuania gain its independence?

The Red Army conquered Lithuania towards the end of the Second World War and subsequently annexed it as the Lithuanian Soviet Socialist Republic. Under *perestroika*, initiated by President Gorbachev of Russia, a Lithuanian independence movement developed in 1987 and eventually achieved its ambition in 1991.

Is Lithuania the home of amber?

Amber, one of the earliest mentions of which is to be found in the writings of Roman historian Tacitus (AD 55–115), is a yellow fossil resin used in the manufacture of jewelry. In Europe it is found mainly along the shoreline of the Baltic States. The largest deposits are located not in Lithuania, however, but in the Russian Kaliningrad region (formerly German Königsberg).

Left: The reading room of Vilnius University, the oldest university in eastern Europe, founded in 1579.

The Verkne and Streva rivers flow through Austadvaris Regional Park, which also has no fewer than 77 lakes.

The Vytis

The Vytis is the attacking white knight adorning Lithuania's coat of arms. It was adopted as the heraldic device of the Lithuanian grand dukes in 1366 and, although banned during the Soviet period, remains the national emblem of Lithuania today.

RUSSIAN FEDERATION

Flag

Currency
1 ruble (RUB) = 100 kopecks

System of government
Presidential republic since 1991

Capital
Moscow

Languages
Russian (official language), the official languages of the republics plus 80 minority languages

Surface area 6.59 million sq miles (17.07 million sq km)

Population 142.4 million

Religion
50% Russian Orthodox, 10% Muslim

Which is Russia's longest river?

The Volga is the longest river in both Russia and Europe. Flowing exclusively through Russia for 2,196 miles (3,534 km), it is the country's most important waterway and has been dammed numerous times along its course. It rises in the Valdai Hills and discharges into the Caspian Sea near Astrakhan via a delta 93 miles (150 km) wide.

Which seas is Russia bounded by?

Russia has 23,396 miles (37,653 km) of coastline along many seas and oceans including the Baltic Sea, the Black Sea, the Caspian Sea, the Sea of Japan, the Sea of Okhotsk, the Pacific Ocean, the Bering Sea, and the Arctic Ocean.

Which are Russia's shortest and longest borders with other countries?

Russia's shortest border is the 12 miles (19 km) of frontier it shares with North Korea while its longest is its 2,265-mile (3,645-km) border with the People's Republic of China.

The Kremlin in Moscow, with its palaces and cathedrals dating from the 15th to 19th centuries, was the residence of the tsars and the seat of the Supreme Soviet.

What are the origins of the name "Russia"?

The historical name of the parts of European Russia, present-day Belarus and present-day Ukraine inhabited by the Slavs was "Rus," from which the widely used Latin name "Ruthenia" was derived in the Middle Ages. Slavic spellings had adopted the second "s" by the 16th century.

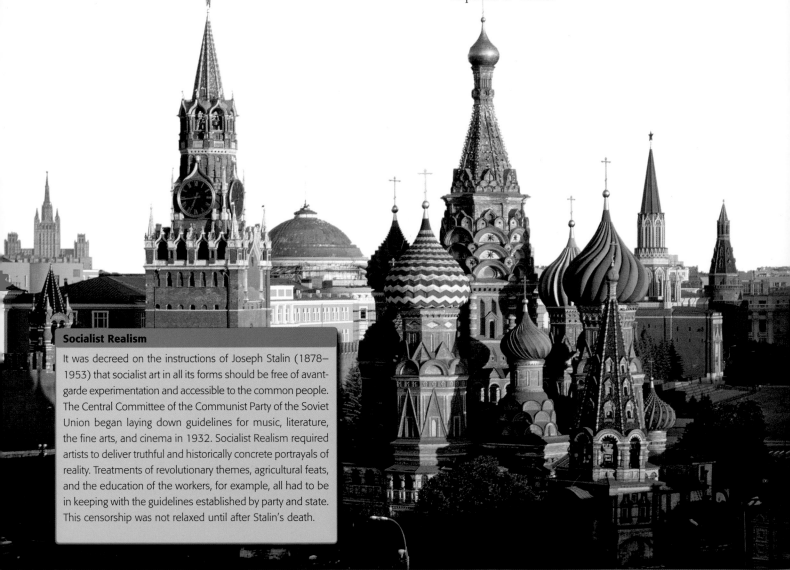

Socialist Realism

It was decreed on the instructions of Joseph Stalin (1878–1953) that socialist art in all its forms should be free of avant-garde experimentation and accessible to the common people. The Central Committee of the Communist Party of the Soviet Union began laying down guidelines for music, literature, the fine arts, and cinema in 1932. Socialist Realism required artists to deliver truthful and historically concrete portrayals of reality. Treatments of revolutionary themes, agricultural feats, and the education of the workers, for example, all had to be in keeping with the guidelines established by party and state. This censorship was not relaxed until after Stalin's death.

Which ethnic groups live in Russia?
Russians make up the overwhelming majority (80 per cent) of the country's population. In addition there are around 100 minority peoples including Tatars, Ukrainians, Armenians, Chuvash, Bashkirs, and Germans.

Who were the first settlers?
Vikings from Sweden sailed along the country's coasts and up its rivers in the 8th century, eventually establishing settlements and interbreeding with the local Slavs. Their descendants were the founders of the east Slavic state of Kievan Rus, the first medieval state on the territory of present-day Russia, Ukraine, and Belarus, whose center was Kiev.

What was the Great Northern War?
The Great Northern War, which started in 1700 and continued for nearly 20 years, was a struggle for supremacy in the Baltic and ended in a victory for Russia, led by Tsar Peter the Great (1672–1725), over Sweden. Hitherto, Russian culture had always been isolated and uninfluenced by European science and arts. In 1703 Peter the Great founded St Petersburg as a symbol of his nation's desire to progress. Russia's victory over Sweden marked its emergence as a major European power.

What does *perestroika* mean?
Perestroika literally means "restructuring." In this context it describes the democratization process involving new electoral laws and constitutional reform initiated by Mikhail Gorbachev (born 1931) upon taking up office as general secretary of the Communist Party in 1988. In 1988/89, this policy of reform stimulated democratization measures in other Warsaw Pact countries. Moreover, disarmament proposals made to NATO resulted

The cathedral of St Sergius in Zagorsk's famous 14th-century monastery.

The Chusovaya River rises on the western side of the Urals and flows into the Kama River 310 miles (500 km) farther on.

A reindeer train led by Nenets crossing the Siberian tundra. The nomadic Nenets, who speak their own language, number around 40,000.

in the removal of all medium-range nuclear weapons from European soil. After an unsuccessful coup by conservative communist elements in August 1991, the final consequence of *perestroika* was the collapse of the Soviet Union itself.

What was the October Revolution?

The government of Aleksandr Fyodorovich Kerensky (1881–1970) that emerged from the February Revolution and the collapse of the Russian Empire was toppled by the Bolsheviks in Petrograd (also known at different times as Leningrad and

St Petersburg) in October 1917. Under the leadership of Leon Trotsky and Vladimir Lenin, the provisional government was replaced by a communist regime with the help of the armed forces. Initially, however, the revolution only secured power for Lenin and Trotsky in the city of Petrograd.

What role did the cruiser *Aurora* play?

The uprising in Petrograd began with a shot fired from the guns of the *Aurora*. Previously part of the imperial fleet, the ship had become a symbol of the revolution. The *Aurora* remained in St Petersburg and was later turned into a museum.

Is Russia now a democracy?

In the view of many critics, Russia is not a pluralist democracy in the Western sense. The Russian political commentator Sergey Markov described the country governed by Vladimir Putin (born 1952) as a "manipulated democracy" while others went even further, calling it a "defective democracy."

Interesting facts

- Russia has the second-highest level of immigration in the world.
- 73 per cent of Russians live in towns and cities.
- Nikita Khrushchev gave Ukraine (then part of the USSR) the Crimean Peninsula in 1954.
- 20–25 per cent of the population now live below the poverty line.

Is Belarus known by any other names?

The area corresponding to present-day Belarus was known historically as "White Russia." When it became a republic of the USSR, it was commonly referred to as "Belorussia." After the break-up of the Soviet Union the government requested that the country be called "Belarus" internationally in order to reflect more accurately the Belarusian form.

How is the population made up?

Belarus is multiethnic. While the vast majority of the population (81 per cent) are native Belarusians, representatives of more than 100 nationalities and numerous different regions live side by side. Russians constitute the largest minority (11 per cent), followed by Poles and Ukrainians.

Interesting facts: History

During the Second World War Belarus's industrial infrastructure was almost entirely destroyed and over 3 million people were left homeless. Prior to the start of hostilities, the population of Belarus had been 10 million; this figure was not reached again until the end of 1980. Around 9 per cent of all Jews murdered by the Nazis came from Belarus.

BELARUS

Flag	**Languages**
	Belarusian and Russian (official languages), Polish in the former Polish areas
Currency	
1 Belarus ruble (BYR) = 100 kapeek	**Surface area**
System of government	80,154 sq miles (207,599 sq km)
Presidential republic since 1991	**Population** 10.3 million
Capital	**Religion**
Minsk	80% Russian Orthodox, 10% Catholic

Who is the most famous Belarusian artist?

The painter Marc Chagall was born Moishe Zakharovich Shagalov in Vitebsk in 1887 and died in St Paul de Vence (France), where he lived most of his life, in 1985. His art is full of mystical and folk elements that tell of his Jewish background.

When did Belarus become an independent state?

Belarus became independent in 1991 and has been under the authoritarian leadership of Aleksandr Lukashenko (born 1954) since 1994. Lukashenko's anti-democratic tendencies have resulted in international isolation for Belarus, which is regarded as Europe's only dictatorship.

Around one fifth of the population of Belarus lives in the capital on the Svislach River. In terms of urban development, Minsk is dominated by monumental postwar architecture.

Right: The "Swallow's Nest" on the south coast of the Crimean Peninsula. This re-creation of a 19th-century Rhineland castle is perched on a cliff top 165 ft (40 m) above the sea.

Who were the Cossacks?

The cradle of the Ukrainian language and Ukrainian culture is the Dnieper region southeast of Kiev, where a short-lived Cossack state was created in the 17th century. The Cossacks were originally Russian and Ukrainian serfs and Tatar deserters who began to form their own communities in the 15th century. In the 18th century Cossack horsemen were incorporated into the Russian army as independent cavalry regiments.

Which great catastrophe occurred in Ukraine at the end of the 20th century?

On April 26, 1986, the second-biggest nuclear disaster (after the accident at Mayak, Russia, in 1957) and the world's greatest-ever environmental catastrophe occurred as a result of a meltdown and explosion in nuclear reactor no 4 at the Chernobyl Nuclear Power Plant. Large sections of the country were exposed to radiation for an extended period of time, and southern and eastern areas of Ukraine accounting for around 25 per cent of the country's total surface area are still affected. The countryside within a radius of

Country folk from the small village of Gidzivkain in Ukraine.

30 miles (50 km) around Chernobyl can still not be farmed due to its prolonged exposure to radiation.

What was the Russian-Ukrainian gas dispute?

In March 2005 Russia increased the price of natural gas. The prices that had applied hitherto had not been market prices but preferential prices based on the historic relationship between the two countries. Ukraine is the fourth-largest importer and sixth-largest consumer of natural gas in the world and was severely affected by the price increase. Its high consumption is due to a poor environmental policy, waste, antiquated infrastructure, and inefficiency. Relative to its gross domestic product Ukraine has the highest energy consumption in the world.

What was the Orange Revolution?

Ukraine has been an independent state since the collapse of the USSR. In 2004 the country experienced a democratic volte-face brought about by the so-called Orange Revolution (after the orange flags and clothing carried and worn during a series of peaceful demonstrations that continued for weeks). Viktor Yushchenko emerged victorious after a number of run-offs. On December 28 he received 51.99 per cent of the votes cast compared to 44.19 per cent for his opponent Viktor Yanukovich.

Is Moldova home to many different peoples?

People of many different ethnic origins live in Moldova. The Romanian Moldovans, making up 65 per cent of the population, are the largest group, followed by Ukrainians and Russians (roughly 13 per cent each). The smaller minorities include the Gagauz and the Bulgars. Many of the country's Russians and Ukrainians live in Transnistria, a region to the east of the Dniester River.

What languages are spoken in the country?

Moldovan was chosen as the country's official language for political rather than linguistic reasons. It is actually a Romanian dialect whose written form is identical with Romanian. The universal language spoken by everyone (and learned by all when under the Soviet Union) is still Russian.

On what is Moldova's economy based?

One of the major cornerstones of the Moldovan economy is agriculture. The warm, dry climate favors the cultivation of grapes and other fruit. In addition to wine and brandy, fruit conserves are made specifically for the export market.

Background: The Palace of Culture in the Moldovian capital, Chişinău

MOLDOVA

Flag

Currency
1 Moldovan leu (MDL) = 100 bani

System of government
Republic since 1991

Capital
Chişinău

Languages
Moldovan (official language), Russian, Ukrainian, Gagauz

Surface area
13,067 sq miles (33,843 sq km)

Population 4.5 million

Religion
98% Orthodox Christian

The conflict in Transnistria

Transnistria, with its population of over 600,000, is a region of Moldova lying to the east of the Dniester River. Under its president Igor Smirnov it declared independence shortly after the dissolution of the Soviet Union but failed to achieve recognition as an independent state and remains unrecognized today. Around a third of Moldova's industrial facilities are located in Transnistria, including textile, shoe and furniture factories, distilleries and hydroelectric plants. Inevitably, these are extremely important to the country as a whole. Armed conflict broke out in summer 1992 causing hundreds of fatalities on either side before a ceasefire was brokered by Belarus. Renewed attempts to create a federal state of Transnistria failed in 2003 as a result of opposition from the Moldovan government. Ukraine is currently mediating between the two countries.

SPAIN

Flag	Valencian, Galician, Basque (official regional languages)
	Surface area
Currency	194,897 sq miles (504,782 sq km)
1 euro (EUR) = 100 cents	**Population** 44.1 million
System of government	**Religion** 90% Catholic
Constitutional monarchy since 1978	**Notable features**
Capital	Also belonging to Spain are the urban
Madrid	exclaves of Melilla and Ceuta in North
Languages	Africa and Llívia in France.
Spanish (official language), Catalan,	

Paella, made with rice and seafood or meat, is the most typical of Spanish dishes.

After France, Spain is the world's favorite holiday destination. Visitors delight in the combination of sun, sea, and sand. Shown here is Portals Nous Beach in the Balearic Island of Mallorca.

What are the origins of the name "Spain"?
The name derives from the Roman name for the peninsula, "Hispania," which in turn came from the Phoenician "Ishapan."

Why does Spain have so many official languages?
Spain also includes the three autonomous regions Catalonia, Galicia, and the Basque Country. Each of these autonomous regions has its own, independent language, which is why four official languages exist alongside one another: Spanish (also known as Castilian), Catalan, Galician, and Basque. In addition to these four, dialects of Catalan are spoken in the autonomous regions of Valencia and the Balearic Islands: Valencian (which has now been recognized as a language in its own right) and Mallorquí (currently fighting for recognition).

What are the origins of the Basque language?
Basque, which is spoken in Spain and France, belongs to no known family of languages and so far philologists have been unable to reconstruct its prehistory.

Spanish cuisine: *Paella*

Originally a humble rural dish, *paella* (which takes its name from the pan in which it is cooked) is familiar throughout the world today. It can be prepared with different ingredients such as rabbit or seafood but always includes either rice or short lengths of spaghetti-like pasta.

How many islands does Spain have?

There are about 20 islands. The main ones are the Balearic Islands in the Mediterranean comprising Mallorca, Menorca, Ibiza, Formentera, and Cabrera, the Canary Islands in the Atlantic consisting of Gran Canaria, El Hierro, La Palma, Tenerife, Lanzarote, Fuerteventura, and La Gomera, the Islas Chafarinas off the Moroccan coast of Peñón de Vélez de la Gomera, Alhucemas, Alborán, and Perejil, and lastly the Columbretes Islands off the coast of Valencia.

Where is Spain's highest mountain?

At 12,198 ft (3,718 m) Pico del Teide on Tenerife in the Canary Islands is Spain's highest mountain. The highest peak on the Spanish mainland is Mulhacén in the Sierra Nevada in Andalucia at 11,424 ft (3,482 m).

What was the Reconquista?

Spain's architecture, food, music, and language were dominated for many centuries (from the 8th to the 15th) by its Arab rulers. The "Reconquista" was literally the reconquest of Spain by a Christian population inspired by religion and nationalism. The process was completed in 1492 by King Ferdinand II (1452–1516) and his wife Isabella (1451–1504), who were known as the "Catholic Monarchs" because of the great ruthlessness with which they drove out the Moors and Jews.

What are Spain's main industries?

Two sectors are of particular importance to the Spanish economy: tourism and construction. Also significant are the communications industry and information technology, mechanical engineering, chemicals, metal-working, and agriculture.

What proportion of Spaniards own their own homes?

It has long been common for Spanish families to own two homes, one in town and one in the country or by the sea. At the end of 2005 there were 1.54 dwellings per household, the highest figure in the world. About 85 per cent of Spanish homes are owner-occupied while just 15 per cent are rented.

Is Spain a popular holiday destination?

After France, Spain is the most popular tourist destination in the world, attracting over seven per cent of all tourists each year. Almost 37 per cent of holidaymakers who visit the country make for Catalonia and the Balearic Islands.

The church of Santa Cruz, dating from 1602, in Cádiz in southern Andalucia.

PORTUGAL

Flag

Currency
1 euro (EUR) = 100 cents
System of government
Republic since 1910

Capital
Lisbon
Languages
Portuguese (official language)
Surface area
35,655 sq miles (92,345 sq km)
Population 10.5 million
Religion 93% Catholic

Fado

Fado is Portugal's best-known musical genre, featuring deeply melancholy songs that deal with themes such as unhappy love, times gone by and *saudade* (longing). Its main centers are Lisbon and Coimbra. *Fado* developed from a combination of Portuguese sailors' songs and African rhythms. The greatest singer of classical *fado* was probably Amália Rodrigues (1920–1999). Today *fado* keeps emerging in new forms, the result of fusions with other musical genres. One of the best known of the new generation of *fado* singers is Marize.

What does the name "Portugal" mean?

The word "cale" in the name Portus Cale, an important port on the delta of the Rio Douro, is thought to stem from the Greek for "beautiful" (*kalos*), which would give the meaning "beautiful port." This developed into "Portugale," which initially designated only the northern part of the country from the Douro to the River Minho, Portugal's present-day border with Spain. The short form "Porto" developed around the same time and became the name of the country's second-largest city. Porto sees itself today as having given Portugal its name.

When was Portugal's golden age?

After the House of Burgundy died out in 1383, John of Aviz, an illegitimate descendant of the royal line, was made king. The claims of the king of Castile to the Portuguese throne were defeated at the Battle of Aljubarrota in 1385, and under the kings of the Aviz line Portugal experienced the most successful period in its history. It became Europe's leading maritime power and, after establishing colonies in South America, Africa, and Asia, the richest nation in the world. In 1580, the House of Aviz died out and Portugal became a Spanish province, losing most of its colonies in the process.

What was the Carnation Revolution?

The Carnation Revolution is the name given to the Portuguese military's revolt against the ruling dictatorship on April 25, 1974. The event became a public celebration during which people placed carnations in the barrels of the soldiers' guns. The new government granted independence to all Portugal's remaining colonies other than Macau. The revolution was not completely without bloodshed, however, as 13 people lost their lives.

Restauradores Square in Lisbon's lower town, the *Baixa*.

Left: Famous Rocha Beach near the small town of Lagos on the Algarve Coast.

Who is the prince of Andorra?

Who is the prince of Andorra? Ever since it was founded in 1278 the tiny state of Andorra has been a principality without a prince. The official duties of the head of state are shared between the bishop of Urgell (Spain) and the president of France as legal successor of the counts of Foix. Since 1993 the government has been headed by a prime minister.

Where is Andorra?

Andorra is one of five European micro-states and is located in a high valley of the eastern Pyrenees between Spain and France. It is extremely mountainous. One third of its surface area lies above the tree line and it has numerous peaks of 6,500 ft (2,000 m) or higher.

What is Andorra's main source of income?

As only two per cent of the surface area is suitable for cultivation, keeping cattle was once the Andorrans' only source of income. Today the population lives mainly on tourism (especially winter sports). It also sells its surplus hydroelectricity to Spain.

ANDORRA

Flag

Currency
1 euro (EUR) = 100 cents

System of government
Constitutional monarchy (principality) since 1993

Capital
Andorra la Vella

Languages
Catalan (official language), Spanish, French

Surface area
181 sq miles (469 sq km)

Population 76,800

Religion 90% Catholic

Is Andorra a tax haven?

There is no income tax or capital gains tax in Andorra and it is therefore highly advantageous for companies to be registered in the principality (even if their registered offices consist of no more than a letter box), while maintaining their headquarters in another country. But Andorra is also financially attractive for tourists as all goods are exempt from duty.

In winter the Vall d'Incles between El Tartar and Soldeu in northeast Andorra is a popular skiing destination.

Interesting facts

- Andorra is not a member of the European Union but has adopted the euro as its official currency.

- To qualify for Andorran nationality applicants must have lived in the country for 25 years.

- Andorra possesses neither an airport nor a railroad network. Buses and taxis are the only available forms of public transportation.

ITALY

Flag	Ladin, Slovenian (official regional languages), various minority languages
	Surface area
Currency	116,358 sq miles (301,366 sq km)
1 euro (EUR) = 100 cents	**Population** 58.1 million
System of government	**Religion** 83% Catholic,
Republic since 1946	13% non-denominational
Capital	**Notable features**
Rome	The two largest islands in the
Languages	Mediterranean, Sicily and Sardinia,
Italian (official language), German,	also belong to Italy.

What is the Italian boot?

What is the Italian boot?
Italy is a peninsula that projects into the Mediterranean Sea in the shape of a boot. The Apennine Mountains extend along the whole length of the country, which is why Italy is sometimes referred to as the "Apennine Peninsula." The highest peaks in the Apennines are around 9,515 ft (2,900 m) while in the north of the country the Italian Alps soar to over 13,125 ft (4,000 m).

Right: The Leaning Tower of Pisa is one of the best-known buildings in the world. Built in the 12th century, it is actually the bell tower of Pisa Cathedral in Tuscany.

Below: The ruins of Pompeii near Naples. The Roman city was destroyed by the eruption of Vesuvius in AD 79.

Italy, cradle of the Renaissance

In the middle of the 15th century science and art in Italy began to undergo a major transformation characterized by a reappraisal of the culture of the ancient world. This period is known as the Renaissance (meaning "rebirth"). Two of the most important Italian artists of this time were Leonardo da Vinci (1452–1519) and Michelangelo (1475–1564). Art took its cue from nature and was once more concerned with naturalistic representation while science replaced traditional beliefs with investigation and experimentation.

Pizza and pasta

Italian cuisine is known and loved the world over. It is based on uncomplicated combinations of basic ingredients of the highest quality. In addition to its outstanding wines, pizza and pasta are among Italy's best-known specialties. Pizza is a flat bread made of yeast dough covered with a variety of savory toppings while pasta is the name given to Italian egg and flour dough processed into a wide variety of shapes.

Does Italy have a high population?

Italy has a relatively large population (the 23rd-largest in the world). Two thirds of Italians live in towns and cities, a consequence of migration from the underdeveloped rural areas of the south. Recently, however, the trend for people to move to the city has started to reverse as city-dwellers move back to the suburbs and small provincial towns.

When did the Italian state emerge?

After the collapse of the Napoleonic empire a national movement developed in Italy called the *Risorgimento* (Italian for "revival"). The most famous revolutionary leader of this time was Giuseppe Garibaldi (1807–1882), whose military successes resulted in Italy's emergence as an independent nation-state under the domination of the Kingdom of Piedmont-Sardinia.

What was the Roman Empire?

The city-state of Rome developed into a mighty empire from around 600 BC onwards. In terms of its system of government it evolved from kingdom (during the early period) to republic to imperium. The Roman Empire achieved its greatest territorial extent under Emperor Trajan (53–117), eventually spreading over three continents. It extended from the British Isles to the North African coast and from Spain to the Black Sea. The empire held on to its authority and the city its status as the center of power in the Mediterranean for more than 1,000 years. Because of its 2,000-year history, Rome is also known as the "Eternal City."

What is Italy's economy based on?

Italy is not well off for raw materials. The mainstay of the economy is its small to medium-sized manufacturing enterprises while winegrowing is a key agricultural segment. Italy is the world's biggest exporter of wine after France, and the fifth most popular tourist destination.

What is the north-south divide?

In Italy there are marked differences between the economically successful north and the underdeveloped south. While northern Italy is one of Europe's strongest economic regions, the Mezzogiorno (southern part of the country) lags significantly behind in terms of industry and is still largely agricultural.

A typical Tuscan scene: A cypress-lined road winds its way through the undulating landscape of the Val d'Orcia.

SAN MARINO

Flag	Languages
	Italian (official language), Emiliano-Romagnolo
Currency	**Surface area** 24 sq miles (61 sq km)
1 euro (EUR) = 100 cents	**Population** 30,000
System of government	**Religion**
Republic since 1599	93% Catholic
Capital	**Notable features**
San Marino	San Marino is the oldest republic in the world.

Where does San Marino take its name from?
Christian stonemason Marinus arrived in the region from Croatia around AD 300. When Emperor Diocletian unleashed the last persecution of Christians a few years later, Marinus and his followers took refuge on Mount Titano. Over the years they were joined by other Christians and established the first community here. Today September 3, 301 is celebrated as the date on which San Marino was founded. In 311 Marinus was made a bishop by Nicodemus and Mount Titano was given him by Roman patrician Donna Felicissima.

Participants in the 2006 Mille Miglia vintage automobile rally in front of the town hall (and state government building) on Piazza della Libertà.

The dying words, in 366, of the saint after whom the state is named were: "I leave you free from both men" and with these words the republic was founded.

Who are the *capitani reggenti*?
The two *capitani reggenti* (captains regent) are elected by parliament to serve as joint heads of state for a period of six months at a time. The periods of office begin on April 1 and October 1 each year.

How did the republic react to Napoleon's offer to extend its territory?
By 1200, San Marino's population had increased to such an extent that it purchased two castles and their lands in the vicinity of Mount Titano. This was to be the last ever expansion. Upon invading Italy, Napoleon is said to have forbidden his troops from crossing San Marino's borders because it was "a model republic" and he offered to extend the republic as far as the coast, but the Sammarinese turned him down on the grounds that they would never again be able to live in peace with their neighbors. Napoleon also presented the republic with two cannons and two loads of grain. The people of San Marino politely returned the cannon while accepting the grain as a gesture of peace.

Arengo
Arengo, which dates back to 1295, was originally a gathering of all the heads of family but now refers to the totality of those entitled to vote. It is summoned twice a year on the Sunday after the assumption of office of the two *capitani reggenti*.

What does the Vatican City comprise?

The Vatican City is the smallest state in the world to have been recognized by the United Nations. It is an enclave within the city of Rome and includes the Basilica of St Peter and Sistine Chapel, St Peter's Square, and the palaces and gardens within the Vatican walls.

Who is the head of the Vatican City?

As well as being the head of the Roman Catholic Church, the Pope, who is elected for life, is the sovereign head (the holder of legislative, executive, and judicial power) of the tiny state. He makes appointments to the government and administrative bodies and represents the Vatican City internationally.

How many citizens does the Vatican City have?

The Vatican City has around 870 citizens. Citizenship is only ever granted for a fixed period of time and is tied to a specific function or office. It does not, however, replace the holder's nationality of birth. Some 60 per cent of Vatican citizens are papal envoys in various parts of the world and therefore live outside the state. Conversely, around 3,000 people who are not citizens of the Vatican City work inside the state—as staff, officials, teachers, or employees of the Vatican Bank or Vatican Radio, for example.

Has the Vatican always been the seat of the popes?

No. Until the return of the popes from Avignon in 1377 and the end of the Schism (the split within the Latin Church) in 1417, the seat of the popes was not the Vatican but the Lateran Palace. "Vatican" is the name of one of Rome's hills (mons vaticanus on the right bank of the Tiber). It is thought to have been the location of Emperor Nero's circus and was also the site of a cemetery believed to contain the tomb of St Peter the Apostle.

Above: Benedict XVI greets onlookers from the balcony of St Peter's shortly after being elected Pope in April 2005.

Right: St Peter's Square was designed and built by Gian Lorenzo Bernini (1589–1680) between 1656 and 1667 (under Pope Alexander VII).

Swiss Guards

The *Guardia Svizzera Pontificia* is the papal army that guards the Papal Palace and entrances to the Vatican City. It is therefore responsible for the security of the Pope. In reality, the guards are more of a security force than an army. Their operational languages are German and Italian. The force of 110 men consists of six commissioned officers, 26 non-commissioned officers, and 78 guardsmen.

VATICAN CITY

Flag	**Surface area** 0.17 sq miles (0.44 sq km)
	Population 870
Currency 1 euro (EUR) = 100 cents	**Religion** 100% Catholic
System of government Sovereign archbishopric since 1929	**Notable features** The Vatican City is the world's smallest state.
Languages Latin, Italian (official languages)	

MALTA

Flag

Currency
1 euro (EUR) = 100 cents

System of government
Republic since 1974
(Commonwealth member)

Capital
Valletta

Languages
Maltese, English (official languages),
Italian

Surface area
122 sq miles (316 sq km)

Population 399,000

Religion
93% Catholic

Notable features
The Republic of Malta comprises six
islands, of which Malta and Gozo make
up 99% of the national territory.

*Valletta was
once one of the
best-protected
cities in the world.
It was built in the
16th century to
plans drawn up
by the Knights
of Malta.*

Where is Malta?
The island republic is located in the
Mediterranean to the south of Sicily. The six islands
belonging to the state are the remnants of an ancient
land bridge that linked Africa with Europe until a little
more than 13,000 years ago.

Why is English an official language?
The British occupied Malta in 1800 during the
Napoleonic Wars and subsequently regarded the island
as a colony. Possession of the island was of strategic
rather than economic interest and, as recently as the
Second World War, Malta was an important base
for the British campaigns against Germany in North
Africa. Malta gained full independence from the
United Kingdom in 1964 but retained English as an
official language.

Is there a connection between the Republic of Malta and the Knights of Malta?
Yes. The Order of Knights of the Hospital of
St John of Jerusalem, whose mission was to protect
Christian pilgrims on their way to Jerusalem, was
founded in 1099. During times of war the knights
wore a red tunic adorned with a white cross of
the same design as the Maltese cross of today.
In 1530 the order was driven back to Malta by
the Ottomans. It has been customary ever since
to refer to the order as the Knights of Malta.

What kind of economy does Malta have today?
In addition to agriculture and fishing, shipbuilding also
plays a major role in the Maltese economy. Europe's
second-largest shipyard, the country's biggest employer,
is in Malta. Tourism is also gaining increasing
importance, as not only are the country's sunny beaches
a big attraction, its English language schools are also
extremely popular, especially with younger people.

Hagar Qim
Starting around 3800 BC a megalithic culture developed on
Malta that was to last for about 1,000 years, leaving behind
a number of ruined temples. One of the most important
archaeological sites is Hagar Qim, where the best-preserved
of the temples was found. Characteristic of this Stone Age
culture on Malta are small sculptures of voluptuous women,
the so-called "Venuses of Malta."

Gyros and ouzo

Gyros (pork meat sliced from a vertical rotating spit), regarded by many tourists as Greece's national dish, was still relatively unknown in Greece at the end of the 1980s. More typical of traditional Greek cuisine are vegetables and lamb-based dishes. The anise-flavored liqueur *ouzo*, on the other hand (although thought to have developed from the Turkish *raki*, which has been made since the 15th century), is not only typically Greek but is only allowed to be made in Greece.

Left: The Greek island of Santorini, with its winding alleyways, provides many examples of the kind of image with which Greece attracts tourists from all over the world.

Is Greece an island state?

No. Although Greece has 9,840 islands, they only make up a quarter of the total surface area. Both mainland and islands are dominated by mountains and hills—no less than 78 per cent of the country is classified as mountainous. Cultivatable plains are found only in Macedonia, Thessaly, and Thrace.

Why is Greece called the "Cradle of Europe"?

Europe's first advanced civilization developed in Ancient Greece. This was the Minoan civilization, centered on the Greek island of Crete, which experienced a golden age around 2000 BC. The very name "Europe" derives from Ancient Greece and its myths. In Greek mythology Europa was a princess who was abducted by Zeus, the father of the gods, disguised as a bull.

Does Greece depend on tourism?

No. Tourism accounts for a mere ten per cent or so of the country's economic output. At 22 per cent the industrial sector alone makes more than twice as large a contribution to Greece's gross domestic product. Another traditionally strong sector that still plays an important role in the country's economic life is shipping. No less than 18.6 per cent of world shipping is Greek owned.

What is the connection between Greece and the Olympic Games?

The very first Olympic Games are thought to have taken place in the Ancient Greek city of Olympia in 776 BC while the first Olympics of modern times (the biggest sporting event since antiquity) were held in Athens in 1896. The International Olympic Committee (IOC) was founded by Frenchman Pierre de Coubertin (1863–1937) in 1894.

The Parthenon, dating from the 5th century BC, survived until 1687, when it was destroyed by a well-aimed shot during the Venetian siege—having been turned into a gunpowder store by the Turks.

TURKEY

Flag	**Capital**
	Ankara
	Languages
Currency	Turkish (official language), Kurdish,
1 Turkish new lira (TRY)	Arabic
= 100 kuruş	**Surface area**
System of government	300,948 sq miles (779,452 sq km)
Republic since 1923	**Population** 69.7 million
	Religion 99% Muslim (mainly Sunni)

A souvenir shop in Turkey. The country is visited by over ten million visitors every year.

Why is Turkey included as part of Europe?
As explained in the Introduction, the allocation of particular countries to larger regions or continents can be relatively arbitrary. Turkey is a good example of this. Although 96 per cent of the country is in Asia and only four per cent lies on the European side of the Sea of Marmara and the Bosporus, for historical and cultural reasons Turkey is always regarded as part of Europe. However, it is often referred to as the "Gateway to Asia."

The Ortaköy Mosque, dating from 1854, and the entertainment district of the same name, with its restaurants, bars and street cafés, are pictured here against the backdrop of modern Istanbul.

Do earthquakes ever occur in Turkey?
Northern Turkey is one of the world's most earthquake-prone regions in the world and has repeatedly suffered major tremors over the last few years. In 1999 there was a devastating earthquake in the province of Kocaeli, just 60 miles (100 km) from Istanbul, which was also affected.

How much coastline does Turkey have?
Three quarters of Turkey is surrounded by the sea: The Black Sea in the north, the Marmara and Aegean seas to the west, and the Mediterranean to the south. To the east and southeast it shares land borders with Syria, Iraq, Iran, Armenia, and Georgia.

Where do most of the Turkish people live?
About 74 per cent of Turks live in the large cities. Turkey is currently experiencing a major internal migration from the countryside to the city, resulting in increasing urbanization of Turkish society.

Who was Atatürk?
Gazi Mustafa Kemal Atatürk (1881–1938) was the first president of the Republic of Turkey, which emerged out of the weakened Ottoman Empire after the First World War. The name "Atatürk," meaning "Father of the Turks," was bestowed on Mustafa Kemal by the Turkish Grand National Assembly in 1934 in recognition of his achievement in modernizing the country along Western lines. He abolished the sultanate and caliphate, created a secular nation in which religious interests were secondary to those of the state, and improved the position in society of women—in 1930 Turkey became one of the first nations in the world to give women the vote.

Orhan Pamuk

Orhan Pamuk (born 1952) is Turkey's best-known writer. His books, which have been translated into 35 languages and are sold in 100 countries, build bridges between the European novel and traditional Asian forms of storytelling. Pamuk was awarded the Nobel Prize for Literature in 2006.

What is the Turkish Republic of Northern Cyprus?

The island of Cyprus is home to two states: the Republic of Cyprus and the smaller Turkish Republic of Northern Cyprus. With over 250,000 inhabitants and a surface area of 2,085 sq miles (3,355 sq km), the northern part of the island is only a third or so of the size of the Republic of Cyprus. The Turkish Republic of Northern Cyprus, whose capital is also the divided city of Nicosia, has not been recognized by any member of the UN other than Turkey.

Which continent does Cyprus belong to?

Geographically Cyprus belongs to Asia but politically to Europe (all the more so since its accession to the EU). Culturally the island can be seen as a meeting point between Asia, Africa, and Europe.

Who are the Maronites?

Founded in Lebanon, the Maronites are one of the oldest Christian communities in the world. The head of their church is the pope.

When was Cyprus divided?

Cyprus became a British crown colony in 1925, having previously belonged to the Ottoman Empire. It gained its independence in 1960. In a move designed to make Cyprus Greek, President Makarios was removed from power in 1974 in a coup sponsored by the Greek junta in Athens. Turkey invaded and in 1983 proclaimed the sector it occupied as the independent Turkish Republic of Northern Cyprus. A strict partitioning of the island ensued and the border was not opened until 2003.

The extensive ruins of Kourion, near the town of Episkopi, are notable for their beautiful and well-preserved floor mosaics.

REPUBLIC OF CYPRUS

Flag

Currency
1 euro (EUR) = 100 cents

System of government
Presidential republic since 1960
(Commonwealth member)

Capital
Nikosia

Languages
Greek, Turkish (official languages)

Surface area
3,572 sq miles (9,251 sq km)

Population 780,000

Religion
82% Greek Orthodox,
15% Muslim, remainder Catholic
and Maronite

Interesting facts: Climate

Cyprus is the warmest but at the same time most densely wooded island in the Mediterranean. Its average summer temperature is 46°F (8°C) higher than that of Mallorca and just 35°F (2°C) below that of Dubai.

CROATIA

Flag	Languages
	Croatian (official language)
	Surface area
	35,134 sq miles (56,542 sq km)
Currency	**Population** 4.5 million
1 kuna (HRK) = 100 lipa	**Religion** 88% Catholic
System of government	**Notable features**
Republic since 1991	Also belonging to Croatia are more
Capital	than 1,200 islands in the Adriatic,
Zagreb	almost all of which are uninhabited.

Can Croatia be divided into different geographical zones?

Yes. The country has three distinct geographical subdivisions. In the east is the Pannonian Basin, in which Zagreb lies. Further west are the Dinaric Alps, which rise in places to significant heights. Finally there is a flat coastal strip along the Adriatic.

Croatia's most beautiful and best-known national park, Plitvice, features 16 small lakes connected to one another by waterfalls.

How long has Croatia existed as a country?

This part of Europe has had a turbulent history and Croatia has belonged to a succession of different countries. For a long time it was part of the Ottoman Empire. Later it fell under the rule of Austria-Hungary. After the Second World War Croatia became a constituent republic of Yugoslavia.

Dubrovnik, the "Pearl of the Adriatic." The districts damaged during the Croatian War of Independence (1991–1995) have since been restored.

It finally gained is independence with the collapse of Yugoslavia in 1991.

How important is tourism for Croatia?

Tourism is a major source of revenue. Croatia attracts around ten million visitors a year, accounting for some 20 per cent of the GDP. Thanks to its long Adriatic coast and many islands, Croatia is one of Europe's most popular holiday destinations. This particular stretch of the Adriatic is considered to be the cleanest part of the Mediterranean and, with nearly 15,000 berths, it is a paradise for sailors too.

Pearl of the Adriatic

The city of Dubrovnik on Croatia's Adriatic coast is often referred to by its nickname the "Pearl of the Adriatic" and is still known in Italian by its Latin name "Ragusa." The city, once an independent republic, can look back on 1,400 years of history. It was the cradle of the Croatian language and Croatian literature and can still be regarded as the center of Croatia's cultural life today. It was added to UNESCO's list of World Heritage sites in 1979.

Is Bosnia and Herzegovina a landlocked country?

Bosnia and Herzegovina forms part of the Balkan Peninsula and for the most part is a country of low mountains and abundant forests. Only in the south does the land flatten out and become suitable for agriculture. It is essentially a landlocked country but a narrow corridor provides access to the Adriatic. Neum is the only town along its 6 miles (10 km) of coastline.

Is Bosnia and Herzegovina a multiethnic state?

Bosnia and Herzegovina is one of the successor states to the former Yugoslavia, itself a multi-ethnic state. The population of Bosnia and Herzegovina is made up of three main ethnic groups: Bosniaks (48 per cent), Serbs (37 per cent), and Croats (13 per cent). None of the groups is classified as a minority. There have been repeated clashes between the different ethnic and religious groups. A civil war that broke out in 1992 finally ended in 1995 with the signing of the Dayton Agreement.

What is the historical significance of Sarajevo?

Sarajevo is where Archduke Franz Ferdinand (heir to the Austrian imperial throne) and his wife were assassinated on June 28, 1914 by a group later known as "The Black Hand." This was the trigger

for the First World War (1914–1918) in which the whole of Europe and later the United States became embroiled.

What is the convertible mark?

The convertible mark is the currency introduced in Bosnia and Herzegovina in 1998. It was pegged to the German D-Mark at par. Initially, German coins and banknotes were also accepted. After the introduction of the euro across the EU the convertible mark was pegged to the euro at a fixed exchange rate.

Constructed in the 16th century, Mostar's single-arch Old Bridge is a masterpiece of engineering.

BOSNIA AND HERZEGOVINA

Flag

Currency
1 convertible marka (BAM)
= 100 pfeninga

System of government
Republic since 1992

Capital
Sarajevo

Languages
Bosnian, Croatian, Serbian
(official languages)

Surface area
31,770 sq miles (51,129 sq km)

Population 4 million

Religion
40% Muslim, 31% Serbian Orthodox,
15% Catholic

The Old Bridge, Mostar

This 16th-century bridge remains the longest single-arch stone bridge in the world. For centuries it has been considered a symbol of the desire for understanding between East and West, Christianity and Islam. In 1993 it was destroyed during the civil war in Bosnia and Herzegovina. After the war it was rebuilt with the help of UNESCO and the World Bank and reopened in 2004.

MONTENEGRO

Flag

Currency
1 euro (EUR) = 100 cents

System of government
Republic since 2006

Capital
Podgorica

Languages Serbian (Montenegrin) (official language), Albanian

Surface area
5,333 sq miles (13,812 sq km)

Population 631,000

Religion
75% Serbian Orthodox, 15% Muslim

Notable features
Montenegro is one of Europe's smallest states

Sveti Stefan is a seaside resort on the Adriatic. It used to be an island connected to the mainland only at low tide—now it is a peninsula.

What are the origins of the country's name?

The literal meaning of the country's Serbo-Croatian name Crna Gora is "black mountain." The international name Montenegro derives not from Italian but from Venetian, an Italian dialect spoken in Venice and the Veneto by around two million people and deviating so markedly from Italian that it is often regarded as a separate language.

When did Montenegro become an independent state?

Montenegro became an independent principality in 1878 and subsequently a kingdom between 1910 and 1918. Between 1945 and 1992 it was a constituent republic (allied with Serbia) of the Socialist Federal Republic of Yugoslavia. In 2003 its relationship with Serbia (by that time the only other Yugoslav republic) was transformed into a state union named Serbia and Montenegro. In May 2006 Montenegro held a plebiscite on independence in which the EU stipulated that 55 per cent of the votes were needed for nationhood. A total of 55.5 per cent voted for independence and Montenegro became a sovereign state.

How important is tourism to the country?

Tourism plays an extremely important role in the country's economic life, currently accounting for 15 per cent of the GDP. In 2006 Montenegro's tourist industry had the highest growth rate of any in the world.

Montenegrin

While most of Montenegro's citizens refer to their country's official language as Serbian, it is described by a minority as Montenegrin. In actual fact Montenegrin is a dialect of Serbian and its speakers are able to communicate with speakers of Serbian, Croatian, and Bosnian with perfect ease. Although the existence of a separate Montenegrin language is disputed by many linguists, language is a political issue and is often used to generate a sense of national identity. Having its "own" language could be useful to a nation as young as Montenegro.

SERBIA

Flag

Currency
1 new dinar (RSD) = 100 para

System of government
Republic

Capital
Belgrade

Languages
Serbian (official language), Albanian, Hungarian, Croatian, Slovenian, Macedonian

Surface area
34,116 sq miles (88,361 sq km)

Population 10.4 million

Religion
85% Serbian Orthodox, 5% Catholic

Interesting facts

- Serbia was one of the first regions in Europe to be settled and cultivated.
- The world's oldest writing system originated not in Mesopotamia, as previously thought, but under the Vinča culture that flourished in the area now covered by Serbia, western Romania, southern Hungary, and eastern Bosnia between 5400 and 4500 BC.

What is the Iron Gate?

The Iron Gate is Europe's longest and deepest gorge, carved by the River Danube into the southern Carpathian mountains on the border between Serbia and Romania millions of years ago. It is also the name of a power station located in the gorge. Until the electricity plant was built in 1972, navigation of this section of the Danube was so hazardous that it was only possible with the help of a guide.

What happened in London on July 17, 1944?

During the turmoil of the Second World War the parents of Serbian Crown Prince Alexander II fled into exile in London. In order that the prince could be born on Serbian soil, however, Winston Churchill declared suite 212 of Claridge's Hotel in London Yugoslavian territory for the duration of July 17.

What was the Socialist Federal Republic of Yugoslavia (SFRY)?

During the Second World War there were two anti-fascist camps in Yugoslavia: the communist movement led by Josip Broz (1892–1980), known as Tito, and the pro-monarchy Chetniks who were supported by the West. It was Tito who emerged victorious. Serbia became one of six constituent republics of the Socialist Federal Republic of Yugoslavia (SFRY) whose president Tito remained until his death. The individual republics were Slovenia, Croatia, Bosnia and Herzegovina, Serbia, Montenegro, and Macedonia. Kosovo and Vojvodina were made autonomous provinces within Serbia in 1974.

When did Yugoslavia begin to fall apart?

After Tito's death in 1980 the artificially created state of Yugoslavia began to crumble and eventually fell apart in 1991 with the declaration of independence of one constituent republic after another. The struggle for autonomy resulted in conflict between the former Yugoslav republics, which in turn escalated into the decade-long Yugoslav wars.

Zemun, a historic district of Belgrade. Celtic tribes first settled in what was then Taurunum in the 3rd century BC.

Below: In rural parts, wool is still spun by older women in the traditional way.

BULGARIA

Flag		**Surface area**	
		42,823 sq miles (110,910 sq km)	
		Population 7.5 million	
Currency		**Religion**	
1 lev (BGN) = 100 stotinki		84% Bulgarian Orthodox,	
System of government		12% Muslim	
Republic since 1991		**Notable features**	
Capital Sofia		Bulgaria is a major transit route	
Languages		between central Europe and the	
Bulgarian (official language), Turkish,		Middle East.	
Greek, Macedonian, Romani			

Above: One of the main landmarks of the Bulgarian capital Sofia is the Alexander Nevsky Cathedral. It can hold 5,000 people and houses a unique collection of icons.

How is Bulgaria subdivided geographically?

Bulgaria forms part of the Balkan Peninsula and is bounded by the Black Sea. The Balkan Mountains bisect the country in an east-west direction, rising in places to heights of 7,875 ft (2,400 m). To the north of this range lies the Danubian Plain while the south of the country is dominated by the Upper Thracian lowland.

Since Bulgaria joined the EU, tourism has boomed. The country's Black Sea beaches, such as this one at Sozopol, are a major attraction.

What is Golden Sands?

Golden Sands (Zlatni Pyasatsi) is a Black Sea beach that extends for over 2 miles (3.5 km) and reaches widths of 330 ft (100 m) in places. This and Sunny Beach (Slanchev Bryag) are Bulgaria's best-known tourist attractions. The season extends from June to August. In winter the beaches and tourist resorts are almost deserted.

Was Bulgaria once ruled by a tsar?

Simeon I became the first tsar of Bulgaria in 913. Tsarist rule lasted until 1398, when Bulgaria fell under Turkish hegemony. The country did not regain its independence until 1878, nearly 500 years later. In 1908 the country's ruling prince readopted the title "tsar." The last tsar was Simeon II (born 1937). Having been forced to abdicate in 1946, he was eventually elected prime minister of the Republic of Bulgaria in 2001 and served a four-year term of office.

Is Bulgaria a member of the EU?

Yes. Romania and Bulgaria joined the European Union on the same day, January 1, 2007. Although the modernization of Bulgaria began in 1950 with its industrialization and the introduction of intensive agriculture, the Bulgarian economy still requires significant levels of investment. This presents foreign investors with good opportunities.

Christo

The best-known Bulgarian artist is Christo Javacheff. Born in Bulgaria in 1935, he later became famous under the name Christo. He and his wife Jeanne-Claude came to international attention by wrapping objects and buildings such as the Reichstag in Berlin (1995) and through actions such as *The Gates* in New York's Central Park (2005). Future projects include the spanning of a 7-mile (11-km) stretch of the Arkansas River (USA) with fabric panels.

Who was Nicolae Ceaușescu?

Nicolae Ceaușescu was president of the Romanian State Council between 1967 and 1974. Towards the end of his tenure he created the office of state president and duly had himself elected president of the Socialist Republic of Romania. He remained in power until 1989, when his repressive regime collapsed. Ceaușescu ruled as a dictator, encouraging a cult of his personality while at the same time leading his country to economic ruin. When the army joined the rebellion in 1989, Ceaușescu and his wife were arrested, sentenced to death in a summary trial, and executed by firing squad.

Which is Romania's most important industrial sector?

As an "original equipment manufacturer" Romania is one of the world's largest manufacturers of

ROMANIA

Flag		**Languages** Romanian (official language), Hungarian, German (regional languages)
Currency		**Surface area**
1 new leu (RON) = 100 bani		92,043 sq miles (238,391 sq km)
System of government		**Population** 22.3 million
Republic since 1991		**Religion**
Capital		87% Romanian Orthodox,
Bucharest		7% Protestant, 5% Catholic

notebook computers, semiconductor applications and WLAN components for different, often competing, markets.

Who was Count Dracula?

Count Dracula is the title character of a novel by the Irish writer Bram Stoker (1847–1912) set in Transylvania in Romania. The fictional character is based on the historical figure of Vlad III Drăculea ("son of the dragon"). Nicknamed "Vlad the Impaler," Drăculea was a 15th-century ruler reputed to have treated his subjects brutally and drunk their blood. The legend surrounding Vlad was further fed by the fact that his remains have never been found—his grave is empty.

The 14th-century stronghold often described as "Dracula's Castle" sits atop a steep, rocky outcrop. It is unlikely that Vlad III Drăculea, the historical figure on whom the fictional Count Dracula was based, ever stepped foot in it, however.

Transylvania

Transylvania is a region of central and western Romania with a particularly turbulent history. In 1734 Holy Roman Emperor Charles VI began deporting Protestants to Transylvania (meaning "beyond the woods") from the Salzkammergut region of Austria because the local population had been depleted by a combination of the Turkish wars and the plague. Another 3,000 Austrians were compulsorily moved to the area in 1770. The German dialect peculiar to Transylvania is still spoken by around 30,000 people.

MACEDONIA

Flag

Currency
1 denar (MKD) = 100 deni

System of government
Republic since 1991

Capital
Skopje

Languages
Macedonian, Albanian (official languages), Turkish, Romani, Serbian, Walachian

Surface area
9,928 sq miles (25,713 sq km)

Population 2 million

Religion
59% Macedonian Orthodox, 28% Muslim

Notable features
There is an ongoing dispute between Macedonia and Greece over the name of the country, as Greece's northernmost province is also called Macedonia. It is often referred to as the Republic of Macedonia.

Macedonia remains an economically underdeveloped country whose industry lags behind that of much of Europe. Many young people are only able to find work in small-scale trades.

How can the country's geography be summed up?

Macedonia is a landlocked country in southeastern Europe with no access to the Mediterranean. It is extremely mountainous and its climate is relatively harsh.

How is Macedonia's population made up?

Macedonia's population is made up of two main ethnic groups and a number of minorities. The largest ethnic groups are the Slavic Macedonians (64 per cent) and the Albanians (25 per cent). The minority groups include Turks, Roma, Serbs, Bosniaks, Vlachs, and Greeks.

How strong is the country's economy?

Macedonia has only modest supplies of raw materials and suffers from the typical problems of collapsed socialist economies: widespread corruption, a large state apparatus, and industrial facilities that fall far short of modern standards. It is one of the poorest countries in Europe.

Does Macedonia have a long history?

Yes. The southern area of the country was part of the ancient Macedonian Empire into which the legendary commander Alexander the Great (356–323 BC) was born. The region covered by present-day Macedonia subsequently endured an extremely checkered history, belonging at various times to Bulgaria, Serbia, the Ottoman Empire, and ultimately Yugoslavia. Macedonia finally gained its independence in 1991.

Lake Ohrid is home to a number of species of fish that are not found anywhere else on the planet. One example is the Ohrid trout, which is now endangered due to overfishing.

Lake Ohrid

Lake Ohrid is located on the border between Macedonia and Albania and is thought to be one of the oldest (at least 2.6 million years) and deepest (up to 948 ft/289 m) lakes in the world. Because of its age, it is a favorite destination of climatologists, who are able to learn about the history of the world's climate from its sedimentary deposits. The lake is also important for fishing and tourism.

Who are the Skipetars?

The Albanians call their country Shqipëria. From this comes the word "Skipetars," an alternative name for the Albanians. It is often translated as "sons of eagles" and a connection is made with the eagle on the Albanian flag. The latest thinking, however, is that the word derives from the Albanian for "to speak" and therefore means "all those who speak Albanian."

Is Albanian a mountainous country?

The eastern part of the country is dominated by a mountain range that is an extension of the Alps. The highest peak is Mount Korab at 9,068 ft (2,764 m). This rugged territory covers some two thirds of the country and offers very few inhabitable regions. The terrain flattens out towards the Adriatic coast in the west and this is where most of the population lives.

Is Albania a poor country?

Yes. Albania is one of Europe's poorest countries. More than half the population live in poverty under the World Bank's definition. The country's agricultural production covers only the country's own needs.

ALBANIA

Flag	**Languages**
	Albanian (official language), Greek, Macedonian
Currency	**Surface area**
1 lek (ALL) = 100 qindarka	11,100 sq miles (28,748 sq km)
System of government	**Population** 3.6 million
Republic since 1991	**Religion**
Capital	70% Sunni Muslim, 20% Albanian
Tirana	Orthodox, 10% Catholic

Is Albania still a largely atheist country?

No. In 1967 President Enver Hoxha (1908–1985) declared Albania "the first atheist state in the world." Religious activity of any kind was banned between 1968 and 1990 and consequently many mosques and churches were destroyed or used for other purposes. Following the collapse of communist rule, however, large numbers of Albanians turned back to their traditional family religion. Despite a diverse religious background, Albania has been free of conflicts, due to its high degree of religious tolerance.

The ruins of the Ancient Greek settlement of Apollonia in Albania. Its archaeological collection was plundered during the turmoil following the collapse of communism in 1990.

Enver Hoxha

Enver Hoxha (1908–1985) was Albania's leader for nearly 40 years. As the son of a well-to-do family he studied law in France and Belgium and upon returning to Albania became a French teacher. In 1941 he founded the Communist Party of Albania and proclaimed the country's independence in 1944. Hoxha remained leader of the Communist Party and the country right up to his death. Politically he leaned towards the Soviet Union initially and the People's Republic of China later.

Japan India Afghanistan

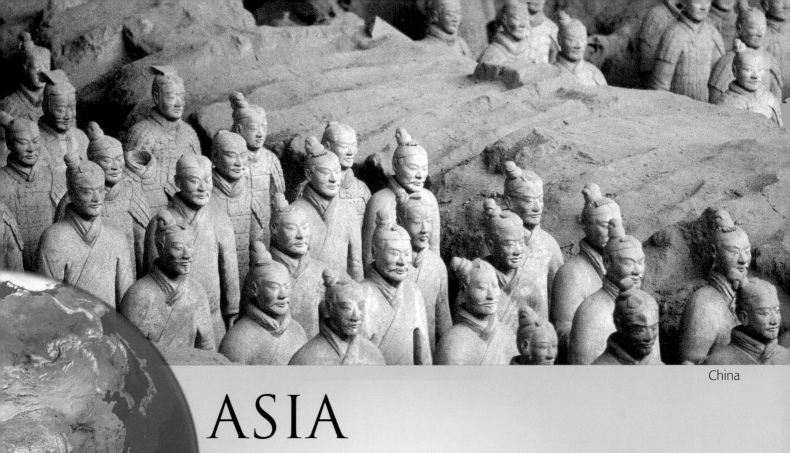

China

ASIA

Asia covers some 30 per cent of the Earth's landmass and is the largest and most populous of the seven continents (17.1 million sq miles/44.4 million sq km and approximately 4 billion inhabitants). It is also the most diverse, featuring arid deserts and humid rainforests, the world's highest peaks (the Himalayas), and depressions such as the Dead Sea, ice that never melts, and tropical beaches. Many of the Earth's geological features owe their existence to volcanic activity and in Asia volcanoes have been responsible for another, immensely sad superlative: the worst natural catastrophes the world has ever seen.

Oman   Israel   Japan

PHYSICAL MAP

1:63 000 000

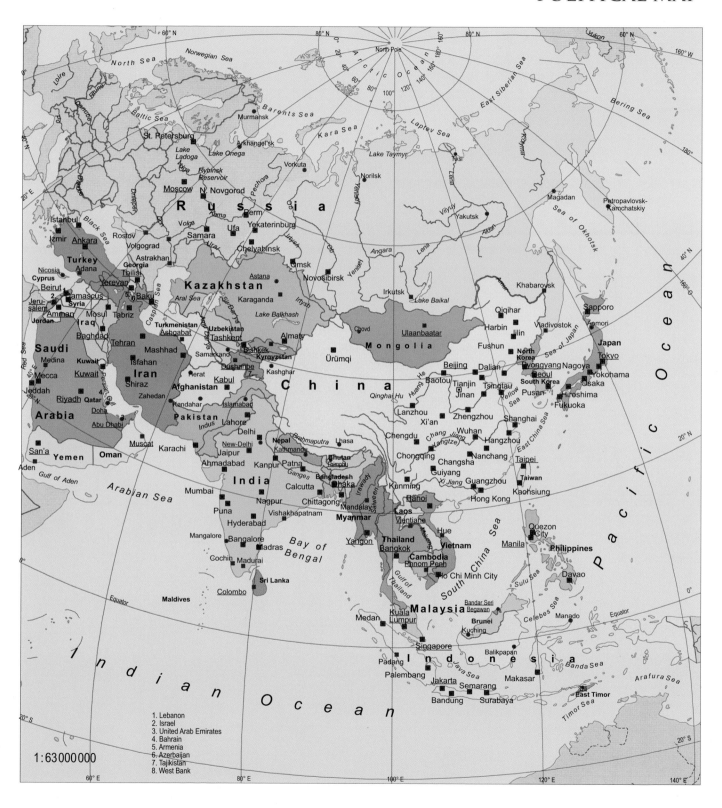

Norwegian Sea
North Sea
Loire
Baltic Sea
Rhine
Danube
Po
Black Sea
Istanbul
Izmir Ankara
Turkey
Nicosia
Cyprus
Adana
Beirut
1.
2. Damascus
Jeru-
salem Syria
Amman
Jordan
Mosul
Iraq
Baghdad
Saudi
Medina
Mecca
Kuwait
Kuwait
Jeddah
Riyadh Qatar
Arabia
Doha
Abu Dhabi
3.
San'a Yemen
Aden
Gulf of Aden

Barents Sea
Murmansk
St. Petersburg
Lake
Ladoga
Lake Onega
Arkhangel'sk
Rybinsk
Reservoir
Moscow
N. Novgorod
R u s s i a
Volga
Vologograd
Rostov
Samara
Ufa
Yekaterinburg
Astrakhan
Chelyabinsk
Georgia
Tbilisi
Yerevan
5.
6.
Baku
Caspian Sea
Tabriz
Turkmenistan
Ashgabat
Mashhad
Tehran
Isfahan
Iran
Shiraz
Zahedan
Herat
Kabul
Afghanistan
Kandahar
Islamabad
Pakistan
Lahore
Indus
Karachi
Muscat
Oman

Kara Sea
Vorkuta
Pechora
Kama
Perm
Ural
Dnieper
Don
Kazakhstan
Aral Sea
Karaganda
Astana
Syr-Darya
Lake Balkhash
Uzbekistan
Tashkent
Samarkand
Dushanbe
7.
Bishkek
Kyrgyzstan
Kashghar
Ürümqi

Lake Taymyr
Norilsk
Yenisey
Omsk
Novosibirsk
Irkutsk
Lake Baikal
Chovd
Mongolia
Ulaanbaatar
Qinghai Hu

Laptev Sea
Lena
Vilyuy
Yakutsk
Angara
Aldan
Amur
Khabarovsk
Qiqihar
Harbin
Jilin
Vladivostok
Fushun
North
Korea
Beijing
Pyongyang
Dalian
Baotou
Tianjin
Tsingtau
Seoul
South Korea
Pusan
Jinan

East Siberian Sea
Kolyma
Magadan
Petropavlovsk-
Kamchatskiy
Sea of Okhotsk
Bering Sea
Yukon

Sapporo
Aomori
Sea of Japan
Japan
Tokyo
Nagoya
Yokohama
Osaka
Hiroshima
Fukuoka

Pacific Ocean

North Pole
Arctic Ocean

China
Qinghai Hu
Lanzhou
Xi'an
Chengdu
Chongqing
Guiyang
Kunming
Huang He
Zhengzhou
Wuhan
Chang Jiang
Yangtze)
Changsha
Xi Jiang
Guangzhou
Hong Kong
Nanchang
Hangzhou
Shanghai
Yellow
Sea
East China Sea
Taipei
Taiwan
Kaohsiung

Lhasa
Brahmaputra
Nepal
Kathmandu
Bhutan
Thimphu
Bangladesh
Dhaka
Irrawady
Salween
Mekong
Mandalay
Myanmar
Yangon
Laos
Vientiane
Hue
Hanoi
Vietnam
Thailand
Bangkok
Cambodia
Phnom Penh
Ho Chi Minh City
Gulf of
Thailand
South China Sea

New-Delhi
Delhi
Jaipur
Ganges
Kanpur Patna
India
Nagpur
Ahmadabad
Mumbai
Puna
Hyderabad
Vishakhapatnam
Mangalore
Bangalore
Madras
Cochin Madurai
Sri Lanka
Colombo
Calcutta
Chittagong
Bay of
Bengal

Arabian Sea

Maldives
Equator

I n d i a n   O c e a n

Quezon
City
Manila
Philippines
Davao
Sulu Sea
Celebes Sea
Manado
Bandar Seri
Begawan
Brunei
Kuching
Malaysia
Kuala
Lumpur
Singapore
Medan
Padang
Palembang
Jakarta
Bandung
Semarang
Surabaya
I n d o n e s i a
Balikpapan
Makasar
Java Sea
Banda Sea
East Timor
Timor Sea
Arafura Sea
Equator

20° E
60° N
80° N
40° N
60° N
160° W
180°
160° E
40° N
20° N
0°
20° S
60° E
80° E
100° E
120° E
140° E

1. Lebanon
2. Israel
3. United Arab Emirates
4. Bahrain
5. Armenia
6. Azerbaijan
7. Tajikistan
8. West Bank

1:63 000 000

Introduction

What is meant by the term "Orient"?
The word "Asia" derives from the Assyrian for "sunrise." This was translated into Latin as "orient," which was eventually adopted into English as a way of referring to the East. In the ancient world it was used to denote the parts of the Roman Empire in Asia Minor.

Which is Asia's longest river?
The longest river in Asia is the Yangtze in China, which is also the third-longest river in the world after the Nile (Africa) and the Amazon (South America). The Yangtze is 3,964 miles (6,380 km) long and navigable for some 1,740 miles (2,800 km).

Where were Asia's earliest advanced civilizations?
The earliest civilizations in the world developed in Mesopotamia (present-day Iraq) (between the Euphrates and Tigris rivers), on the Indus River in present-day Pakistan and in northern China in the vicinity of the Yellow River.

What cultural achievements were these civilizations responsible for?
These Asian civilizations invented writing systems, the decimal system, irrigation, astronomy, the wheel, the chariot, and complex social structures.

Below: Evening prayers at the Mosque of the Prophet in Medina. Nearly two million pilgrims a year visit the city during the annual *hajj* (pilgrimage to Mecca).

The Aral Sea
In the 1930s the Soviet Union began irrigating large areas of Central Asia for cotton production. The Karakum irrigation canal opened in 1956 and diverted such a vast quantity of water from the Amu Dar'ya that the river was reduced to virtually a trickle by the time it reached the Aral Sea. The Aral Sea has been shrinking steadily ever since. By 1997 it had lost 40 per cent of its original surface area and the shoreline has now retreated some 50 miles (80 km). Millions of tons of salts, mineral particles, and sand are blown through the region every year by strong winds. This has severe consequences for the health of the local people, including cancer of the throat, eye diseases, and increased infant mortality. At 25,830 sq miles (66,900 sq km) the Aral Sea was once the fourth-largest lake in the world. It is now predicted that although it will not disappear altogether, it will gradually shrink to a tenth of its original size.

Do any traces remain of these civilizations?
Evidence of Asia's ancient civilizations is scattered throughout the continent. One of the most famous survivors is the Great Wall of China. Most of what we see today was built between the 14th and 17th centuries (during the Ming Dynasty). Other surviving traces of ancient civilizations include roads such as the Silk Road, which traversed the continent from end to end, and ruins of great cities such as Ubar in Oman, or Angkor (built between

the 9th and 13th centuries and boasting a population of over one million), the capital of the Khmer people, in northeast Cambodia.

Is Israel part of Asia?

Geographically Israel is indeed part of Asia but in terms of culture it is usually counted as European because a large proportion of its population comes from Europe. Israel enters the Olympic Games and soccer World Cup, for example, as a European nation.

How did the Himalayas come into being?

The world's highest mountain range was created by a collision between the Indian and Eurasian tectonic plates. These plates are still moving closer and closer together.

How many countries do the Himalayas straddle?

The Himalayas (sometimes referred to as the "Roof of the World") encompass parts of northeastern Pakistan, northern India, Nepal, Bhutan, and China.

Where is the Taklimakan Desert?

The Taklimakan Desert stretches across two thirds of the Xinjiang area of northwest China. Covering some 115,830 sq miles (300,000 sq km), it is the second-largest sandy desert in the world after the Sahara in north Africa. The prevailing climate is

A small delivery truck in Pakistan that has been converted into a taxi. It can carry a far greater load of goods and passengers than would seem possible.

extremely dry. This is due partly to the region's remoteness from the nearest sea and partly due to the fact that it lies in the rain shadow of a range of high mountains.

Are there any active volcanoes in Asia?

In many Asian countries, such as Japan, China, Indonesia, and the Philippines, the population lives in constant fear of the power of the Earth. It is in Asia that the majority, and most violent, of the world's volcanic eruptions occur—with devastating consequences.

Background: Chang Tang Plateau in Tibet with Namtso Lake in the background.

Water: Asia's biggest problem

Water is of immense importance for both the health and prosperity of communities. Along Asia's drought belt, water for domestic consumption, agriculture, and industry is in extremely short supply. The countries of the Middle East and Central Asia suffer from a particularly chronic water shortage and are incapable of agreeing on how to distribute this precious resource fairly. Countries are constantly seeking to secure not only their own but also their neighbors' water reserves. India, China, and other large nations build dams, thereby cutting off the flow of water to countries downstream. There is a persistent threat of war breaking out over water. In 1997 and 1998 exceptionally dry weather was the cause of enormous fires in Indonesia that destroyed forests and practically suffocated neighboring countries.

water. Today the island of Samosir, which eventually formed in the middle of the lake, is surrounded by water up to 2,000 ft (600 m) deep. Samosir is now an idyllic holiday resort.

What were the environmental consequences of the First Gulf War?

Of Kuwait's 1,000 or so oil wells, an estimated 800 were damaged during the First Gulf War. About 600 of these were set on fire. Oily smoke formed large clouds that hung in the air for a long time before falling to Earth over cities and natural habitats.

Interesting facts

- The geographical center of Asia is located outside Kysyl in the autonomous Russian republic of Tuva in southern Siberia.
- Asia has 51,140 miles (82,300 km) of coastline.
- With an area of 143,244 sq miles (371,000 sq km), the Caspian Sea is the largest inland body of water in the world.
- All the so-called "world religions" originated in Asia.
- Asia has repeatedly witnessed the development of large empires and has never been as fragmented as Europe.
- The word "Asia" derives from the Assyrian language and means "sunrise."
- The continent stretches for more than 5,600 miles (9,000 km) along its east-west axis and over 4,350 miles (7,000 km) north to south.
- After Africa, Asia contains the second-highest number of developing countries in the world.

A vegetable seller in a street souk *(market) in Muscat, Oman.*

Where is Lake Toba?

Lake Toba is located in north central Sumatra in the Barisan Mountains. It is 60 miles (96 km) long, 18 miles (29 km) wide and was formed by the collapse (one of the Earth's largest ever) of a very old volcano following a series of eruptions. Once the volcano became extinct, its crater filled with

The world's largest Buddha statue dominates the temple complex at Dambulla in Sri Lanka.

The mouth of Hindu monkey god Lord Hanuman in New Delhi, India.

Not only were large expanses of land contaminated and harvests ruined, the inhabitants of the affected areas were exposed to significant health risks, in particular an increased likelihood of cancer. The oil that discharged into the Persian Gulf formed the largest oil slick in industrial history (3 billion gallons/11 billion liters) killing millions of creatures and damaging the environment for many years to come—and in some places irreparably.

How is Asia's population expected to develop over the foreseeable future?

With around four billion inhabitants, Asia is already the world's most populous region. Experts estimate that this figure will grow by a further 1.5 billion over the next 50 years. India alone will see an increase of 600 million, the largest in the world, by then.

In which countries has economic development been hindered by war?

Countries whose progress has been hindered by wars and corruption include Afghanistan, Bangladesh, Myanmar, North Korea, Laos, Cambodia, and Vietnam. In these places, but also in many countries of the former Soviet Union, agriculture is the only significant source of income.

Kuwaitis inspecting a desalination plant. Facilities of this kind consume vast amounts of energy in rendering seawater drinkable.

KAZAKHSTAN

Flag

Currency
1 tenge (KZT) = 100 tyin

System of government
Presidential republic since 1991

Capital
Astana (since 1997, previously Almaty)

Languages
Kazakh (state language), Russian (lingua franca)

Surface area 1.05 million sq miles (2.72 million sq km)

Population 15.2 million

Religion
47% Sunni Muslim,
46% Russian Orthodox

A *yurt* is a domed tent erected for festive occasions. The one shown here is furnished with sumptuous red carpets of various patterns.

How does Kazakhstan like to portray itself?
Kazakhstan sees itself as the center of Eurasia. As mentioned in the Introduction, the definition of a country as part of one continent or another is sometimes a matter not only of geography but of perspective too. If we see the Ural River as the border between Asia and Europe, some 5.4 per cent of Kazakhstan's surface area could be regarded as belonging to the extreme east of Europe.

What is the Khan Tengri?
Located in the Tien Shan range where the borders of China, Kyrgyzstan, and Kazakhstan meet, the Khan Tengri is the country's highest mountain at 22,950 ft (6,995 m).

Does Kazakhstan have enough water?
In Kazakhstan's border areas water is in plentiful supply while its interior is relatively dry. The country has around 4,000 lakes (many of which are located in the north) although most of these are salt lakes. Kazakhstan's largest lake is the Caspian Sea.

What kind of climate does Kazakhstan have?
Kazakhstan has a decidedly continental climate with significant differences in temperature between

Agriculture
In Soviet times Kazakhstan accounted for a fifth of all the Soviet Union's agriculturally productive land. It produced 13 per cent of the USSR's grain, seven per cent of its meat, and 23 per cent of its wool. The major grain-producing areas are located in the north, where the amount of land under cultivation was greatly expanded in the 1950s. Tobacco, sunflowers, and, most importantly, cotton are also grown in Kazakhstan's fertile soil.

the seasons. In the city of Almaty, situated at 2,790 ft (850 m) above sea level, the temperature ranges from 108°F (42°C) in summer to −54°F (−48°C) in winter.

Does Kazakhstan have environmental problems?
Yes. An area near the city of Semeypalatinsk was contaminated with radiation as a result of nuclear weapons testing under the Soviet Union. In other places the groundwater has been polluted with fertilizer and pesticides, creating health risks in certain areas, and the extreme loss of water from the Aral Sea (see Asia Introduction) has also endangered the local population.

What type of landscape does Uzbekistan have?

Most of Uzbekistan is covered by desert. Its agricultural areas are to be found in the east of the country, in the great oases of Samarkand, Tashkent, and Bukhara, which are also the country's most densely populated regions.

What is Uzbekistan's climate like?

Uzbekistan has a continental desert climate with very little precipitation. Annual rainfall across most of the country is only 20–80 in (50–200 mm), rising to a maximum of 400 in (1,000 mm) in the mountains.

How did Uzbekistan come to have a German minority?

In 2001, Uzbekistan had a German minority of some 24,000 people. These are the families and descendants of around 40,000 Volga Germans deported to Tashkent by Stalin in the 1940s.

What is Uzbekistan's main agricultural produce?

Uzbekistan is the world's third-largest exporter of cotton. Around 80 per cent of its agricultural land

is used for the cultivation of this crop. Irrigation of the fields relies on the extraction of vast quantities of water from the country's two largest rivers, the Amu Dar'ya and the Syr Dar'ya (both of which discharge into the Aral Sea), causing serious ecological damage.

The Shir Dor Madrasa (1619–1636) is one of Samarkand's main sights. A *madrasa* is an Islamic school attached to a mosque.

UZBEKISTAN	
Flag	**Surface area** 172,742 sq miles (447,400 sq km) **Population** 26.9 million
Currency 1 Uzbekistan som (UZS) = 100 tiyin	**Religion** 90% Muslim (mostly Sunni)
System of government Presidential republic since 1992	**Notable features** Not only is Uzbekistan landlocked, it is separated from the ocean by two borders.
Capital Tashkent	
Languages Uzbek (official language), Karakalpak (a Turkic language)	

Samarkand

Samarkand was founded as an oasis settlement by the Persians in the 14th century BC. Thanks to its position on the Silk Road (see People's Republic of China), it grew into an extremely prosperous city. In 329 BC Samarkand was conquered by Alexander the Great and in 1220 it was destroyed by Genghis Khan's Mongol army. Because of its impressive examples of Islamic architecture, Samarkand has been made a UNESCO World Heritage site.

KYRGYZSTAN

Flag

Currency
1 Kyrgyzstan som (KGS) = 100 tyiyn

System of government
Presidential republic since 1991

Capital
Bishkek

Languages
Kyrgyz, Russian (official languages)

Surface area
76,641 sq miles (198,500 sq km)

Population 5.1 million

Religion
75% Sunni Muslim,
20% Russian Orthodox

Is Kyrgyzstan mountainous?
Yes. Three quarters of the country lies above 4,925 ft (1,500 m) and a good half above 9,850 ft (3,000 m). The mountains cross the country in a mainly east-west direction.

What are the Celestial Mountains?
The term "Celestial Mountains" is a translation of the Chinese name for one of the world's highest mountain ranges, the Tien Shan. Partly forest-clad

Women weaving on a portable loom in front of their *yurt* (a domed tent typical of this region).

and partly covered by glaciers, the highest peak in Kyrgyzstan is the Pobeda at 24,406 ft (7,439 m).

Who are the Kyrgyz people?
The Kyrgyz ethnic group came into being as a result of crossbreeding between Turkic and Mongol peoples which started during the days of Mongol rule. The Kyrgyz make up around 65 per cent of the country's population.

What were the consequences for Kyrgyzstan of the collapse of the USSR?
Already poor, the country experienced a drastic reduction in its GDP following the disintegration of the Soviet Union. In 1991/92 industrial production dropped by 27 per cent and agricultural production by 24 per cent. By 1993 the national income had fallen by 38 per cent. Today around 40 per cent of the population live below the official poverty line. Despite the existence of certain mineral resources (mercury, petroleum, and coal), this state of affairs is not expected to change in the foreseeable future as only around seven per cent of the country's surface area can be used for agriculture (most of the land is too mountainous). Kyrgyzstan does, however, possess uranium. A plant for the manufacture of enriched uranium is to be built in a joint venture with Kazakhstan financed by Russia.

Kyrgyz literature: Chinghiz Aitmatov

Kyrgyz writer Chinghiz Aitmatov was born in 1928 in the village of Sheker in northern Kyrgyzstan close to the border with Uzbekistan. His father was executed in a Stalinist purge in 1937. Aitmatov studied veterinary medicine but turned to journalism and literature in the 1950s. His best-known work is *Jamila*, a love story set in 1943 during the Second World War that was also made into a film. Many of Aitmatov's books have been translated into English.

TURKMENISTAN

Flag

Currency
1 Turkmen manta (TMM)
= 100 tennesi

System of government
Presidential republic since 1991

Capital
Ashgabat

Languages Turkmen

Surface area
172,742 sq miles (488,418 sq km)

Population 5 million

Religion
89% Sunni Muslim, 9% Russian
Orthodox

Notable features
90% of the country's surface area
is desert.

What are Turkmenistan's main economic sectors?
As the country with the world's third-largest petroleum reserves, oil and natural gas extraction play a major role in the country's economy. The second-biggest contributor to Turkmenistan's gross domestic product is agriculture, the main crops being wheat and cotton.

Why are parts of Turkmenistan's interior described as "lunar landscapes"?
Almost 90 per cent of the country consists of scree and sandy deserts. The driest of these is the Karakum Desert, which covers some 115,850 sq miles (300,000 sq km). The areas referred to as "lunar landscapes" are some of the lowest-lying terrain on Earth—as low as 266 ft (81 m) below sea level in places.

Are human rights respected in Turkmenistan?
Turkmenistan is continually being accused of gross human rights violations and alongside North Korea and Myanmar is widely regarded as one of the world's worst dictatorships. For cultural and religious reasons, the country's Russian minority is one of the most severely repressed groups. The Turkmen secret service and military stifle any attempt at free expression and the people as a whole are denied the Internet and freedom to travel. Religious freedom is also very restricted. The ruling classes, who profit from the country's abundant gas reserves, are unconditionally loyal to the regime and corruption is one of the country's biggest problems.

Left:
Turkmenistan's ruler Saparmurat Niyazov promoted a preposterous personality cult. His image is seen here adorning vodka bottles.

In the 3rd century BC Nisa was the capital of the mighty kingdom of Parthia.

Turkmenistan's rulers throughout history

The region covered by present-day Turkmenistan has had every imaginable kind of ruler over the centuries. It was conquered in the 4th century BC by Alexander the Great, the Seljuks arrived in the 11th century, and Ghengis Khan's Mongol army invaded two centuries later. In the 14th century the Turkmen people fell under the influence of the Timurids and between the 17th and 19th centuries the region was fought over more or less continually by the Persian shahs, the Chinese khans, the emirs of Bukhara, and the rulers of Afghanistan. It eventually fell under Russian hegemony in 1881.

TAJIKISTAN

Flag

Currency
1 somoni (TJS) = 100 diram

System of government
Presidential republic since 1994

Capital
Dushanbe

Languages
Tajik (official language), Russian

Surface area
55,251 sq miles (143,100 sq km)

Population 7.3 million

Religion
85% Sunni Muslim, 5% Shiite and Ismaili Muslims

Almost all of Tajikistan lies at over 9,850 ft (3,000 m). The Pamir Highlands consist of extensive pastureland that gradually rises, culminating in the highest point in the country.

Does Tajikistan possess significant mineral resources?

Yes. Around 14 per cent of the world's uranium resources are located in Tajikistan. The country also possesses gold, petroleum, and natural gas. However, profitable exploitation is hindered by a poorly developed infrastructure.

When did Tajikistan gain its independence?

In 1886 it became a Russian colony and later a constituent republic of the Soviet Union. Tajikistan declared its independence in 1991 but degenerated almost immediately into a civil war between Islamic fundamentalists and the government of Emomali Rahmon, who is still president.

What did the country's highest mountain used to be called?

About 70 per cent of the country is covered by high mountains, nearly half of them over 9,850 ft (3,000 m). Tajikistan's highest point is the Ismail Samani Peak in the Pamir Highlands, at 24,590 ft (7,495 m). In Soviet times this mountain was known as Communism Peak.

The Volga Germans

This term is used to describe an ethnic minority group of German origin in the former USSR. Between 1763 and 1767 Catherine II of Russia encouraged German farmers to move to the country to cultivate the steppes in the Volga region. In return for their agricultural expertise they were granted the right of self-government and linguistic self-determination. When Nazi Germany invaded the Soviet Union in 1941, the Volga Germans were accused of collaboration and deported to Siberia and Central Asia, where they were housed in labor camps or permitted to establish villages of their own, such as Thälman in Tajikistan. In 1979 39,000 Volga Germans lived in Tajikistan but by 2006 this number had dwindled to 1,700. Today they are one of the poorest sections of the population.

A mother and child in the Pamir Highlands.

AFGHANISTAN

Flag

Currency
1 afghani (AFN) = 100 puls

System of government
Presidential republic since 2004

Capital
Kabul

Languages
Dari, Pashto (official languages), Uzbek

Surface area
250,001 sq miles (647,500 sq km)

Population 29.9 million

Religion
84% Sunni Muslim,
5% Shiite Muslim

Why is Afghanistan considered inaccessible?
Afghanistan is dominated by the Hindu Kush Mountains with peaks of up to 24,600 ft (7,500 m). Only ten per cent of the country lies below 2,000 ft (600 m). Furthermore, it has no access to the sea. The only plains are located in the north while the south is mostly desert.

Is Afghanistan the land of the Pashtuns?
The Pashtuns were Afghanistan's traditional rulers. Although they now only make up around 40 per cent of the population, they were the founders of Afghanistan and gave the country its name. The Tajiks, who are of Persian origin, are the next-largest ethnic group, constituting 30 per cent of the population. The Hazara, at 20 per cent, are Afghanistan's third-largest group.

Do all women have to wear the veil?
Over 99 per cent of the Afghan population are Muslims. The form of Islam practiced in Afghanistan has always been the most conservative kind and it was customary for women in the towns and cities to wear the burka, which covers the whole body. In rural areas the burka impeded work in the fields and was therefore less common.

Does Afghanistan's economy depend on the cultivation of illegal drugs?
Afghanistan's economy has been largely destroyed by decades of warfare. Furthermore, only six per cent of its land is suitable for agriculture. In 2002 around one half of the country's GDP relied on the illegal cultivation of opium poppies. In 2006 Afghanistan was responsible for 92 per cent of the world's opium production.

The province of Bamyan in central Afghanistan was of strategic importance even in ancient times because the Silk Road passed through it.

The Taliban

Between 1979 and 1989 a guerilla war was fought in Afghanistan between the Islamic mujahideen and Soviet occupation forces. When the Russians withdrew, the conflict developed into a civil war from which the Taliban, a radical Islamic group, emerged victorious. The Taliban established a strict Islamist regime under which all men had to wear beards, all women had to wear the burka (a loose garment covering the entire body), and girls were forbidden to attend school. The Taliban remained in power until they were overthrown (because of their support for terrorism) by a US-led military intervention following the terrorist attacks of September 11, 2001 on New York and Washington DC.

GEORGIA

Flag

Currency
1 lari (GEL) = 100 tetri

System of government
Presidential republic since 1995

Capital
Tbilisi

Languages
Georgian (official language),
23 languages from six different
language families

Surface area
26,911 sq miles (69,700 sq km)

Population 4.7 million

Religion
75% Georgian Orthodox,
11% Muslim, 8% Armenian Apostolic

Notable features
Georgia lies on the border between
Europe and Asia although the border
follows no universally recognized
precise course.

What is the nature of Georgia's historical relationship with Russia?

Tsarist Russia conquered the territory covered by present-day Georgia little by little from the 17th century onwards. The Red Army finally occupied the remainder of the country in 1921. Georgia declared its independence in 1991 as the Soviet Union was breaking up.

What are Georgia's economic prospects?

Prior to independence Georgia's economy relied on tourism (Black Sea and Caucasus), winegrowing and the cultivation of citrus fruits and tea. As for the future, hopes of an economic upturn rest on petroleum and gas pipelines that will pass through Georgia on their way from Azerbaijan to Turkey. Ever since independence, however, the country has had to contend with an outflow of well-educated Georgians wanting to escape poverty.

Are there any regional independence movements within Georgia?

The autonomous Abkhaz Republic in the northwest of Georgia (on the border with Russia) continues to be recognized by the UN as part of Georgia but in practice is no longer under Georgia's control. Abkhazia is demanding independent statehood, as is South Ossetia, situated on Georgia's northern border.

The Voronya Cave

Voronya Cave, the deepest known cave in the world, is located in the western Caucasus region of Georgia. The entrance of this limestone cave, which contains underground waterfalls, lakes, and swamps, lies at 7,380 ft (2,250 m). It has so far been explored to a depth of 7,100 ft (2,164 m) but is thought to be considerably deeper. At a depth of 5,610 ft (1,710 m) the cave opens out into a large gallery.

A bistort-filled mountain pasture in the Caucasus. More than 6,000 species of flowering plant are indigenous to the Caucasus.

AZERBAIJAN

Flag

Currency
1 Azerbaijani manat (AZN)
= 100 gopik

System of government
Presidential republic since 1995

Capital
Baku

Languages
Azerbaijani (official language), Russian

Surface area
33,436 sq miles (86,600 sq km)

Population 7.9 million

Religion 75% Shiite Muslim,
25% Sunni Muslim

Notable features
The Azerbaijani exclave of Nakhichevan
lies in neighboring Armenia.

Nagorno-Karabakh

The region of Nagorno-Karabakh lies inside Azerbaijan's national borders but is inhabited mainly by Armenians. Following the dissolution of the Soviet Union, armed conflict broke out between an independence movement that was demanding the creation of an independent republic of Nagorno-Karabakh and the newly founded Republic of Azerbaijan. The Armenian government initially provided the independence movement with military support but has recently held back in order not to inflame the situation further.

What kind of landscape does Azerbaijan have?

The Kura-Araks Plain extends over the center of the country. It is bounded by the Talysh Mountains to the south and the Caucasus Mountains to the north. Azerbaijan's highest peak is Bazardüzü (Caucasus), which rises to 14,652 ft (4,466 m). Around half the country's land is used for agriculture.

What is the connection between Azerbaijan and the Battle of Stalingrad?

The decisive battle in Germany's Russian campaign of 1942/3 was ultimately about control of the Baku petroleum fields. In 1848 the Azerbaijani capital had been the scene of the first ever attempt to drill for oil. By the beginning of the 20th century the petroleum fields outside the city were the most extensive in the world and were responsible for half the world's production.

Is Azerbaijan a petroleum-rich country?

The significance to the world economy of the oil wells outside Baku is currently still small. Petroleum is nevertheless the country's main economic sector, accounting for 67 per cent of gross domestic product. Future profits from the industry are to be used to promote other branches of the economy.

How important is Islam in Azerbaijan?

Almost 100 per cent of the population profess to Islam but only ten per cent describe themselves as practicing Muslims. Between 1920 and 1991, when Azerbaijan was part of the Soviet Union, it was forbidden to practice a religious faith.

The art of knotting carpets has a long tradition in Azerbaijan and can be traced back to antiquity.

A petroleum field near the capital Baku, the starting point of an oil pipeline opened in 2005 terminating in the Turkish port of Ceyhan.

ARMENIA

Flag

Currency
1 dram (AMD) = 100 luma

System of government
Presidential republic since 1991

Capital
Yerevan

Languages
Armenian (official language), Yezidi,
Russian

Surface area
11,506 sq miles (29,800 sq km)

Population 3.0 million

Religion
94% Armenian Apostolic
(the "Gregorian Church")

Notable features
The region of Nagorno-Karabakh
in neighboring Azerbaijan has a
predominantly Armenian population.

When did Armenia become independent?

Present-day Armenia was previously a republic
of the USSR. The Armenian Soviet Socialist
Republic declared its independence under the name
"Republic of Armenia" in 1991. However, the
greater part of the historical Armenian homelands
remained under Turkish rule.

When was the Armenian genocide perpetrated?

An earlier struggle for Armenian independence
developed in the dying days of the Ottoman Empire
during the First World War. Political forces that
wanted the Ottoman Empire to be succeeded by
a Turkish nation-state attempted to suppress this
struggle for independence and somewhere between
600,000 and 1.5 million Armenians were killed in
the years 1915 to 1921.

Is Armenia an earthquake zone?

A major earthquake in 1988 was the first time the
Soviet Union allowed foreign assistance into the
country. Armenia is a mountainous land whose
average height above sea level is 5,900 ft (1,800 m).
The reason earthquakes occur repeatedly here is that
the country is located at the meeting point between
the Eurasian and Arabian tectonic plates. Armenia
is still suffering from the consequences of the 1988
earthquake today.

Background: Mount Ararat is 16,854 ft (5,137 m) high and was first
climbed in 1829.

Below: Pomegranates on a market stall in capital Yerevan. Their juice
has been used for centuries to dye oriental carpets.

Noah's Ark

According to the Bible the patriarch Noah survived the
Flood in a ship that ran aground on Mount Ararat when
the waters receded. Today the mountain lies inside Turkey's
borders but in an area formerly settled by Armenians, which
explains why it figures prominently on the Armenian coat of
arms. The image shows the summit of Mount Ararat with
Noah's Ark resting on it. Mount Ararat attracts a steady flow
of amateur archaeologists hunting for remains of the Ark,
although opinions diverge as to the possible location of the
resting Ark.

The Khajenafas fishery produces its famous caviar from salted sturgeon roe in Bandar Torkaman on the Caspian coast in northern Iran.

IRAN

Flag		**Languages**
		Persian (Farsi) (official language), Azerbaijani, Turkmen, Kurdish, others
Currency		**Surface area** 0.63 million sq miles
1 rial (IRR) = 100 dinars		(1.64 million sq km)
System of government		**Population** 68.7 million
Islamic republic since 1979		**Religion**
Capital		90% Shiite Muslim,
Tehran		10% Sunni Muslim

What is the difference between the names "Iran" and "Persia"?

Both names are closely intertwined with the history of the country. The name "Persia" stems from the 2nd century BC, when Indo-Iranian Persians settled in the southwest of present-day Iran and named their new territory "Pârs" after themselves. After being conquered by the Islamic Arabs "Pârs" became "Fâars" as there is no letter "P" in Arabic, hence also the name of the new Persian language Farsi. The name "Iran" derives from "Eran-Schar," meaning the "Empire of the Arya (Aryans)."

"Persia" remained the country's official name until 1934, when Rezah Shah ordered that it be changed to "Iran."

What is the Guardian Council?

Since 1979 Iran has been an Islamic republic and all legislation has to conform to Islamic Law. The Guardian Council of the Constitution consists of six religious jurists (proposed by the country's religious leader and voted in by parliament) whose job is to ensure that religious law is upheld. Islamic Law allows the supreme religious leader (Ayatollah Ali Khameinei since June 1989) to restrict the power of the politicians.

Evening prayers at the shrine of Imam Reza in Mashhad.

IRAQ

What is the Shatt al-Arab?

The Shatt al-Arab is a waterway formed by the confluence of the Euphrates and Tigris rivers. Forming part of the border between Iran and Iraq, it is around 95 miles (150 km) long and flows into the Persian Gulf.

Why is Iraq described at present as a "part-sovereign" state?

Since the Iraq War of 2003 the country has been occupied by the military forces of an international coalition led by the United States. The establishment of normal, fixed national and democratic structures is not currently in prospect. For this reason the country is considered to be a part-sovereign state, i.e. ultimate decision-making authority does not rest with the Iraqi government.

What is the difference between the Sunnis and the Shiites?

The Sunni Muslims are the larger of the two main Islamic groups. They recognize the caliphs (successors to the Prophet Muhammad who were not of his family line) as the legitimate leaders of Islam. Their doctrine and concept of Islamic duty rests on the Prophet's *Sunna* (Arabic for "custom," the main source of Islamic teaching after the Qu'ran). The Shiites, on the other hand, recognize only Muhammad's cousin and son-in-law Ali and his descendants (the imams) as the legitimate leaders of Islam. The imams' teaching is based on the *Shia* (Arabic for "faction"). As has been seen in Iraq and India, the tension between these two groups expresses itself periodically in outbreaks of violence.

Saddam Hussein

Saddam Hussein (1937–2006) was Iraq's state president between 1979 and 2003 and prime minister between 1979 and 1991, and 1994 and 2003. As a dictator he was responsible for dragging his country into a series of military conflicts that cost hundreds of thousands of lives, for gross infringements of human rights, for the murder of thousands of Kurds with poison gas, and for the abduction and execution of political opponents. During the Iran-Iraq War (1980–1988) he was supported by the United States but this support turned to opposition when his forces invaded Kuwait. Hussein was executed in Baghdad on December 30, 2006 for crimes against humanity.

A spiral-shaped minaret at the Great Mosque in Samarra. Minarets of this kind are based on the ziggurats that existed in ancient Babylon. The Tower of Babylon has traditionally been depicted in this form.

Does Syria have a stable population?

After the First World War Syria's population was around 1.5 million. Since then it has increased by a factor of 13. One of the main reasons for this has been the strong flow of immigrant workers and refugees into the country. The immigrant workforce comes from the surrounding Arab nations while the refugees are predominantly Kurds from Turkey and Iraq, and Iraqis fleeing the chaos of war.

What are the mainstays of Syria's economy?

Syria has a positive balance of trade. In good years agriculture accounts for a third of the country's economic output. The main exports are petroleum, foodstuffs, and textiles. Petroleum is responsible for approximately 70 per cent of export income but deposits are being rapidly exhausted.

Is Syria a tourist destination?

Syria attracts mainly cultural tourists interested in its ancient sites but it also has adequate facilities for holidaymakers looking for sun, sea, and sand along its 125 miles (200 km) of Mediterranean coastline.

Two men praying in front of a shrine in the Umayyad Mosque in the old town of Damascus.

SYRIA

Flag

Currency
1 Syrian pound (SYP) = 100 piastres

System of government
Presidential republic since 1973

Capital
Damascus

Languages Modern Standard Arabic (official language), Levantine Arabic, Armenian, Kurdish

Surface area
71,498 sq miles (185,180 sq km)

Population 20.1 million

Religion
90% Muslim (74% Sunni, 7% Alawite), 9% Christian

What is the Muslim Brotherhood?

The Muslim Brotherhood—also known as the Muslim Brothers—is a revolutionary Islamist movement founded in 1928 by the Egyptian Hassan al-Banna (1906–1949) as part of the struggle against British and Western "decadence." The slogan of the Muslim Brothers is: "Allah is our goal. The Prophet is our leader. The Qur'an is our law. Jihad is our path. To die in the service of Allah is our greatest hope." The Muslim Brothers have carried out a number of serious attacks on Syrian soil, including the killing of 50 cadets at a military academy in 1979. In 1982 the Brotherhood instigated riots in Hama which resulted in heavy fighting that claimed the lives of 1,000 soldiers and possibly as many as 30,000 civilians.

LEBANON

Flag

Currency
1 Lebanese lira (LBP) = 100 piastres

System of government
Republic since 1926 (when a
consitution was approved), but an
Independent Republic since 1943

Capital Beirut

Languages Arabic (official language),
French, English, Armenian

Surface area
4,036 sq miles (10,452 sq km)

Population 3.8 million

Religion
60% Muslim (32% Shiite, 21% Sunni,
7% Druze), 40% Christian
(25% Maronite, 15% Greek Orthodox)

What are the "Mashreq" countries?

Lebanon is one of the Mashreq countries in the Middle East. The word means "where the sun rises," the opposite of Maghreb ("where the sun sets"). Egypt, Jordan, Syria, Lebanon, Iraq, and the countries of the Arabian Peninsula are all Mashreq states.

What were the events that triggered the Lebanese Civil War?

In 1970 the armed forces of the PLO (Palestine Liberation Organization) were expelled from Jordan and established themselves in Lebanon. This created a religious imbalance that eventually led to the outbreak of hostilities (preceded by attacks and massacres) between the Christian militia and the PLO in 1975. In 1976 the Syrians intervened on the side of the Christian militia, as did Israel in 1978 and again in 1982, when it invaded southern Lebanon and drove the PLO out of the region.

What was the Taif Agreement?

The 1989 Taif Agreement provided a basis for the ending of the 15-year Lebanese Civil War (1975–1990). It provides for an equal distribution of political power between the different religious groups, hence the Lebanese president is always a Maronite, the prime minister is always a Sunni and the speaker of parliament is always a Shiite.

Baalbek

Baalbek is one of the largest ancient temple complexes in the world. The Temple of Venus, the smallest of the temples, is bigger than the Parthenon on the Acropolis in Athens. Although very little is understood of Baalbek and its origins, it is known that the Babylonians and Phoenicians maintained holy shrines here for the worship of their gods Baal and Moloch. The ruins we see today are unmistakably of Roman origin, however. Baalbek is famous above all for its immense foundation stones. The Stone of the South is 69 ft (21 m) long and 14 ft (4.3 m) high and wide and weighs around 1,650 tons (1,500 metric tonnes). This makes it the largest building block in the world.

The Temple of Bacchus in Baalbek.

To what extent is the Dead Sea dead?

Due to its high rate of evaporation, the Dead Sea, which extends over some 394 sq miles (1,020 sq km), has a salt content ranging between 27 and 31 per cent. This makes it impossible for anything but micro-organisms to survive in it. It is situated at 1,300 ft (396 m) below sea level, making it the lowest point on Earth.

When was the State of Israel founded?

David Ben Gurion (1886–1973) proclaimed the creation of the State of Israel on May 14, 1948, the day the British mandate in Palestine expired. The United States recognized it instantly, followed by the Soviet Union two days later. Egypt, Saudi Arabia, Jordan, Lebanon, Iraq, and Syria declared war immediately.

Zionism

Zionism is a political movement created at the end of the 19th century that strives for the establishment of the State of Israel and the uniting of the Jewish people. It was a response to the rampant anti-Semitism in many European countries at the time. Zionism was developed into a properly organized movement by Hungarian Theodor Herzl (1860–1904), who organized the first Zionist congress in Basel in 1897. As a consequence, European Jews began to migrate to Palestine and by 1898 5,200 had settled there.

ISRAEL

Flag	**Languages** Hebrew, Arabic (official languages), Yiddish, Russian, English, French, German
Currency 1 new shekel (ILS) = 100 agorot	**Surface area** 8,105 sq miles (20,991sq km)
System of government Parliamentary republic	**Population** 6.3 million
Capital Jerusalem	**Religion** 76% Jewish, 16% Muslim (mostly Sunni)

What was the result of the first Arab-Israeli war?

The war lasted from May 1948 to July 1949 and brought Israel substantial gains in western Galilee and northern Negev, allowing it to expand its original territory considerably. Approximately 850,000 Arabs fled or were driven out of the country.

Where do most of the immigrants come from?

A fifth of the world's Jews live in Israel. The initial wave of immigration (up to 1960) was from Europe, the Middle East and North Africa. Since the creation of the State of Israel the national population has grown to five times its original size. Most of the immigrants now come from the former Soviet Union, from where around 800,000 people entered the country in the 1990s alone.

The Dome of the Rock in Jerusalem was built in the 7th century on the spot from which, according to Muslim tradition, Prophet Muhammad ascended to heaven. It is also where Abraham (in the Christian tradition) was told to sacrifice his son Isaac.

JORDAN

Flag

Currency
1 Jordanian dinar (JOD) = 1,000 fils

System of government
Constitutional monarchy since 1952

Capital
Amman

Languages
Arabic (official language), English, Bedouin dialects

Surface area
35,637 sq miles (92,300 sq km)

Population 5.8 million

Religion
90% Sunni Muslim, 6% Christian

What is the West Bank?

The West Bank has been under Israeli occupation since the Six Day War of June 1967. In 1988 Jordan relinquished all its national ties and claims to the area in favor of a Palestinian state even though this meant sacrificing economically important territories. Almost half the population of the West Bank have since emigrated to Jordan and many Palestinians are currently living in refugee camps.

What is rain-fed agriculture?

Jordan is an extremely arid country—less than five per cent of its total surface area is cultivable. The little productive land that exists is located mostly in the mountainous east, the only region in which rain-fed agriculture (whereby crops are not artificially irrigated but get all their water from rainfall) is possible. While wheat, vegetables, and melons are grown, the yields do not meet the needs of the population, making it necessary to import food on a large scale.

Why were Jordanian immigrant workers expelled from the Gulf States?

During the Iran-Iraq War (1980–1988) Jordan adopted a pro-Iraq stance. As a result, large numbers of Jordanian immigrant workers were expelled from the oil-producing Gulf States and the country forfeited significant foreign earnings that would otherwise have been wired to relatives back home. (It is very rare for a whole family to immigrate to a foreign country for work purposes. Normally the men go alone and stay for a fixed period.)

The famous rock tombs of Ed-Deir in the ancient city of Petra

Petra

Petra (famously described as the "red-rose city") was built in 312 BC by the Nabataeans, a group of nomadic tribes from northwest Arabia, as their capital. The Pharaoh's Treasury, rock tombs, and rock temples have all been preserved. The mighty façades of these tombs and temples were hewn out of the rock face and decorated with intricate carvings. Petra is a unique cultural monument and was designated a UNESCO World Heritage site in 1985.

The Prophet Muhammad is known to have prayed in the *mihrab*, a niche inside the Prophet's Mosque in Medina, which faces Mecca.

SAUDI ARABIA

Flag	**Languages** Arabic (official language), English
Currency 1 Saudi riyal (SAR) = 100 halalas	**Surface area** 0.86 million sq miles (2.24 million sq km)
System of government Islamic absolute monarchy since 1932	**Population** 26.4 million
Capital Riyadh	**Religion** Muslim (mostly Sunni)
	Notable features Saudi Arabia has the most extensive oil reserves in the world.

of the holy book are strictly enforced and the penalty for murder, adultery, treason, sex offenses, blasphemy, drug dealing, and homosexuality is capital punishment.

What are the origins of the country's wealth?
Saudi Arabia is the world's largest exporter of crude oil and possesses the most extensive known petroleum reserves in the world.

Are there any holy cities in Saudi Arabia?
Both Mecca and Medina, each of which has a population of over one million, are holy. Mecca is the home of Islam's greatest holy shrine, the Kaaba, which is visited by millions of pilgrims every year. When praying, Muslims throughout the world face the Kaaba. The Islamic calendar started in Medina in 622, when Prophet Muhammad left Mecca and settled in the oasis of Yathrib, known today as Medina. This is where Muhammad was buried. Non-Muslims are denied entry to the holy cities.

Where does Saudi Arabia's labor force come from?
When slavery was officially abolished in Saudi Arabia in 1963, the slaves were replaced by immigrant workers who now make up nearly 21 per cent of the population. Most of them come from the neighboring Arab countries as well as from southeast Asia and Africa. The country's oil industry also attracts many Europeans and Americans.

What is the basis of the constitution?
Since 1993 Saudi Arabia has had a written constitution based on the Qur'an. The injunctions

Lawrence of Arabia

Thomas Edward Lawrence (1888–1935) was a British amateur archaeologist, military strategist, and writer. During the First World War (from 1916 onwards) he provoked and supported a rebellion by the Emir of Mecca against the Ottoman Empire, which controlled the Arabian Peninsula at that time. The revolt was backed financially by the British Empire as part of its efforts to secure influence over a large area of the Middle East. After the successful outcome of the revolt, northern Arabia was divided into French and English zones of influence. Lawrence's account of the Arab revolt, entitled *The Seven Pillars of Wisdom*, has become a classic of world literature.

A vast expanse of sand dunes in the Rub' al-Khali desert.

KUWAIT

Flag

Currency
1 Kuwaiti dinar (KWD) = 1,000 fils

System of government
Hereditary monarchy (emirate)
since 1962

Capital Kuwait

Languages
Arabic (official language), English,
Persian

Surface area
6,880 sq miles (17,818 sq km)

Population 2.5 million

Religion
65% Sunni Muslim,
35% Shiite Muslim

Does Kuwait have any other significant industrial sectors besides the petroleum industry?

The petroleum industry is the most important factor in the country's prosperity. It accounts for around half the country's GDP as well as 80 to 90 per cent of export earnings and government revenue. On top of this, significant levels of foreign investment also generate substantial revenue streams. The country sees its industrial future in the expansion of its domestic refining capacity and the creation of a petrochemical industry.

How many islands does Kuwait have?

Kuwait has nine islands: Auhah, Failaka, Kubbar, Qaruh, Umm al Maradim, Miskan, Warbah, Umm an Namil, and the largest, Bubiyan (connected to the mainland by a bridge and converted after 1991 into a military base which is off-limits to civilians).

Where does the Kuwaiti population live?

Kuwait has an urbanization level of 94 per cent, one of the highest in the world, and a high proportion of foreigners (over 60 per cent), most of whom work in the oil industry.

A US-led coalition of international troops liberated Kuwait in 1991. The withdrawing Iraqi forces destroyed industrial facilities and set oil wells alight as they retreated.

The Gulf wars

Iraq, which shares a 150-mile (240-km) border with Kuwait, refused to recognize the emirate's declaration of independence in 1961, claiming it instead as Iraqi territory. As early as the summer of 1961 the prime minister of Iraq, Abd al-Karim Qasim, threatened to invade Kuwait but his plans were thwarted by the United Kingdom, which sent troops to the region. Over the following years there were frequent border incidents during which Iraqi units occupied various parts of the country. Nevertheless, Kuwait supported Iraq (as did the US) during the Iran-Iraq War, which broke out in 1980, and a number of its tankers were destroyed in Iranian aerial bombardments.

The Gulf War also began with border skirmishes. This time a petroleum field was the subject of the dispute. On August 2, 1990, Iraqi troops invaded and annexed Kuwait and removed its government. The UN Security Council set January 15, 1991 as the deadline for an Iraqi withdrawal and on February 27, US-led coalition forces invaded and liberated Kuwait in Operation Desert Storm. The country's infrastructure and industrial facilities were badly damaged by the withdrawing Iraqi troops. During the Second Gulf War of 2003 (Iraq War), Kuwait was used as the starting point for the invasion of Iraq.

BAHRAIN

Flag		Languages
		Arabic (official language), Persian, Urdu, English
Currency		**Surface area**
1 Bahraini dinar (BHD) = 1,000 fils		275 sq miles (711 sq km)
System of government		**Population** 689,000
Constitutional monarchy since 2002		**Religion**
Capital		81% Muslim, 9% Christian
Manama		

What does the word "Bahrain" mean?

The word "Bahrain" is Arabic for "two seas." This refers on the one hand to the Persian Gulf, which surrounds the islands that make up the country, and on the other to the country's plentiful supply of groundwater in contrast to its neighbors. This group of islands is formed mainly of limestone bedrock in which water collects in karst springs and artesian wells that prevent evaporation.

Who is the king of Bahrain?

Bahrain's current king, Sheikh Hamad ibn Isa al-Khalifah (born 1950), comes from the royal Al-Khalifah family that has ruled the country since 1783. After a spell as a British Protectorate, Bahrain eventually achieved independence from the United Kingdom in 1971. Since 2002 Bahrain has been a kingdom with a constitutional monarchy.

Is Bahrain a petroleum nation?

Petroleum extraction and refining is still Bahrain's main industry with over 250,000 barrels of crude refined per day. Its petroleum refinery, one of the largest in the Middle East, is also used to process imported petroleum. Since its petroleum reserves are predicted to run out by 2015, however, the country is currently making substantial efforts to develop other industries including the service sector.

Is Bahrain a tourist destination?

No. Although Bahrain is one of the most liberal of the Gulf States, and due to the decline of its petroleum reserves is very interested in developing a tourist industry, there is still a long way to go. The country is still strongly influenced by Muslim traditions and a beach holiday in the Western sense would only be possible in special clubs.

Left: A woman has had her hand intricately painted for a wedding. Henna can be used to produce shades ranging from orange to mahogany brown.

The new Al-Fateh Mosque in Manama is the largest building in the country. It can hold up to 7,000 worshippers and is fitted out with fine Italian marble.

The Bahrain Grand Prix

In 2004 Manama started hosting an annual Formula One World Championship race. The circuit was rebuilt at a cost of 150 million dollars. Its location in the desert poses a problem to the competitors as the fine sand can damage the engines and gearboxes. The winner's traditional Champagne shower has to be dispensed with in order not to offend the religious sensitivities of the Muslim hosts.

QATAR

Flag

Currency
1 Qatar riyal (QAR) = 100 dirhams

System of government
Absolute monarchy (emirate)
since 1971

Capital Doha

Languages
Arabic (official language), English,
Persian, Urdu

Surface area
4,399 sq miles (11,437 sq km)

Population 863,000

Religion
77% Sunni Muslims,
8% Christians

This sculpture of an oyster shell and a pearl is a reminder of the famous pearl divers of Qatar.

What is Qatar's climate like?
Qatar's climate is hot (up to 113°F/45°C in summer and 63°F/17°C in winter) and damp (due to its proximity to the Persian Gulf). Despite the very high atmospheric humidity (around 85 per cent), precipitation is negligible and the land is therefore very dry. The *shamal*, a dry and dusty northwesterly wind that can cause sandstorms, is common. Qatar's vegetation is correspondingly sparse and the only trees are to be found at the oases.

Is any agricultural produce grown in Qatar?
Agriculture is only possible with artificial irrigation. At present this applies to some one per cent of the country's surface area. The water is provided by seawater desalination plants. Mainly fruit and vegetables (tomatoes, pumpkins, dates, citrus fruits) and some cereals are grown, meeting around 60 per cent of the country's needs. Whereas at one time livestock was farmed exclusively nomadically, Qatar now has a number of livestock farms. These are only able to satisfy a proportion of the country's meat requirements, however.

When was petroleum first pumped in Qatar?
Qatar's first petroleum deposits were discovered at Jabal Dukhan in 1939 but it was not until 1949 that extraction and exportation began. Qatar joined OPEC (the Organization of Oil Producing and Exporting Countries) in 1961. The most important fields are at Dukhan in the west and off the country's east coast. It has been estimated that these deposits will be exhausted in 30 years' time although Qatar also possesses major natural gas fields off its northern coast.

Social welfare system and population
The per capita income in Qatar is among the highest in the world and the country benefits from an extremely good social welfare system. Anyone who cannot work receives a fixed monthly income regardless of age, and medical care and education are free of charge. Only around 20 per cent of the population are Qatari. The rest are foreigners and include large numbers from Pakistan and India (which is why Urdu is widely spoken). Many immigrant workers also come from other Arab countries and Iran.

What are the names of the seven states that make up the United Arab Emirates?

The United Arab Emirates (UAE) comprises Abu Dhabi, Dubai, Sharjah, Ajman, Umm al-Quwain, Ras al-Khaimah, and Fujairah. The largest emirate is Abu Dhabi and the smallest is Ajman.

Why does the region have such an extreme climate?

The interior of the UAE has a desert climate while along the coasts atmospheric humidity can reach extreme levels, above all in summer. The region as a whole has one of the warmest climates in the world and it is not unusual for rain to fall on only one or two days a year.

What is the main mode of transport?

The automobile is the most widely used mode of transport. The UAE benefits from an excellent road network that is illuminated all night long. In 2004 road accidents were the second-largest cause of death in the UAE.

How does the UAE obtain its drinking water?

Drinking water is obtained predominantly by means of salt-water desalination. After the USA and Canada, the UAE has the third-largest water consumption per person in the world.

Background: Burj Al Arab, the most expensive hotel in the world. It is the world's only seven-star hotel to date.

Below: Camel traders at a market in Al Ain.

UNITED ARAB EMIRATES

Flag

Currency
1 dirham (AED) = 100 fils

System of government
Federation (Ittihad) of seven autonomous emirates since 1971

Capital
Abu Dhabi

Languages
Arabic (official language), Pashtu, Somali, Hindi, Urdu, Farsi, English

Surface area
30,000 sq miles (77,700 sq km)

Population 5.3 million

Religion
96% Muslim (80% Sunni, 16% Shiite and others)

Interesting facts: Government

The *CIA World Factbook* describes the UAE's system of government as "a federation with specified powers and other powers reserved to member emirates." Power is always invested in one of the emirs of the seven states in the role of president. The first-ever elections to the national assembly, the Federal National Council, were held in December 2006.

Interesting facts: Population

The UAE's population is growing at a faster rate than any other country's. When founded in 1971, the seven emirates had a total population of just 181,000. By the end of 2006 this number had increased almost 30-fold. This extreme growth is mainly explained by a rapid increase in the number of immigrant workers, who now make up more than three quarters of the population. Most are from India, Pakistan, and Bangladesh, with smaller numbers from Southeast Asia.

OMAN

Flag	Languages
	Arabic (official language), Baluchi, Persian, Urdu, English
Currency	**Surface area**
1 Omani rial (OMR) = 100 baizas	119,499 sq miles (309,500 sq km)
System of government	**Population** 2.6 million
Monarchy (sultanate)	**Religion**
Capital	54% Muslim, 28% Hindu,
Muscat	15% Christian

Women performing the traditional Quriat dance in Muscat.

How is Oman's population made up?

Three quarters of Oman's population are Omanis, the majority of them Arabs. The remainder are East Africans, Pakistanis, Indians, Bangladeshi, Filipinos, and Europeans who have come to work in the country. More and more Indian languages are being spoken in the country as a result.

When was Oman's historical golden age?

After the expulsion of the Portuguese, who had occupied Oman's coastal cities in the 16th century, the country developed into a maritime power and conquered parts of the East African coast including the sultanate of Zanzibar. The re-separation of the sultanates of Oman and Zanzibar in 1860 was the beginning of a period of steady decline that only came to an end when the petroleum industry came on stream in 1967.

When was petroleum first extracted in Oman?

Oman began to export and extract petroleum in 1967. "Black gold" is now the country's main export, accounting for 85 per cent of the total. Oman also possesses extensive reserves of natural gas. These have barely been tapped as yet, although the government is currently planning to increase its exploitation of this sector.

Interesting facts

- Political parties are banned in Oman.
- In the coastal areas of northeastern Oman the hottest time of day is the morning.
- All cars are equipped with an alarm that emits an acoustic signal if the driver exceeds the 75 mph (120 km/h) speed limit.

Ubar

Ubar is an ancient city in the south of present-day Oman. It was buried under the sand dunes centuries ago after having been abandoned by its inhabitants and was eventually rediscovered by British explorer Ranulph Fiennes (born 1944) in 1992. Archaeologists found the remains of watchtowers, city walls, earthenware pots, and houses in the settlement of Shisar that had apparently grown up over the buried city. It is thought that Ubar had been a major trading station on the Silk Road between 2800 BC and AD 300 before eventually declining in importance and falling into ruin.

The sand dunes of the Ramlat al-Wahiba desert cover an area of some 5,800 sq miles (15,000 sq km).

What is the mainstay of Yemen's economy?

Yemen's economy is based on agriculture, with subsistence farming still playing an important role. Both the western highlands and the *wadi* of southern Yemen benefit from sufficient precipitation for the cultivation of vegetables, cereals, fruit, tobacco, and cotton. Livestock farming is also important and in the coastal areas extensive fishing generates export income.

What is the country's second-largest source of income?

Much of the labor working in the Gulf petroleum-producing countries is provided by Yemen. The money sent home by these workers plays an important part in the country's economy.

Has Yemen experienced a golden age?

Yemen's economic golden age began in the 13th century under the Turkic Rasulid dynasty (1228–1455). It experienced an enormous increase in prosperity as a result of its role as middleman in the trade between the Mediterranean region and India. With the end of Rasulid rule, a decline in Yemen's fortunes set in that was sealed by the Portuguese discovery in the 16th century of the sea route to India. Only with the opening of the Suez Canal in the 19th century did the great powers turn their attention back to Yemen.

Does Yemen have petroleum deposits of its own?

Relatively minor oil fields have been discovered in the vicinity of Masila. These deposits are being exploited by US, South Korean and French companies and are expected to be exhausted by 2016.

YEMEN

Flag

Currency
1 Yemeni rial (YER) = 100 fils

System of government
Islamic presidential republic since 1991

Capital Sanaa

Languages
Arabic (official language), Yemeni Arabic

Surface area
203,850 sq miles (527,970 sq km)

Population 21 million

Religion
99% Muslim (Sunni and Zaidi)

Background: Bab al-Yaman. The multistory residential buildings protected by mighty city walls in Sanaa, Yemen, are now a UNESCO World Heritage site.

Wadi

Wadi is an Arabic word meaning a dry valley or riverbed that carries water only temporarily after heavy rainfall. As rivers of this kind are often torrential, they can carve a path up to 330 ft (100 m) deep through the dry desert.

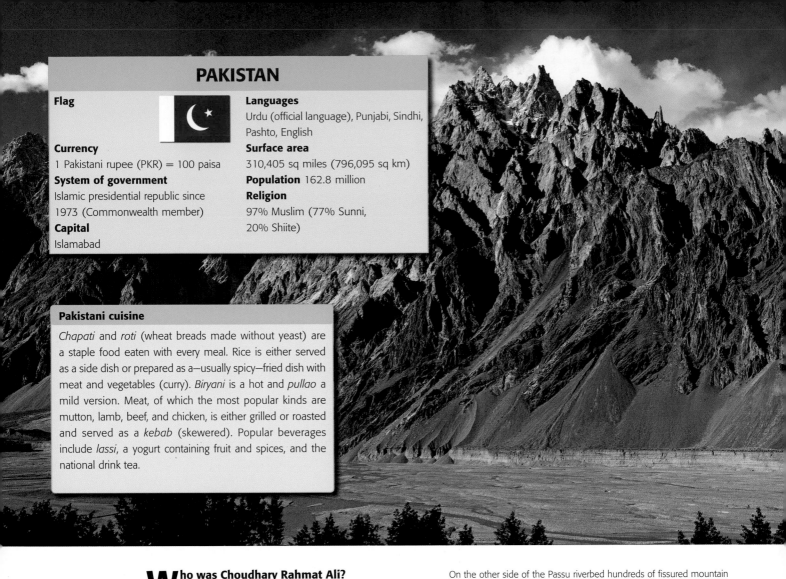

PAKISTAN

Flag

Currency
1 Pakistani rupee (PKR) = 100 paisa

System of government
Islamic presidential republic since
1973 (Commonwealth member)

Capital
Islamabad

Languages
Urdu (official language), Punjabi, Sindhi,
Pashto, English

Surface area
310,405 sq miles (796,095 sq km)

Population 162.8 million

Religion
97% Muslim (77% Sunni,
20% Shiite)

Pakistani cuisine

Chapati and *roti* (wheat breads made without yeast) are
a staple food eaten with every meal. Rice is either served
as a side dish or prepared as a—usually spicy—fried dish with
meat and vegetables (curry). *Biryani* is a hot and *pullao* a
mild version. Meat, of which the most popular kinds are
mutton, lamb, beef, and chicken, is either grilled or roasted
and served as a *kebab* (skewered). Popular beverages
include *lassi*, a yogurt containing fruit and spices, and the
national drink tea.

Who was Choudhary Rahmat Ali?

Choudhary Rahmat Ali (1897–1951) was one
of the founders and namers of Pakistan. In 1933
he devised an acronym out of the names of the
provinces of the future independent state: **P**unjab,
Afghania, **K**ashmir, **S**indh, and Baluchi**stan**. An "i"
was inserted in order to simplify pronunciation but
as the first letter of the word "Islam" it also serves
as a reminder of the importance of religion in what
was the first Islamic republic in the world.

On the other side of the Passu riverbed hundreds of fissured mountain
peaks soar into the sky above the Khunjerab pass in the Himalayas.

What are the country's highest mountains called?

The three highest mountain ranges in the world,
the Hindu Kush, the Karakoram, and the
Himalayas, converge on northern Pakistan. Five
of the world's 14 8,000-m (26,250-ft) peaks lie in
Pakistani territory, including K2, the second-highest
mountain in the world at 28,251 ft (8,611 m), and
Nanga Parbat at 26,657 ft (8,125 m).

Who was Benazir Bhutto?

Benazir Bhutto (1953–2007) was the prime minister
of Pakistan from 1988 to 1990 and 1993 to 1996
and the first female premier of an Islamic country.
Benazir Bhutto was dismissed as prime minister in
the wake of a number of corruption scandals and
exiled herself to Dubai in the United Arab Emirates
in 1998. She returned to Pakistan in October 2007
to campaign in the general elections. On December
27, 2007, she was assassinated by a gunman during
an election rally in Rawalpindi.

Lavishly and inventively decorated trucks used for cross-country transport.

What are the two main population groups in India?

India's population is so diverse in terms of religion and ethnicity that it is impossible to talk of a single Indian people. Two main groups can be identified, however: the light-skinned Indids, who make up over 70 per cent of the population, speak mainly Indo-Aryan languages and live mostly in the northern and middle parts of the country, and the dark-skinned Melanids, who speak Dravidian languages such as Tamil and Telugu, and live mainly in the south.

Is school attendance compulsory in India?

Yes. India requires all children to attend school but in practice the size of the population, linguistic, ethnic and significant social differences, and a shortage of teaching staff and premises make this so difficult that around 60 per cent of Indians are still illiterate.

To what extent does India depend on agriculture?

Although India is one of the ten leading industrial nations in the world, it is still a fundamentally agrarian country. Two thirds of the workforce are tenant farmers or smallholders and around half the country's surface area is arable land (a quarter of it irrigated). The cultivation of rice takes up around a third of the available farmland.

What is the Land of Five Rivers?

"Land of Five Rivers" is a translation of the name of the northern Indian state of Punjab. The five rivers in question are all tributaries of the Indus: the Jehlam, the Chenab, the Ravi, the Beas, and

INDIA		
Flag		**Languages** Hindi, English, 17 regional languages of equal status (official languages)
Currency 1 Indian rupee (INR) = 100 paise		**Surface area** 1.27 million sq miles (3.28 million sq km)
System of government Federal republic since 1950 (Commonwealth member)		**Population** 1.12 billion
		Religion
Capital New Delhi		80% Hindu, 13% Muslim, 2% Christian

With its slender minarets and elegant dome, the Taj Mahal mausoleum in India is one of the most beautiful buildings in the world.

the Sutlej. When India gained its independence from the United Kingdom in 1947, the Punjab was divided between the Indian Union and Pakistan (the former colony's successor states). The new border ran centrally but more or less indiscriminately between the two most important cities in the region, Lahore (Pakistan) and Amritsar (India). This division led to a flood of refugees: Hindus and Sikhs from West Punjab (Pakistan) wanting to pass into India, and Muslims from East Punjab (India) wanting to pass into Pakistan. In certain places there were outbreaks of civil war-like violence. Today Punjab is both a Pakistani province (and the country's most populous region) and an Indian federal state. A similar problem exists in Kashmir, which is claimed by both Pakistan and India.

Hindus taking a ritual bath in the sacred River Ganges in Uttar Pradesh.

Population growth

India's biggest problem is its exploding population. Life expectancy and birth rate are rising in tandem with general economic progress and the concomitant improvements in medical care. Measures such as enforced sterilization (introduced in the 1970s) had barely any effect. The country has a particularly large proportion of young people—approximately 40 per cent are under 15 years old. As a result, an average of around 40 million individuals need to be absorbed by the employment market every five years, the impossibility of which in turn exacerbates the glaring social inequalities. While China has succeeded in bringing its population relatively well under control, this is hardly the case in India, with the result that by 2045 its population will have overtaken China's as the largest in the world.

Bollywood

The word "Bollywood," an amalgam of "Bombay" (now Mumbai) and "Hollywood," has become a byword for the Indian film industry. Like Hollywood, Bollywood is not, as is commonly supposed, a genre, but an indication of where the films originate. Around 250 films are made a year in Mumbai, roughly a quarter of India's total annual output (the largest of any country in the world). Indian films have a character all their own. They are strikingly different to films made in the West and are all expected to include song, dance, and music. Just like Hollywood, the Indian film industry is constantly creating new stars. Those in greatest demand at the moment are Aishwarya Rai and Arjun Rampal. Amitabh Bachchan, known as "Big B," is still considered the biggest Bollywood star of all time.

Elephants are
painted with
elaborate designs
on festive occasions.

What is the Sardar Sarovar Project?

The Narmada is considered India's second-most sacred river after the Ganges. It rises in central India and flows for 815 miles (1,310 km) before discharging into the Arabian Sea. The government is planning to build a total of 30 large, 135 medium-sized, and 3,000 small dams along its course. Since work began in 1961 the Sardar Sarovar Project has been the country's largest construction project. The resettlement of 20,000 people is necessary in order to complete the project. The dam project came to international attention as a result of the protests of those affected, who have been voicing their opposition for more than a decade. In 1993 the protestors managed to persuade the World Bank to withdraw its financial support for the project. Work continues, however, despite major ecological concerns and despite the fact that most of the dams have been declared unsafe.

Hawa Mahal, the "Palace of Winds"

The Hawa Mahal is an extraordinary building in Jaipur (the capital of the Indian state of Rajasthan), some 205 miles (330 km) south of Delhi. It was built in 1799 by Maharaja Sawai Pratap Singh and its unique, almost opulent architecture offers a fascinating insight into the lives of the Rajput princes. The façade of this five-story red sandstone building presents a honeycomb structure. It is made up of 953 small windows (many of them projecting forward oriel-fashion) furnished with richly decorated latticework. The purpose of this design was to maximize the circulation of air inside the building (hence the name: *hawa* means "wind" and *mahal* means "palace") while simultaneously permitting the ladies of the harem to observe the daily comings and goings on the street and royal processions through the town without being seen themselves.

NEPAL

Flag

Currency
1 Nepalese rupee (NPR) = 100 paisa

System of government
Constitutional monarchy since 1990

Capital
Kathmandu

Languages Nepali (official language), Maithili, Bhojpuri, 18 languages with numerous dialects

Surface area
54,124 sq miles (147,181 sq km)

Population 28.3 million

Religion
86% Hindu, 8% Buddhist, 4% Muslim

Notable features
Eight of the highest mountains in the world are in Nepal, including the very highest, Mount Everest, at 29,028 ft (8,848 m).

What are the origins of the word "Sherpa"?

The Sherpas are a Tibetan people that fled to Nepal from the north around 1500. Today this ethnic group comprises around 60,000 members. Ever since climbers began ascending the peaks of 8,000 m (26,250 ft) and more in the early years of the 20th century, Sherpas have been used as bearers and guides, creating the misapprehension that the word "Sherpa" actually means mountain porter.

What are castes?

The word "caste" derives from the Portuguese word *casta* ("race"), which in turn comes from the Latin *castus*, meaning "pure." The caste system originated as a social phenomenon in India and also played an important role in Nepali society for a long time. Although the system differentiates between a large number of social groups, it is based on four basic distinctions. At the top are the Brahmins (priests), followed in descending order by the Kshatriya

The Himalayas, the "Roof of the World," in the Kumba region.

Sadhu, literally "good man," is the collective term for Hindu monks who lead an ascetic lifestyle. Shown here is a *sadhu* in Kathmandu.

(warriors, nobility, the king), Vaisya (merchants and farmers), and finally Sudra (those in menial occupations), who were forbidden to enter other people's houses. Today discrimination of this kind is prohibited by law.

Who are the Gurkhas?

The Gurkhas are a Nepalese clan that has traditionally provided the British army with large numbers of soldiers. Around 200,000 Gurkhas served under the Union Jack in the First World War and around 50,000 in the Second. Gurkhas were once feared for their brutality and their skills in close combat.

Interesting facts

- Nepal is the only country whose state religion is Hinduism.
- The pagoda style of architecture originated in Nepal, from where it spread to China and Japan.
- Over 50 per cent of Nepalis are illiterate.
- 300,000 tourists travel to Nepal every year.
- Around 1,000 tourists have been killed in Nepal since 1979.

Is Bhutan in the Himalayas?

Yes. The northern part of the country along the border with China is in the Himalayas. To the south the mountains give way gradually to the Duars Plain, part of the Ganges-Brahmaputra lowlands that form the border with India, Bhutan's neighbor to the south.

Who is the ruler of Bhutan?

The Ngalong people, who migrated from Tibet in the Middle Ages, are the dominant population group in Bhutan. The royal house (the Wangchuk dynasty, which has provided the country's rulers since 1907) also belongs to this group. The fifth king in this line, Jigme Khesar Namgyel Wangchuk, who studied politics at Oxford University, ascended the throne in 2006.

What is meant by "Bhutanization"?

Since the end of the 19th century large numbers of Nepalis have migrated to the south of Bhutan. By 1980 they made up 50 per cent of the population. Fearful of being overwhelmed by foreigners, the government introduced a policy of "Bhutanization" in 1988 under which immigrants are required to wear local costume, speak the Ngalong language and adopt traditional Ngalong rules of behavior. The government brought in the army and police to quell the ensuing protests.

What does the population live on?

Because Bhutan is a predominantly mountainous country, its agriculture is relatively unproductive. Its rice production does not even meet the nation's own needs and its only foreign currency earnings are from the supply of electricity to India and Bangladesh. In 2005 the Chukha power station alone contributed 40 per cent of the national budget.

BHUTAN

Flag

Currency
1 ngultrum (BTN) = 100 chetrums

System of government
Absolute monarchy since 1969

Capital
Thimphu

Languages
Dzongkha (official language), local dialects, English

Surface area
17,954 sq miles (46,500 sq km)

Population 2.2 million

Religion 75% Buddhist, 22% Hindu

Notable features
80% of the country lies above 6,500 ft (2,000 m).

The small town of Paro in Bhutan holds an annual dance festival called the Tsechu, at which groups from the surrounding villages perform dances in traditional costume.

A smoke-free country

In December 2004 Bhutan became the first country in the world to prohibit not only smoking in public places but also the selling of tobacco. The government's aim was to make Bhutan a non-smoking country. The penalty for infringing the law is a heavy fine. Although tobacco can still be imported from other countries for private use, it is subject to 100 per cent customs duty.

BANGLADESH

Flag

Currency
1 taka (BDT) = 100 poisha
System of government
Republic since 1991
(Commonwealth member)
Capital
Dhaka

Languages
Bengali (official language), English
Surface area
56,977 sq miles (147,570 sq km)
Population 144.3 million
Religion 83% Muslim, 16% Hindu
Notable features
Bangladesh has the highest
population density of any country
(excluding city-states) in the world.

What is the relationship between Bangladesh and Pakistan?

When British colonial rule came to an end on the Indian subcontinent in 1947, two large countries were initially formed: India, which was mostly Hindu, and Pakistan, to the northwest, which was predominantly Muslim. As Bengal, in the northeastern corner of India, also had a Muslim population, it was made a part of Pakistan. In 1971 East Pakistan, as it had become known, achieved independence and changed its name to Bangladesh ("Land of the Bengalis").

Is Bangladesh overpopulated?

With a population density of approximately 2,500 people per sq mile (1,000 people per sq km),

Bangladesh is the most densely populated nation (excluding city-states) on the planet. Because of the high birth rate, its population has increased by 25 million over the last 20 years. It is also one of the poorest countries in the world.

Why is the country subject to continual floods?

Bangladesh is an extremely flat land, most of which lies in the delta area of the Ganges and Brahmaputra rivers. Floods occur on a regular basis whenever the rivers run high. Between spring and autumn Bangladesh is also vulnerable to tropical monsoons that blow up over the Bay of Bengal to the south. The tidal waves triggered by these storms cause repeated flooding with catastrophic effects.

Grameen Bank

More than 60 million people live below the poverty line in Bangladesh. In 1983 Bangladeshi economist Muhammad Yunus founded Grameen Bank in order to provide poor sections of the population with microcredit as a way of helping people help themselves. The bank grants loans without demanding the usual safeguards, and 97 per cent of its loans are made to women. The initiative earned the bank and its founder a joint Nobel Peace Prize in 2006.

Women and children removing the air bladder from small fish in order to extract fish oil.

How many islands are there in the Maldives archipelago?

This South Asian island state comprises around 2,000 coral islands fringed by reefs and arranged in groups of atolls. These islands extend for 541 miles (871 km) in a north-south direction, straddling the Equator, and rarely rise more than 8 ft (2.5 m) above sea level. Only 220 of the islands are inhabited.

What is the country's main source of income?

Since the 1980s the Maldives' main source of income has been tourism, which has brought a degree of prosperity to the islands but also created a number of problems, such as the progressive destruction of the coral reefs. Over 200,000 tourists visit the islands every year but are mostly restricted to 60 specially equipped tourist islands offering hotels and bungalow complexes. It is only possible for tourists to visit the so-called "local islands" with special authorization.

When did Islam reach the Maldives?

In the middle of the 12th century travellers persuaded the king to convert to Islam and he ordered the islanders to do the same. Until then the dominant religion was Buddhism. Hardly any traces of the islands' Buddhist past remain today.

Have the islands had colonial rulers in the past?

Portugal made a number of unsuccessful attempts to colonize the sultanate in the 16th century. In 1887 it became a British Protectorate. The Maldives gained internal autonomy in 1948 and full independence in 1965.

Of the 2,000 islands that make up this island state off the southern tip of India, only 60 are accessible to tourists without special authorization.

MALDIVES

Flag

Currency
1 rufiyaa (MVR) = 100 laari

System of government
Presidential republic since 1968

Capital
Male

Languages
Dhivehi (Maldivian) (official language), English (lingua franca)

Surface area
115 sq miles (298 sq km)

Population 350,000

Religion
99% Sunni Muslim

Dhivehi

The country's national language is Dhivehi. Dhivehi is related to Sinhala, an Indo-European language belonging to the Indo-Aryan group and spoken by the largest ethnic group on neighboring Sri Lanka.

SRI LANKA

Flag

Currency
1 Sri Lankan rupee (LKR)
= 100 cents

System of government
Presidential republic since 1978
(Commonwealth member)

Capital Colombo

Languages
Sinhala, Tamil (official languages),
Malay, English

Surface area
25,332 sq miles (65,610 sq km)

Population 20.2 million

Religion
77% Buddhist, 8% Muslim,
8% Hindu, 6% Catholic

A rich selection of fruits on a market stall in Colombo.

What mineral resources does Sri Lanka have?

Sri Lanka is very rich in mineral resources. In addition to iron ore, tin, manganese, molybdenum, nickel, cobalt, arsenic, tungsten, tellurium, and gold, precious stones are also found on the island (rubies, sapphires and beryl).

What kind of climate does Sri Lanka have?

Sri Lanka's climate is tropical across the whole island although there are significant differences in rainfall from region to region. The southwest is wet all year round, with the southwest monsoon bringing the heaviest rainfall in May and October. The east and northeast coasts have low levels of precipitation at these times of year while their wettest months are

Working elephants at Pinnewala near Kegalla.

November and December (northeast monsoon). In the mountains temperatures often fall beneath freezing.

What is Adam's Bridge?

Until some time between 6000 and 3500 BC Sri Lanka was connected to the Indian mainland. Adam's Bridge, as the link is known, is still visible today in the form of coral reefs and islands.

What happened on December 26, 2004?

Sri Lanka was hit by an enormous tidal wave known as a tsunami, which destroyed large parts of the east and southeast coast and killed tens of thousands of people.

The civil war in Sri Lanka

The Tamils and the Singhalese have both lived on Sri Lanka for over 2,000 years. During colonial times the British gave the Tamils (the island's largest minority, making up 18 per cent of the population) preferential treatment over the Singhalese. Following independence this special status was abolished as part of the process of democratization and in 1983 an armed conflict broke out between the Tamil separatists in the north and east, who demanded an independent Hindu Tamil state, and the Sri Lankan army and various paramilitary groups. It is estimated that the conflict has cost well over 70,000 lives to date. The situation calmed down in 2001 but no solution is yet in sight as neither side is prepared to make any concessions.

Is Mongolia a land of climatic extremes?

Yes. Mongolia boasts both the most southerly permafrost and the most northerly desert in the world. Only ten per cent of the country is forest and no more than one per cent of the land is suitable for cultivation. Mongolia's extreme temperatures, which range from −13°F to 68°F (−25°C to 20°C), are due to its dry continental climate. There are also big differences (as much as 90°F/32°C) between daytime and night-time temperatures.

Does Mongolia suffer from environmental problems?

Yes. The country is facing major environmental problems and there are as yet few signs of it adopting a responsible approach towards the environment. Thermal power stations of Soviet design and many businesses (for example in the mining sector and textile and leather industries) consume vast quantities of water, which is a scarce resource in Mongolia. Barely half the country's wastewater is treated and the rivers in industrial areas are therefore heavily polluted. Unofficial garbage disposal sites are popping up all over the country. The one consolation is that Mongolia is the most sparsely populated country on the planet.

MONGOLIA

Flag

Currency
1 tugrik (MNT) = 100 möngö

System of government
Republic since 1992

Capital
Ulaanbaatar

Languages Mongolian (official language), Russian, Kazakh

Surface area 0.60 million sq miles (1.56 million sq km)

Population 2.8 million

Religion
90% Buddhist

Notable features
Mongolia's population includes significant numbers of nomads.

What is shamanism?

Shamanism is the ancient belief of the people of the Mongolian steppes. Its religious and magical ideas and practices are based on a belief in spirits and human beings with extraordinary powers known as shamans, who receive instructions from the other world with a view to restoring the proper relationship between men and gods.

Demonstrations of horsemanship were held in 2006 as part of the celebrations held to mark the 800th anniversary of the founding of Mongolia by Genghis Khan.

Genghis Khan

In the Middle Ages Genghis Khan (1162–1227) united the Mongolian tribes into a single people, subjugated neighboring lands, and eventually created the biggest empire that ever existed, stretching from the Sea of Japan to the Caspian. Genghis Khan had a special form of writing developed in order to facilitate the administration of his empire and issued laws that applied equally to all his subjects. After his death the empire was divided between his sons and simultaneously expanded. By 1240 it extended as far as central Europe. The Mongol Empire eventually fell apart another two generations later.

PEOPLE'S REPUBLIC OF CHINA

Flag

Currency
1 renmimbi yuan (CNY) = 10 jiao
System of government
Socialist People's Republic since 1949
Capital
Beijing
Languages
Chinese (official language),

Chinese dialects (e.g. Fujian, Hakka), 55 minority languages
Surface area 3.69 million sq miles (9.57 million sq km)
Population 1.3 billion
Religion
Majority non-denominational, 10% Buddhist
Notable features
China is frequently visited by natural catastrophes.

ascended the throne at the age of two) resigned in response to the proclamation of the republic.

When was the People's Republic of China founded?
Mao Zedong proclaimed the People's Republic of China in October 1949 following the end of the civil war between the Communist Party of China and the Kuomintang (Chinese Nationalist Party).

Who was Mao Zedong?
As chairman of the Communist Party of China, Mao Zedong (1893–1976) determined the history of the People's Republic of China for nearly 30 years. An estimated 35 million people died as a result of economic mismanagement or persecution while he was in power.

Where is the Silk Road?
The Silk Road is the legendary trading route between China and Syria that has been used since Roman times.

Lion dance during the Chinese New Year celebrations, the country's most important holiday, which starts on the first day of the lunar calendar.

How long did the Chinese Empire last?
The first empire was founded by Emperor Qin Shihuang in 221 BC. Imperial rule continued uninterrupted for 2,133 years until 1912, when the last emperor (Pu Yi, who had

Jing Jing is the name of the panda chosen as the mascot for the 2008 Olympic Games.

Not only were basic commodities and luxury goods transported along its caravan routes, the trading links also brought about a cultural exchange between Central Asia and Europe.

Is China frequently hit by natural catastrophes?

Yes. China has suffered and continues to suffer from devastating natural catastrophes, particularly earthquakes and floods. Millions of people have perished in disasters such as the Shaanxi (1556), Sichuan (1850), Gansu (1920), and Tangshan (1976) earthquakes and the Banqiao Dam and Yellow River floods.

What was the Long March?

In 1934/5 the communists, under the leadership of Mao Zedong, were forced to flee Chiang Kai-shek's nationalists. Their 6,000-mile (10,000-km) trek to Shaanxi in northwestern China took over a year and was accomplished in conditions of unutterable deprivation. Of the 130,000 people who set out, barely 30,000 reached the destination.

What was the Great Leap Forward?

This was the official name of the policy pursued by Mao Zedong between 1958 and 1962. Under the Great Leap Forward China was to become an economic superpower with the largest steel production in the world. As labor was organized centrally, however, this policy led to a severe shortage of farmers, resulting in the worst famine in history.

What was the Cultural Revolution?

The Cultural Revolution was a large-scale reorganization of society unleashed by Mao Zedong between 1965 and 1976. Its main objective was to do away with bourgeois thinking and values. In addition to the destruction of classical "bourgeois" cultural artifacts, the first three years of the program saw large numbers of people killed and persecuted. The main tool used by Chairman Mao was the Red Guard.

Causeway Bay in Hong Kong. Since 1997 the former British crown colony has been a part of the People's Republic of China.

Initiated in Beijing, the Cultural Revolution was a call to arms against the "old order." Everything that was capitalist, feudal, reactionary or revisionist had to be destroyed, above all the vehicles and artifacts of Chinese culture.

Interesting facts: Population

While the People's Republic of China is slightly smaller than the United States, it has a bigger population. Indeed, China's population is the largest in the world and the country also has some of the most densely populated regions on the planet. It has a long history of overpopulation and the concomitant problem of food supply. Famine has repeatedly triggered economic and political crises. The country's current population policy is based on just one child per family. China has enormous conurbations, all along its coasts, and around half the population now live in around ten per cent of the country.

The Great Wall of China is the longest and largest man-made structure on Earth.

What are the consequences of the one-child policy?
Countless female fetuses are aborted, leading to a gender imbalance whereby men significantly outnumber women. For every 100 girls brought into the world, 120 boys are born. Ultrasound scans to determine gender are now punishable by law.

When did the Tiananmen massacre take place?
The massacre brought an end to the month-long occupation of the "Square of Heavenly Peace" in Beijing, which borders the parliament building. The occupying students were violently driven out on June 3 and 4, 1989. In the square itself and throughout the whole of Beijing there were 3,000 deaths, according to the Red Cross. In the follow-up

The Great Wall of China

The Great Wall of China is 30 ft (9 m) high and runs for over 3,000 miles (4,800 km) from close to the mouth of the Yellow River to northwest China. It consists of a series of fortifications erected over a period of more than 2,500 years in order to defend China against incursions from the north. The surviving parts were built during the Ming Dynasty (1364–1644).

What is the Terracotta Army?

The Terracotta Army is a collection of over 7,000 terracotta soldiers that were buried with Emperor Qin, China's first emperor (who came to power in 221 BC), in a series of underground chambers attached to Qin's mausoleum. The figures were discovered in 1974 during excavations at Xian. In addition to soldiers there are also figures of horses and riders as well as artifacts such as swords, arrowheads, and crossbows. One of the fascinating things about the figures, many of which are life-size, is that no two figures are identical.

Does the People's Republic of China have the death penalty?

Nowhere in the world are more people executed than in China. A number of crimes are punishable by death, including drug offenses and economic crime, corruption, and treason, which includes the dissemination of information on the spread of HIV/AIDS.

Left: Lines of brightly colored prayer flags and ceremonial scarves (*katags*) are a common sight in the highlands of Central Asia.

The famous Terracotta Army at Xian.

operation, activists and intellectuals were arrested and 49 (the official figure) were executed.

What is the attitude of the People's Republic towards Taiwan?

The People's Republic of China regards Taiwan as a part of mainland China. On March 13, 2005 a so-called anti-secession law was introduced that provides for military intervention should Taiwan formally proclaim its independence or should reunification with the People's Republic appear impossible.

What is Beijing opera?

Beijing opera is the best-known form of Chinese opera, in which different genres such as dance, song, martial arts, and drama rub shoulders in popular plays. Beijing opera is heavily ritualized and the masks and costumes of the players are all the more striking for the sparseness of the stage. It developed during the Tang Dynasty (618–906) and has survived in its essentials to the present day—even some of the same works are performed—although its future is now uncertain due to sagging audience numbers.

DEMOCRATIC PEOPLE'S REPUBLIC OF KOREA (NORTH KOREA)

Flag

Currency
1 won (KPW) = 100 chon

System of government
People's republic since 1948

Capital
Pyŏngyang

Languages Korean (official language), Russian, Chinese

Surface area
47,399 sq miles (122,762 sq km)

Population 22.9 million

Religion
Buddhist and Confucianist but the majority of the population are thought to be atheist.

What is a Juche state?

"Juche" is a Korean word meaning "self-reliance." In terms of ideology it represents a strand of Marxist-Leninist thought developed by the Workers' Party of North Korea in the 1940s whereby the interests of one's own country are placed above those of the international communist movement. Unconditional loyalty and, in the case of North Korea's current leader, Kim Jong-il (born 1941), boundless adoration of the head of state (personality cult) are demanded of the citizen of a Juche state.

Where is Korea's demilitarized zone?

The end of the Korean War in 1953 brought not only a ceasefire but also the creation of a demilitarized zone between North and South Korea. This is 154 miles (248 km) long and approximately 2.5 miles (4 km) wide and runs through the two countries in an east-west direction. Through the middle of this zone runs the actual North-South border. This frontier is virtually impenetrable and the only possibility of escape is through China, where up to 300,000 North Korean refugees are currently thought to live.

The 560-ft (170-m) Juche Tower on the eastern bank of the Taedong River in Pyŏngyang (completed in 1982) was erected to celebrate the 70th birthday of Kim Il-sung.

Does North Korea have nuclear weapons?

One of North Korea's most ambitious development programs is aimed at the acquisition of a nuclear arsenal. The country conducted its first nuclear weapons test (underground) on October 9, 2006 and claims to be able to deliver nuclear warheads as far as the West Coast of the United States by means of its newly developed transcontinental rockets. North Korea's nuclear ambitions have attracted international condemnation.

Interesting facts

- The population of North Korea has almost doubled since 1970.
- Life expectancy has fallen markedly as a result of famine and inadequate medical care.
- North Korea has the lowest proportion of foreigners of any country in the world.
- Human rights are barely respected in North Korea.

Rice has been grown in Korea for 4,000 years. In North Korea it is still cultivated using the simplest of tools.

When did South Korea come into existence?

The two Korean states came into being in 1948 during the early days of the Cold War. This division of Korea was sealed by the Korean War (1950–1953). No peace treaty has been signed since the end of the war—the only existing treaty is the ceasefire agreement of 1953.

What is the Saemangeum?

The Saemangeum is an area of mudflats (the second-largest in the world after those of the North Sea) on South Korea's west coast, in the estuary of the Donjing and Manyeon rivers in the Yellow Sea.

Does South Korea suffer from frequent earthquakes?

No. Although there are around 20 earthquakes a year in South Korea, only half of them measure more than 3 on the Richter Scale (the point at which earth tremors can be detected by human beings). By comparison, Japan registers around 1,200 tremors a year with a magnitude of 3 or more.

Is there a gender imbalance in South Korea?

As in other Asian countries, male children are generally favored in South Korea. The country therefore has a greater proportion of men than women although women have a longer life expectancy (79.5 years for women compared to 72 years for men). As a result, the population is aging

rapidly and it is assumed that it will stop growing after 2028.

What are *chaebols*?

Chaebols are large, family-controlled business conglomerates, the best-known being LG, Samsung, Hyundai, and Daewoo. In South Korea these corporations are far more diversified than abroad and often include real estate and insurance corporations, wholesale and retail chains, etc.

What is the KTX?

KTX stands for Korea Train Express, a high-speed train (based on French TGV technology) that was brought into service in 2004. It operates on the Seoul-Pusan and Seoul-Mokpo routes and transports over 100,000 passengers a day at speeds of up to 150 mph (240 km/h).

REPUBLIC OF KOREA (SOUTH KOREA)

Flag

Currency
1 won (KRW) = 100 chon

System of government
Presidential republic since 1948

Capital
Seoul

Languages
Korean (official language), English, Japanese

Surface area
38,345 sq miles (99,313 sq km)

Population 48.6 million

Religion
20% Buddhist, 15% Protestant, 7% Catholic

The soccer stadium in Pusan, built for the 2002 World Cup.

JAPAN

Flag

Currency
1 yen (JPY) = 100 sen

System of government
Constitutional monarchy since 1947

Capital
Tokyo

Languages
Japanese (official language), English

Surface area
145,884 sq miles (377,837 sq km)

Population 127.4 million

Religion
84% Buddhist and Shinto

Of how many islands is Japan made up?
Japan consists of over 3,000 islands. The four principal islands, on which all the large cities are located, are Honshu, Hokkaido, Kyushu, and Shikoku.

Is there any volcanic activity in Japan?
Japan is one of the countries worst affected by earthquakes. The Japanese Archipelago is the mountain ridge that rises from over 13,000 ft (4,000 m) below sea level and culminates in the volcanic peak of Mount Fuji on Honshu Island at 12,388 ft (3,776 m). Of Japan's 250 volcanoes, some 60 are still active.

What were the consequences of the Kobe earthquake?
At 5:46 on the morning of January 17, 1995 an earthquake occurred on the Nojima Fault on Awaji Island at a depth of 10 miles (16 km) below ground. Although the tremor, which measured 7.2 on the Richter Scale, lasted no more than 20 seconds, it was

Below: The temple complex of Kiyomizu-dera in eastern Kyoto has been designated a UNESCO World Heritage site. Its history goes back to 798.

one of the most destructive of all time. Buildings in the city of Kobe in southern Japan collapsed, roads were ripped up like paper, and factories and railroads were destroyed. Over 6,000 people lost their lives and more than 30,000 were left homeless.

When were the atomic bombs dropped on Hiroshima and Nagasaki?

On the morning of August 6, 1945 a B-29 bomber named *Enola Gay* took off for Hiroshima under the command of Captain Paul W. Tibbets. It was carrying the first atomic bomb ever to be detonated in other than test conditions. *Little Boy*, as it had been named, was dropped over Hiroshima and exploded with the destructive power of around 22,000 tons of TNT at an altitude of 2,000 ft (600 m). The city was razed to the ground. No fewer than 75,000 people died in the explosion and a further 250,000 succumbed to the aftereffects. Never in the history of mankind had a single weapon claimed so many lives. Two days later, on August 8, a plutonium bomb

Background: The Chuo-ohashi Bridge in Tokyo. With almost 13 million inhabitants, Tokyo is Japan's largest city and one of the largest and most modern in the world.

Below: View of a traditional Japanese house in Tokyo.

South Kuril Islands

The Kurils are a chain of over 30 islands that stretch for approximately 750 miles (1,200 km) off the northeastern tip of Hokkaido. The waters around the islands are among the richest in fish of any in the world. In 1945, towards the end of the Second World War, the Kuril Islands were occupied by Soviet troops and the Japanese population (some 18,000 people) driven out. On February 2, 1946 the USSR declared the islands to be Soviet sovereign territory.

In the peace treaty of 1951 between Japan and the Allies (to which the USSR was not a party), Japan renounced all rights to the Kuril Islands. No geographical borders were specified but to all those involved it was clear that the four South Kuril Islands in question (Iturup, Kunashir, Shikotan, and the Habomai group of islands) were being treated as Japanese sovereign territory rather than included with the rest of the Kurils. Japan is still claiming these islands today.

Interesting facts

- 160,000 people have died in tsunamis in Japan over the last 1,000 years.

- Rice, Japan's main crop, was originally introduced into the country from Korea.

- Japan's largest ethnic minority are roughly 650,000 Japanese of Korean descent who do not have Japanese nationality because in order to acquire it they would have to adopt the Japanese form for their names, which Korean national pride prevents them from doing.

- In Article 9 of the Japanese constitution Japan renounces its right as a sovereign state to wage war—the only time any country in the world has undertaken such a commitment.

- There is no compulsory military service in Japan, yet in terms of military expenditure the country ranks sixth in the world.

- 44 death sentences were carried out in Japan in 2006.

An actor in the Kabuki tradition (meaning something like "singing and dancing"), whose origins go back to the early Edo period (17th century).

named *Fat Man* was dropped on Nagasaki, exposing the industrial city to unimaginable temperatures of 540,000°F (300,000°C). The pressure wave destroyed half the city and killed 50,000 people. A week later Emperor Hirohito signed the surrender document.

What are the problems associated with Japan's low birth rate?

Japan's population growth is just 0.14 per cent. As a result, in 2005 Japan became the most aged country in the world with 21 per cent of its population aged 65 or above. If the birth rate does not rise, the population could fall by 30 per cent over the next 50 years. In 2007 the issue came to a head when health minister Hakuo Yanagisawa referred to Japan's women as "child-bearing machines" whose responsibility it is to do "their utmost" to increase the birth rate.

Where are the weaknesses in Japan's economy?

In addition to raw materials and petroleum, another of Japan's chief imports is food. Because the terrain is mostly mountainous, only 15 per cent of the land can be used for agriculture and the soil is farmed extremely intensively in order to increase profitability.

Iwo Jima

In 1877 Japan annexed the uninhabited island of Iwo Jima in the Pacific Ocean approximately 750 miles (1,200 km) south of Tokyo. It settled the volcanic island of just 8 sq miles (21 sq km) and turned it into a military base. In 1945 around 100 civilians lived on Iwo Jima when on February 19, following a 50-hour bombardment, US troops landed and one of the bloodiest battles of the war in the Pacific ensued, costing the lives of 21,000 Japanese and around 7,000 US soldiers. Today the island is again uninhabited.

There is a similar problem with the generation of energy and as a result 90 per cent of the nation's energy needs have to be imported. This dependence on imports has led to growing concerns about Japan's ability to remain competitive in the future.

What is a *ryokan*?

A *ryokan* is an inn in which visitors can acquaint themselves with the traditional Japanese way of life. Guests sleep on futons (cotton-filled mattresses) laid on floors covered only by *tatamis* (straw mats), wear typical *yukatas* (the type of kimono worn on such

occasions), and bathe in *onsens* (hot spring baths). There is no better way of coming into contact with Japanese traditions, culture, and customs than in a *ryokan*.

What is Minimata disease?

Japan's rapid development into one of the world's leading industrial nations soon brought enormous environmental problems. Minimata disease is the result of poisoning by certain mercury compounds and first appeared in the vicinity of the coastal town of Minimata. Its symptoms are fatigue, headaches, and aching limbs followed by signs of paralysis, psychosis, and coma. In extreme cases the illness can be fatal.

Other "Japanese" illnesses caused by environmental damage include itai-itai disease (chronic pain as a result of cadmium poisoning) and Yokkaichi asthma (chronic asthma caused by industrial pollutants). The latter was named after the city of Yokkaichi, a center of the petrochemical industry.

Above: *Sushi* is traditionally served with soy sauce and hot, green *wasabi* paste.

A view of Mount Fuji from across Lake Kawaguchi with cherry blossom in the foreground.

REPUBLIC OF CHINA (TAIWAN)

Flag

Currency
1 New Taiwan dollar (TWD) = 100 cents

System of government Republic

Capital
Taipei (de facto), Nanjing (official)

Languages
Mandarin (official language), Min, Hakka

Surface area
13,900 sq miles (36,000 sq km)

Population 22.8 million

Religion 93% Buddhist, Confucianist, Taoist

At 1,667 ft (508 m) the Taipei 101 tower is one of the tallest office buildings in the world and dominates the metropolis.

What was Taiwan's previous name?
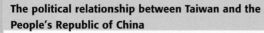

What was Taiwan's previous name? The island was discovered by the Portuguese in 1583 and named Ilha Formosa ("beautiful island"), by which it was known for centuries in the West. In China, on the other hand, the name "Taiwan," borrowed from the language of the Gaoshan, the island's original inhabitants, was adopted in the 16th century to refer to both the island and its capital.

What was the San Francisco Peace Treaty?
The civil war between the communists and the Chinese Nationalist Party (Kuomintang) ended in 1949, whereupon the Chinese government, under the leadership of General Chiang Kai-shek, fled to the island of Taiwan. The San Francisco Peace Treaty, signed in 1952, stipulated that the right of self-determination of the Taiwanese people had to be respected by mainland China. The United States declared itself to be Taiwan's protector but broke off relations with the country in 1978, when it began to draw closer to the People's Republic. Taiwan is still not officially recognized by the United States.

What are Taiwan's main industrial sectors?
In the 1950s agriculture provided the basis for Taiwan's economic growth but by the 1990s accounted for only four per cent of the GDP. Today Taiwan is the world's largest producer of Wireless LAN components, semiconductor applications, and PC circuit boards and electronic notebooks.

The political relationship between Taiwan and the People's Republic of China

The relationship between the People's Republic of China and Taiwan is extremely tense and complex. Since 1971 most nations have recognized the People's Republic while only 24 have established official diplomatic relations with Taiwan.

Between 1912 and 1949 the name "Republic of China" designated the whole of China but since the founding of the People's Republic, the territory under its control has been restricted to Taiwan plus the islands of Kinmen, Matsu and the Pescadores. The constitutions of both countries lay claim to the entire Chinese territory although Taiwan gave up officially pursuing its claim in the 1990s. The People's Republic did not follow suit and on the contrary regards Taiwan as a breakaway province, threatening military action should Taiwan formally proclaim its independence (see People's Republic of China).

MYANMAR

Flag	**Languages** Burmese (official language)
	Surface area 261,228 sq miles (676,577 sq km)
Currency 1 kyat (MMK) = 100 pyas	**Population** 54 million
System of government Socialist republic since 1974	**Religion** 89% Buddhist, 4% Christian,
Capital Naypyidaw	4% Muslim

Why was the capital moved?

Myanmar's largest city, Yangon (Rangoon), was also its capital until 2005. In December of that year the government moved to Pyinmana, 200 miles (320 km) farther north. The new capital, renamed Naypyidaw ("City of the Kings") in March 2006, is closed to civilians and foreigners. It is thought that this move was motivated by a fear of seaborne invasion by foreign forces.

Why did Burma change its name to Myanmar?

In 1988, after brutally suppressing a popular uprising, the military took control of the country and turned it into a military dictatorship. In 1989 the name of the country was changed to Myanmar in order to distance it from its own traditions—above all the English name imposed by its former colonial masters—and mark the new beginning.

Is the rate of HIV infection increasing?

Although no reliable statistics are available, it is thought that the number of people infected with HIV/AIDS has increased dramatically over the last few years. The military junta is covertly operating a form of state-sponsored prostitution and it is believed that a sizable proportion of the population suffers from drug addiction, which is also contributing to the increase in infection rate.

What position is the country in economically?

Myanmar is one of the poorest countries in the world, due largely to economic mismanagement by the military dictatorship. While it had previously been considered the "granary of Southeast Asia" and enjoyed a positive balance of payments, the junta now spends over 50 per cent of the national budget on the military, police and secret services and has ruined the once prosperous nation with its restrictive policies.

The Kakku pagoda complex, approximately 43 miles (70 km) from Nyaung Shwe. It is renowned for its 2,500 temples and stupas arranged in straight lines and covering an area of 0.4 sq miles (1 sq km).

Aung San Suu Kyi

Aung San Suu Kyi (born 1945) is a political activist committed to the nonviolent democratization of Myanmar. She stood in the 1990 general election as leader of the National League for Democracy, but, although her party won, the result was not recognized by the military. She had already been placed under house arrest the year before and, other than a few short suspensions, this has been maintained ever since. In 1991 Aung San Suu Kyi was awarded the Nobel Peace Prize for her work.

Is there drugs trafficking in Myanmar?

The dictatorship is believed to be financed by trafficking of heroin and, most importantly over the last few years, amphetamines. These drugs are produced by the ton in jungle locations and distributed throughout the world via Thailand and China.

A woman of the Kayan tribe in Myanmar. Brass rings start to be worn by Kayan girls at the age of five. The number of rings is gradually increased until their weight exerts downward pressure on the collarbone, making the neck longer.

THAILAND

Flag

Currency
1 baht (THB) = 100 satang

System of government
Constitutional monarchy since 1932

Capital
Bangkok

Languages
Thai (official language), Chinese, Malay, English

Surface area
198,115 sq miles (513,115 sq km)

Population 65.4 million

Religion
94% Buddhist, 5% Muslim

What does the name "Thailand" mean?
Previously known as Siam, the country adopted its new name, meaning "Land of the Free," in 1939. Thailand is the only country in Southeast Asia never to have been colonized.

What is Thailand's "narrow neck"?
The southern part of Thailand extends along the long, thin Malay Peninsula that separates the Gulf of Thailand (part of the Pacific) from the Indian Ocean. Thailand's coasts, which have been almost completely opened up to tourism, are lined with beautiful beaches and dotted with small islands. The narrowest point between the two oceans is the Isthmus of Kra (the "narrow neck") at just 40 miles (64 km) wide.

Why are there only three seasons in Thailand?
In Thailand the seasons are characterized not by differences in temperature but by differences in precipitation. Three distinct phases can be identified:
a) Between November and February the country is dominated by dry, cooler air introduced by northerly and northwesterly winds.
b) Between March and May is the pre-monsoon season and hottest period of the year, with temperatures exceeding 95°F (35°C).
c) During the monsoon (rainy) season between June and October the weather is dominated by southwesterly winds.

Is tourism important for Thailand's economy?
After rice-growing (Thailand is one of the world's largest rice exporters), tourism is Thailand's main economic sector. Over 14 million people visit the country each year. Unfortunately many of them are dreaming not only of sun, palm trees, and the sea, but of sex too. Sex tourists are drawn to specific locales and the Thai sex industry turns over an estimated 27 billion dollars per year.

Thai cuisine

Thai cuisine is a fusion of East Asian and European influences that has developed gradually over the centuries and which is widely appreciated today. It is particularly well-known (notorious even) for its spiciness and hotness. It is interesting to note, however, that hot chilies were only introduced into the country (by Portuguese missionaries) in the 18th century.

Thai food is eaten with a fork and a spoon, whereby the fork is used to push food onto the spoon. Lifting the fork to one's mouth and eating from it is considered ill-mannered. Equally frowned upon are table noises such as slurping or the clattering of cutlery or crockery.

The Wat Pra Thong Temple on the island of Phuket. The 2004 tsunami caused severe damage here.

Does Laos have a homogeneous population?

No. The population of Laos displays considerable ethnic diversity and comprises more than 60 ethnic groups. The biggest of these is the Lao-Lum (lowland dwellers), who make up 50 per cent of the populace, followed by the Lao-Tai (highland dwellers) and the Lao-Theung (meaning "those who draw close to the summits," clearly also mountain dwellers).

What is the Golden Triangle?

Geographically the Golden Triangle denotes the place where the Ruak River flows into the Mekong, which forms much of the border with neighboring Thailand. In a wider sense it has come to mean the region of Thailand, Laos, and Myanmar where opium poppies are cultivated and made into heroin. As narcotics production has soared in Afghanistan, however, the Golden Triangle has diminished appreciably in importance.

What are the consequences of the Vietnam War?

Between 1964 and 1973 around two million tons of bombs were dropped on Laos across around 50 per cent of its national territory. Many of these bombs failed to explode and still lie buried in the soil. No country in the world has as many unexploded bombs as Laos. Because the country is dominated by agriculture, Laotians are repeatedly being killed and injured in explosions.

The Akha are an ethnic group who originated in China but now live in the mountains of Southeast Asia. Shown here is an Akha village in northwest Laos.

LAOS

Flag

Currency
1 kip (LAK) = 100 ats

System of government
People's republic since 1975

Capital
Vientiane

Languages
Lao (official language), French, Chinese, Vietnamese

Surface area
91,429 sq miles (236,800 sq km)

Population 6.2 million

Religion
60% Buddhist, 33% Animist, 1% Christian

Monsoon

The word "monsoon" derives from the Arabic for "season" and refers to wind systems that change with the seasons. While the summer monsoons usually bring abundant precipitation, the winter monsoons are generally dry. The monsoon is caused by seasonal changes in general atmospheric circulation. Laos has a tropical monsoon climate. During the wet and warm season between May and October the southwest monsoon brings rainfall of up to 67 in (1,700 mm) per year and up to 157 in (4,000 mm) in mountainous regions. The hottest season is the pre-monsoon season between March and May.

CAMBODIA

Flag		**Capital** Phnom Penh
		Languages
		Khmer (official language)
Currency		**Surface area**
1 riel (KHR) = 100 sen		69,900 sq miles (181,040 sq km)
System of government		**Population** 13.6 million
Constitutional monarchy since 1993		**Religion**
		94% Buddhist

What is Angkor Thom?

Angkor Thom, founded around the 9th century AD, was the political and religious capital of the Khmer Empire. The city was abandoned in 1431, when its residents were forced to flee invading Thai tribes. It was eventually covered over by primeval forest. Angkor Thom was "discovered" in 1861 by French explorer Henri Mouhot. The main structure is Angkor Wat, a temple built by King Suryavarman II (1113–1150). Featuring five towers and surrounded by an artificial lake, Angkor Wat is a wonderful example of Khmer architecture.

The ruined city of Angkor Thom became famous the world over as a wonderful example of Khmer architecture. This illustration shows the Pre Rup temple complex.

What is the Tonle Sap?

What is the Tonle Sap?
The Tonle Sap is a Cambodian river and lake (the largest in Southeast Asia and one of the country's richest fishing lakes). During the monsoon season the lake acts as a type of overflow pool for the Mekong River, which is connected to the Tonle Sap. At this time of year the Mekong runs so high that it changes direction, flows inland and swells the lake to some 1,200 sq miles (3,000 sq km), many times its normal size. The land surrounding the lake is extremely fertile as a result.

Did Henri Mouhot really discover the city?

Apparently not, as it had never actually been forgotten. Angkor Wat had continued to be used as a temple and Portuguese sailors had visited the city in the jungle in the 16th century. Nevertheless, Mouhot's book *Voyage à Siam et dans le Cambodge* (1868, "Journey to Siam and Cambodia") put the site on the European map and wove a wonderful sense of mystery around it that endures to the present day.

The Khmer Rouge dictatorship

The civil war of the early 1970s ended in victory for the Khmer Rouge (supported by North Vietnam and the People's Republic of China). Prime Minister Pol Pot (1928–1998) subsequently embarked on a radical and dictatorial reorganization of the country, which was still at that time suffering from the consequences of the Vietnam War. Over the next few years three million people were murdered and died of hunger, disease, and torture inflicted or caused by the totalitarian regime. Pol Pot was eventually removed from power by Vietnamese troops in 1979. The Khmer Rouge remained at large until well into the 1990s, however, keeping the country in a state of turmoil through guerilla activities. The Khmer Rouge finally fell apart in 1996.

Why has Vietnam been described as "two rice bowls on a bamboo stick"?

Vietnam has over 2,100 miles (3,400 km) of coastline. It is long and narrow but in the north and south there are two fertile river deltas—the Red River Delta and Mekong Delta—which are connected by a thin strip of unproductive (mountainous and forested) land.

Is Vietnam heavily polluted?

During the Vietnam War (1964–1975) the United States used dioxin and other environmental pollutants. Not only did these destroy the country's flora (which took decades to recover), they also found their way into the human food chain and are still causing cancer, miscarriages, stillbirths, and deformations today.

What are Vietnam's principal raw materials?

Vietnam's most important raw materials are antimony, bauxite, chrome, iron, petroleum, natural gas, gold, coal, phosphate, tin, and zinc.

What are the most important religions?

The most widespread religion in Vietnam (officially an atheist state) is Buddhism, which arrived overland from China in the 2nd century. The second-largest religion is Catholicism, which was introduced into the country by French, Spanish, and Portuguese missionaries from the 17th century onwards. There are around 6,000 churches in Vietnam and around seven per cent of the population are Catholic.

VIETNAM

Flag

Currency
1 dong (VND) = 100 xu

System of government
Socialist republic since 1980

Capital
Hanoi

Languages
Vietnamese (official language),
Chinese, Khmer

Surface area
120,894 sq miles (313,114 sq km)

Population 83.5 million

Religion
55% Buddhist, 7% Catholic

Notable features
The country is still suffering from the late effects of the Vietnam War of 1964–1975.

Hmong women prepare for a wedding in Lun Chu.

Below: The rural district of Hon.

Vietnam's biggest festival

The Chinese New Year celebrations, known as the Têt, are the country's biggest festival. It starts on the last day of the lunar calendar and continues for a whole week. Because fireworks are prohibited by law, the New Year is ushered in with drums.

PHILIPPINES

Flag

Currency
1 Philippines peso (PHP)
= 100 centavos

System of government
Presidential republic since 1987

Capital
Manila

Languages
Filipino (Tagalog) (official language),

English (lingua franca), 168 languages
(including Waray-Waray and Bicol)

Surface area
115,831 sq miles (300,000 sq km)

Population 89.4 million

Religion
83% Catholic, 9% Protestant,
5% Muslim

Notable features
The state comprises 7,107 islands.

What does "Tagalog" mean?

The Tagalog people are the Philippines' single largest ethnic group, making up approximately 28 per cent of the population. Their tongue, Tagalog, forms the basis for the country's official language, Filipino.

What have been the consequences of population growth?

At the beginning of the 1960s the population was 28 million. It now stands at nearly 90 million. This population explosion is one of the main reasons for the severe economic difficulties the country is facing (despite being an aspiring nation). Several hundred thousand jobs need to be created each year, which is well beyond the country's capabilities, and food has to be imported.

The Taoist temple in Cebu City contains the writings of Chinese philosopher Lao-tzu (6th century BC).

What is the Pacific Ring of Fire?

Volcanoes are often to be found at the point where tectonic plates collide because the Earth's crust is thinner there. Around half the world's 550 or so active volcanoes are located in the Pacific Ocean, where they form the so-called "Ring of Fire." The Philippines are located on this ring and are home to 20 active volcanoes. To the east of the islands is the Philippine Trench, which in places is over 33,000 ft (10,000 m) deep. Seaquakes occurring at these enormous depths are liable to cause tsunamis.

Ferdinand Edralin Marcos

Ferdinand Edralin Marcos (1917–1989) took up office as his country's tenth president in 1965 but soon established a dictatorship in which he had unlimited powers. When the populace rose up against him, he fled to the United States.

Marcos's career as a dictator began in 1972, when he imposed martial law, had 30,000 opposition members imprisoned, and forced congress, publishers, and broadcasting companies to close. The ostensible reason for resorting to these measures had been an attack on defense minister Juan Ponce Enrile but in 1986 Enrile admitted the attack had been faked. During his dictatorship Marcos and his wife Imelda accumulated millions of US dollars in foreign bank accounts.

Interesting facts: The country and its people

- Of the 7,107 Philippine islands, only 880 are inhabited.
- Spanish rule lasted approximately 330 years, yet the Spanish language never caught on.
- Filipino cuisine is a fusion of Spanish, Chinese, Indian, Japanese, and American traditions.
- Divorce is illegal in the Philippines.
- Foreigners are not allowed to buy land in the Philippines.

What is Malacca?

What is Malacca? **M**alacca (after the Sultanate of Malacca) is the name by which the Malay Peninsula was formerly known. It derived originally from a city on the west coast, however, which also gave its name to the busy, strategically important straits between Sumatra and the mainland that are the subject of continual disputes.

What are Malaysia's main industries?

Although agro-industries remain important (Malaysia is responsible for 25 per cent of the world's production of rubber and is one of the leading producers of palm oil), this fast-developing nation has succeeded since the 1960s in freeing itself from dependence on a plantation and raw materials-based economy. Thanks to Japanese intervention the country has developed into a leading electronics manufacturer and also produces petroleum and, increasingly, natural gas too. Malaysia has now become an "Asian Tiger" (see Singapore) alongside South Korea, Hong Kong, Taiwan, and Singapore.

MALAYSIA

Flag

Currency
1 Malaysian ringgit (MYR) = 100 sen

System of government
Constitutional elective monarchy since 1963 (Commonwealth member)

Capital
Kuala Lumpur

Languages
Malay (official language), Chinese, Tamil, English (lingua franca)

Surface area
127,317 sq miles (329,750 sq km)

Population 23.9 million

Religion
60% Sunni Muslim, 19% Buddhist, 9% Christian, 6% Hindu

Notable features
Malaysia has one of the oldest rain forests in the world but this is under severe threat from slash-and-burn and commercial felling: Malaysia is one of the world's biggest exporters of tropical wood.

Since 2000 the 1,483-ft (452-m) Petronas Twin Towers in Kuala Lumpur have been connected at a height of 558 ft (170 m) by the 190-ft-long (58-m) "Skybridge."

Borneo

Borneo is the largest island in the Malaysian Archipelago and the third-largest island in the world. Indonesia possesses the biggest share of the island at 208,495 sq miles (540,000 sq km), followed by the two Federation of Malaya states Sarawak and Sabah at 76,448 sq miles (198,000 sq km), and lastly Brunei at 2,226 sq miles (5,765 sq km). The island is blessed with abundant minerals and is almost completely covered by hot, humid rainforest. Borneo is home to the second-largest orangutan population in the world after the Indonesian island of Sumatra.

SINGAPORE

Flag	**Languages** Malay, Tamil, Chinese, English (official languages)
Currency 1 Singapore dollar (SGD) = 100 cents	**Surface area** 270 sq miles (669 sq km)
System of government Republic since 1959 (Commonwealth member)	**Population** 4.4 million
Capital Singapore	**Religion** 43% Buddhist, 15% Muslim, 15% Christian, 9% Taoist

Right: The richly decorated façade of a Hindu temple in Singapore.

What does the name "Singapore" mean?
"Singapore" is Sanskrit and means "city of the lion." In the 7th century the island had been called Temasek ("city by the sea"). Legend has it that the city changed its name when the Merlion, a sea monster with the head of a lion, emerged from the sea during a mighty storm and saved the inhabitants by calming the winds. The Merlion was subsequently adopted as the city's emblem.

How important is land reclamation for Singapore?
Singapore's surface area is very small and land reclamation is correspondingly important. The earth and rubble needed for land creation is extracted on the island or from quarries in neighboring states or else dug up from the seabed. In 1960 Singapore's surface area was 224.5 sq miles (581.5 sq km). It is now 270 sq miles (699 sq km) and by 2030 a further 39 sq miles (100 sq km) are expected to have been added.

The Merlion statue—the city-state's emblem.

What is being done to control the growth in the number of automobiles in Singapore?
Automobiles are extremely expensive in Singapore—around two and a half times as expensive as in Europe. The government also holds permit auctions as a way of controlling the growth in vehicle numbers. Permits apply to specific vehicles and are valid for ten years.

Who was Sir Stamford Raffles?
The stage for Singapore's development was set when Sir Stamford Raffles (1781–1823) established a British East India Company trading post there in 1819. Hitherto, the island had been inhabited by 20 or so Malay families but otherwise served merely as a bolt-hole for pirates. In 1824 the island was bought from the Sultan of Johor for 60,000 US dollars and became a British crown colony. By 1881 Singapore was home to 170,000 people.

What is a durian?
The durian is the fruit of the durian tree (*Durio zibethinus*). Its name is derived from the Malay word for "thorn." This nutritious fruit rich in vitamins is also known as the "civet fruit" because of its strong odor. In 2002 Singapore received a new landmark: the Esplanade cultural center, designed in the shape of a durian.

Asian Tigers

The term "Asian Tigers" was coined in the 1980s to describe four Asian states that were experiencing phenomenal growth: South Korea, Hong Kong, Taiwan, and Singapore. In a short space of time these four states had transformed themselves from developing to industrial nations with a tiger-like dynamism.

Where is Brunei?

Brunei is located on the South China Sea coast on the island of Borneo. On the land side, the tiny state is completely surrounded by Malaysia and divided into two by a river valley belonging to Malaysia. Brunei's capital is Bandar Seri Begawan, which means "harbor of the revered leader."

Was Brunei once a colony?

Brunei is an ancient sultanate that experienced a golden age from the 15th to the 17th centuries, during which time it extended across the whole of Borneo and the southern Philippines. In 1888 Brunei became a British Protectorate, a status that lasted until the Japanese invasion during the Second World War. After the war (1946) it became a British colony before demanding independence in 1984.

Is Brunei a rich country?

Brunei has prospered thanks to its enormous natural gas and petroleum reserves. It has no foreign debts, offers wide-ranging tax exemptions, and provides its people with comprehensive social benefits. Basic healthcare and school and university education are free of charge.

BRUNEI

Flag	**Surface area**
	2,228 sq miles (5,770 sq km)
Currency	**Population** 372,361
1 Brunei dollar (BND) = 100 sen	**Religion**
System of government	67% Muslim, 13% Buddhist,
Islamic monarchy (sultanate) since	Taoist, and Confucianist,
1984 (Commonwealth member)	10% Christian
Capital	**Notable features**
Bandar Seri Begawan	Brunei's state territory is divided by a
Languages	river valley that belongs to Malaysia.
Malay (official language), Chinese, English	

Who is the sultan of Brunei?

The reigning sultan of Brunei (the 29th) is Hassanal Bolkiah. He was born in 1946 and became sultan in 1967. The royal line can be traced back to 1405. The sultan of Brunei reigns as an absolute monarch and is simultaneously head of state, prime minister, finance minister, and defense minister.

The Omar Ali Saifuddin Mosque in Bandar Seri Bagawan, completed in 1958, was built on an artificial lagoon.

The largest palace on Earth

The sultan of Brunei is one of the richest men in the world. His palace offers 2,152,782 sq ft (200,000 sq m) of accommodation and no fewer than 1,800 rooms, making it the largest palace on Earth. The sultan also possesses the most extensive collection of luxury automobiles in the world—between 3,000 and 5,000 vehicles. His private plane (a Boeing 747) features stables and gold taps.

INDONESIA

Flag	Languages
	Indonesian (official language), Javanese, Malay, around 250 regional languages
Currency	
1 rupia (IDR) = 100 sen	**Surface area** 0.74 million sq miles (1.91 million sq km)
System of government	
Presidential republic since 1945	**Population** 242 million
Capital	**Religion**
Jakarta	88% Muslim, 8% Christian

A Komodo dragon in the national park on Komodo Island.

Of how many islands is Indonesia made up?

Indonesia consists of more than 17,000 islands with a total coastline of 50,549 miles (81,350 km). Around 6,000 of these are inhabited. The largest islands are Java, Sumatra, Borneo, Sulawesi, Bali, Lombok, and Flores.

Is there any volcanic activity in Indonesia?

Paddy fields and volcanoes on the idyllic island of Bali.

Many of the islands consist of volcanic rock. Hundreds of volcanoes, of which 70 are still active, follow in succession along the 3,170-mile (5,100-km) chain of islands from Sumatra to the Maluku Islands. The best-

Komodo dragon

The Komodo dragon is a giant lizard belonging to the Varanidae family. It is the largest surviving lizard on the planet. Komodo dragons grow up to 10 ft (3 m) long and can weigh up to 110 lb (50 kg)—with empty stomachs. Because these lizards can eat up to 80 per cent of their body weight very quickly, however, they can sometimes weigh as much as 200 lb (90 kg). The creatures live for 30 to 50 years and are marked by their foul smell, which has been ascribed to remnants of decaying carcass in the mouth. This also means that bites from Komodo dragons (which are known to attack and eat humans) are very hard to heal. Today Komodo dragons only inhabit the islands of Komodo, Flores, Rinca, and Gili Motang.

known of these is Krakatoa in the Sunda Strait between the islands of Sumatra and Java. Approximately 36,000 people lost their lives when it erupted in 1883.

What is the biggest problem currently facing Indonesia?

The country's main problem is its extremely uneven population distribution. More than two thirds of the total population live on Java (just seven per cent of the surface area). Ever since the middle of the 20th century attempts have been made (with little success) to move people to the less densely populated islands. In Java the population density is over 5,180 people per sq mile (2,000 people per sq km) in rural areas and over 28,490 people per sq mile (11,000 people per sq km) in the capital.

Is tourism important to Indonesia's economy?

Yes. Tourism is a very important source of revenue. Around four million tourists (mainly from Australia, the USA, and Europe) visit the country every year.

What does the name "East Timor" mean?

The country's official name is "Timor-Leste," which literally means "east-east" as both "Timor" and *leste* (in Portuguese) mean "east." In Tetum the name of the country is Timor Loro Sa'e, meaning "Timor of the Rising Sun."

What are the "Men's Sea" and "Women's Sea"?

To the north of East Timor lies the calm Banda Sea and to the south the choppy Timor Sea. The former is known in East Timor as the Taci-Mane or "Men's Sea" and the latter as the Taci-Feto or "Women's Sea."

What raw materials does East Timor possess?

The Timor Sea was identified long ago as the location of the richest petroleum deposits in the Asian-Pacific region. During the Indonesian occupation of East Timor (1975–1999) Indonesia and Australia signed the Timor Gap Treaty, which divided the petroleum between the two states. In 2004, after the end of the Indonesian occupation, Australia confirmed the agreement, which effectively shifted the sea boundary (and with it the oil) in Australia's favor. Despite East Timor's petroleum resources, it remains Asia's poorest country according to a UN study.

EAST TIMOR

Flag

Currency
1 US dollar (USD) = 100 cents

System of government
Presidential republic since 2002

Capital
Dili

Languages
Tetum, Portuguese (official languages), numerous minority languages and dialects

Surface area
5,794 sq miles (15,007 sq km)

Population 947,400

Religion 93% Catholic

Notable features
Despite rich petroleum deposits, East Timor remains Asia's poorest country.

Indonesian occupation

Just nine days after East Timor was granted its independence by Portugal on November 28, 1975, Indonesia annexed the new state and initiated a reign of terror. To lend weight to its claim to East Timor, Indonesia pursued a policy of systematic rape and compulsory sterilization. Women were also forced to have abortions and contraception was imposed as a means of population control. During Indonesia's 24-year occupation around one third of the region's 800,000 inhabitants were killed. East Timor was finally recognized as an independent sovereign state in 2002.

After a few years of uncertainty East Timor's independence was at last officially recognized in 2002. Groups of East Timorese are shown here parading through the streets of the capital Dili on Independence Day in 2004.

USA

Cuba

Costa Rica

USA

NORTH AMERICA

North America is the northern part of the double continent of America. Two major mountain ranges, the Rocky Mountains and the Appalachian Mountains, run along the length of the land mass in a north-south direction, separated by vast open landscapes. It is bounded by the Atlantic Ocean to the east, the Pacific Ocean to the west, and the Caribbean to the south. North America covers an area of 9.36 million sq miles (24.23 million sq km), making it the third-largest continent after Asia and Africa. In terms of population it is the fourth-largest with 454.23 million inhabitants. It comprises 23 countries.

Dominican Republic

Nicaragua

Canada

PHYSICAL MAP

Arctic Ocean
Greenland Sea
Iceland
Reykjavík
Greenland
Bering Sea
Beaufort Sea
Brooks Range
Baffin Bay
12,139 ft
Gunnbjörn Fjeld
10,600 ft
Alaska
Yukon
Ellesmere Island
Devon Island
Parry Islands
Alaska Range
20,335 ft
Mount McKinley
Banks Island
Victoria Island
Baffin Island
Nuuk
Gulf of Alaska
Mackenzie Mountains
19,524 ft
Mount Logan
Great Bear Lake
Mackenzie
Great Slave Lake
Southampton Island
Labrador Sea
Peace
Lake Athabasca
Canadian Shield
Hudson Bay
Labrador
Athabasca
Reindeer Lake
Churchill
Newfoundland
Rocky
Lake Winnipeg
14,409 ft
Mount Rainier
Columbia
Missouri
Lake Superior
Lake Huron
Ottawa
St. Lawrence
Lake Ontario
Atlantic Ocean
14,163 ft
Mount Shasta
13,786 ft
Gannett Peak
Snake
Great Salt Lake
7,241 ft
Black Hills
Mississippi
Great Basin
Lake Michigan
Lake Erie
Appalachian Mountains
Washington
Mountains
Great Plains
14,505 ft
Mount Whitney
Colorado
14,423 ft
Mount Elbert
Colorado Plateau
Arkansas
Ohio
Mississippi
6,690 ft
Mount Mitchell
Sargasso Sea
Baja California
Sierra Madre Occidental
Rio Grande
Sierra Madre Oriental
Gulf Coast Plains
Florida
Bahamas
Nassau
Pacific Ocean
Gulf of Mexico
Havana
Cuba
Lesser Antilles
Hispaniola
San Juan
Puerto Rico
Santo Domingo
Port-au-Prince
Mexico City
17,887 ft
Popocatépetl
Yucatán
Jamaica
Kingston
Caribbean Sea
Netherlands Antilles
Belmopan
Tegucigalpa
Caracas
Guatemala
San Salvador
Managua
Lake Nicaragua
Panamá
Orinoco
Magdalena
San José
Bogotá
Equator

Hawaii
20° N
160° W

1 : 47 000 000

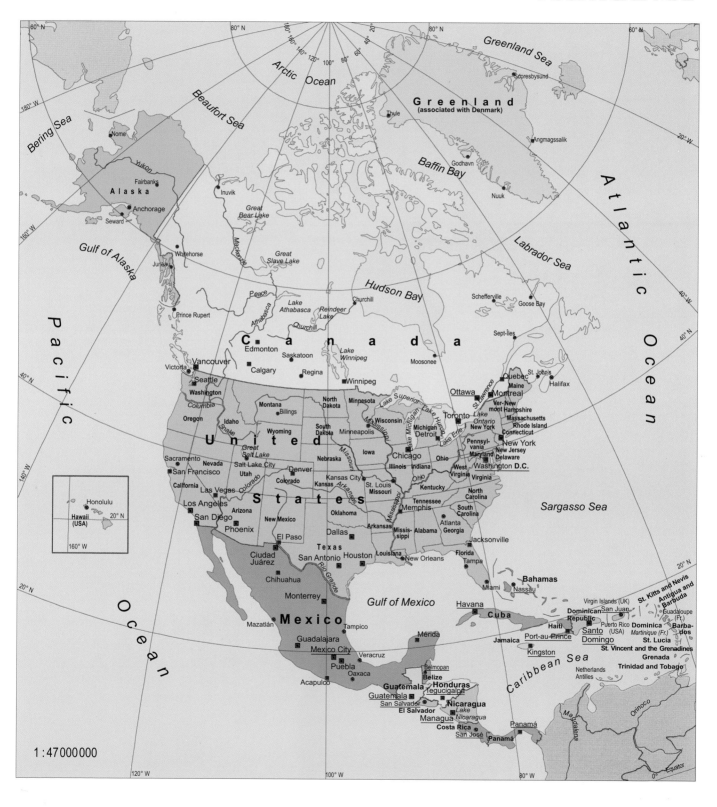

1 : 47 000 000

Introduction

Who gave America its name?

The first person to realize that the land discovered in 1492 by Christopher Columbus (1451–1506) was a separate continent was the Italian merchant, seafarer, and cartographer Amerigo Vespucci (1454–1512). He drew a map of the region and signed it with his first name, thereby christening the new continent.

Why were America's original inhabitants called "Indians"?

Columbus undertook his journey of discovery in order to find a sea route to India. When he landed in America, he was convinced he had arrived in India and named the indigenous people accordingly.

Is Central America a separate continent?

The southernmost country in North America is Panama. Looking north from here there are 13 states and island nations that are often—wrongly—regarded as a continent (Central America) rather than simply a region. North America is often thought to comprise just the two northernmost (and also largest and richest) countries, the United States and Canada, mainly because they often refer to themselves in this way.

Where is the center of North America?

The small town of Rugby in the US federal state of North Dakota has been acknowledged since 1931 as

Background: The Golden Gate Bridge seen from Marin County in California. San Francisco can be seen in the background on the left.

Below: The Pyramid of the Magician at Uxmal (Mexico), a ruined Maya city on the Yucatán Peninsula.

the geographical center of North America. The exact position is marked with a 15-ft-high (4.5-m) obelisk.

How did America's original inhabitants live?
America's indigenous peoples—originally called "Indians" and now known by the politically correct term "Native Americans"—lived a settled rather than a nomadic existence, sometimes in large cities and often farming the land and practicing animal husbandry. European settlers introduced diseases against which the local populations had no resistance. Some 90 per cent of Native Americans succumbed to these illnesses and died. Vastly inferior in number, they were then subjugated by the settlers and forced into reservations.

What are the names of the best-known tribes of Native North Americans?
The best-known names are the Aztecs, the Maya, the Olmecs, the Zapotecs, the Huron, the Apaches, the Sioux, the Cherokees, the Iroquois, the Mohawk, and the Comanche.

Who were the first Europeans in America?
It is now known that the first Europeans to reach Newfoundland in the north of the continent were Vikings under the leadership of Leif Erikson (circa

970–1020). They arrived in or around the year 1000 in open ships up to 80 ft (24 m) long rowed by up to 40 men. They named the new country Vinland ("Wineland") and established settlements here and there but left hardly any trace of themselves behind.

Palm-fringed Playa Carrillo on the Nicoya Peninsula on Costa Rica's Pacific coast.

Which Europeans were the first to settle the continent in large numbers?
Following its discovery by Christopher Columbus (1451–1506) the new continent was settled, logically

Interesting facts

The following islands off the coast of North America do not belong to the continent politically:

- Anguilla, the Cayman Islands, Montserrat, the Turks and Caicos Islands, the British Virgin Islands, and Bermuda are all overseas territories of the United Kingdom.

- Aruba and the Netherlands Antilles belong to the Kingdom of the Netherlands.

- Guadeloupe, Martinique, and St Pierre and Miquelon are French overseas departments and regions.

- Navassa, Puerto Rico, and the US Virgin Islands are unincorporated overseas territories of the United States.

Are there any political conflicts between the countries of North America?

There have been wars and major political disputes between the United States and its southern neighbors over the years—some of which remain unresolved today. The United States has repeatedly sought to demonstrate to its neighbors its economic and political pre-eminence: between 1846 and 1848 it annexed territory in the Mexican-American War; in 1989 it safeguarded its influence over the canal zone by invading Panama; it asserted its political supremacy throughout the region with its invasion of Grenada and intervention in Nicaragua and remains at loggerheads with Cuba due to ideological differences.

Rocky Mountains

The Rocky Mountains stretch for over 3,000 miles (5,000 km) in a north-south direction from Alaska, through Canada and the United States to Mexico. The mountain system includes a number of volcanoes (such as Mount St Helens, which erupted in 1980) and its highest peak is Mount McKinley in Alaska at 20,322 ft (6,194 m). The Rocky Mountains are actually part of the Cordillera system that continues in South America as the Andes. There are a number of important national parks along the length of the Rockies (including Yellowstone) and the mountains are rich in minerals such as lead, gold, copper, silver, tungsten, zinc, coal, natural gas, petroleum, and oil shale. Parts of the range have been developed for tourism and some of the United States' and Canada's most attractive skiing areas are to be found here.

The Rocky Mountains near Lake Louise in Alberta, Canada.

enough, by the Spanish. They gradually moved from the larger islands to the mainland and, after defeating the Aztecs, became the rulers of the whole of Central America and Mexico.

The northern parts of the continent were settled over the following years by the Swedish and Dutch and then in greater numbers by the English and French.

The Maya ruins of Tulum on the Yucatán Peninsula overlook some of Mexico's most beautiful Caribbean beaches.

Why are southern parts of North America plagued by hurricanes?

Climatologists have discovered that, due to the greenhouse effect, temperatures on Earth are steadily rising. Most significantly, the surface temperature of the oceans has warmed by an average of around 33°F (0.5°C) over the last 20 years. Scientists have ascertained that this is a contributory factor where hurricanes are concerned. At surface temperatures of around 79°F (26°C) and above, enough water evaporates to be able to generate and sustain a hurricane. The higher the air temperature, the more humidity the air can absorb, thereby increasing the power of the hurricane even further. The water in the Gulf of Mexico is some of the warmest in the world. Over the last 20 years not only has the number of tropical hurricanes risen, their strength and duration have also increased. One of the most devastating of all time was Hurricane Katrina in 2005.

The Grand Teton National Park in western Wyoming is a paradise for hikers and mountaineers.

Polar bears in Manitoba, Canada, making their way across a freezing Hudson Bay to their winter hunting grounds.

Greenland

At 0.83 million sq miles (2.16 million sq km) Greenland, in the North Atlantic, is the largest island in the world. It is an autonomous province of Denmark but belongs geographically to North America. Greenland has a total population of 57,000 and a population density of just 0.067 people per sq mile (0.026 people per sq km), one of the lowest in the whole world. Only 131,931 sq miles (341,700 sq km) of the island—an area roughly the size of Germany—are not covered by ice. Greenland's ice sheet is up to 13,125 ft (4,000 m) thick, the second-thickest in the world after Antarctica. If all this ice were to melt, sea levels all round the world would rise by 20 ft (6 m).

Flag 	Surface area
Currency	3.85 million sq miles (9.98 million sq km)
1 Canadian dollar (CAD) = 100 cents	**Population** 32.3 million
System of government	**Religion**
Federal constitutional monarchy since 1931 (Commonwealth member)	43% Catholic, 35% Protestant, 17% non-denominational
Capital	**Notable features**
Ottawa	As a consequence of Canada's colonial
Languages	past (see below), French is the main
English, French (official languages), Inuktitut and other Native American languages	language spoken in the eastern province of Quebec while English is the main language throughout the rest of the country.

Is Canada bigger than the United States?

Yes. Canada is slightly bigger than the United States and second only to Russia in the list of the world's largest countries. It stretches for 2,900 miles (4,600 km) north to south and 3,400 miles (5,500 km) east to west.

Policeman's Creek near Canmore in the province of Alberta in western Canada.

What are Canada's main geographical features?

Other than the province of British Columbia in the west, Canada's landscape is extremely uniform: flat or gently hilly with abundant rivers. Its southern regions are forested while the colder north features rocky outcrops, ice, and treeless tundra.

When did Canada's colonial history begin?

The first Europeans to arrive in Canada were the Vikings in around AD 1000. They were followed after a long gap by English and from 1534 French explorers. Frenchman Jacques Cartier (1491–1557) claimed the eastern part of Canada as a colony of France called "New France." In 1763 Great Britain gained possession of all French territories in North America. Although Canada was able to act independently in international affairs by the beginning of the 20th century, the process of acquiring independence was not fully completed until 1982.

How densely is the country populated?

With a population density of 8.3 people per sq mile (3.2 people per sq km), Canada is one of the most sparsely populated countries in the world. On top of this, the population is very unevenly distributed with almost 80 per cent of Canadians living in towns and cities. The rural population is confined to a narrow strip along the country's southern border while the north is almost uninhabited.

Do Native Americans still live in Canada?

Yes. Indigenous ethnic groups are generally known in Canada as the "First Nations." As of 2001 there were nearly 700,000 native Canadians belonging to 612 tribes. Most still live on reservations.

The Eskimo peoples living on Canadian territory are known as the Inuit. They are related to the Kalaallit in Greenland and the Yupik in Siberia. Total numbers across all these regions are around 150,000, with around 50,000 living in northern Canada.

Does the country offer opportunities to immigrants?

Immigration to Canada is strictly regulated. A points system is in operation whereby applicants need to accumulate a specific score in order to be admitted. Points are awarded for educational attainments and language skills, for example, and also for job offers from Canadian employers. Applicants also have to demonstrate that they have sufficient financial resources to provide for themselves for a transitional period.

Is Canada a rich country?

Yes. Canada is eighth in the list of per capita income by country. Its economic structure has changed markedly over the last decade. Whereas the Canadian economy used to be based on raw materials and agriculture, it has developed a strong bias towards services and new technologies. Canada also possesses the largest oil reserves in the world after Saudi Arabia.

What is the significance to Canada of the maple tree?

Canada is a tree-rich country and exploitation of its forests has been an important economic factor throughout its history. The most widespread variety is the sugar maple (*Acer saccharum*), whose hard, cream-colored wood (the tree is also known in Canada as "hard maple") has a reddish tinge. As well as yielding a timber that is ideal for furniture-making, the maple tree has also long been used as a source of sugar—indeed, techniques for making maple syrup were known to the native Canadians. The maple leaf was adopted as Canada's national symbol by the beginning of the 19th century and incorporated into the national flag in 1965.

An Inuit hunter aligns his dog sled team. The Inuit live mainly in the northern territory of Nunavut.

This photograph from 1890 shows gold prospectors in the vicinity of Dawson.

The last great prospecting frenzy to grip America was the Klondike gold rush at the end of the 19th century. It began with finds in the Klondike River in northwest Canada in 1896 and reached its climax just two years later. The journey to this remote region was extremely arduous and many prospectors arrived after the richest seams had already been abandoned. Dawson City came into being during the gold rush and grew rapidly until its population reached around 40,000. Only around 1,250 live in the small town today.

UNITED STATES OF AMERICA

Flag

Currency
1 US dollar (USD) = 100 cents

System of government
Presidential federal republic
since 1789

Capital Washington DC

Languages
US English (national language, no specific
official language), Spanish (regional)

Surface area 3.72 million sq miles
(9.63 million sq km)

Population 300 million

Religion
52% Protestant, 24% Catholic, 2%
Mormon, 12% other

How many federal states does the United States have?

The United States has a total of 50 federal states, with Alaska and Hawaii lying outside the borders of the national heartland. The continental United States comprises 48 states plus the District of Columbia (DC)—the government district incorporating the federal capital Washington DC.

What effect does the country's geography have on its climate?

Unlike Europe, the main mountain systems run in a north-south direction, resulting in extremely cold winters (as the cold is able to penetrate southwards unimpeded) and very hot summers. This explains why the temperature in New York City, which lies on the same latitude as Rome, can drop to −22°F (−30°C) in winter and climb to above 95°F (35°C) in summer.

Why is the United States referred to as a "melting pot"?

The reason the US has been described as a melting pot is that its indigenous peoples have been joined over the centuries by French, English, German-speaking, Irish, Italian, Scandinavian, and eastern European (including many Jewish) settlers and immigrants. Americans of European descent make up 70 per cent of the population, descendants of African slaves 13 per cent, Asians around four per cent, and Latinos (immigrants from Central and South America) 13 per cent. These different groups merged together culturally and linguistically to form a new nation—the United States of America.

How was the territory of North America divided up in the 17th century?

Although the first European settlement was founded by the Spanish (St Augustine in Florida) in 1565, from the 17th century onwards the continent was divided up by the English and French. The French controlled the north as far as Canada while the English controlled New England and as far south as Virginia.

A young Navajo in traditional tribal dress.

When was the Declaration of Independence signed?

The American Declaration of Independence was signed on July 4, 1776 following the War of Independence with Britain. With French support, the United States forced Great Britain to accept US independence in 1783 and the Treaty of Paris was duly signed. In 1787 a constitution was drawn up in Philadelphia and signed by George Washington (1732–1799), the first president of the United States of America.

What does the Statue of Liberty commemorate?

The Statue of Liberty—a sculpture of a female figure carrying a torch positioned at the entrance to New York Harbor—was a gift from France to mark the 100th anniversary of the American Declaration of Independence of July 4, 1776. It was created by French sculptor Frédéric Auguste Bartholdi (1834–1904) and constructed of copper on a steel frame. It was dismantled and shipped from France in 1885 and finally erected on Bedloe's Island (as Liberty Island was known until 1960) in 1886. The Statue of Liberty is 153 ft (46.5 m) high without its plinth and 335 ft (103 m) high with.

What is the significance of the Civil Rights Act of 1866?

The Civil Rights Act of 1866 sealed the end of slavery and granted full citizenship to former slaves.

It had been preceded by the American Civil War (1861–1865), a conflict primarily about the abolition of slavery fought between the northern states and the southern states that wanted to secede.

What happened on "Black Friday" in 1929 and what were the consequences?

Black Friday in October 1929 was the day the New York Stock Exchange crashed, plunging the world into an economic crisis. Among other things, the

The Morning Glory Pool is the best-known and most beautiful geothermal pool in Yellowstone National Park. Its magnificent colors are caused by bacteria.

Background: Looking down into the Grand Canyon, Arizona, from the famous South Rim.

Interesting facts: Population

- As recently as 2000, the biggest single population group in the United States consisted of people with a Germanic background.

- As a federal republic the United States has no specific official language.

- Many states are officially bilingual (English and Spanish).

- Native Americans were not awarded full citizenship until 1924.

- Over 41 million US citizens (nearly 14 per cent) do not have medical insurance.

- Between 1901 and 1950 US scientists were very much in the minority among Nobel Prize winners but since 1950 they have won half of all prizes awarded in the natural sciences.

- More than two thirds of US citizens live in the large cities.

The legendary Hollywood sign on Mount Lee, Los Angeles' highest peak.

Macy's Thanksgiving Parade is held on the last Thursday in November on New York's Broadway.

right after the Japanese attack on Pearl Harbor on December 7, 1941. Thanks to its great industrial might, the United States eventually decided the war in the Allies' favor. After the war in Europe had ended (May 8, 1945) the United States dropped two atomic bombs on the Japanese cities of Hiroshima and Nagasaki, thereby bringing the Second World War to a definitive end.

What dangerous confrontations took place during the Cold War?

The most dangerous confrontations of the Cold War to break out between the United States and the countries of the communist Eastern Bloc (under the leadership of the Soviet Union) were the Korean War (1950–1953) and the Cuban Missile Crisis of 1962, which pushed the world to the brink of a third world war.

When did the Vietnam War begin and end?

The origins of the Vietnam War go back to the start of the resistance against the French colonial power in 1946. In 1964 the United States entered the war with the intention of furthering its interests (with respect, in particular, to communism) in Southeast Asia. In 1973 the United States quit Vietnam in defeat, and the two halves of the country (north and south) reunited under communist rule.

Which three assassinations shook the United States in the 1960s?

The "series" of assassinations began in 1963 with the shooting of President John F. Kennedy in his open-topped limousine in Dallas, Texas. Martin Luther King, the Black civil rights leader and advocate of nonviolent struggle, and Robert F. Kennedy, the Democratic presidential candidate and younger brother of John, were both shot in

Wall Street Crash demonstrated how important an economic position the United States had attained worldwide. Some 15 million workers lost their jobs as a result of the crash, provoking a domestic political crisis.

Why did the United States enter the Second World War and what influence did it have?

When the Second World War broke out, the United States initially remained neutral but in 1941 began to supply the United Kingdom with weapons on an enormous scale. It entered the war in its own

Thanksgiving is a national holiday in the United States and is regarded by many as the most important festival of the year. Ever since 1868 it has been celebrated on the fourth Thursday in November and unites all Americans of all creeds. It is the only day of the year when all businesses without exception are closed and the whole family gets together for a celebratory meal, the centerpiece of which is traditionally roast stuffed turkey.

Americans generally tell of the origins of the festival as follows: a group of English pilgrims had drifted off course and ran aground near Plymouth Rock, Massachusetts. Out of thanks for the help of the Wampanoag Indians, without which they would never have survived the winter, they celebrated a three-day harvest festival in the autumn of 1621.

1968. The United States and the world at large were deeply shaken by the three assassinations, none of which has been conclusively solved.

When did the "war on terror" begin?
Following the attacks by radical Islamists on the World Trade Center in New York and the Pentagon in Washington DC on September 11, 2001, George W. Bush declared a worldwide war on terrorism. Taking his cue from former president Ronald Reagan (1911–2004, president 1981–1989), who described the Soviet Union as the "evil empire," President Bush used the expression "axis of evil" to describe "rogue states" such as Iran, Iraq, and North Korea in a speech given on January 29, 2002.

What role does Congress play in the political life of the United States?
Congress is the legislative body of the United States. It is made up of elected representatives from the 50 federal states and has two chambers: the House of Representatives and the Senate which total 535 members. Under the US Constitution, Congress has authority over budgetary matters and the power to enact legislation. Only Congress may pass federal laws, declare war, and ratify treaties with foreign nations. While the president signs all international agreements, and makes nominations to public offices (such as justices of the Supreme Court and cabinet posts), all such decisions have to be approved by the Senate, the upper house of Congress.

How high is the minimum wage in the United States?
When it was first introduced in the United States in 1938, the minimum wage was set at 0.25 US dollars per hour. It is now 5.85 dollars per hour although in a number of US states it has been set at a higher level.

What are the most popular sports in the United States?
The three most popular sports in the United States are American football, baseball, and basketball.

The Statue of Liberty by French sculptor F. A. Bartholdi, a gift from France to the United States, has stood at the entrance to New York Harbor since 1886.

The United States' road, rail, and air networks radiate outwards from its major cities. Most journeys are made by road—in particular by private automobile, although buses (such as the famous Greyhound buses) are also popular for cross-country travel. The railroads played an extremely important role in opening up the West but, other than for the transportation of goods and mass transit within the urban conurbations, have dwindled in importance over time. The other main means of transportation for private journeys around the country is the airplane—even the smaller cities generally have their own airports.

MEXICO

Flag

Currency
1 Mexican peso (MXN)
= 100 centavos

System of government
Presidential federal republic
since 1917

Capital
Ciudad de Mexico (Mexico City)

Languages
Spanish (official language), Amerindian languages (including the Aztec language Nahuatl, Maya, Zapotec, and Mixtec)

Surface area 0.76 million sq miles
(1.97 million sq km)

Population 108 million

Religion 89% Catholic, 6% Protestant

Which mountain ranges dominate Mexico?

WTwo mountain ranges run through Mexico from north to south: the Sierra Madre Oriental along its eastern edge and the Sierra Madre Occidental in the west. In the middle is a plateau with an average elevation of 3,937 ft (1,200 m). Sierra Madre del Sur extends across the south and Sierra Madre de Chiapas runs northwest to southeast through the southern state of Chiapas, after which it is named.

Teotihuacán, Mexico's legendary Aztec city, literally means "where the gods live."

Are there any volcanoes in Mexico?

Yes. There is abundant volcanic activity in Mexico. The highest of the country's many volcanoes form what is known as the Trans-Mexican Volcanic Belt in the central highlands: Citlatépetl (also called Pico de Orizaba), which is the country's highest mountain at 18,405 ft (5,610 m), Popocatépetl, which is active and rises to 17,887 ft (5,452 m), and Itzaccihuatl at 17,342 ft (5,286m). The last two are located just outside Mexico City.

What are tequila and mescal?

Tequila is a liquor distilled from the heart of the blue agave (*Agave tequilana*) and displays the strong natural flavor of that plant. It owes its name to the town of Tequila in the Mexican state of Jalisco on the Pacific coast. It normally has an alcohol content of 38 per cent. Mexico's indigenous people were familiar with the effects of the distillate and called the heart of the agave "mescal" which literally translates as "house of the moon." This is the generic term for liquors made from the agave plant outside the Tequila region. The "worm" (actually a caterpillar) found in bottles of mescal is a marketing gimmick that was introduced in 1950. Tequila, on the other hand, is "worm"-free.

Home to more than 25 million people and extending over more than 772 sq miles (2,000 sq km), Mexico City is currently the largest city in the world.

Who was Hernán Cortés?

Between 1519 and 1521 the Spanish explorer and *conquistador* Hernán Cortés (1485–1547) conquered Mexico with just a few hundred soldiers, destroying the Aztec Empire and its capital Tenochtitlán in the process. He defeated the last Aztec ruler Montezuma II and founded the Viceroyalty of New Spain on the mainland. This Spanish colony destroyed the region's indigenous cultures with fire and sword.

Does corruption exist in Mexico?

According to a survey carried out by Transparency International, an organization whose mission is to expose corruption throughout the world, 1.5 billion dollars were paid out in bribes in Mexico in 2005. This amount does not include bribes paid out to businesspeople or politicians.

What is Teotihuacán?

For a long time it was believed that the oldest city on the American continent had been built by the people who gave it the name by which it is known today. In the Aztec language of Nahuatl, "Teotihuacán" means "where the gods live." However, it was not until the 14th century that the Aztecs penetrated into Mexico's high valley and established their capital Tenochtitlán (present-day Mexico City) there. Nearby Teotihuacán, meanwhile, is much older and could not, therefore, have been founded by the Aztecs. The city experienced its heyday between AD 150 and 600. During this time it became prosperous and grew to around 200,000 inhabitants, making it the sixth-largest city of its day. Who its actual founders were is still not known.

Mexican Revolution

In 1910 Francisco Madera (1873–1913), the son of a wealthy landowner and industrialist, called from Texas (where he had fled after serving a prison sentence) for a revolution to oust dictator Porfirio Diaz (1830–1915). After victory by the revolutionary forces led by Emiliano Zapata (1879–1919) and Pancho Villa (1878–1923), Madera became president. Diaz had been defeated in a decisive battle outside the city of Ciudad Juárez and had gone into exile in Paris. Madera remained in office until his assassination in 1913. As a result of disagreements between the various revolutionaries, Mexico remained in a state of turmoil for many years, with military coups by General Huerta and subsequently Venustiano Carranza. It was 1929 before peace was established.

A typical *tasca* (bar) in the old part of Oaxacas in southwest Mexico.

GUATEMALA

Flag

Currency
1 quetzal (GTQ) = 100 centavos

System of government
Presidential republic since 1986

Capital
Guatemala (Guatemala City)

Languages
Spanish (official language), Amerindian languages (including Maya languages)

Surface area
42,042 sq miles (108,889 sq km)

Population 14.7 million

Religion
60% Catholic, 30% Protestant

Notable features
Guatemala was once the heartland of Mayan culture.

A coffee picker harvesting high-quality coffee beans with which Guatemalan producers are hoping to break into the international fine coffee market.

What are the main aspects of Guatemala's topography?

The northeast of the country is covered by tropical rainforest and is sparsely populated. Central Guatemala is mountainous with volcanoes of up to 13,800 ft (4,200 m). In the southwest the country possesses a narrow but fertile Pacific coastal strip while the Caribbean coast to the northeast is notable for its long sandy beaches.

What is Tikal?

The pyramid-shaped Mayan temples at Tikal are comparatively steep. Shown here is Temple II in the Main Plaza.

Tikal was one of the most important cities of the Mayan civilization. Its ruins are located in the rainforest of northern Guatemala. The city reached its cultural high point in the 5th century AD, when it was the seat of a dynasty of powerful rulers. Tikal was abandoned in the 9th century.

What factors are inhibiting the country's economic development?

Guatemala was ravaged by a civil war that lasted for 36 years. The conflict, which hindered the economic development of the country, finally ended in 1996. It claimed the lives of 200,000 people and forced one million Guatemalans into exile. Mass murders were perpetrated against certain indigenous groups, putting them at risk of extinction.

What are Guatemala's main economic sectors?

Guatemala's economy is based on exports of textiles and coffee and, to a lesser extent, sugar, bananas, tobacco, rubber, and cardamom. The country's tourist industry has also been able to develop since the end of the civil war.

The quetzal

The quetzal is a bright green bird with scarlet breast feathers. It is the national bird of Guatemala and has also given its name to the country's currency. It lives in the cloud forests of Central America but its habitat is being destroyed by the steady clearing of the land for agricultural purposes. As a result, it is protected under the Washington Endangered Species Act.

What are the country's main geographical features?

Belize is located on the east coast of Central America. It is the only nation in Central America without a Pacific coastline. It is hilly rather than mountainous and the land rises gently from the coast to the interior, reaching elevations of no more than 3,600 ft (1,100 m). Temperatures range from 61°F to 97°F (16°C to 36°C) throughout the year and the prevailing wind blows from the Caribbean.

Why is Belize City no longer the capital?

After the coastal city was almost completely destroyed by a hurricane in 1961 the decision was taken to build a new capital in a more secure location. Belmopan, in the interior of the country, has been Belize's capital since 1970 but still has just 15,000 inhabitants (mostly officials). Belize City remains the country's largest city as well as its economic and cultural center.

When was Belize known as British Honduras?

Having served in the 17th century as a base for English pirates preying on Spanish cargo ships in the Caribbean, the region eventually became a British crown colony (British Honduras) in 1862. It changed its name to Belize in 1973 and achieved independence from the United Kingdom eight years later.

BELIZE

Flag

Currency
1 Belize dollar (BZD) = 100 cents

System of government
Constitutional monarchy since 1981 (Commonwealth member)

Capital
Belmopan

Languages
English (official language), Creole, Spanish, Garifuna, Maya languages, Plautdietsch

Surface area
8,867 sq miles (22,966 sq km)

Population 280,000

Religion
50% Catholic, 25% Protestant

Notable features
Belize is the only Central American country without access to the Pacific.

Can Belize survive on tourism alone?

No. Tourism accounts for just ten per cent of the economy. The tourist industry lacks hotel capacity and an adequate infrastructure. The country is extremely poor, with a third of the population living below the poverty line. The economy of Belize depends mainly on the export of high-grade woods, in particular mahogany.

Belize's unspoiled rainforests are home to Central America's biggest jaguar population. The big cat is protected by a hunting ban.

Mayan culture

From around 2000 BC the area covered by present-day Belize was settled by the Maya, whose descendants make up 11 per cent of the current population. Cultural tourists can visit important archaeological sites such as Cuello, Altun Ha, and Xunantunich.

HONDURAS

Flag

Currency
1 lempira (HNL) = 100 centavos

System of government
Presidential republic since 1982

Capital
Tegucigalpa

Languages
Spanish (official language), Amerindian languages, English Creole

Surface area
43,433 sq miles (112,492 sq km)

Population 7 million

Religion
85–90% Catholic

Why is the currency called the lempira?
The national currency was named after the 16th-century Amerindian ruler Lempira, who led the fight against the Spanish invaders.

What form does the country's population take?
Around 90 per cent of Hondurans are Mestizos of mixed European and Amerindian ancestry. Most of the people live in the northwest and in the cities. The population growth rate is very high and the average age very low at 19.

A banana plantation in the interior of the country.

Are gangs of youths a significant problem in Honduras?
Yes. Honduras has a high rate of unemployment and is one of the poorest countries in Central America. The gangs are a consequence of the lack of prospects for the country's young people. Some of them are responsible for terrorizing entire cities. The largest of these gangs has some 40,000 members, who proclaim their allegiance through distinctive tattoos.

What economic problems is the country facing?
Honduras is the poorhouse of Central America. On the one hand its small farmers often own too little land to be able to provide adequately for their families, and on the other, big landowners frequently leave large areas of productive land fallow.

Banana Republic

The term "Banana Republic" refers to countries whose economies are dominated by agricultural plantations owned by foreign corporations. Honduras is a typical example. For many decades American United Fruit exerted a pervasive influence over the country's economy, which resulted in undue political influence, corruption, and bribery.

Flag	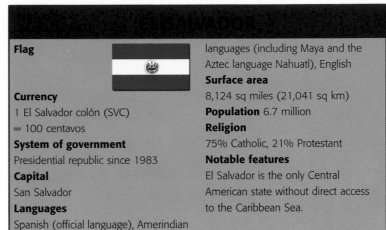	languages (including Maya and the Aztec language Nahuatl), English

Currency
1 El Salvador colón (SVC)
= 100 centavos

System of government
Presidential republic since 1983

Capital
San Salvador

Languages
Spanish (official language), Amerindian

Surface area
8,124 sq miles (21,041 sq km)

Population 6.7 million

Religion
75% Catholic, 21% Protestant

Notable features
El Salvador is the only Central American state without direct access to the Caribbean Sea.

What are El Salvador's main geographical features?

Situated on the west coast of Central America, El Salvador is the region's smallest country. It is located in an earthquake region and also has numerous volcanoes. The highest of these, at 7,759 ft (2,365 m), is Santa Ana. It is an active volcano and last erupted on October 1, 2005.

How is El Salvador's population made up?

Mestizos of mixed European and Amerindian descent make up 90 per cent of the population. About nine per cent of the population have European ancestry while indigenous peoples account for just one per cent of the total. More than 75 per cent of Salvadorans are Roman Catholic.

What was La Matanza?

In 1932 there was a revolt by Amerindian peasants that was bloodily suppressed by the president, General Maximiliano Hernández Martinez (1882–1966). No less than 30,000 people were killed in a massacre (*matanza*) that almost wiped out the country's indigenous population.

Who was Oscar Romero?

Oscar Romero (1917–1980) became Archbishop of San Salvador in 1977. He campaigned against the oppression of the people and publicly condemned the crimes perpetrated by the ruling military dictatorship. In 1980 he was murdered by an assassin acting on behalf of the regime. This marked the start of a civil war that lasted for 12 years and claimed the lives of 75,000 people. Among other things, Romero is remembered for his famous declaration: "They may be able to kill me but they can't kill the voice of justice."

Santa Ana volcano, also known as Ilamatepec, is the highest volcano in El Salvador.

Above: A statue of Christ is carried by Catholics through the Amerindian village of Panchimalco during a Palm Sunday procession.

The Soccer War

In 1969 the relationship between the neighboring states of Honduras and El Salvador was strained as a result of 300,000 economic refugees from El Salvador settling on tracts of fallow land in Honduras. After a soccer match between the two national sides (won by El Salvador), violence broke out in Honduras directed against the unpopular immigrants. El Salvador responded militarily in order to try to secure the right of residence for the Salvadoran immigrants. After three days of fighting, the OAS (Organization of American States) forced El Salvador to end the war.

NICARAGUA

Flag

Currency
1 córdoba (NIO) = 100 centavos

System of government
Presidential republic since 1987

Capital Managua

Languages
Spanish (official language), Amerindian languages (including Miskito, Chibcha and Sumo)

Surface area
49,998 sq miles (129,494 sq km)

Population 5.6 million

Religion
73% Catholic, 17% Protestant

Notable features
Nicaragua is known as the "Country of a Thousand Volcanoes."

Is Nicaragua prone to earthquakes?

Yes. The country suffers frequent earthquakes due to a chain of active volcanoes that runs through the country parallel to its Pacific coast. This geological feature has earned Nicaragua the nickname "Country of a Thousand Volcanoes."

What special animals live in Lake Nicaragua?

Lake Nicaragua contains bull sharks that have adapted fully to their freshwater habitat. Measuring around 11 ft 6 in (3.5 m) and weighing up to 440 lb (200 kg), they were trapped in what was previously an ocean bay when it became cut off from the Pacific. Lake Nicaragua is the sixth-largest freshwater lake in the world.

What was the Somoza clan?

The Somoza clan was the family of Nicaraguan dictators that ruled the country for over 40 years. In 1937 Anastasio Somoza Garcia (1896–1956) led a coup against his uncle, the liberal Juan Bautista Sacasa, and then had himself elected president. While in power the members of the clan lined their own pockets at the expense of the state. When an earthquake devastated Managua in 1972, costing the lives of over 10,000 people, international aid was diverted by the clan members into their own bank accounts. In 1977 the Sandinista National Liberation Front rose up against the ruling dictator Anastasio Somoza Debayle (1925–1980). The dictatorship, which had been supported by the United States, was finally overthrown in 1979 after two years of civil war.

> **Augusto César Sandino**
>
> Augusto César Sandino (1895–1934) was Latin America's first guerilla leader and led the Nicaraguan resistance against the USA. He was assassinated in 1934 after being invited to a formal dinner by Anastasio Somoza Garcia and his closest officers, dying from a shot in the back. He gave his name to the revolutionary movement that was ultimately responsible for the downfall of dictator Anastasio Somoza Debayle in 1979.

An early-morning view of León (situated to the northwest of Managua) showing its cathedral towers. León was Nicaragua's capital until 1852.

Why are Costa Ricans referred to as Ticos?

A common nickname for Costa Ricans is "Tico" ("Tica" for the women). This developed from a linguistic habit peculiar to the Costa Ricans. Instead of adding "ito/ita" to the end of words as is common in Spanish, they add "ico/ica." *Chiquitito* (meaning "tiny"), for example, becomes *chiquitico*. It is an affectionate nickname and is not perceived by the recipients as insulting.

When was Costa Rica discovered?

Although the east coast was discovered by Christopher Columbus (1451–1506) in 1502, it was not colonized by the Spanish until 1560. As it lacked natural resources and did not possess any great strategic importance, the colony always remained relatively underdeveloped.

Does Costa Rica depend on coffee and banana exports?

No. The importance of its traditional export commodities is gradually diminishing although Costa Rica remains the world's second-largest exporter of bananas. Until the early 1930s, 90 per cent of foreign earnings came from its coffee and banana exports. Since then, tourism and the high-tech

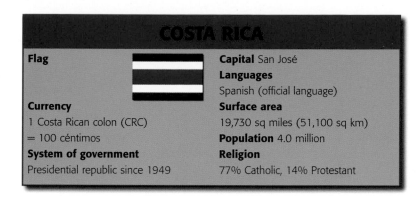

COSTA RICA

Flag	**Capital** San José
	Languages
	Spanish (official language)
Currency	**Surface area**
1 Costa Rican colon (CRC)	19,730 sq miles (51,100 sq km)
= 100 céntimos	**Population** 4.0 million
System of government	**Religion**
Presidential republic since 1949	77% Catholic, 14% Protestant

sector have taken over and now bring significantly more money into the country. The Intel corporation operates a microchip factory in Costa Rica.

Why is Costa Rica called the "Switzerland of Central America"?

The country enjoys a high standard of living and education relative to the other countries in the region. Its illiteracy rate is very low at 4.2 per cent. Democracy has been functioning well in Costa Rica for the past 50 years and, thanks to the abolition of the army in 1949, Costa Rica has also been spared military coups.

The Irazú Volcano National Park near the city of Cartago. At 11,260 ft (3,432 m), the Irazú is Costa Rica's highest and most dangerous volcano.

Ecotourism

Costa Rica was one of the first countries to recognize the importance of the environment and its protection and has introduced a tax aimed at protecting its tropical forests. Conservation areas cover 27 per cent of the land and there are over 20 nature parks. This has also brought benefits for the economy. An estimated 1.5 million ecotravelers (who value a form of tourism that is not harmful to the environment) journey to Costa Rica from all over the world each year.

Flag

Currency
1 balboa (PAB) = 100 centésimos

System of government
Presidential republic since 1912

Capital
Panama City

Languages
Spanish (official language), English Creole, Amerindian languages (including Buglere and Ngäbere)

Surface area
30,193 sq miles (78,200 sq km)

Population 3.2 million

Religion
85% Catholic, 10% Protestant

When did Panama achieve independence?

Panama became part of the Republic of Gran Colombia forged by Simón Bolívar (1783–1830) in 1821. The United States became interested in the country at an early stage as a platform from which to control the canal zone. They encouraged and supported Panama in proclaiming its independence from Colombia in 1903.

Who was Manuel Noriega?

Noriega's pockmarked face earned him the nickname "Pineapple Face." Manuel Antonio Noriega Moreno (born 1934) was the head of the secret service organization operated by Panama's

military. Between 1983 and 1989 he was the most powerful man in Panama and the United States' closest ally in the fight against Colombia's drug dealers. When it became clear that Noriega was himself closely associated with organized crime and was simultaneously in the pay of the CIA, the United States decided to get rid of him. In 1990 he was sentenced to 40 years in prison and is still serving his sentence in a federal jail in Miami.

What was Operation Just Cause?

Under President George Bush senior (born 1924) the United States invaded Panama in December 1989. The official reason for the operation, which was called Operation Just Cause, was to depose Noriega. It was the largest airborne operation since the Second World War. For three whole days access to the bombed areas was denied to neutral observers, the media, and the Red Cross.

The Panama Canal is an artificial waterway extending for approximately 50 miles (80 km) and comprising a sequence of 46 locks, channels, and mountain cuts that link the Caribbean Sea to the Pacific Ocean. It was constructed between 1904 and 1914 by US Army engineers.

A container ship on the 50-mile-long (80-km) Panama Canal, which was built between 1904 and 1914.

CUBA

Flag

Currency
1 Cuban peso (CUP) = 100 centavos

System of government
Socialist republic since 1959

Capital La Habana (Havana)

Languages
Spanish (official language)

Surface area
42,803 sq miles (110,860 sq km)

Population 11.3 million

Religion
40% Catholic,
55% non-denominational

Notable features
Cuba has been regarded for several
decades as a model socialist state.

Why was Cuba nicknamed "Sugar Island"?
Cuba was once the world's biggest exporter
of raw sugar. The only parties to benefit from the
substantial profits from the trade, however, were US
corporations and a small section of the Cuban elite.
The bulk of the rural population carried on living
under the same very basic conditions. Sugar remains
the country's biggest export today.

What was the Cuban Missile Crisis?
In 1962, the Soviet Union installed nuclear missiles
on Cuba and as a result the US government ordered
a naval blockade of the island in order to prevent
any further military equipment from reaching Cuba.
In October 1962, the world was teetering at the edge
of a third world war. Tough negotiations eventually
led to the removal of the missiles and a resolution of
the crisis.

Cohibas

The Cohiba is a brand of cigar exported by the Cuban firm
Habanas and famous the world over for its supreme quality.
It was originally produced for the sole use of President Fidel
Castro and as a gift for state visitors. Cohibas, which are
completely handmade, only became available on the open
market in 1982.

Is Cuba a communist state?
Yes. In 1959 a revolution overthrew the dictatorship
of President Fulgencio Batista (1901–1973) of
Cuba. Its leaders included President Fidel Castro
(born 1926) and popular hero Ernesto "Che"
Guevara (1928–1967). From 1961 onwards
Castro established a socialist dictatorship in Cuba
under the aegis of the Communist Party. The
subsequently adopted policy of nationalization
affected, among others, big US corporations.
This led the US to impose an economic embargo
that is still in place today.

Old American cars
are a common
sight on Cuba.
They arrived on the
Caribbean island
with the flood of
tourists decades ago.

Farmers carrying
fresh tobacco
leaves that are
dried for up to
50 days in drying
sheds.

BAHAMAS

Flag

Currency
1 Bahamian dollar (BSD) = 100 cents

System of government
Constitutional monarchy since 1973
(Commonwealth member)

Capital Nassau

Languages
English (official language), Creole

Surface area
5,382 sq miles (13,940 sq km)

Population 302,000

Religion
32% Baptist, 20% Anglican,
19% Catholic

How many islands does the Bahamas comprise?
The Bahamas consists of around 700 islands and 2,400 coral reefs, which are known as "cays." Only 30 of these islands are inhabited. The Bahamas belongs to the West Indies group of islands, which are located to the southeast of the United States. Geographically they are part of Central America.

The yacht harbor and magnificent beach at Hopetown on one of the northern Bahamian islands. Its red-and-white striped lighthouse is a famous landmark.

Who discovered the Bahamas?
The first New World land on which Christopher Columbus (1451–1506) set foot on October 12, 1492 was a Bahamian island. The natives called it Guanahani. Whether this was San Salvador or the uninhabited island of Samana Cay is still a subject of dispute today.

What does the population live on?
As the Bahamas is poor in raw materials, tourism offers the only opportunity for economic development. With its idyllic beaches and wonderful diving locations, the country offers the best possible basis for this, and 60 per cent of its population work in the tourism industry. The Bahamas has also become a center of the cruise industry.

Why is the Bahamas regarded as a tax haven?
In addition to tourism, another of the Bahamas' main sectors is banking. Due to the advantageous taxation laws, many banks and investment companies have moved their headquarters to the Bahamas and the island nation has developed into an international financial center as a result.

Blackbeard
Blackbeard (circa 1680–1718) has entered history as one of the most notorious British pirates of the Caribbean. He liked to present himself bristling with pistols and knives and was reputed to wear lighted matches in his beard before a battle. He was feared for his cruelty and became a byword for the redoubtable pirate. He established a base on the Bahamas and was captured and beheaded while trying to seize a ship in 1718. Blackbeard's life has been the subject of numerous films.

	JAMAICA	
Flag		Jamaican (patois)
		Surface area
		4,244 sq miles (10,991 sq km)
Currency		**Population** 2.7 million
1 Jamaican dollar (JMD) = 100 cents		**Religion**
System of government		56% Protestant, 5% Catholic
Constitutional monarchy since 1962		**Notable features**
(Commonwealth member)		Santiago de la Vega (currently known
Capital Kingston		as Spanish Town) was Jamaica's
Languages		capital between 1535 and 1872.
English (official language),		

Did reggae originate in Jamaica?

Yes. Reggae originated in Jamaica at the end of the 1960s, influenced by American musical trends. Its most famous protagonist was Jamaican musician Bob Marley (1945–1981), who is honored in his home country as a national hero.

Left: Reggae musician Bob Marley wearing a characteristic hand-crocheted cap over his rasta dreadlocks.

Rastafari

The Rastafari are members of a Christian movement that developed in the 1930s and is common today in Jamaica. Members worship the former Ethiopian emperor Haile Selassie (1892–1975) as a messiah who freed his people from colonial oppression. Certain branches of the movement renounce tobacco and alcohol while others use cannabis as an aid to meditation.

The Rio Cobre is one of the many small rivers that flow through Jamaica.

What are the main features of the country's topography?

Jamaica is a predominantly mountainous island in the Caribbean. The Blue Mountains in the east of the country rise to heights of 7,402 ft (2,256 m). Most of the island is covered by a karst plateau. The south of the country is dominated by coastal plains.

Was Jamaica a pirate island?

At the beginning of the British colonial period (1655–1962) the island was an important bolt-hole for pirates who, tolerated by the British authorities, plundered Spanish ships in the Caribbean. Their base was Port Royal, which was destroyed in a major earthquake in 1692.

What are the main economic sectors?

Until the 1940s the export of bananas, coffee, and sugar cane was Jamaica's only source of revenue. Since then, however, the mining and export of the aluminum ore bauxite has grown significantly. Tourism has also developed into an important industry. A not insignificant role is played here by day-trippers from cruise ships.

Flag		Languages
	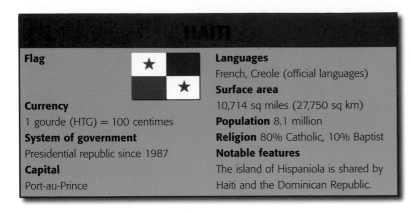	French, Creole (official languages)
		Surface area
Currency		10,714 sq miles (27,750 sq km)
1 gourde (HTG) = 100 centimes		**Population** 8.1 million
System of government		**Religion** 80% Catholic, 10% Baptist
Presidential republic since 1987		**Notable features**
Capital		The island of Hispaniola is shared by
Port-au-Prince		Haiti and the Dominican Republic.

Do the people of Haiti inhabit a dream island?
No. On the contrary, Haiti is the least-developed country of either American continent. Life expectancy is very low at just 53 years and there is a very high rate of infant mortality. Until the second half of the 1990s over 50 per cent of the population were illiterate.

Why are nearly all Haitians Black?

After the island of Hispaniola was discovered by Christopher Columbus (1451–1506) in 1492, its indigenous population was almost completely wiped out in a few short decades. In the 17th century African slaves were brought to the island to help work the sugar-cane plantations. Their descendants now make up 95 per cent of the population.

Does Haiti have a long tradition of republicanism?

Yes. In the 18th century Haiti was the richest of France's colonies. But a slave revolt in 1791 led eventually to the creation an independent state (13 years later). Slavery was abolished in the independent republic.

What state is the country's economy in?

Haiti can currently be described as economically bankrupt. It had to buy its independence from France with a commitment to pay large amounts of compensation, with the result that its former wealth gradually dwindled away. This was exacerbated by long periods of dictatorship and mismanagement of the economy that eventually turned Haiti into America's poorhouse. The crime rate in the capital Port-au-Prince is correspondingly high.

Voodoo

Voodoo is a religion that originated in Africa and involves animal sacrifices and black magic. It arrived in Haiti with African slaves who were only free to practice it after the revolution in 1804. Haiti later became a bastion of the religion outside Africa. Even though they belong to the Christian church, around 70 per cent of the country's inhabitants practice voodoo as well.

During a voodoo ceremony, women carry baskets of food on their heads.

What do Haiti and the Dominican Republic have in common?

The two countries share Hispaniola, the second-largest island in the West Indies. Haiti occupies the western half of the island while the Dominican Republic occupies the eastern half. Columbus discovered and named Hispaniola in 1492.

What makes the Dominican Republic so attractive to tourists?

Its tropical climate and the diversity of its flora and fauna make the Dominican Republic a popular travel destination. Tourists flock to the republic from all over the world, above all North America (50 per cent) and Europe (40 per cent). In the 1990s the Dominican Republic was regarded as Europe's cheapest package holiday destination. Since then the country has tried to change its image by offering a more sophisticated range of facilities.

Sosúa

Sosúa is located on the north of the island and is popular with tourists for its beautiful beaches. In the 1940s the little town became a destination for Jewish refugees who had managed to flee persecution by the Nazis in Germany. Reminders of the German Jews are still present today in the form of street names and a number of products that are still sold in the butchers' and bakers' shops.

DOMINICAN REPUBLIC

Flag		**Languages** Spanish (official language), French, Haitian Creole
Currency 1 Dominican peso (DOP) = 100 centavos		**Surface area** 18,696 sq miles (48,422 sq km)
		Population 9 million
System of government Presidential republic since 1966		**Religion** 75% Catholic, 4% Protestant
Capital Santo Domingo		**Notable features** The Dominican Republic shares the island of Hispaniola with Haiti.

Where is America's oldest cathedral located?

The cathedral of Santa María de la Encarnación in Santo Domingo, the oldest of the American cities founded by the Europeans, was consecrated in 1540, making it the oldest cathedral in the New World. Until 1992 the cathedral housed the tomb of Christopher Columbus (1451–1506).

What social problems does the country have?

The Dominican Republic has a relatively high poverty rate (10–15 per cent). It also has a high unemployment rate (30 per cent), with a large proportion of the country's inhabitants working only part-time. Many of the inhabitants depend on money wired home by relatives living abroad.

A farmer and his son on their way to market carry their products (including a live turkey) on horseback with them.

ST KITTS AND NEVIS

Flag

Currency
1 East Caribbean dollar (XCD) = 100 cents

System of government
Constitutional monarchy since 1983 (Commonwealth member)

Capital
Basseterre

Languages
English (official language), English Creole

Surface area
St Kitts 68 sq miles (176 sq km), Nevis 36 sq miles (93 sq km), total area 104 sq miles (269 sq km)

Population 390,000

Religion
34% Anglican, 31% Methodist, 8% Catholic, 9% Moravian

Above: The ruins of the fortress at Brimstone, St Kitts, which date back to the 18th century. Today the fortress is a UNESCO World Heritage site.

Right: St Kitts's main crop is sugar cane. Harvests are transported to the factory for processing.

What are the islands' main topographical features?

Both islands are of volcanic origin. St Kitts consists of three groups of volcanoes separated from each other by narrow gorges. Mount Liamuiga is the island's highest peak at 3,793 ft (1,156 m). Nevis is a mere 2 miles (3 km) away and its highest mountain is Mount Nevis, which rises to 3,576 ft (1,090 m).

When were the islands awarded to Britain?

The two islands were discovered by Christopher Columbus (1451–1506) on his second trip to the New World (1493–1496) but were only settled (by the French and English) in 1620. In 1783 the islands were awarded to Great Britain under the Treaty of Versailles. They finally achieved independence in 1983.

What are the mainstays of the country's economy?

The country's main crop is sugar cane. It also has relatively modest textile and electronic parts industries that manufacture goods for export mainly to the United States. St Kitts and Nevis also rely on tourism. The islands are especially popular with US holidaymakers.

The West Indies Federation was a nation that existed for just four and a half years, between January 3, 1958 and May 31, 1962. It was established as an autonomous federal state under British overall control with the hope that it would one day enable the 12 former British colonies of which it was formed to achieve independence as a unit. The federation collapsed, however, due to the inability of the different nations to coexist as federal states. The entities involved were Antigua and Barbuda, Barbados, Cayman Islands, Dominica, Grenada, Jamaica, Montserrat, St Christopher-Nevis-Anguilla (today St Kitts and Nevis is a single country and Anguilla is another), St Lucia, St Vincent and the Grenadines, Trinidad and Tobago, and Turks and Caicos Islands.

How is population distributed between the islands?

Around 98 per cent of the country's population lives in Antigua. Barbuda, most of which is a nature reserve, has a population of some 1,500.

Who were and are the country's inhabitants?

Antigua was settled by various Amerindian peoples as early as 10,000 BC. The island was discovered by Christopher Columbus in 1493 and the indigenous people were subsequently forced into slavery. The majority of today's inhabitants (91 per cent) are descendants of the African slaves who were brought to the island in the 17th century to work on the sugar-cane plantations.

King of Redonda

The Kingdom of Redonda is a disputed term for the uninhabited island. The title of "king" was adopted by Montserrat businessman Matthew Dowdy Shiell (1824–1888) when he landed on the uninhabited island in 1865. Although the island is less than 1 sq mile (2.5 sq km) in size, numerous claims to the kingship remains.

ANTIGUA AND BARBUDA

Flag

Currency
1 East Caribbean dollar (EC$) = 100 cents

System of government
Constitutional monarchy since 1981 (Commonwealth member)

Capital
St John's

Languages
English (official language), Creole

Surface area
171 sq miles (442 sq km)

Population 69,000

Religion
74% Protestant, 11% Catholic

Notable features
In addition to the Islands of Antigua and Barbuda, the uninhabited rocky island of Redonda is also part of the country.

How do the people of Antigua and Barbuda earn their living today?

After being grown on the islands for 100 years, sugar cane stopped being cultivated in 1972. In an attempt to release the country from its dependence on expensive imports, the government promoted the cultivation of fruit and vegetables instead. Today the population depends almost exclusively on tourism for its living. The annual regatta attracts sailors from all over the world.

The English Harbour on Antigua's south coast. One of its main attractions is Nelson's Dockyard, a large open-air museum.

DOMINICA

Flag

Currency
1 East Caribbean dollar (XCD)
= 100 cents

System of government
Republic since 1978
(Commonwealth member)

Capital
Roseau

Languages
English (official language), French
Creole (patois), Cocoy (Pidgin English)

Surface area
290 sq miles (751 sq km)

Population 69,000

Religion
80% Catholic, 15% Protestant

A group of some of the region's last surviving indigenous people in the Carib reservation on Dominica.

Why is Dominica called the "Nature Island"?
This mountainous island is home to
an extremely rich flora and fauna and boasts
numerous nature parks. About 60 per cent of
Dominica is covered by tropical rainforest and the
island's boiling lakes and fumaroles are reminders
of its volcanic origins. These conditions make it
an ideal destination for environmentally friendly
ecotourism. This potential has been recognized and
efforts have been made to establish an ecotourism
industry in Dominica.

Is the country a popular tourist destination?
No. So far Dominica has been unable to establish
itself as a tourist destination. Its efforts have been
hampered by two main factors: firstly the country

does not have a large international airport, and
secondly it does not possess expanses of attractive
sandy beaches capable of luring tourists to
the islands.

Are there any survivors of the island's original inhabitants?
Some 400 survivors of the Carib race, from which
the Caribbean takes its name, live in a reservation
on the island. They represent the single largest
group of indigenous people left in the region,
as nearly all the Caribbean's other indigenous
populations have died out.

What economic problems does the country face?
Dominica's economy relies heavily on the
cultivation of tropical fruits, particularly bananas.
But the island is vulnerable to hurricanes, which
can cause extensive damage to crops. This was the
case in 1995, for example, when two hurricanes
almost completely destroyed the banana harvest,
severely damaging the island's economy.

A small wooden
hut on a
Dominican banana
plantation. It is
built on stilts to
protect it from
the heavy tropical
downpours.

Ma Pampo

Dominica has a relatively large number of centenarians and
Ma Pampo, otherwise known as Elizabeth Israel, was one
of them. When she died in 2003, she was thought to be
128 years old, although her age could not be confirmed for
lack of clear documentary evidence and is therefore disputed.
Instead, French-born Jeanne Calment is widely accepted as
holding the record. It has been proved beyond doubt that she
had reached the age of 122 when she died in 1997.

What are the origins of the island's name?

According to one theory, a group of French seamen were stranded on the island after being shipwrecked on December 13, 1502. They named the island after St Lucy of Syracuse, whose feast day it was. December 13 was adopted as St Lucia's national holiday. The original Amerindian population called their island Iouanalao ("Land of the Iguana").

Who was the first European to settle on the island?

The first European to settle on the island was the notorious French pirate François Le Clerc, better known as Jambe de Bois ("Peg Leg"). He used the island as a base from which to target mainly Spanish ships.

What is patois?

In addition to English, the island's official language, patois is also spoken on St Lucia. It is a French-based Creole that is widespread throughout the Caribbean. As the number of patois speakers is rapidly declining, concerted efforts are being made to revitalize it.

Flag		Capital Castries
		Languages
		English (official language),
Currency		French Creole (patois)
1 East Caribbean dollar (XCD)		**Surface area**
= 100 cents		238 sq miles (616 sq km)
System of government		**Population** 168,000
Constitutional monarchy since 1979		**Religion**
(Commonwealth member)		68% Catholic, 7% Protestant

What are St Lucia's main economic sectors?

St Lucia heavily relies on its banana monoculture, which is highly vulnerable to the hurricanes that regularly strike the island. In addition to agriculture, tourism is also gaining in importance thanks to improvements in the country's infrastructure.

What are the Twin Pitons?

The Grand Piton and Petit Piton, volcanic mountains that rise steeply out of the sea off St Lucia's west coast, are the island's landmark. This is the only place on the planet where visitors can drive their cars into an active volcano crater.

A view of Castries, the capital and St Lucia's largest port, from one of the surrounding mountains.

ST VINCENT AND THE GRENADINES

Flag

Currency
1 East Caribbean dollar (XCD)
= 100 cents

System of government
Constitutional monarchy since 1979
(Commonwealth member)

Capital
Kingstown

Languages
English (official language), English and
French Creole (patois)

Surface area
131 sq miles (339 sq km)

Population 118,000

Religion 47% Anglican,
28% Methodist, 13% Catholic

Notable features
The country comprises 33 islands
in the Windward Islands group
(Lesser Antilles).

A Carib woman in front of her home on the Grenadine island of Petit Martinique to the south of St Vincent.

What are the origins of the main island's name?
When Christopher Columbus reached the island in 1498, he named it after St Vincent of Saragossa whose feast day it was (January 22).

Who brought the breadfruit to the island?
William Bligh (1754–1817), the famous captain of the *Bounty*, introduced the breadfruit tree to the island during his Second Breadfruit Voyage in 1793. Due to the ever-increasing number of slaves brought to St Vincent to work the plantations, new sources of food were needed and the tree provided a solution.

A typical "Victorian" house on St Vincent.

When was slavery abolished?
After the abolition of slavery in 1838 a new society emerged in St Vincent consisting of former slaves and their descendants, East Indian contract laborers and Portuguese. Today's population is made up of the descendants of these groups, and a proportion also have Amerindian blood.

What is the Whaleboner Bar and where is it?
The Whaleboner Bar is a pub whose entire bar and furniture is made out of whale bones. It is located on Bequia, the island next to St Vincent, and is a favorite meeting place for sailors.

Breadfruit

The breadfruit tree produces three harvests a year of a green fruit weighing up to 4 lb (2 kg) whose white flesh is a staple food in many parts of the world. The fruit contains 22 per cent starch and 1–2 per cent protein. Breadfruit trees can grow up to 65 ft (20 m) high and live for about 70 years.

How is the current population of Barbados made up?

Around 90 per cent of the inhabitants are Black and are descendants of the African slaves who were brought to the island by the British to work sugar-cane plantations. The rest of the population is Caucasian or mixed-race.

What happened to the island's indigenous people?

The indigenous people of Barbados were the Arawak, who arrived as early as AD 350. From 1536 onwards they were transferred as slaves to other islands by the Spanish invaders. When the British finally arrived in 1625, they found the island deserted.

What are the origins of the island's name?

In the 16th century Portuguese sailors were struck by the hanging roots of the fig trees. They likened them to beards and named the island Los Barbados, meaning "the bearded men." Fig trees have become rare on the island today.

Sam Lord's Beach, one of the many fantastic beaches in Barbados. Because of the strong winds, this bay is also a popular destination for surfers.

BARBADOS

Flag

Currency
1 Barbadian dollar (BBD) = 100 cents

System of government
Constitutional monarchy since 1966 (Commonwealth member)

Capital
Bridgetown

Languages
English (official language), Bajan (colloquial language)

Surface area
166 sq miles (430 sq km)

Population 279,000

Religion
70% Anglican

Notable features
Unlike many of its Caribbean neighbors, Barbados is not a volcanic but a coral island.

Why is Barbados considered a tourist paradise?

The island's magnificent climate attracts tourists from all over the world, who fall in love with the stunning bays of the south and west coasts. Barbados has a tropical oceanic climate with very little variation between the seasons and average daytime temperatures of 82°F (28°C) throughout the year. Tourism has been the country's most important industry since 1990.

Chattel houses

Characteristic of the island are its brightly colored chattel houses. These modest wooden dwellings were constructed in such a way that they could be dismantled and moved. They date back to the abolition of slavery, when freed slaves could lease and farm their own patches of land. When a lease ran out, the tenant's house could simply be moved to another location. The chattel houses provide a stark contrast with the magnificent residences built by the former plantation owners.

GRENADA

Flag

Currency
1 East Caribbean dollar (XCD)
= 100 cents

System of government
Constitutional monarchy since 1974
(Commonwealth monarchy)

Capital
St George's

Languages
English (official language), English and
French Creole (patois)

Surface area
133 sq miles (345 sq km)

Population 90,000

Religion
53% Catholic, 30% Protestant

Notable features When Christopher
Columbus discovered the island in
1498, he named it Concepción.

Nutmeg blossom drying in the sun. When harvested, the flowers are red or crimson but gradually turn yellow.

What is Grenada's colonial history?

Although it was discovered by Christopher Columbus (1451–1506) in 1498, the island remained unoccupied until some 150 years later, when it was sold to French traders by the local chiefs. In 1674 it came under French colonial rule before being ceded to the British in 1763. Grenada finally achieved independence within the Commonwealth of Nations in 1974.

Why did the United States invade the island in 1983?

In 1983 Grenada's ruling military junta was emphatically left-leaning, giving rise to US fears that it might move closer to Cuba or Nicaragua, which had also by then embraced socialism. The US invaded under the pretext that they were protecting US citizens on the island. Some months later, in 1984, elections were held and Herbert Blaize (1918–1989) was elected prime minister. He had very close ties with the United States and pursued a rigorous economic policy that made him unpopular.

How important is the tourist industry?

Tourism is Grenada's most important source of income. Around 400,000 tourists visit the country every year, mainly from Great Britain and the United States. One of the island's most famous and popular beaches is Grand Anse, widely regarded as one of the most beautiful in the Caribbean. Over recent years the government has recognized the benefits of ecotourism, using the beauty of Grenada's national parks and coral reefs to market the island as a holiday destination.

The Spice Isle

Grenada's main export, nutmeg, has earned it the nickname "Spice Isle." Grenada is the second-largest producer of nutmeg in the world, responsible for 20 per cent of world trade compared with Indonesia's 75 per cent. Nutmeg is a spice used in potato dishes, soups and stews. Just how important it is to the country's economy is seen by the fact that it features on the national flag.

What are the origins of the islands' names?

Christopher Columbus discovered the two islands in the summer of 1498. Because of one of its three very striking mountain peaks, Trinidad was named after the Holy Trinity (*trinidad* in Spanish). Tobago was originally named Bella Forma by Columbus. Its current name is derived from the Spanish word for tobacco (*tabaco*), which is grown on the island.

How is the islands' population made up?

Both islands have very mixed populations, although Trinidad displays greater ethnic variety than Tobago, whose population is mostly Black. Trinidad's population can be divided into three groups: those descended from Africans (43 per cent), those descended from Asians, mostly from India and China (40 per cent), and those descended from Europeans and immigrants from the Middle East.

In the 18th and 19th centuries the islands were a slave-trading center. This is still evident in people's names today as numerous citizens bear surnames that are the English first names given to their ancestors. Two notable examples are the national soccer players Stern John and Kelvin Jack.

Is the country prone to hurricanes?

Like many other Caribbean islands, Trinidad and Tobago belong to the Windward group of islands. However, as they are on the southern tip of the hurricane zone they are considered relatively safe compared with the others.

What are the origins of the islands' prosperity?

The discovery of petroleum in Pitch Lake on Trinidad generates a modest level of prosperity. However, as reserves are expected to run out soon, attempts are being made to expand natural gas production. Natural gas liquefaction is one of many industries that have grown up in this sector. Trinidad is one of the most industrialized islands in the Caribbean.

A group of stilt-walkers parading in Port of Spain, Trinidad, where the carnival is celebrated in flamboyant style.

What is a steelpan?

The steelpan is a drum made out of an oil barrel and is Trinidad's and Tobago's national musical instrument. More than 100 bands take part in the Panorama steelpan competition held during the extravagantly celebrated carnival, and some of them comprise over 100 musicians. The steelpan is a favorite instrument for playing calypso on, a musical genre that originates from these parts.

TRINIDAD AND TOBAGO

Flag

Currency
1 Trinidad and Tobago dollar (TTD) = 100 cents

System of government
Presidential republic since 1976 (Commonwealth member)

Capital
Port of Spain

Languages
English (official language), Hindi, Creole

Surface area
1,980 sq miles (5,128 sq km)

Population 1.1 million

Religion
31% Catholic, 23% Hindu, 14% Protestant, 12% Anglican, 7% Muslim

▲ Bolivia

Venezuela

Chile

Brazil

SOUTH AMERICA

At 6.9 million sq miles (17.8 million sq km), South America forms the smaller half of the double continent of America. In terms of population it is the fourth-largest continent with 355.07 million inhabitants. Mountains stretch from the Panama Canal to Cape Horn. The Incas, highland Indians of the Andes (which rise to nearly 23,750 ft/ 7,000 m and extend for 4,500 miles/7,240 km), had a highly developed culture of their own prior to the discovery of America by the Europeans in 1492, but today most of the nations of South America are influenced above all by the cultures of Spain and Portugal.

Guyana

Colombia

Argentina

PHYSICAL MAP

Guatemala
Tegucigalpa
San Salvador
Managua
Lake
Nicaragua
San José
Panamá

Caribbean Sea

Atlantic Ocean

Caracas

▲16,411 ft
Pico Bolívar

Georgetown
Paramaribo
Cayenne

Cordillera Occidental

Cordillera Oriental

Magdalena

Bogotá

Llanos

Orinoco

Guiana Highlands

Rio Branco

Vaupés

▲9,888 ft
Neblina

Equator

Quito

▲20,702 ft
Chimborazo

Galápagos Islands

Japurá

Rio Negro

Içá

Amazon

Amazon

Tocantins

Rainforest

Marañón

Tapajós

Ucayali

Purús

Xingu

Pacific

Teles Pires

Madeira

Juruena

Mato Grosso
Plateau

Araguaia

Tocantins

São Francisco

Lima

Guaporé

A n d

Paraguay

Brazilian

Brasília

Lake
Titicaca

▲21,463 ft
Sajama
Sucre

Paranaíba

Highlands

Pico da Bandeira
9,777 ft ▲

Rio Grande

Atacama

e

s

Gran Chaco

Paraná

Paraná

▲22,572 ft
Ojos del Salado

Asunción

Aconcagua
▲22,835 ft

Pampas

Paraná

Santiago

Buenos Aires

Montevideo

Ocean

Colorado

▲12,388 ft
Lanín

Patagonia

Atlantic

Falkland Islands

Ocean

South Georgia

Tierra del Fuego

1:40 000 000

80° W

60° W

40° W

0°

0°

20° S

20° S

40° S

40° S

100° W

80° W

60° W

40° W

20° W

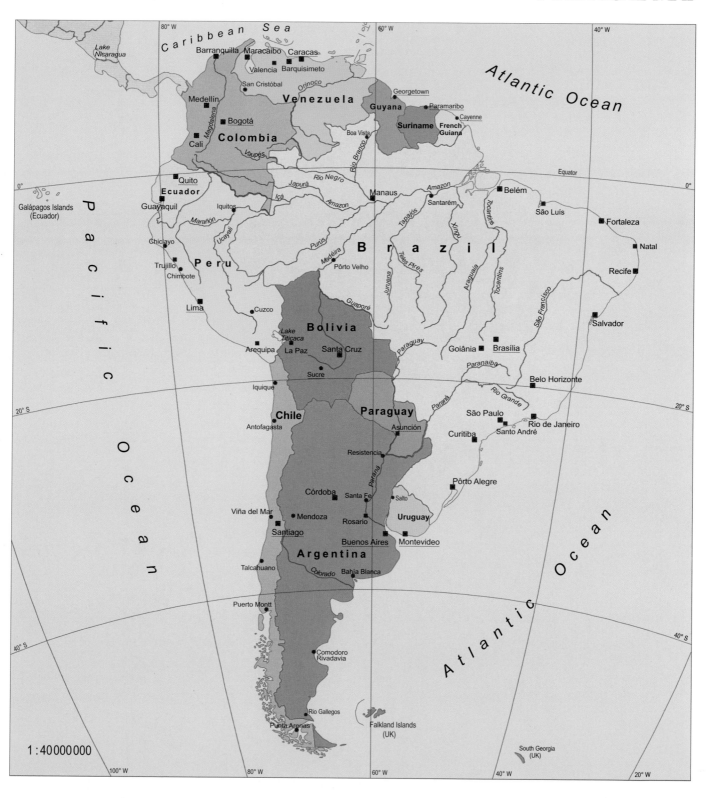

Lake Nicaragua

Caribbean Sea

Barranquilla   Maracaibo   Caracas
Valencia   Barquisimeto
San Cristóbal   *Orinoco*
Medellín   **Venezuela**   Georgetown
Bogotá   **Guyana**   Paramaribo
Magdalena   **Suriname**   Cayenne
Cali   **Colombia**   Boa Vista   **French Guiana**
Vaupés

Equator

Quito   *Rio Negro*   *Amazon*   Belém
Ecuador   *Japurá*   Manaus
Guayaquil   *Içá*   Santarém   São Luís
Iquitos   *Amazon*
Marañón   *Purús*   **B r a z i l**   Fortaleza
Chiclayo   *Ucayali*   *Madeira*   *Tapajós*   *Xingu*   *Tocantins*   Natal
Trujillo   **Peru**   Pôrto Velho   Recife
Chimbote   *Juruena*   *Teles Pires*   *Araguaia*   *São Francisco*   *Tocantins*
Lima   Cuzco   Salvador
Bolivia   *Guaporé*
Lake Titicaca   Goiânia   **Brasília**
Arequipa   La Paz   Santa Cruz   *Paraguay*
Sucre   *Paranaíba*   Belo Horizonte
Iquique   *Paraná*   *Rio Grande*
20° S   São Paulo   Rio de Janeiro
Chile   **Paraguay**   Curitiba   Santo André
Antofagasta   Asunción
Resistencia   Pôrto Alegre
Paraná
Córdoba   Santa Fe   Salto
Viña del Mar   Mendoza   Rosario   **Uruguay**
Santiago   **Buenos Aires**   Montevideo
Argentina
Talcahuano   *Colorado*   Bahía Blanca

Puerto Montt

Comodoro Rivadavia

Río Gallegos
Punta Arenas   Falkland Islands (UK)

South Georgia (UK)

P a c i f i c   O c e a n

Atlantic Ocean

A t l a n t i c   O c e a n

Galápagos Islands (Ecuador)

1:40 000 000

100° W   80° W   60° W   40° W   20° W

Introduction

What was the Treaty of Tordesillas?

On June 7, 1494, just two years after the discovery of the West Indies by Christopher Columbus, Pope Alexander VI split the world into two halves—one Spanish, the other Portuguese—in the Treaty of Tordesillas. Spain and Portugal were the superpowers of the day and the pope's intention was to prevent war from breaking out between them. Thus, the western part of South America became Spanish and the eastern part Portuguese. This explains why people speak Portuguese in Brazil and mainly Spanish throughout the rest of South America.

What languages are spoken in South America other than Spanish and Portuguese?

French is spoken in French Guiana, Dutch is the official language of Suriname, which was a Dutch colony until 1975, and English is the official language of Guyana, a British colony until 1966. Of the indigenous American languages spoken today, Aymara, Quechua, and Guaraní are the most widespread.

Background: The Amazon Basin in Brazil, home to the largest and most biodiverse tropical rainforest in the world and the Amazon River, which has the biggest flow of any river in the world.

Geysers at 14,108 ft (4,300 m) above sea level in the extinct Tatio volcano (Atacama Desert, Chile).

Inca civilization

Inca civilization flourished between 1200 and 1532, the year the Spanish invaded. Its territory extended over present-day Colombia, Ecuador, Bolivia, Argentina, Chile, and Peru and its capital was Cusco. The Inca Empire was notable for its highly sophisticated culture. The rulers of the empire regarded themselves as the direct descendants of the sun god Inti and named themselves accordingly. According to legend, the founder of the Incas, Manco Cápac—the son of the sun—and his sister Mama Ocllo had been sent by their father to the Island of the Sun in Lake Titicaca. Their mission was to improve the world. They were given a golden staff by Inti, who instructed them to settle wherever the staff should sink into the earth. They are said to have founded the city of Qusqu (Cusco), the "navel of the Earth," in 1200.

How many countries are there in South America?

There are 12 countries in total plus two autonomous territories: the Falkland Islands which still belong to the United Kingdom despite being claimed by Argentina, and French Guiana which is an overseas department of France.

What is unusual about the Amazon River?

With its numerous tributaries, the Amazon River passes through regions of Brazil, Venezuela, Colombia, Ecuador, Peru, and Bolivia. Flowing for 4,050 miles (6,518 km), it is second in length to the River Nile but is the world's biggest river by volume—11 trillion liters of water discharge into the Atlantic Ocean every day. From the Andes in the

west to its delta on the Atlantic coast the river is fed by around 1,100 major and 9,000 minor tributaries. The enormous Amazon Basin—the lowland plains in the north of the subcontinent—covers nearly half the total surface area of South America. Its floodplain alone is twice as big as the United Kingdom and is home to the largest and most biodiverse tropical rainforest in the world.

What is the reason for South America's great diversity of plant and animal species?

Half the world's animal and plant species originated in South America. This may be due to the continent's wealth of contrasting terrains and ecological extremes ranging from flatlands to hot and humid tropical forests and glacier-covered mountains.

What is the Atacama Desert?

The Atacama Desert is the driest place on Earth and stretches from southern Peru into northern Chile not far from the Pacific Ocean. Some areas have had no rain since records began. The desert lies within the Andes' rain shadow and is also influenced by the cold Humboldt Current that flows along the coast. Because of the region's numerous volcanoes, the Atacama is rich in volcanic mineral salts. In addition to nitrates, which are used for making fertilizers and explosives, copper ores are also mined here.

What is Aconcagua?

At 22,835 ft (6,960 m) Aconcagua is not only the highest mountain in Argentina but also the

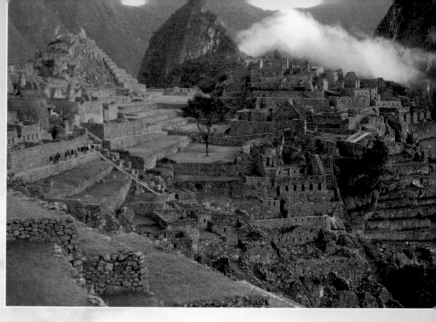

Machu Picchu, the legendary city of the Incas, is located in the Peruvian Andes at an altitude of around 7,900 ft (2,400 m).

highest peak in the whole of South America. It is located just over 1¼ miles (2 km) from the Chilean border in the Argentine Province of Mendoza and suffers from extreme weather conditions. At its summit the temperature can drop as low as –36°F (–38°C) while the plains of San Felipe, just 40 miles (64 km) away, are free of snow all year round. The Chilean capital Santiago de Chile, meanwhile, is a mere 80 miles (130 km) away and yet enjoys a mild Mediterranean climate. Aconcagua is very popular with mountain climbers.

Typical reed boats on Lake Titicaca in Peru.

Background: 3,215 ft (980 m) high and with a free drop of 2,650 ft (807 m), Angel Falls in Canaima National Park in Venezuela is the world's highest waterfall.

What are *tepuis*?

In the language of the Pemón Indians of Venezuela *tepui* means "mountain." The word is used in English to denote the towering table mountains with vertical sides, of which there are more than a hundred in Venezuela and Guyana. Up to now fewer than half of them have been explored as they are often located in rugged and inaccessible areas. Geologically the *tepuis* were formed by a process of erosion that began 20 million years ago whereby the soft sedimentary sandstone was washed away while the harder rock was left behind in the form of steep cliffs. The mountains are covered with thick forest and act as a kind of ark for plants and animals of all kinds. The *tepuis* are inaccessible and cut off from the rest of the world. They stand there untouched, guarding their precious "cargo."

What is the name of the world's highest waterfall and where is it?

The world's highest waterfall is the Angel Falls, which plunges over the cliffs of Auyán Tepui ("Devil's Mountain") in Venezuela. It is 3,215 ft (980 m) high and is fed by regular torrential rain that falls on the cliff top before plunging into the depths of the Cañon del Diablo ("Devil's Canyon").

Who was Manuela Sáenz?

Manuela Sáenz de Thorne (1797–1856) was Simón Bolívar's mistress. She was also known as the Libertadora del Libertador ("Liberator of the Liberator") because she protected Bolívar from an assassination attempt by mutinous officers on September 25, 1828. Historians consider her to be South America's most important female freedom

fighter and many people even regard her as the continent's first feminist. Due to her popularity, she is often compared with Evita Perón. After Bolívar's death, Sáenz spent her last 25 years despised and destitute in the Peruvian coastal village of Paita, eking out a living selling tobacco. She died of diphtheria in 1856.

What is Valdívia culture?

Valdívia culture is the oldest known Native American fishing and farming culture. The Valdívia people had already settled on the southern coast of Ecuador by the 4th century BC. For a long time it was believed they were of Japanese origin but recent pottery discoveries have led to the rejection of this hypothesis.

What is the largest city in South America?

With its 11 million or more inhabitants living in the city itself, not only is São Paulo the largest city in South America, it is also the largest in the Southern Hemisphere and one of the biggest metropolises in the world. Its satellite communities—consisting for the most part of shantytowns dotted around the periphery—accommodate another 20 million or so people not included in the census.

Is South America a rich continent?

South America is very rich in natural resources but ever since the continent was discovered, its wealth has been unequally distributed, creating a very wide gap between rich and poor. In many countries a rich minority owns around 20 per cent of the land and 60 per cent of the wealth while the poor majority owns less than five per cent. The average unemployment rate is around 11 per cent. With the exception of Argentina, Chile, and Uruguay, where social inequalities are not as significant, the outskirts of the cities usually consist of slums that contrast strongly with the luxurious buildings of the city centers.

Llamas are South America's only representatives of the camelid family. They are seldom used as beasts of burden any more and as a result are now found almost exclusively in southern Peru, northern Bolivia and northern Argentina.

Latin American music and dance

"Latin American" is a collective term for the musical styles of South and Central America. Numerous dances in South America are named after a particular style of music. The main ones are the salsa, calypso, merengue, and bachata from Colombia; the bossa nova and samba from Brazil; the tango and cuarteto from Argentina; and the tipico, cumbia, and vallenato from (mainly) Venezuela. The conga arrived in the country with African slaves while carnevalito is a musical genre that originated with the Indians of the Andes.

COLOMBIA

Flag

Currency
1 Colombian peso (COP)
= 100 centavos

System of government
Presidential republic since 1886

Capital
Santa Fe de Bogotá (Bogotá)

Languages Spanish (official
language), Amerindian languages
(including Chibcha and Quechua)

Surface area
0.44 million sq miles (1.14 million
sq km)

Population 45.6 million

Religion
91% Catholic

Notable features
The Colombian islands of San Andrés
and Providencia lie 434 miles
(700 km) off Colombia's Caribbean
coast. As they are just 124 miles
(200 km) from Nicaragua's coast, the
latter is also claiming the islands.

Background: A
coffee plantation
in the mainly
agricultural
department
of Quindio,
Colombia's
smallest province.

What are Colombia's main topographical features?

Colombia is located in northern South America
and possesses two coastal strips along the Caribbean
Sea and Pacific Ocean. The west of the country
is dominated by the Andes, which rise to a height
of 18,947 ft (5,775 m). The east is flat and is part
savanna and part rainforest.

A plantation worker harvesting coffee beans. Coffee is Colombia's
main crop.

What countries were part of Gran Colombia?

In the 16th century the Spanish conquered northern
South America and established the Viceroyalty
of New Grenada there. Under the leadership of
freedom fighter Simón Bolívar (1783–1830) the
Spanish invaders were driven out of the country at
the beginning of the 19th century. In 1813 Bolívar
founded the Republic of Gran Colombia, although
by 1830 this had disintegrated into Venezuela,
Ecuador, and Colombia. In 1903 Panama also went
its own way.

What do Colombia and the Netherlands have in common?

They are the largest flower exporters in the world,
with Colombia leading in the carnation trade.
Colombia has also specialized in the cultivation of
orchids and now has 3,500 different species.

What is the basis of the country's economy?

Apart from flowers, other products important to the
economy include coffee, bananas, and potatoes, all
of which contribute to the country's high volume
of exports. Colombia's raw materials include
emeralds, bituminous coal, and nickel. The country
is also more than self-sufficient in petroleum and is
able to export the surplus. This accounts for a not
inconsiderable 30 per cent of total exports.

The Medellín Cartel

From 1978 to 1993 the Medellín Cartel was the world's
largest exporter of cocaine. It was based in the Colombian city
of Medellín and its head was Pablo Escobar (1949–1993).
During its heyday the cartel generated annual revenues
of up to 35 billion US dollars and did not shy away from
committing political murders. Under pressure from the United
States, Colombia started to break up the drug trafficking
organization in 1989, employing measures that at times
resembled military operations. In 1993 Escobar was killed
while on the run. His death brought a definitive end to the
cartel's power.

What are the origins of the name Venezuela? The native stilt houses built in and over the water reminded Italian explorer Amerigo Vespucci (1454–1512) of buildings in Venice and so he named the region "little Venice."

When did Venezuela achieve independence?

In 1498 Christopher Columbus declared the region a possession of the Spanish crown. Over time, however, the Spanish began to neglect their grip on the colony as no significant amounts of gold had been found there. The forces striving for independence gradually grew stronger during the early years of the 19th century and in 1821 Simón Bolívar (1783–1830) succeeded in liberating the country from Spanish rule after winning the Battle of Carabobo.

What are the origins of Venezuela's wealth?

Petroleum accounts for four fifths of the country's exports and half its total revenue. Unlike most other Latin American countries, Venezuela has no debts with the International Monetary Fund (IMF) or World Bank, which makes it completely economically independent.

VENEZUELA

Flag

Currency
1 Bolívar (VEF) = 100 céntimos

System of government
Presidential republic since 1961

Capital Caracas

Languages
Spanish (official language), Amerindian languages (including Goajiro, Guaraúno, Cariña, and Pemón)

Surface area
352,144 sq miles (912,050 sq km)

Population 26.7 million

Religion
84% Catholic, 5% Protestant

Notable features
Venezuela is the fifth-largest petroleum exporter in the world and possesses the largest reserves of natural gas in South America.

Where are Venezuela's petroleum reserves located and what does petroleum mean for the country?

Venezuela's largest petroleum reserves are located under the eastern shores of Lake Maracaibo and in the Orinoco lowlands in the east of the country. Venezuela is the eighth-largest oil producer in the world and the fifth-largest exporter, so petroleum is an essential source of income. The largest importer of Venezuelan petroleum is the United States.

A group of Warao Indians shown here in their village of stilt houses in the Orinoco River Delta in southeastern Venezuela.

Is Lake Maracaibo really a lake?

No. Lake Maracaibo, which has a surface area of 5,019 sq miles (13,000 sq km), is actually an inland sea connected to the Gulf of Venezuela by a 47-mile-long (75-km) strait known as the Canal de San Carlos. However, because it is almost completely separate from the Caribbean Sea it is usually described as a lake.

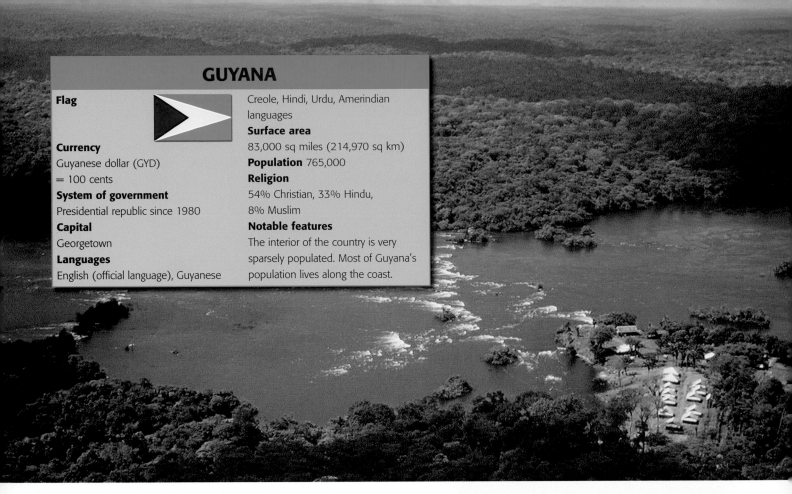

GUYANA

Flag

Currency
Guyanese dollar (GYD)
= 100 cents

System of government
Presidential republic since 1980

Capital
Georgetown

Languages
English (official language), Guyanese

Creole, Hindi, Urdu, Amerindian languages

Surface area
83,000 sq miles (214,970 sq km)

Population 765,000

Religion
54% Christian, 33% Hindu,
8% Muslim

Notable features
The interior of the country is very sparsely populated. Most of Guyana's population lives along the coast.

The tropical rainforest is the Earth's most humid vegetation zone. Large areas of Guyana are covered by impenetrable rainforest.

Where is Guyana?

Guyana is located on the Atlantic coast in the northeastern corner of South America. It is almost as big as the United Kingdom but its population is a mere 1.3 per cent of the UK's. Large expanses of the country's interior are covered with tropical rainforest and populated only by small Indian tribes.

What form did the country's colonial history take?

British and Dutch trading stations were established along the coast of present-day Guyana as early as the 17th century. Over the ensuing period the region came under alternating British and Dutch control. The region only became a British crown colony (British Guiana) in 1831. Guyana achieved independence from the United Kingdom in 1966.

Why are there so many Hindus in the country?

After the abolition of slavery a large number of laborers were imported from India. Their descendants make up the majority (51 per cent) of the current population. Guyana's culture is therefore heavily influenced by Hinduism.

Which commodities form the basis of Guyana's economy?

In addition to exports of gold, sugar, and shrimps, the country's economy is based on the extraction of

The Canaima National Park, which contains some of the world's highest waterfalls, is located on the border between Venezuela and Guyana.

The Kaieteur Falls

The Kaieteur Falls are among the most impressive in the world. The Potaro River plunges down a 738-ft (225-m) cliff from the Guyanese highlands before flowing through the Potaro Gorge. German biologist Carl Eigenmann (1863–1927) came across the Kaieteur Falls during a 1908 expedition and discovered a number of hitherto unknown species of fish there.

bauxite (a raw material used in the production of aluminum). Guyana is the eleventh-largest exporter of bauxite in the world.

What happened as a result of the Treaty of Breda?

The Treaty of Breda was signed on July 31, 1667 at the end of the Second Anglo-Dutch (naval) War, and what is now known as Suriname—previously Dutch Guiana—became a colony of the Netherlands. England received New Amsterdam (present-day New York) in return.

When was slavery abolished in Suriname?

Slavery was officially abolished on July 1, 1863 although the colony's 35,000 freed slaves were forced to carry on working on the plantations (albeit for money) for the next ten years. The Netherlands paid former slave owners compensation of 300 guilders for every worker they lost. As of that date each slave also had to be given a surname by the colonial administration.

What is the most important means of transportation in Suriname?

The main means of transportation is not by road but by water. A total of 745 miles (1,200 km) of rivers and other waterways link the coast to the inaccessible interior. The country's most important rivers are the Maroni (which forms the boundary with Guyana), the Courantyne (which forms the boundary with French Guiana), and, most importantly, the Suriname (which flows through the capital Paramaribo).

What are the country's main sources of income?

In addition to bauxite (see Guyana) the country possesses petroleum reserves that have been exploited since 1982. By the end of January 2004 around 55 million barrels had been extracted. There are further reserves offshore, which are being exploited in a joint venture with Spanish petrochemical company Repsol YPF SA.

SURINAME		
Flag		**Languages**
		Dutch (official language), Hindi, Javanese, Sranan (Taki-Taki), English Creole
Currency		
1 Surinamese dollar (SRD) = 100 cents		**Surface area** 63,039 sq miles (163,270 sq km)
System of government		**Population** 438,144
Presidential republic since 1987		**Religion** 27% Hindu, 23% Catholic,
Capital Paramaribo		22% Muslim, 17% Protestant

Many Dutch colonial-style buildings can still be found in Suriname's capital Paramaribo.

The Surinamese brain drain

Suriname's independence in 1975 was followed by a period of political unrest. Following a coup d'état in 1980 and a series of assassinations of political opposition figures in December 1982, around 350,000 Surinamese emigrated to the Netherlands alone. This was a great loss to the country as it was Suriname's well-educated and well-trained citizens who left the country or chose not to return after studying abroad.

ECUADOR

Flag 	**Languages** Spanish (official language), Quechua
	Surface area 109,483 sq miles (283,560 sq km)
Currency 1 US dollar (USD) = 100 cents	**Population** 13.2 million
System of government Presidential republic since 1978	**Religion** 90% Catholic
	Notable features
Capital Quito	The Galápagos Islands also belong to Ecuador.

Above: The capital Quito lies almost on the Equator. Because of its high elevation, it enjoys a temperate climate that has earned it the sobriquet "City of Eternal Spring."

Below: An iguana on Fernandina Island, one of the Galápagos Islands. There are 700 species of iguana in the world, of which the longest can grow up to 6 ft 6 in (2 m) long.

What different geographical regions does Ecuador have?

Ecuador, through which the Equator runs, is located on the west coast of South America and is divided into three clearly defined geographical zones: in the west the coastal area (Costa) is dominated by fertile plains, further east the country is traversed by two Andean mountain ranges (Sierra), and the easternmost part of the country (Oriente) comprises a section of the Amazon Basin and is covered by rainforest.

Is the capital Quito also Ecuador's largest city?

No. Quito is located in a high valley between two Andean mountain ranges at an elevation of 8,202 ft (2,500 m). The city was founded in 1534 by the Spanish *conquistadors* and currently has a population of 1.4 million. Ecuador's largest city, and also its biggest port, is Guayaquil, which has around three million inhabitants. Guayaquil is located in the west of the country on the hot and humid coastal plain.

Is Ecuador a poor country?

Yes. Although it possesses petroleum reserves in the Amazon Basin that are responsible for half its economic output, Ecuador is still one of South America's poorest countries. Most of the population live below subsistence level and almost 25 per cent of Ecuadorians live abroad as immigrant workers.

Why doesn't Ecuador have its own currency?

Until 1999 Ecuador had its own currency, the sucre. At that time the exchange rate was 6,500 sucres to the US dollar. Soaring inflation led the government to abandon the sucre in favor of the dollar and in 2000 the Ecuadorian currency was definitively replaced by the dollar at a rate of 25,000 sucres to the dollar. The US dollar has been the national currency of Ecuador ever since.

Galápagos

The Galápagos Islands are located in the Pacific Ocean around 620 miles (1,000 km) west of Ecuador, to which they belong. The islands' fauna includes many endemic species. As a result, a trip to the Galápagos is the dream of every biologist. Charles Darwin (1809–1882) made a series of exciting discoveries there that helped him develop his theory of evolution. Today 97 per cent of the surface area of the Islands is a conservation area.

What are Quechua and Aymara?

Quechua and Aymara are the names of two of Peru's Amerindian peoples that still make up nearly 50 per cent of the population. They are also the names of their languages.

How many climate zones does Peru have?

Peru is divided into three very different climate zones:
• Costa (11 per cent). Coastal deserts under the influence of the cold Humboldt Current. The driest desert in the world, the Atacama, is located in southern Peru.
• Sierra (15 per cent). Andean uplands with rivers and snowcapped peaks of over 19,700 ft (6,000 m) featuring a dry climate.
• Selva and Montaña (64 per cent). A tropical area covered by impenetrable, hot and humid rainforests characterized by high temperatures and high rainfall. The source of the Amazon River.

What is so special about Lake Titicaca?

Lake Titicaca, which plays a prominent role in Inca mythology, has a surface area of 3,200 sq miles (8,288 sq km) and is located at an elevation of 12,500 ft (3,810 m) above sea level, making it the world's highest commercially navigable lake. It is extremely rich in fish and its islands are considered to be the birthplace of Inca culture.

What was the Viceroyalty of Peru?

In 1532 the Spanish invaded the Andes and founded the Viceroyalty of Peru, which at its peak covered most of South America, extending all the way from Panama to Tierra del Fuego. During the 18th century, however, it gradually diminished in size and importance due to the creation of the viceroyalties of New Granada and Rio de la Plata. It finally came to an end in 1818 with the independence of Chile and Peru.

The funerary towers (known as *chulpas*) of Sillustani, on the shore of Lake Titicaca, were the final resting places of Incas of noble birth.

PERU

Flag	**Surface area** 0.50 million sq miles (1.29 million sq km)
	Population 28.3 million
Currency	**Religion**
1 nuevo sol (PEN) = 100 céntimos	92% Catholic
System of government	**Notable features**
Presidential republic since 1980	Located between the towns of Nazca
Capital	and Palpa are the so-called Nazca
Lima	lines, enormous geoglyphs or earth
Languages	drawings whose origins have been the
Spanish, Quechua (official languages),	source of much speculation since their
Aymara	discovery in the 1920s.

BOLIVIA

Flag

Currency
1 boliviano (BOB) = 100 centavos

System of government
Presidential republic since 1967

Capital
Sucre (constitutional, judicial),
Le Paz (administrative)

Languages
Spanish, Quechua, Aymara (official languages)

Surface area 0.42 million sq miles (1.09 million sq km)

Population 8.8 million

Religion 92% Catholic

Notable features
The border with Peru runs through Lake Titicaca, one of the highest lakes on Earth.

Has Bolivia always been a landlocked country?
No. After Bolivia declared its independence from Spain under the leadership of South American freedom fighter Simón Bolívar (1783–1830), Bolivia claimed the coastal region of Atacama, which had originally belonged to Chile. It was not until after saltpeter began to be mined there in 1860 that Chile demanded the territory back. Chile occupied the coastal region during the Saltpeter War (1879–1883) and Bolivia lost its access to the Pacific Ocean.

How is Bolivia's population made up?
Bolivia's population is made up of four roughly equal groups: the indigenous Quechua and Aymara peoples, the Mestizos of mixed Indian and European ancestry, and the descendants of Spanish settlers. These four groups are united by their common faith: 92 per cent of the population are Roman Catholic.

Can Bolivia be described as a mountainous country?
Yes. Bolivia's topography is dominated by two Andean mountain ranges with peaks of up to 21,325 ft (6,500 m). Between these two chains lies the central Altiplano upland at elevations of between 10,000 ft (3,000 m) and 13,100 ft (4,000 m). This high plateau is where 80 per cent of the population live.

Why is the population so poor?
Bolivia has hardly any export goods. Most of its people depend for their livelihoods on subsistence farming in the Altiplano. Two thirds of Bolivians live on less than one US dollar a day. The country's industry remains relatively undeveloped.

Above: A ceremony of the indigenous Aymara people. Although Catholic, the Aymara still maintain many of their own pre-Christian traditions.

Background: Salar de Uyuni in southwest Bolivia is one of the world's largest salt lakes. Hot, glaringly bright days give way to dark and bitterly cold nights here.

El Mutún

Hopes for Bolivia's economic future rest on the region of El Mutún on the Brazilian border, the site of the world's largest iron ore deposits. Although the ore is located relatively close to the surface, attempts to work the deposits have failed up to now partly due to a lack of investment and partly because of the region's remoteness. A project is currently underway to power the blast furnaces that would need to be constructed there with natural gas sourced within Bolivia itself. The project stands a good chance of success as Bolivia possesses the second-largest natural gas reserves in South America.

How did the country get its name?

Brasil was the word used by one of the region's indigenous peoples to denote the dark rosewood common in these parts. This wood was once the country's main export article and it is only natural that it should give the nation its name. The export of Brazilian rosewood has been banned since 1968. This high-grade hardwood was greatly sought-after for fine furniture

Why is Portuguese spoken in Brazil?

In 1494 the Treaty of Tordesillas divided the newly discovered American lands into Spanish and Portuguese spheres of interest. Portugal was allocated areas along the coast of present-day Brazil, parts of which were still unexplored. It was another 100 years or so, however, before Portugal gained control (as colonial ruler) of the entire country of Brazil as it exists today.

Has Brazil ever had an emperor?

In 1807 Napoleon's troops occupied Portugal and King João VI fled with his entire court to

Brazil, where he lived in Rio de Janeiro. In 1821 he returned to Portugal, leaving his son Pedro as regent in Brazil. In 1822 the latter declared himself Pedro I, emperor of an independent Brazil. He was forced to abdicate in 1831 following a military coup and likewise returned to Portugal. His son in turn became the new emperor of Brazil at just five years of age and reigned until the proclamation of the

BRAZIL		
Flag	**Amerindian languages** (including Tupi, Guaraní, Gê, Arawak, and Carib)	
Currency 1 real (BRL) = 100 centavos	**Surface area** 3.29 million sq miles (8.51 million sq km)	
System of government Presidential federal republic since 1988	**Population** 186.4 million	
Capital Brasília	**Religion** 70% Catholic, 15% Protestant	
Languages Portuguese (official language),	**Notable features** Brazil covers 47% of the total surface area of South America.	

Most Brazilian children are enthusiastic soccer players. The number 10 shirt is worn in honor of national soccer hero Pelé.

Soccer in Brazil

The most popular sport in Brazil is soccer. A career as a soccer player is the dream of countless children living in shantytowns and, for many of them, the only means of escaping poverty. Young children playing soccer with an improvised ball on patches of sandy ground is a common sight in Brazil. It is into this enormous reservoir that Brazilian soccer dips to find talented youngsters. The Brazilian national team has been world champion five times and is thus the most successful in the world. For many soccer fans the Brazilian Edson Arantes do Nascimento, otherwise known as Pelé (born 1940), is and will always remain the best player of all time.

Republic in 1889. The abolition of slavery in 1888 was Pedro II's last major achievement but also led to his downfall.

Is Brazil an immigration destination for Europeans?
Under Portuguese colonial rule more than one million Portuguese emigrated to Brazil. This continued during the imperial era and was further boosted by immigration from Italy, Spain, and Germany. Between 1800 and 1950 more than five million Europeans emigrated to Brazil. Today most Brazilians are dark-skinned, the descendants of African slaves who were brought to Brazil during the 16th to 19th centuries.

What are *favelas*?
Favelas are the poor districts that have sprung up on the outskirts of Brazil's cities. They can be distinguished from slums—urban areas that have become dilapidated over time—in that they are zones of unregulated dwellings around the edge of cities. A great influx into the cities occurred after the

Above: Ipanema Beach, *the* beach in Rio de Janeiro, where young people from the city's more prosperous districts mix with holidaymakers from all over the world.

Below: The biodiversity of Brazil's Amazon region attracts numerous tourists who can cruise along the Rio Negro through primeval forest near the city of Manaus.

Interesting facts

- Brazil is the world's fifth-largest country.
- Brazil has 13 cities of over one million inhabitants.
- Brazil's highest mountain is Pico da Neblina at 9,888 ft (3,014 m).
- The Corcovado (meaning "hunchback") in Rio de Janeiro is the country's most famous mountain, known throughout the world for its 98-ft-high (30-m) statue of Christ (the city's emblem) that has stood on its summit since 1931.
- Penedos de São Pedro e São Paulo ("St Peter and St Paul Rocks"), a group of rocks located some 500 miles (800 km) east of the Brazilian coast, also belongs to Brazil. A lighthouse is the only man-made structure on these uninhabited islands.

abolition of slavery in 1888. The *favelas* tend to be under the de facto control of the drug lords rather than that of the municipalities to which they belong.

Is the Amazon region ecologically intact?

The Amazon Basin is dominated by tropical evergreen rainforest. Indeed, the region accounts for more than half the world's total rainforest. Over the past few years threats to this region of key importance to the Earth's ecosystem have come not only from large-scale deforestation but also increasingly from river pollution. Around 10,000 tributaries feed into the Amazon. Of these, 17 are longer than many of Europe's major rivers such as the Rhine. In their quest to find gold, prospectors are increasingly using highly poisonous mercury. This is then simply flushed into the river, where it causes untold damage.

Is Brazil a poor country?

No. Brazil has the biggest economy in America after the United States. The industrial sector already contributes 40 per cent of the GDP and, based on the country's wealth of raw materials (iron ore, tin, aluminum, gold, phosphate, platinum, uranium, manganese, copper, and coal), its potential would appear to be far from exhausted. Among Brazil's main agricultural exports are meat, coffee, and cacao.

When did Brasília become the national capital?

Just a few years after the end of the Brazilian Empire in 1889, it was established in the national constitution that Brazil should have a new capital. A new site in the interior of the country was chosen in order to promote growth there. Although the foundation stone was laid in 1922, the project only began in earnest in 1956. Brasília officially replaced Rio de Janeiro as the national capital in 1960.

The parade in the Sambadrome in Rio de Janeiro is the climax of the Brazilian Carnival. Thousands of people attend the event and millions more watch it live on television.

CHILE

Flag		

Currency
1 Chilean peso (CLP)
= 100 centavos

System of government
Presidential republic since 1925

Capital Santiago (Santiago de Chile)

Languages
Spanish (official language),
Amerindian languages (including
Mapudungun, Quechua and Aymara)

Surface area
292,260 sq miles (756,950 sq km)

Population 16.3 million

Religion
72% Catholic, 13% Protestant

Notable features
Chile is claiming sovereignty over part
of Antarctica.

Background: Chile's
mountainous
coastline is
punctuated by
numerous inlets
such as Garibaldi
Fjord shown here,
which extend
far inland.

Below: This
impressive row of
15 standing *Moais*
is located at Ahu
Tongariki on the
southeast coast of
Easter Island.

Is Chile a country of geographical extremes?

Yes. Chile is a South American country that extends an enormous 2,700 miles (4,300 km) from north to south but only 150 miles (240 km) from east to west at its widest point. Despite this lack of width the difference in elevation between east and west is extreme. The country rises from sea level along its Pacific coastline to heights of over 19,700 ft (6,000 m) in the Andes. Chile also possesses the world's highest active volcano, Ojos del Salado, at 22,572 ft (6,880 m).

Is the population evenly distributed?

No. Almost one third of the population live in the greater Santiago de Chile region (national capital).

The desert areas of the north and the stormy south are barely populated. The population is very homogeneous: 90 per cent of Chileans are of European descent or are Mestizos, in other words have mixed European-Amerindian ancestry.

What was the Saltpeter War?

When the South American colonies achieved independence from Spain at the beginning of the 19th century, the question of which of the three new countries (Chile, Peru, or Bolivia) owned the Atacama Desert on the Pacific coast remained unresolved. When vast deposits of high-quality saltpeter were discovered there in 1860, the dispute assumed explosive proportions due to the economic importance of the area. During the Saltpeter War (1879–1883), also known as the War of the Pacific, Chile eventually conquered the region and Bolivia lost its access to the Pacific Ocean. The region currently boasts the largest opencast copper mine in the world.

Is Chile a poor country?

No. Chile is the richest country in South America although nowhere else on the continent is the gap between rich and poor more marked. Chile is a prime example of a pure market economy at work, although over the last few years the government has attempted to soften the impact of the extreme social inequalities by setting up effective social insurance systems such as the "Chile Solidario" program.

Easter Island

Easter Island is an isolated island that belongs to Chile even though it is located 2,300 miles (3,700 km) off Chile's Pacific coast. The island has a population of just 4,000. It is famous for its *Moais*, which are giant stone sculptures of uncertain origin. The island's Rapa Nui National Park was designated a UNESCO World Heritage site in 1995.

Of which different population groups is Argentina made up?

More than 90 per cent of Argentinians are the descendants of European immigrants (mainly from Spain and Italy). The indigenous peoples who inhabited the region when it was colonized were almost completely wiped out by the Spanish invaders. Their descendants make up only a small minority.

Does the tango come from Argentina?

Yes and no. At the beginning of the 20th century travelers from Buenos Aires took the Tango Argentino to Paris, where it was rejected by society's conservative elite who found it excessively "wild" and "indecent." It was subsequently modified in the United Kingdom until it satisfied European social norms. In its new form it became one of the five standard dances of the international dance repertoire.

Falklands War

Geographically the Falkland Islands in the South Atlantic are part of South America but politically they belong to the United Kingdom. Argentina has claimed the islands since 1833 and occupied them militarily in 1982, thereby triggering the Falklands War. The United Kingdom sent a task force to the region and reconquered the islands seven weeks after the start of the Argentinian occupation. The war cost more than 1,000 lives.

ARGENTINA

Flag

Currency
1 Argentine peso (ARS)
= 100 centavos

System of government
Presidential federal republic since 1853

Capital Buenos Aires

Languages
Spanish (official language),
Amerindian languages (including Quechua and Guaraní)

Surface area 1.07 million sq miles (2.77 million sq km)

Population 38.7 million

Religion 92% Catholic

Notable features
Before the Spanish arrived in the region there were around 30 different indigenous peoples living in present-day Argentina.

Where is Tierra del Fuego and what are the origins of its name?

Tierra del Fuego ("Land of Fire") is a group of islands at the southern tip of South America. The eastern side belongs to Argentina and the western side to Chile. The islands were named by Ferdinand Magellan (1480–1521) who discovered them in 1520 when he was looking for the southern passage around South America. During the voyage he would watch the campfires of the local people for days on end and named the region after them.

Tango Argentino is basically an improvised dance with no fixed steps. The dancers can choose from a multitude of "figures."

Evita Perón

Eva Maria Duarte de Perón (1919–1952), commonly known as Evita, was the second wife of Argentinian president Juan Perón (1895–1974). Although she did not hold any official political position, she was a passionate champion of women's rights and defender of the poor. As a result, she achieved enormous popularity far beyond Argentina's borders. Her life story has been both filmed and turned into the musical *Evita*.

PARAGUAY

Flag	**Languages** Spanish, Guaraní (official languages)	
	Surface area 157,047 sq miles (406,750 sq km)	
Currency 1 guaraní (PYG) = 100 céntimos	**Population** 6.2 million	
System of government Presidential republic since 1967	**Religion** 90% Catholic, 6% Protestant	
Capital Asunción		

Right: A young Guaraní man. The Guaraní are Paraguay's biggest minority. While they only represent one per cent of the population, 80 per cent of Paraguayans speak their language.

Below: Itaipú is the largest hydroelectric power plant in the world. It is operated jointly by Brazil and Paraguay. Some 363 sq miles (940 sq km) of forest and farmland were flooded to create the reservoir.

What does the word "Paraguay" mean?

The country name is taken from the language of the Guaraní, the indigenous inhabitants of the region, and means "water that flows to the water." The water towards which the river flows is the ocean, which is a considerable distance from this landlocked country.

How is the population of Paraguay made up?

The majority of Paraguayans (around 90 per cent) are Mestizos, in other words persons of mixed Spanish and Indian descent. At the beginning of the 20th century European, Brazilian, and Argentinian immigrants arrived in the country. The indigenous Guaraní are the country's biggest minority. Although the Guaraní represent only one per cent of the population, 80 per cent of Paraguay's inhabitants speak their tongue as it is the country's second official language after Spanish.

What is Plautdietsch?

Plautdietsch is an East Low German dialect spoken more or less as it was in eastern Europe during

Guaraní and Jesuit reservations in Paraguay

The Guaraní are indigenous Amerindians who settled in South America (in areas covered by present-day Paraguay, Bolivia, Argentina, Uruguay, and Brazil) prior to the arrival of Christopher Columbus (1451–1506). The first Spanish governor encouraged interbreeding between the Amerindians and the Spanish. The Jesuits started performing missionary work in South America at the beginning of the 17th century, and in order to protect the Guaraní from exploitation and slavery, they built what became known as "Jesuit reductions," effectively the continent's first reservations for the indigenous population. Only invited guests were allowed to enter these reservations, which came under direct jurisdiction of the Spanish crown. In 1767, as a result of conflicts with big landowners and the colonial regime, the Jesuits were expelled under King Charles III and the Amerindians became fair game for exploitation. The destruction of the Jesuit reservations by the Spanish colonial rulers was the subject of the 1986 film *The Mission*, starring Robert De Niro.

the 16th and 17th centuries. In the 18th century Mennonite emigrants spread the dialect all over the world. Plautdietsch is currently spoken by around 50,000 people in northwest Paraguay (nearly seven per cent of the population is of German descent), making it the country's third language. In the United States the dialect is also known as Mennonite Low German.

What is the country's main source of energy?

Paraguay's most important source of both energy and revenue is Itaipú, the largest hydroelectric power plant in the world, which is jointly operated by Paraguay and Brazil. The facility meets nearly all the country's energy needs and the surplus is sold mainly to Brazil.

When was Uruguay first settled?

When Prehistoric archaeological finds have demonstrated that people settled here in small nomadic groups as early as 7000 BC. The first people to display any kind of sophisticated civilization were the Charrúas, who were almost completely wiped out by the Spanish in the 19th century.

What is the basis of Uruguay's agricultural success?

The Spanish colonial rulers had hoped to discover large amounts of silver in Uruguay but they were disappointed as the country is poor in minerals. The Spaniards released the horses and cattle they had brought with them by sea. These animals thrived in the Pampas and developed into large herds. Stockbreeding is now an important branch of what is Uruguay's main economic sector: agriculture.

Is there a national sport in Uruguay?

If any sport deserves to be called the national sport of Uruguay, it is surely soccer. The national team won gold in the Paris and Amsterdam Olympic Games in 1924 and 1928 respectively. On July 30, 1930 they became the first soccer world champions in the Centenario Stadium in Montevideo (the biggest stadium in the world at the time, with 93,000 seats) when they beat Argentina 4–2. Twenty years later they won the title again when they beat Brazil 2–1 in Rio de Janeiro's Maracanã Stadium in 1950.

URUGUAY

Flag

Currency
1 Uruguayan peso (UYU)
= 100 centésimos

System of government
Presidential republic since 1967

Capital
Montevideo

Languages
Spanish (official language)

Surface area
68,039 sq miles (176,220 sq km)

Population 3.5 million

Religion
66% Catholic

Notable features
Uruguay is the smallest Spanish-speaking country in South America.

What are Uruguay's culinary specialties?

Uruguay's national dish is *asado*, which consists of any cuts of beef, lamb, or pork that can be grilled over an open charcoal fire. The traditional ingredients are black pudding (*morcillas*), veal sweetbreads, kidneys, and liver. The most popular dessert is *dulce de leche*, which is made with caramelized sweetened milk and eaten by itself, with cake or as an ice cream. *Dulce de leche* is a favorite throughout the whole of South America.

Punta del Este, located 90 miles (140 km) from Montevideo, is a holiday destination on the southern tip of Uruguay visited by thousands of tourists every year between Christmas and the end of January.

Interesting facts

- In Uruguay there is a strict division between church and state and so religious holidays have been given an additional secular name. Christmas, for example, is also called "Family Day."

- Uruguay is one of the few countries with an all-digital telephone network. All towns of 2,000 or more inhabitants are equipped with fiberglass telephone cables and the number of Internet connections per person is the highest in the whole of South America.

- Public hospitals are free of charge, thereby guaranteeing medical care for the whole population.

▲ Ivory Coast

Morocco

Ethiopia

South Africa

AFRICA

Africa, the second-largest continent and three times the size of Europe, was exploited for centuries by colonial rulers. Since the middle of the 20th century the "Dark Continent," as it was nicknamed by its European overlords, has increasingly been going its own way after fighting hard for independence—and grappling with the numerous problems that independence has brought. 53 nations have emerged in which the speakers of nearly 200 languages are working to build a common future.

São Tomé

Mauritius

Angola

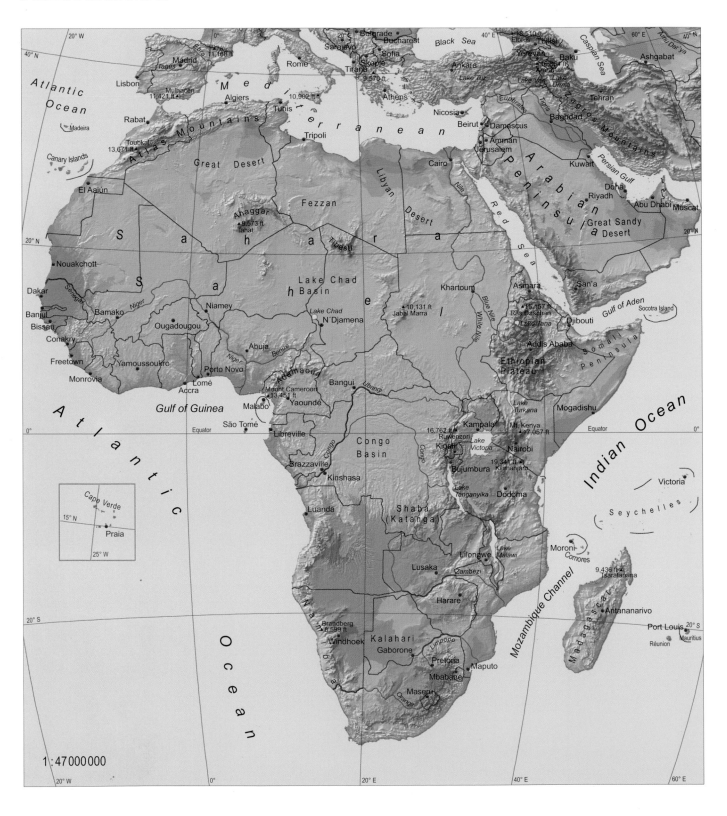

1:47 000 000

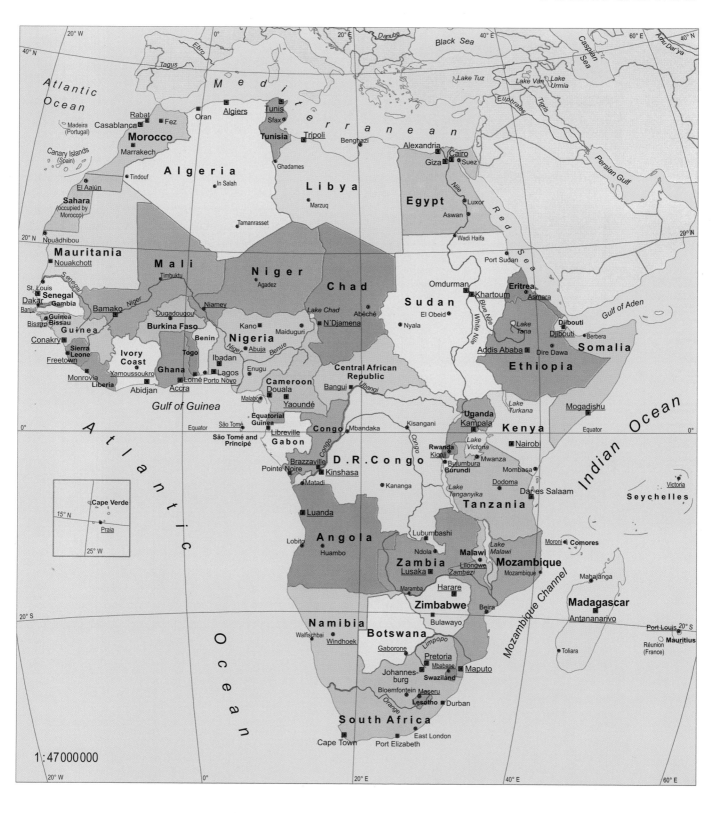

1:47 000 000

Introduction

What are the main problems facing Africa at the beginning of the 21st century?

Africa's most severe problems are currently drought, famine, disease (above all HIV/AIDS), an antiquated economic infrastructure, corruption, poverty, and armed disputes over territory and political power.

What are the main religions in Africa?

Around 40 per cent of the population are Muslim and another 40 per cent Christian. Buddhism, Hinduism, Judaism (mainly non-African sections of the community), and folk religions account for the remaining 20 per cent.

What are Africa's main mineral resources?

Among Africa's most important mineral resources are gold, diamonds, copper, and chrome. However, Africa's processing industries are poorly developed—largely because of the difficulty of creating the efficient transportation networks needed in order to open the continent up—and so most of the processing takes place outside Africa. Many of the continent's rich mineral deposits are waiting for the kind of infrastructure that would allow for efficient mining.

Background: Drifting dunes such as those shown here (Algeria) are a feature of sandy deserts. The Arabic word *erg* is sometimes used to denote the shifting sands of the Sahara.

Below: Children in a famine zone in Somalia.

Canary Islands

While the Canary Islands belong to Africa geographically, politically they are part of Spain. The seven islands (Tenerife, Gran Canaria, Fuerteventura, El Hierro, La Gomera, Lanzarote, and La Palma) have had a turbulent history. They were known to the Ancient Greeks as the Hesperides and, in one of his labors, Hercules had to fetch the eternal-life-bestowing Apple of the Hesperides for the goddess Athena from here. In the Treaty of Alcáçovas of 1479 the Canary Islands were promised to Queen Isabella I of Castile but they continued to be fought over until Tenerife was finally conquered in 1496 and they became Spanish for good. The original inhabitants of the islands, the Guanches (whose language is related to the Berber languages), are thought to have arrived from North Africa in reed boats.

How big is the River Nile's drainage area?

The Nile is thought to be the longest river in the world. It flows for 2,589 miles (6,671 km) and its drainage area encompasses some 1 million sq miles (2.5 million sq km). It rises in the mountains of Rwanda and Burundi and flows through Tanzania, Uganda, Sudan, and Egypt before discharging into the Mediterranean Sea. The main branch of the Nile is the White Nile, which merges with the lesser branch, the Blue Nile, near Khartoum in Sudan. The most fertile section of the river is its 8,700-sq mile (22,500-sq km) delta in Egypt. For millions of Africans the Nile is a life-bringer, just as it was to the Ancient Egyptians.

What is the Afar Triangle?

The lowest point in Africa occurs in a geological depression in the Horn of Africa (where the Gulf of Aden meets the Arabian Sea). Lake Asal, on the border between Djibouti and Ethiopia, is 512 ft (156 m) below sea level and has an area of 21 sq miles (54 sq km). This depression, known to geologists as the Afar Triangle, is the meeting point of three tectonic rifts (fractures in the Earth's crust). Were these to break, magma would erupt along Djibouti's coast and form new landmasses.

What is the name of Africa's highest point?

At 19,340 ft (5,895 m) Uhuru, the eastern summit of Mount Kilimanjaro, is Africa's highest peak. The smaller Mawenzi, to the west, rises to 16,890 ft (5,148 m). Kilimanjaro, situated close to the Equator, is a dormant volcano covered by glaciers. Coffee, cereals, and vegetables are grown on its slopes.

What are *ergs*?

Ergs are star-shaped sand dunes that extend like a thick carpet over the borders of three countries. They can attain a diameter of 2,600–3,300 ft (800–1,000 m) and a height of up to 5,250 ft (1,600 m). Because of their inhospitability, these areas are avoided even by the fearless Tuaregs (see p216). This kind of terrain is pitiless, where ice-cold nights alternate with lethally hot days. Sandstorms can blow up without warning and the only water is a mirage.

The Amboseli National Park in southern Kenya is famous for its view of the snowcapped summit of Mount Kilimanjaro, Africa's highest mountain at 19,340 ft (5,895 m).

Is the "Sahel zone" a precisely defined region?

No. *Sahel* is the Arabic word for "coast" and denotes the band of semi-desert 200–700 miles (320–1,130 km) wide that forms the transition between desert and the more fertile regions to the south. The actual breadth of the Sahel zone depends on a number of factors including drought, sudden rainfall, and desertification caused by man.

How big is the Sahara Desert?

The Sahara covers some 3.5 million sq miles (9 million sq km), in other words more than a third of North Africa. Moreover, it is continuing to grow—creeping slowly and surely southwards.

Why is Africa so often the victim of famine?
Famine in Africa is mainly a politico-economic problem and less a problem of food production. The West African Sahel zone, for example, produces enough food for the region's population, but inadequate infrastructure and a lack of political cooperation prevent this food getting to where it is needed. The situation is aggravated by war and corruption on the part of those in power.

Above: Cairo, the capital of Egypt, is located on the banks of the Nile in the northeast of the country.

A group of warriors of the Ethiopian Hamer tribe patrol the border along Lake Chew Bahir.

Does the Sahara consist of sand alone?
Although the Sahara is famous for its drifting sand dunes, it is actually composed primarily of scree and stone resting on enormous slabs of rock. The desert comprises both high mountains and depressions descending to 100 ft (30 m) below sea level.

Which are Africa's largest cities?

Africa's largest city is the Egyptian capital Cairo, which has 15.7 million inhabitants. It is followed by Lagos in Nigeria with 11.2 million people, and Kinshasa in the Democratic Republic of Congo with 8.1 million.

Which African authors have won the Nobel Prize for Literature?

Wole Soyinka became the first African author to win the Nobel Prize for Literature in 1986. He was followed by Naguib Mahfouz from Egypt in 1988, South African Nadine Gordimer in 1991, and South African J. M. Coetzee in 2003.

What is a tonal language?

A tonal language is a language in which a complex system of pitches is used to distinguish between different meanings. The same word can have a range of meanings and the right one has to be inferred from the degree of accentuation attached to it within a sentence. In Africa tonal languages include numerous dialects plus Afro-Asiatic languages such as Hausa in West Africa, Nilo-Saharan languages such as Kanuri, and a large number of Niger-Congo languages.

Interesting facts: Colonialism

- Following the discovery of America in 1492, Africa became attractive to Europeans primarily as a source of slaves.
- Against the background of imperialism, the major European powers developed a renewed economic interest in Africa around 1877 and within 20 years virtually the entire continent had been divided up between European rulers.
- By 1912 most African peoples had lost their freedom.
- The last colony in Africa was Djibouti, which gained its independence from France in 1977.
- In South Africa the Black majority has only been represented in government since 1994.
- There are still a number of islands that belong to Africa geographically but Europe politically.
- Africa's national boundaries were drawn up arbitrarily by the continent's colonial rulers and as a consequence many African states have found it impossible to develop a sense of nationhood.

Because of its rich and unique flora and fauna, Ngorongoro Crater in Tanzania (one of the largest volcano craters in the world not to have flooded since becoming extinct) has been made a UNESCO World Heritage site.

MOROCCO

Flag

Currency
1 dirham (MAD) = 100 centimes

System of government
Constitutional monarchy since 1972

Capital
Rabat

Languages
Arabic (official language), French,
Spanish, Berber languages

Surface area
172,413 sq miles (446,550 sq km)

Population 32.7 million

Religion
99% Muslim (mainly Sunni)

Notable features
Morocco currently administers the
territory of Western Sahara, which is
seeking independence.

Casablanca
The economic heart of Morocco is Casablanca on the Atlantic
coast. Casablanca lies to the south of the national capital Rabat
and with nearly three million inhabitants is the country's largest
city. It achieved international fame through the 1942 film
of the same name. One of Casablanca's famous sights is
the Hassan II Mosque, whose minaret rises to over 650 ft
(200 m), making it the tallest in the world.

*The Carpet Souk in
Marrakech. Souks
are designed to
provide traders and
craftsmen with a
place to do business.
People do not
generally live there.*

What does the word "Maghreb" mean?
The Arabic word "Maghreb" is derived from
gharaba ("to sink"—of the sun) and denotes the
African countries Tunisia, Algeria, and Morocco.
In the Arabic world, however, it is often used to
refer to Morocco (the westernmost Arabic country)
alone.

What is the High Atlas?
The High Atlas is one of the mountain ranges of
the Atlas Mountains, with peaks of over 13,000 ft
(4,000 m). It runs through Morocco from southwest
to northeast. Geologically speaking it is a young
system. The Atlas Mountains divide Morocco's
Atlantic coast from the interior, which is dominated
visually by the Sahara.

Who is the king of Morocco?
The current king is Mohammed VI of the Alouite
dynasty, who has been on the throne since 1999. The
Alouites have ruled Morocco since 1640, initially
as sultans and since 1957 as kings of Morocco.
Although the king has wide-ranging powers in the
country, day-to-day political affairs are managed by
a prime minister.

Does the country possess mineral wealth?
Yes. Of particular importance to the economy
are the country's phosphate deposits. Morocco is
responsible for 75 per cent of world phosphate
mining. However, money transfers from Moroccan
emigrant workers (one million of whom live in
Europe alone) are the country's biggest source of
foreign currency earnings.

*Ait-Ben-Haddou, a fortified village in southeastern Morocco, is famous for
its interlocking casbahs (fortified dwellings) made of earth.*

How is Algeria subdivided geographically?

Along its Mediterranean coast Algeria has only a narrow strip of fertile flat land before the Tell Atlas mountains begin. The coastal plains and parts of the mountains, which rise to around 7,500 ft (2,300 m), constitute Algeria's entire habitable area. South of the mountains begins the Sahara Desert, which covers 85 per cent of the country.

Why is Algeria called a "young country"?

Around 34 per cent of Algerians are under 15 years old. A high rate of youth unemployment, however, has led large numbers of young Algerians to leave the country—the destination of choice is France.

When did the Algerian War take place?

The Algerian war of independence against French rule (the colonial power since 1830) began in 1954. The war was conducted brutally by both sides. Algeria's independence was not recognized by France until 1962.

ALGERIA

Flag

Currency
1 Algerian dinar (DZD)
= 100 centimes

System of government
Presidential republic since 1962

Capital
Algiers

Languages
Arabic (official language), French, Berber languages

Surface area 0.9 million sq miles (2.4 million sq km)

Population 32.5 million

Religion 99% Sunni Muslim

Notable features
80% of the land is devoid of vegetation.

What is the Casbah?

Casbah is an Arabic word meaning "fortress." The entire old quarter of the Algerian capital, which was made a UNESCO World Heritage site in 1992, is also known as the Casbah.

A Bedouin caravan in the Algerian Sahara. The nomadic Bedouins are mainly animal herders.

Algerian petroleum

Algeria has the third-largest reserves of petroleum in Africa and crude oil, natural gas, and petroleum products make up 98 per cent of Algeria's export earnings. A proportion of the petroleum revenue has been invested in prestigious real estate projects. A significant amount of the profits has remained in the hands of the upper strata of Algerian society.

TUNISIA

Flag

Currency
1 Tunisian dinar (TND)
= 1,000 millimes

System of government
Presidential republic since 1956

Capital
Tunis

Languages
Arabic (official language), Berber languages, French

Surface area
63,170 sq miles (163,610 sq km)

Population 10.1 million

Religion
98% Sunni Muslim

A typical spice stall at a village market in Tunisia.

What are Tunisia's main industries?

Tunisia has three main economic sectors:
a) Agriculture. Around 50 per cent of the surface area is used for agriculture. After the destruction of Carthage in the Third Punic War (149–146 BC), Tunis became one of Ancient Rome's key granaries (Egypt was another). Tunisia is also one of the biggest exporters of olive oil. The country's wine production, on the other hand, is declining.
b) Mineral resources. Tunisia's main mineral resources are petroleum, natural gas, and phosphates, which are processed into phosphoric acid and fertilizer.
c) Tourism. Tunisia's tourist industry started to develop in the early 1970s and the country now attracts around four million visitors a year. The most popular destinations are the coastal towns and resorts of Hammamet, Nabeul, Monastir, and the island of Djerba.

These traditional silos for the storage of grain are called ghorfas.

Where is the world's oldest synagogue?

El Ghriba synagogue on the island of Djerba was built more than 1,000 years ago. Its name means something like "bizarre" and it is thought to be the oldest functioning synagogue in the world. On the 33rd day after Pessach, which is celebrated at the same time as Easter, pilgrims make their way here from all over the world in what is North Africa's biggest Jewish pilgrimage. There are now only 2,000 Jews living in Tunisia, and 98 per cent of the population are Sunni Muslims.

Do women have the vote in Tunisia?

Female suffrage was introduced in Tunisia in 1959, making Tunisia the first Arabic country in which women have had the vote since the nation was founded. There is a strict separation of state and religion in Tunisia. The government has placed an emphasis on equal status for women and as a result around 33 per cent of women are employed.

What is *malouf*?

Malouf is Tunisia's best-known musical genre. It was imported by Andalusian refugees following the Spanish conquest of Tunisia in the 15th century. *Malouf* combines Arabic and Spanish elements with quotations from Berber music. A typical ensemble consists of violin, drum, sitar, and lute.

How is the country's population distributed?
Libya's population lives almost exclusively in towns and cities on the Mediterranean coast. The Sahara Desert covers 85 per cent of the country and is almost uninhabited other than in a few oases.

What is the Gulf of Sidra?
The Gulf of Sidra is the wide bay that constitutes Libya's Mediterranean shoreline. The coastal towns where the pipelines from the country's interior terminate are not only petroleum and natural gas entrepôts but also important transshipment points.

Does Libya have a long history?
Yes. The Libyan people have been documented since antiquity and from around 945 BC provided the 22nd Dynasty of Egyptian pharaohs. The Libyans were also known to the Ancient Greeks and large parts of Libya later belonged to the Roman Empire. During the Middle Ages Libya was part of the Ottoman Empire.

What is the Great Man-Made River Project?
The Great Man-Made River Project is an enormous engineering project (the largest of its kind in the world) started in 1984 whereby "ice-age" water from beneath the Libyan desert is transported to the country's population centers in a pipeline. Among the aims of the project are to provide irrigation for agriculture and more generally to invest in the country's economic future in the knowledge that its petroleum deposits will not last for ever.

The ruins of Leptis Magna. During the Roman Empire, Leptis Magna was an important trading center for exotic animals. The lions for the circus games in Rome were bought here.

Muammar al-Qadaffi
Colonel Qadaffi (born 1942) has been Libya's head of state since 1969, when he deposed reigning King Idris in a military coup. He subsequently set about transforming the former kingdom into a socialist state and strove—ultimately in vain—to create a union of African states. Qadaffi's suspected links with international terrorist organizations led to Libya's isolation from the Western industrial states. Only recently has this situation begun to ease.

LIBYA

Flag

Currency
1 Libyan dinar (LYD) = 1,000 dirhams

System of government
Islamic socialist people's republic since 1976

Capital
Tripoli

Languages
Arabic (official language), Berber languages

Surface area 0.68 million sq miles (1.76 million sq km)

Population 5.8 million

Religion
97% Muslim

Notable features
Libya is a dry country without a single river that flows all year round.

EGYPT

Flag

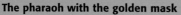

Currency
1 Egyptian pound (EGP) = 100 piastres

System of government
Presidential republic since 1953

Capital Cairo

Languages
Arabic (official language), Nubian

Surface area 0.39 million sq miles
(1.0 million sq km)

Population 77.5 million

Religion
90% Sunni Muslim,
9% Coptic Christian

Notable features
The population lives almost exclusively
along the Nile Valley and in the Nile
Delta.

The pharaoh with the golden mask

Tutankhamun was an Egyptian pharaoh of the 18th Dynasty who reigned from around 1333 to 1323 BC and died at the age of 18. His tomb was discovered in the Valley of the Kings by British archaeologist Howard Carter (1874–1939) in 1922. The discovery caused a worldwide sensation as the tomb was largely intact. Many of the burial objects—most impressively the death mask, which covered the pharaoh's head, shoulders, and chest—were made of gold. Archaeologists are still puzzling over the significance of many of the artifacts found in the tomb and theories abound concerning the sudden death of the young pharaoh.

The pyramids of Giza are some of the oldest man-made structures on the planet. Even in the ancient world they were ranked among the Seven Wonders of the World.

Is Egypt a desert nation?
Around 95 per cent of the country is covered by desert; The Libyan Desert on the western side of the Nile and the Arabian Desert on the eastern side. To the northeast is the Sinai Peninsula, a desert separated from the rest of Egypt by the Suez Canal and geographically more Asian than African. Egypt's highest point, Mount Catherine (8,652 ft/2,637 m), is located on the Sinai Peninsula.

Why is the Nile referred to as Egypt's lifeline?
Egypt's only productive land is along the banks of the river that separates the western and eastern deserts from one another. These areas are cultivated with the help of irrigation systems. Fertile land makes up just five per cent of Egypt's surface area and is therefore of great significance to the country.

How often does it rain in Egypt?
Egypt has a predominantly desert climate with virtually no precipitation. While to the south of Cairo it hardly ever rains, in the Nile Delta and along the Mediterranean coast there is some rainfall in winter, when cooler temperatures prevail.

Is the Nile the longest river in the world?
At 4,145 miles (6,671 km) in length, the Nile is probably the longest river in the world. The only river that might be longer is the Amazon in South America. As it is impossible to clearly identify the source of the Amazon, the question of which river is longer remains open. The Nile rises in the mountains of Rwanda and Burundi. It then flows through Tanzania, Uganda, and Sudan before discharging into the Mediterranean via a large delta.

When was the source of the Nile discovered?
Numerous attempts to reach the source of the Nile were undertaken during the 19th century. The most famous explorer to join the quest was the Briton David Livingstone (1813–1873), who thought the source was Bangweulu Lake. He was wrong. In 1893 the source of the Luvironza River was found, which is now considered to be the source river of the Nile.

Who built the pyramids?
Many of the Old Kingdom pharaohs (circa 2680–2180 BC) were buried in pyramids. The

shape evolved from flat-topped structures known as *mastabas* to step pyramids and eventually to the true pyramid shape of the three Great Pyramids of Giza. There are around 80 known pyramids in Egypt, of which the largest is the Pyramid of Cheops at Giza, with base measurements of 755 × 755 ft (230 × 230 m).

Was Cairo the capital of the Egyptian Empire?
No. The capitals of Ancient Egypt were Thebes and Memphis. Cairo only became the capital (of the Muslim Fatimid Empire) in 973. With 15.7 million inhabitants, it is now not only the capital of modern Egypt but the largest city in the Arabic world.

Does Egypt depend on tourism?
No, but along with revenue from the Suez Canal and petroleum and natural gas exports, tourism is one of the country's most important sources of foreign currency earnings. Egypt's antiquities attract visitors from all over the world. Over recent times, however, the tourism industry has suffered as a result of terrorist attacks on major tourist attractions. Most

recently, 23 people were killed in April 2006 during an attack at Dahab (Sinai).

What role does Islam play in Egyptian life?
Islam is the state religion in Egypt and nearly 90 per cent of Egyptians are Sunni Muslims.

Aswan High Dam
The Aswan High Dam (Sadd el-Ali) near the city of Aswan in southern Egypt was built between 1960 and 1971. It dams the Nile to form the enormous Lake Nasser, which stretches south as far as neighboring Sudan and holds some 5,297 billion cu ft (150 billion cu m) of water. The dam was constructed with the help of 2,000 Soviet engineers and 30,000 laborers. No less than 100,000 people had to be moved so that their settlements could be flooded. During construction the archaeological site of Abu Simbel 175 miles (280 km) south of Aswan came to worldwide attention. Two rock temples dedicated to Ramses II were dismantled into over 1,000 individual sections and reassembled on ground 210 ft (64 m) higher in order to preserve them from the water. The temples are now UNESCO World Heritage sites.

The Temple of Luxor. Only one obelisk remains in front of the two seated figures representing Pharaoh Ramses II. The other is in the middle of Place de la Concorde in Paris.

Above: The Sultan Hasan Mosque in Cairo. There are several hundred mosques in the city, many of which are architecturally outstanding.

Girls at the Qur'an school in Dakhla, a collection of 14 villages comprising one of Egypt's most attractive oases.

Although the form of Islam practiced in Egypt is on the whole progressive, there are also centers of Islamic fundamentalism whose adherents regard violence against "unbelievers" as part of a legitimate struggle. A significant minority of Egyptians are Coptic Christians, who see themselves as the direct descendants of the Pharaonic Egyptians.

What is the significance of the Suez Canal?

The Suez Canal opened in 1869 and connects the Mediterranean with the Red Sea and thus Europe with the Middle East and Far East. Because of its economic and strategic importance, the canal has been the cause of repeated armed confrontation throughout its history. Today around 14 per cent of world shipping passes through the Suez Canal.

Fellahin

Members of Egypt's indigenous rural population who work the fields are known as the *fellahin* (singular: *fellah*). The *fellahin* farm the fertile land along the Nile Valley, in the Nile Delta, and in individual oases. Egypt is no longer able to grow enough food to feed its growing population, however, and in 1980 three times as much wheat had to be imported as was produced at home.

What are the White and Blue Niles?

The White and Blue Niles converge at Khartoum in Sudan to form the River Nile proper. Contrary to popular belief, neither is actually the source river of the Nile as the White Nile has two source rivers of its own (the Albert Nile and the Victoria Nile) and the Blue Nile, which rises in the highlands of Ethiopia, is regarded as more of a tributary today. The Blue Nile takes its name from the dark, earthy color of the fertile soil it picks up in Ethiopia and carries along with it.

Where is Nubia?

The region between Karima and Khartoum is often described as South Nubia. Nubia was long regarded as the place where Egypt (seen as belonging to the Mediterranean world) met "Black" (i.e. sub-Saharan) Africa. Nubia was a supplier of gold and slaves to Ancient Egypt. In the 10th century BC this region saw the emergence of the Kush Empire, whose princes ruled Egypt for a brief period. Kush survived until around AD 300.

Sharia

Other than in the south, *sharia* (Islamic law) applies in Sudan. *Sharia* means "the path (to God)" and embraces virtue, faith, and religious duty as well as comprising a system of civil and criminal law based on the Qur'an. Under *sharia* law, sexual offenses (including homosexuality), defamation, and the consumption of liquor are officially punishable by death. The penalty for theft is amputation of the hand, and in the case of recidivism, the foot. Adultery committed on the part of adult, married Muslims is punishable by lifelong house arrest although a God-given "way out" may be offered—in practice usually stoning. Though Islamic law is interpreted differently across times, places, and scholars, Muslim scholars believe it should be legally binding on all Muslims.

SUDAN

Flag

Currency
1 Sudanese dinar (SDG) = 100 piastres

System of government
Islamic republic since 1986; military government since 1989

Capital
Khartoum

Languages
Modern Standard Arabic (official language), Sudanese Arabic, Dinka

Surface area 0.97 million sq miles (2.51 million sq km)

Population 40.2 million

Religion
70% Sunni Muslim, 25% traditional religions, 5% Christian

Notable features
Sudan is the largest country in Africa.

What are Sudan's main economic sectors?

Despite possessing abundant natural resources such as petroleum, marble, uranium, and gold, Sudan remains one of the world's poorest countries. Its biggest overseas investor is the People's Republic of China, as much as eight per cent of whose petroleum imports are from Sudan.

What is the nature of the conflict that has been raging for years in Sudan?

With independence in 1956 came the outbreak of domestic disputes that developed into a full-blown civil war (1983–2005). At the heart of the war were religious and ethnic differences between the Arabic-Muslim north and the Christian-Black African south. The conflict prevented exploitation of the recently discovered petroleum fields in the southeast of the country. By April 2006 more than 300,000 refugees had fled to Chad from the Darfur region, where dreadful living conditions prevail.

By April 2006 nearly 300,000 people had been displaced by the civil war that raged without interruption between 1983 and 2005.

ERITREA

Flag

Currency
1 nakfa (ERN) = 100 cents

System of government
Republic since 1983

Capital
Asmara

Languages
Arabic, Tigrinya (official languages),
English

Surface area
46,842 sq miles (121,320 sq km)

Population 4.6 million

Religion
50% Christian, 50% Sunni Muslim

Notable features
Eritrea displays a wide variety of
climatic conditions ranging from
hot, dry coastal plains to temperate
highlands.

What does the name "Eritrea" mean?
The name "Eritrea" derives from the Greek for
"Red Sea" and refers to the country's geographical
location in East Africa on the coast of that body of
water. It shares borders with Sudan, Ethiopia, and
Djibouti.

When was Eritrea created?
Previously a patchwork of smaller territories ruled
by local princes (with the Eritrean Highlands under
the control of the Ethiopian emperor), Eritrea
became an Italian colony between 1890 and 1941.
When Italian colonial rule came to an end, the
United Nations federated Eritrea with Ethiopia.
A 30-year war of independence between 1960
and 1990 ended with Eritrea's emergence as an
independent state in 1993.

Is the country in a good economic state of health?
No. Eritrea has an extremely high rate of
unemployment (50 per cent). Of those with jobs,
50 per cent work in agriculture, which contributes no
more than 15 per cent to the economy. Food has
to be imported in order to meet the needs of the
population. The country possesses natural resources
such as gold, silver, copper, and petroleum, but
these remain largely unexploited and industry is
developing only slowly.

Do the Eritreans form a homogeneous ethnic group?
No. There are nine different ethnic groups in
Eritrea, of which the largest are the Tigrinya (41 per
cent) and the Tigre (32 per cent). Neither is there
any uniformity in terms of faith, as the population is
split equally between Christianity and Islam. Despite
these differences, the people of Eritrea constitute a
cohesive national unit.

A baby is weighed. Famine is an ever-present danger in Eritrea. Aid
organizations help to look after the population.

Female circumcision

Eritrea is one of the countries in which female circumcision
is still practiced. Ninety per cent of girls are subjected to this
cruel procedure for which there are no medical grounds.
The tradition of female circumcision has been exposed to
more and more public criticism recently. According to the
WHO (World Health Organization), between five per cent and
ten per cent of girls die during the procedure and a further
20 per cent from long-term complications.

The Ethiopian Orthodox Church (1.7 million members) has 1,500 churches (such as this one in Addis Ababa) and 22 monasteries in Ethiopia.

ETHIOPIA

Flag 	**Surface area** 0.44 million sq miles (1.13 million sq km)
Currency 1 birr (ETB) = 100 cents	**Population** 73.1 million
System of government Federal republic since 1994	**Religion** 55% Christian, 40% Sunni Muslim, 5% traditional religions
Capital Addis Ababa	**Notable features** Over 80 languages are spoken in Ethiopia.
Languages Amharic (official language), Oromo, English	

Ethiopian cuisine

An important staple of Ethiopian cuisine is the cereal grass teff. This ancient type of grain is known to have been grown in Ancient Egypt but is not now cultivated outside Ethiopia. Teff flour is used to make the Ethiopian national dish *injera*, a soft flatbread of about 20 inches (50 cm) served with a variety of sauces that are conveyed to the mouth with small pieces of the bread (no cutlery is used). The meal is heavily spiced with *berbere*.

A group of women carrying water back from Lake Tana (Africa's highest lake) in the Abyssinian Highlands.

What and where is Abyssinia?

Although Ethiopia is frequently referred to as Abyssinia, strictly speaking this name only applies to the mountains of central and northern Ethiopia. The Abyssinian Highlands are between 6,560 and 15,160 ft (2,000 and 4,620 m) high and extend for some 600 miles (1,000 km) north to south and 300 miles (500 km) east to west, which makes them roughly the same area as the Alps.

Is Ethiopia a Christian country?

Along with Armenia, Ethiopia was one of the earliest countries to adopt Christianity. Ethiopian Christians make up 45 per cent of the population with Protestant and Catholic Christians accounting for a further ten per cent. Forty per cent of Ethiopians are Muslims.

Who was Haile Selassie?

Haile Selassie I (1892–1975) was the last emperor of Ethiopia. He also bore the titles "King of Kings" and "Lion of Judah" and regarded himself as the 225th direct heir of the biblical King Solomon. Haile Selassie was deposed by the Ethiopian army in 1974 and died soon after while in detention.

MAURITANIA

Flag

Currency
1 ougiuya (MRO) = 5 khoums

System of government
Islamic presidential republic
since 1960

Capital
Nouakchott

Languages
Arabic (official language), French,
English

Surface area 0.40 million sq miles
(1.03 million sq km)

Population 3.1 million

Religion 99% Muslim

Is Mauritania a desert nation?
Yes. Most of the interior consists of sand dunes
and scree. Mauritania has only one river that runs
all year round: the Sénégal, in the south, which also
forms the boundary with Mauritania's southern
neighbor Senegal.

Is Mauritania a poor country?
Yes. Its hot and dry desert climate makes most of the
country unsuitable for agriculture. Eighty per cent of
inhabitants live in 15 per cent of the surface area in
the south. Mauritania is one of the poorest countries
in the world.

Does Mauritania have a long colonial history?
No. The coastline is not easily accessible, nothing
was known of any mineral wealth, and so the
colonial powers had little interest in the region.
The country was only incorporated into French
West Africa in 1904, mainly in order to facilitate
communications between France's North African
and West African colonies. Mauritania gained its
independence in 1960.

Today large parts of the ancient trading center of Chinguetti have been
abandoned to the desert.

Chinguetti
For centuries Mauritania was known as the "Land of
Chinguetti." Chinguetti, in northwestern Mauritania, is almost
1,000 years old and was an important Islamic cultural center
and a gathering point for West African pilgrims on their way to
Mecca. This small city was also at the crossroads of a number
of trading routes that ran through the Sahara. It still has five old
libraries housing medieval Qur'anic manuscripts. Chinguetti
has been designated a UNESCO World Heritage site.

What does the future hold for Mauritania's economy?
In addition to fishing and ore mining, Mauritania's
economy is based on agriculture, which only meets
the needs of the Mauritanian people. Only 0.2 per
cent of the surface area—predominantly in the
Sénégal valley—is suitable for agriculture. Hope for
the future rests in new dam projects that will enable
the irrigation of further expanses of land.

What was the Mali Empire?

The Mali Empire controlled large parts of West Africa in the 13th and 14th centuries. Its rulers bore the title Mansa, meaning "King of Kings." It achieved its greatest extent under Mansa Musa around 1320, when it stretched from the Atlantic to present-day Nigeria. Its rulers were renowned for their spectacular wealth.

What are the country's main physical features?

Mali is mostly flat and more than 60 per cent of the country is a desert, which covers the whole of the northern part of the country. The south has a more tropical climate, making agriculture possible. The most important river is the Niger, which flows through the south of the country.

What made Timbuktu legendary?

Today Timbuktu is a small oasis city in central Mali with around 30,000 inhabitants. In its heyday it was the capital of the Mali and Songhai empires and home to as many as 100,000 people. The city was the center of the gold and salt trade and became a byword for fabulous wealth.

MALI

Flag

Currency
1 Communauté Financière Africaine
CFA franc (XOF) = 100 centimes

System of government
Presidential republic since 1960

Capital Bamako

Languages
French (official language), Bambara, Fulfulde, Songhai

Surface area
0.48 million sq miles
(1.24 million sq km)

Population 12.3 million

Religion
90% Muslim, 8% traditional religions

Notable features
The Niger River forms a large inland delta called the Macina, a marshy depression that extends for some 280 miles (450 km).

Is Mali still a wealthy country?

No. Mali is one of the poorest and least developed countries in the world. Eighty per cent of its population work the land although only two per cent of the surface area is cultivable. The harvest is repeatedly threatened by long periods of drought. More than 80 per cent of the adult population are illiterate.

The Great Mosque of Djenné, built of clay bricks, was one of the most important centers of Islam in the Middle Ages.

The Great Mosque of Djenné

The Great Mosque in the city of Djenné in Mali is the world's largest clay-brick structure and one of Africa's best-known works of architecture. The current mosque was begun in 1906 but is based on a 13th-century model. It was designated a UNESCO World Heritage site in 1988.

NIGER

Flag

Currency
1 Communauté Financière Africaine
CFA franc (XOF) = 100 centimes

System of government
Parliamentary democracy

Capital Niamey

Languages
French (official language), Hausa, Zarma, Fulfulde

Surface area 0.49 million sq miles (1.26 million sq km)

Population 11.7 million

Religion
95% Muslim, 5% traditional religions and Christian

Much of the salt trade was previously in the hands of the Tuareg. Tuareg women enjoy a high social status and are regarded as the custodians of Tuareg culture.

Tuareg

The word "Tuareg" derives from Arabic and is widely—though probably inaccurately—interpreted as being cognate with *tarqi*, meaning "repudiated by God." The Tuareg's own names for themselves are Kel Tagelmust, meaning "People of the Veil," and Imuschaq, meaning "the Free." They are also occasionally referred to as the "Blue People" because of their indigo clothing. The Tuareg people are Berber in origin and have lived for centuries as nomads in areas of the Sahara and Sahel zone covered by present-day Mali, Niger, Burkina Faso, Mauritania, Nigeria, and Algeria. They are thought to number around 500,000. The Tuareg in Niger are in rebellion against the government, which is trying to force them to change their traditional nomadic way of life.

Why is the Republic of Niger repeatedly struck by famine?

Niger is one of the world's poorest and least developed nations. Two thirds of the country is covered by the Sahara and only a narrow strip along the border with Nigeria in the south can be used for agriculture.

What causes the problem of soil erosion?

General clearing and the felling of trees for firewood exposes the forest floor and fields to the full power of the sun. This causes the ground to dry out and prevents fertilizer from having any effect, leading to increased erosion and the loss of nutrients in the soil. In order to avoid wholesale desertification, a program of large-scale planting was initiated in the 1980s. The acacia species *Faidherbia albida* has proved particularly suitable and some 7.5 million acres (3 million hectares) have been planted. Further deforestation has been prevented and large areas of land have been won for agricultural use.

CHAD

Flag	
Currency	**Surface area**
1 Communauté Financière Africaine	0.49 million sq miles
CFA franc (XAF) = 100 centimes	(1.28 sq million km)
System of government	**Population** 9.8 million
Presidential republic since 1960	**Religion**
Capital N'Djamena	50% Muslim, 30% Christian,
Languages	20% traditional religions
Modern Standard Arabic, French	**Notable features**
(official languages), Chad Arabic, Maba	Chad is around five times the size of Wyoming but has only 250 miles (400 km) of constructed roads.

Surface area
0.49 million sq miles
(1.28 sq million km)
Population 9.8 million
Religion
50% Muslim, 30% Christian,
20% traditional religions
Notable features
Chad is around five times the size of
Wyoming but has only 250 miles
(400 km) of constructed roads.

Does Chad have adequate water supplies?
No. The dry regions (the Sahara and Sahel zone in the north and center of the country) far outweigh the almost tropical regions of the south, the only areas of the country to benefit from any substantial rainfall. Because of the strong population growth and frequent drought years, wells are being dug unchecked, creating the long-term problem of a drop in the water table. This in turn results in a reduction in the water level of, for example, Lake Chad in the southwest.

How many languages are spoken in the country?
Members of over 200 ethnic groups live in Chad, many of whom have their own languages or dialects. As a result, over 100 languages and dialects are spoken, with the majority of Chadians speaking more than one. The main language is Arabic, which is spoken by 26 per cent of the population. French, the other official language, is only spoken by an educated minority.

What is the country's biggest political problem?
Since 2003 increasing numbers of refugees from the war-torn region of Darfur in western Sudan have been pouring over the border (more than 300,000 up to April 2006). Without international aid Chad is not in a position to cope with this stream of refugees. Furthermore, armed clashes with rebel forces from Sudan have claimed hundreds of lives as well.

Left: The United Nations has called Darfur the greatest humanitarian crisis facing mankind. The children shown here are refugees from Sudan and are living in a camp in Farchana.

Interesting facts

- The study into corruption published by Transparency International in 2006 ranks Chad 157th of the 163 states investigated, indicating that it has one of the highest levels of corruption in the world.

- Due to inadequate medical care, thousands die of meningitis, malaria, cholera, and measles each year.

- 80 per cent of the population live in absolute poverty.

The Ennedi Massif in northern Chad may have been the original source of the Amazon when this region was part of the supercontinent Gondwana 130 million years ago.

CAPE VERDE

Flag

Currency
1 Cape Verdean escudo (CVE)
= 100 centavos

System of government
Republic since 1975

Capital
Praia

Languages
Portuguese (official language), Creole

Surface area
1,558 sq miles (4,036 sq km)

Population 495,000

Religion
90% Catholic, 10% Protestant

Notable features
This island nation consists of 15 islands, of which nine are inhabited.

Tarrafal
The name of Tarrafal, a municipality on Santiago, the largest of the Cape Verde islands, was once enough to make the Portuguese shudder with fear. Between 1933 and 1974 it was the site of a concentration camp in which political opponents of the Salazar dictatorship in Portugal were held.

What are the origins of the people of Cape Verde?
Prior to their discovery by the Portuguese in 1456, the islands were uninhabited. Thereafter they attracted repeated waves of settlers from Portugal but large numbers later left the islands due to famine. The current population is descended from the offspring of Portuguese settlers and African slaves although more Cape Verdeans now live overseas than on the islands themselves.

Why were the Cape Verde islands important to Portugal?
The islands were used by the Portuguese mainly as military outposts from which further voyages of discovery could be protected. In the 16th century the island of Santiago in particular acquired a role as a slave-trading post on the route between America and Africa. Cape Verde gained its independence from Portugal in 1975.

What are the problems facing the national economy?
Cape Verde has no natural resources and, due to its dry desert climate, agriculture is almost impossible. As a result, over 90 per cent of food has to be imported. Money transfers from Cape Verdean emigrants account for some 20 per cent of the population's income.

How important a role does tourism play?
The tourist industry is still very underdeveloped and contributes only ten per cent of the national economy. So far it has only succeeded in luring beach lovers, sailors, and surfers to the islands. There are no real attractions for nature lovers and cultural tourists.

A small fishing port on Santo Antão, the second-largest of the Cape Verde islands. The catch is sold from the harbor itself.

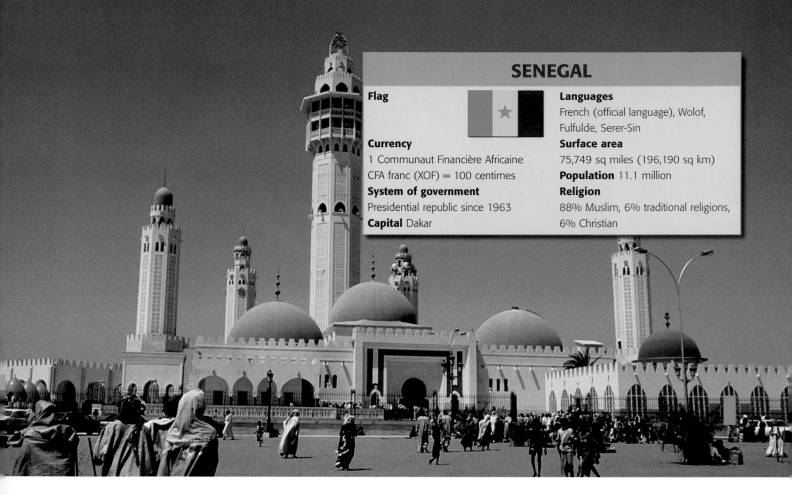

SENEGAL

Flag	**Languages** French (official language), Wolof, Fulfulde, Serer-Sin
Currency 1 Communaut Financière Africaine CFA franc (XOF) = 100 centimes	**Surface area** 75,749 sq miles (196,190 sq km) **Population** 11.1 million
System of government Presidential republic since 1963	**Religion** 88% Muslim, 6% traditional religions,
Capital Dakar	6% Christian

What was the Casamance conflict?

This is the name given to the armed conflict between the Senegalese government and the Mouvement des Forces Démocratiques de la Casamance (MFDC). The conflict started with a declaration of independence by the people of the Casamance region of southern Senegal. The Jola people had been organizing peaceful pro-independence demonstrations until their leaders were imprisoned in 1982, when a civil-war-like conflict broke out that cost several thousand lives.

What happened to the ferry *La Joola*?

The ferry *La Joola*, named after the Jola ethnic group, was the most important ferry service linking Dakar with the Casamance region. This vessel was designed to carry 550 passengers, 13 vehicles, and 275 tons (250 tonnes) of cargo. On September 26, 2002 *La Joola* capsized with the loss of 1,863 lives. Only 65 people could be saved. The accident led to a crisis in Senegal and the dismissal of the government by President Abdoulaye Wade.

What is special about Lake Retba?

The French name for this salt lake of 1.15 sq miles (3 sq km) outside Dakar is called Lac Rose, "the pink lake." Separated from the sea by nothing but a sand dune, the lake has taken on this hue due to certain cyanobacteria and microorganisms that live in the salt. The shores of the lake are lined with mounds of salt, which is harvested here. Because of its extremely high salt content (over 3 lb per gallon/400 g per liter), swimmers can float effortlessly on the water as in the Dead Sea. Lake Retba is the final destination of the Dakar Rally.

The faithful on their way to prayers in the Great Mosque of Touba.

A group of fishermen sit under the spreading boughs of a fig tree on the bank of the Casamance River in Kafountine.

GAMBIA

Flag

Currency
1 dalasi (GMD) = 100 bututs

System of government
Presidential republic since 1970
(Commonwealth member)

Capital
Banjul

Languages English (official language),
Mandingo, Wolof, Fulfulde

Surface area
4,361 sq miles (11,295 sq km)

Population 1.6 million

Religion 90% Muslim, 9% Christian

Notable features
Other than along its Atlantic coastline,
Gambia is completely surrounded by
Senegal.

A Senegambian stone circle. Visitors place pebbles on the megaliths for good luck.

What are the origins of the country's name?
Gambia is located in West Africa along the shores of the Gambia River. The name is believed to have originated with the Portuguese word *câmbio*, meaning "exchange" or "trade." This would have referred to the mouth of the river, where Portuguese sailors traded with the local people.

Which colonial powers played a role in Gambia's history?
Portuguese merchants had begun visiting the coast of West Africa as long ago as the 15th century. In the 17th and 18th centuries the French and the British vied for control of the rivers in Senegal and Gambia. Great Britain won control of Gambia in 1763 and transported ivory, gold, and slaves from the interior by river.

Does Gambia possess natural resources?
No. Gambia has no economically significant mineral wealth. The population depends for its living on agriculture, tourism, and fishing. Peanuts are the country's main agricultural export. Gambia is one of the poorest countries in the world.

What are Senegambian stone circles?
Along the Gambia River there are more than 1,000 megaliths weighing around a ton each arranged in a circle or double circle. These stones range in height up to around 8 ft (2.5 m). Archaeologists have not been able to ascertain who built these stone circles or what their significance was. It is possible that they are the tombs of ancient rulers. They were added to UNESCO's list of World Heritage sites in 2006.

Sacred crocodiles

In Gambia the crocodile is of enormous symbolic importance. Throughout West Africa the shapes visible on the surface of the moon are interpreted as crocodiles. Just outside Bakau is the sacred crocodile pool of Kachikally, which is believed to have been looked after by the Bojang family since the 13th century. The crocodile is regarded as a symbol of fertility and adorns Gambia's coins.

Why is Portuguese spoken in Guinea-Bissau?

The Portuguese occupied the coastal strip as early as 1466 and the rest of the country only much later. They named their territory Portuguese Guinea. Guinea-Bissau gained its independence from Portugal in 1974. Only 14 per cent of the population speak Portuguese proper; the majority speak Portuguese Creole, a simplified form of Portuguese supplemented by elements of the local tribal languages.

Is Guinea-Bissau a developed country?

No. Guinea-Bissau is one of the ten poorest countries in the world. The population depends on agriculture for its livelihood but the country is unable to produce enough food to feed itself. There is no industry. In recent times the country has become a major exporter of cashew nuts. Guinea-Bissau does possess petroleum deposits but these have so far proven too expensive to develop.

Bissagos Archipelago

The Bissagos Archipelago is a group of 88 islands off the coast of Guinea-Bissau. Before the arrival of the Portuguese in the 15th century, the inhabitants of the archipelago had built up a large fleet of boats. They played an important role in West African trade and even managed to defend themselves against the Portuguese. It was not until 1936 that the islands were (in part) annexed by Portugal. After gaining independence in 1974 the islands became part of Guinea-Bissau.

A fisherman scoops water out of his traditional canoe made from a single tree trunk.

GUINEA-BISSAU

Flag

Currency
1 Communauté Financière Africaine CFA franc (XOF) = 100 centimes

System of government
Presidential republic since 1973

Capital Bissau

Languages
Portuguese (official language), Portuguese Creole, Fulfulde, Mandingo

Surface area
13,946 sq miles (36,129 sq km)

Population 1.4 million

Religion
50% Muslim, 40% traditional religions, 10% Christian

Notable features
The Bissagos Archipelago makes up 22% of the surface area of Guinea-Bissau.

Grain drying on platforms constructed of wood and palm leaves.

Does Guinea-Bissau have a state-run school system?

Officially children are required to attend school for six years. In practice, however, few children go to school, either because their parents need them to help in the fields or the nearest school is too far away. As a result, Guinea-Bissau has an illiteracy rate of 61 per cent. The country's only secondary schools are in the capital Bissau and there is no university.

GUINEA

Flag

Currency
1 Guinea franc (GNF) = 100 centimes

System of government
Presidential republic since 1991

Capital
Conakry

Languages
French (official language), Fulfulde, Malinka

Surface area
94,922 sq miles (245,847 sq km)

Population 9.5 million

Religion
85% Muslim, 8% Christian, 7% traditional religions

Notable features
At 5,748 ft (1,752 m) Mount Nimba is Guinea's highest mountain. It is also the Ivory Coast's highest peak as the border runs across its summit.

What are Guinea's different population groups?
There are around 20 different ethnic groups in Guinea. The main ones are the Fulbe (40 per cent) and the Malinke (30 per cent) peoples. The Fulbe are relatively light-skinned and there is some evidence that their forefathers originated in Egypt. The Malinke were the main ethnic group in the Mali Empire, whose heyday was the 15th century and which was fabled for its wealth.

Is Guinea a poor country?
Yes. It is one of the poorest countries in the world. Eighty per cent of the population work in agriculture, which serves mainly to meet the country's own needs, making up only two per cent of the country's exports. Guinea's industry is relatively undeveloped.

Does Guinea have natural resources?
Yes, in abundance. Guinea is thought to have almost half the world's bauxite deposits and the country is the world's second-largest supplier of the aluminum ore after Australia. It also possesses iron ore, uranium, diamonds, and gold. Mineral resources account for 85 per cent of Guinea's exports.

Fishermen in dug-out canoes. Small boats made from a single tree trunk are used not only by primitive peoples but by modern societies too.

When did Guinea gain its independence?
Having been a French colony since 1892, Guinea eventually became fully independent in 1958 when, under the direction of Charles de Gaulle, France held a referendum where its colonies could choose independence. The other countries in French West Africa did not achieve this status until 1960.

Sékou Touré
Sékou Touré (1922–1984) led Guinea to independence in 1958 and became the first president of the new nation. Independence was followed by a split with France and Touré propagated a form of pan-African socialism. In Guinea he established one of Africa's cruelest dictatorships, from which at least two million people were forced to flee. Current president Colonel Lansana Conté came to power in 1984 after Touré's death.

SIERRA LEONE

Flag	**Languages**
	English (official language), Mende, Temne
Currency	**Surface area**
1 leone (SLL) = 100 cents	27,699 sq miles (71,740 sq km)
System of government	**Population** 6 million
Presidential republic since 1978	**Religion**
(Commonwealth member)	70% Muslim, 15% traditional religions,
Capital	15% Christian
Freetown	

Why is the country called Sierra Leone?

The coastline was named Sierra Leone (meaning "lion mountains") by the Portuguese when they came upon it for the first time in 1460. From the sea, two rounded mountains resemble a sleeping lion.

How did Freetown acquire its name?

Sierra Leone's capital Freetown was established in 1787 as a settlement for freed slaves. A British organization named the Black Poor Society helped Africans who had fought for the United Kingdom during the American War of Independence in 1776 and had been left without any means of support to return home.

Where are the Banana Islands?

These three small islands are located off the tip of the Freetown Peninsula. The two main islands, Dublin and Rickets, are linked by a causeway. The third island, Mes-Meheux, is uninhabited. The islands are a paradise for divers thanks to their white sandy beaches and clear waters.

Does Sierra Leone possess mineral resources?

Sierra Leone is very rich in mineral resources but due to the civil war that raged throughout the 1990s, for the last decade or so it has been one of the world's poorest and least developed nations.

Interesting facts: Diamond smuggling

Sierra Leone's bloody civil war, which lasted from 1991 until 2002, was financed by the diamond trade and diamond smuggling. When the war ended, the shady dealing continued. In 2003 70 nations signed a certification agreement aimed at putting an end to the black marketeering but this did not succeed either. It is estimated that around 50 per cent of all uncut diamonds originating in Sierra Leone are traded illegally. The legal trade in diamonds is worth some 140 million US dollars per year.

Above: Exotic and colorful species thrive in Sierra Leone's tropical climate.

Workers in a diamond mine. During the civil war, official prospecting came to a virtual standstill.

LIBERIA

Flag	**Surface area**
	43,000 sq miles (111,370 sq km)
	Population 3.5 million
Currency	**Religion**
1 Liberian dollar (LRD) = 100 cents	40% Christian, 20% Muslim,
System of government	40% traditional religions
Presidential republic since 1847	**Notable features**
Capital	Liberia extends back from the coast
Monrovia	in three stages. The coastal plain
Languages	is succeeded by a central plateau
English (official language), Mande, Kru,	covered by rainforest, which is in turn
others	followed by the mountainous interior.

Liberia's lengthy civil war caused thousands of Liberians to flee their homes. In many cases they were only able to take what they could physically carry themselves.

Why is Liberia's flag similar to the USA's?

At the beginning of the 19th century the American Colonization Society, under the chairmanship of US president James Monroe (1758–1831), purchased land in West Africa on which to settle freed Afro-American slaves. In 1822 the society founded the city of Monrovia (named after James Monroe). When Liberia became independent in 1847, its flag was chosen in honor of the United States.

How many of the population are descended from Afro-American slaves?

Only around 2.5 per cent of the current population are descended from freed slaves. Until 1980, however, they held all the important offices and positions and at times behaved like colonial rulers towards the majority of the population. This pre-eminence was brought to an end by a coup in 1980, albeit at the cost of a long-drawn-out civil war.

Does Liberia possess mineral resources?

Yes. There are substantial deposits of iron ore in the Nimba Mountains. These once formed the basis of Liberia's economy but during the civil war the mining facilities were destroyed and extraction came to a standstill. Current president Ellen Johnson-Sirleaf has won an agreement from ArcelorMittal, the world's largest steel company, to invest one billion US dollars in resuscitating the iron ore industry. It is hoped that the project will create 20,000 new jobs and attract additional investors to the country.

Flag of convenience

Many shipping companies find it makes sense to register their vessels in a foreign country. Not only can this offer tax advantages, it also allows them to circumvent stringent regulations governing the remuneration and social welfare benefits of their crews. Two of the main flags of convenience are offered by Panama and Liberia. Around 1,600 ships throughout the world are registered under the Liberian flag.

IVORY COAST

Flag

Currency
1 Communauté Financière Africaine
CFA franc (XOF) = 100 centimes

System of government
Presidential republic since 1960

Capital Yamoussoukro

Languages
French (official language), 70 national languages

Surface area
124,502 sq miles (322,460 sq km)

Population 17.3 million

Religion
34% Christian, 27% Muslim, 15% traditional religions

Notable features
The elephant, from whose tusks the country takes its name, is now extremely rare and under strict protection.

Notre Dame de la Paix

The first president of Ivory Coast, Félix Houphouët-Boigny (1905–1993), was responsible for the construction in the capital Yamoussoukro of a cathedral based on St Peter's in Rome—in Italian marble. Constructed between 1986 and 1989, Notre Dame de la Paix became the largest place of Christian worship in the world and was consecrated by Pope John Paul II in 1990. The project was heavily criticized for wasting money that would have been more wisely spent on eradicating the country's economic and social problems.

Left: Thousands of illegal workers continue to prospect for diamonds in the disused diamond mine in Tortiya.

The elephant is Ivory Coast's heraldic animal.

What are the origins of the country's name?

The country takes its name from what was once its biggest export product and dates back to French colonial times. The country's official name is Côte d'Ivoire, and, in the country itself, use of any other version is a punishable offense.

What does the country export?

Until the 1990s Ivory Coast was one of the world's biggest cocoa producers and was regarded as a prosperous country. A collapse in world cocoa prices created economic difficulties that in turn brought about a deep political crisis.

Who governs Ivory Coast?

Since September 2002 the country has effectively been split into two. The north is controlled by rebel factions of the army, the south by government troops. A large contingent of UN forces has been deployed to Ivory Coast to keep the opposing sides apart. All attempts to disarm the belligerent parties have so far failed.

When did Abidjan cease to be the capital?

The port of Abidjan was the capital under French rule and remains Ivory Coast's largest city by far. Its population has exploded from 65,000 in 1950 to 3.7 million in 2005. In 1983 Félix Houphouët-Boigny, Ivory Coast's first president, decided to move the capital to his place of birth. Yamoussoukro is located in the interior and has around 200,000 inhabitants.

BURKINA FASO

Flag

Currency
1 Communauté Financière Africaine
CFA franc (XOF) = 100 centimes

System of government
Presidential republic

Capital
Ouagadougou

Languages
French (official language), Mossi, Dioula

Surface area
105,869 sq miles (274,200 sq km)

Population 14 million

Religion 50% Muslim, 40%
traditional religions, 10% Catholic

Notable features
Burkina Faso was called Upper Volta
until 1984.

Was Burkina Faso once under colonial rule?

The country came under French colonial rule in 1888. From 1919 it was known as Upper Volta but was subsequently partitioned between neighboring French possessions for a time. Upper Volta gained its independence in 1960 and changed its name to Burkina Faso in 1984.

What is the basis of Burkina Faso's economy?

Burkina Faso's poor farmers grow millet, sorghum, rice, and corn primarily to satisfy their own needs, in other words at a subsistence level, and the country still relies on food imports. Cotton is grown for export and the nation's only developed industries are in the food processing and textiles sectors.

Burkina Faso is home to around 60 different ethnic groups. Many villages still have the traditional round huts.

Is Burkina Faso a poor country?

This landlocked country in West Africa is one of the poorest nations on the planet. It is located on a high plateau and extends as far north as the Sahel zone. Most of its people live off the land and suffer enormously from the regular periods of drought that afflict the country.

What is Ouaga 2000?

There are very few modern buildings in Ouagadougou, which looks more like an enormous village than a capital city. Most of the city is without electricity or running water. In order to make space for a modern development project, all single-story buildings in the center have been demolished and a new administrative district is being built on the southern edges of the city. Ouaga 2000 will include new presidential offices and a major sports arena.

Africa's Che Guevara

Thomas Sankara (1949–1987), Burkina Faso's fifth president, was a left-wing leader who was particularly well admired by the country's youth and women, whose status he strove to improve. In 1987 he was killed in a military coup. Because of the similarity between his ideas and those of the South American revolutionary, he was nicknamed "Africa's Che Guevara."

The Old Mosque in the village of Larabanga dates from 1421. It is thought to be the oldest building in Ghana.

What was Gold Coast?

Gold Coast was a British colony and part of British West Africa from 1878 to 1958. The crown colony covered the southern portion of present-day Ghana. It was called "Gold Coast" because of a major find of that precious metal in the interior.

What is the "Star of Hope"?

After independence a black, five-pointed star was incorporated into the flag of the new country to symbolize the hope of economic progress. The star also features on Black Star Arch, a triumphal arch in the capital Accra that commemorates the achievement of independence.

Does Ghana still benefit from its gold?

Although Ghana's share of the worldwide gold trade is very modest today, its gold exports are still of immense economic importance to the country, making up around 30 per cent of total exports. Total export earnings are very low, however, meaning that Ghana is still one of the poorest countries in the world.

How do the Ghanaians support themselves?

Ghana is still an agrarian country and the majority of Ghanaians are subsistence farmers—around 60 per cent of the people work in agriculture and fishing. It is hoped that tourism will bring a boost to the economy.

The world's largest reservoir

Lake Volta, some 60 miles (100 km) northeast of Ghana's capital Accra, is the largest reservoir in the world, with a surface area of 3,282 sq miles (8,501 sq km). It was completed in 1966 as a hydroelectricity facility but also provides protection against flooding. The passenger ferries and goods vessels that now ply across Lake Volta play an important role in the regional communications network.

Young women carry heavy loads around Accra for 3 US dollars a day.

TOGO

Flag

Currency
1 Communaut Financière Africaine
CFA franc (XOF) = 100 centimes

System of government
Presidential republic since 1967

Capital Lomé

Languages
French, Kabiyé, Ewe (official languages)

Surface area
21,925 sq miles (56,785 sq km)

Population 5.7 million

Religion
50% traditional religions,
35% Christian, 15% Muslim

Members of
the Tamberma
tribe in Togo
live in two-story
stronghold-like
dwellings made of
mud called *tatas*.
Similar structures
are also found in
Burkina Faso
and Benin.

Who were the colonial powers in Togo?
Between 1884 and the end of the First World War Togo and the eastern part of Ghana formed a German colony (Togoland). After the war, control of the colony passed to France. Togo achieved independence in 1960.

What are Togo's main exports?
Togo's main exports are palm oil, palm kernels, corn, cotton, rubber, cocoa, coffee, and peanuts. Germany is the recipient of around two thirds of the country's total production.

A small Roman Catholic church in Togoville. Christians are outnumbered in Togo by followers of traditional religions.

What was the difference between a protectorate and a colony?
There was often no difference. The term "protectorate" was generally a euphemism. White overlords would set foot on African soil and swear to look after and protect a land and its people but in reality they pursued only their own interests and protected the land only against other colonial powers. To start with, private trading companies were often the first to arrive in a particular territory and would sign agreements with indigenous rulers in which they undertook to protect the land and its people. The interior would then be conquered by force. During the second half of the 19th century in particular, it was often a question of one colonial power vying with another (mainly the United Kingdom against France and vice versa).

Togo's rich fauna
Among Togo's biggest animal populations are giraffes, water buffalo, rhinoceros, hyena, warthogs, and baboons. Elephants and lions have become very rare in the country's savannas and rainforests as a result of extreme deforestation.

Why was Benin formerly known as Dahomey?
The French conquered the Kingdom of
Dahomey, which covered the area of present-day
Benin, at the end of the 19th century. Until 1960
the region was part of French West Africa (capital:
Dakar in what is now Senegal). After independence
the country was called Dahomey until 1975, when
its name was changed by the Marxist-Leninist
government of the day to the People's Republic
of Benin.

Is there a high rate of illiteracy in Benin?
Yes. In 2005 60 per cent of men and 75 per cent
of women were illiterate. Literacy is an important
goal in the fight against poverty. There is still a
significant difference between the numbers of girls
and boys attending primary school.

What economic goods does the country produce?
Benin's economy is based almost entirely on
agriculture, on which 90 per cent of the people
depend for their livelihood. Traditional crops
such as corn, cassava, and yams are grown on a
small scale and cotton is virtually the only export.
Livestock farming plays only a marginal role in the
economy.

BENIN		
Flag	**Languages** French (official language), 90 local languages and dialects	
Currency 1 Communauté Financière Africaine CFA franc (XOF) = 100 centimes	**Surface area** 43,483 sq miles (112,620 sq km)	
System of government Presidential republic since 1991	**Population** 7.5 million	
Capital Porto Novo	**Religion** 50% traditional religions, 21% Catholic, 20% Muslim	

What is voodoo?
Voodoo is a religion that originated in West
Africa and is now common in Benin, Ghana, and
Togo. It is practiced by 17 per cent of Benin's
population. In the West the term "voodoo" is
associated mainly with black magic and
voodoo dolls, which were originally
representations of the religion's
deities.

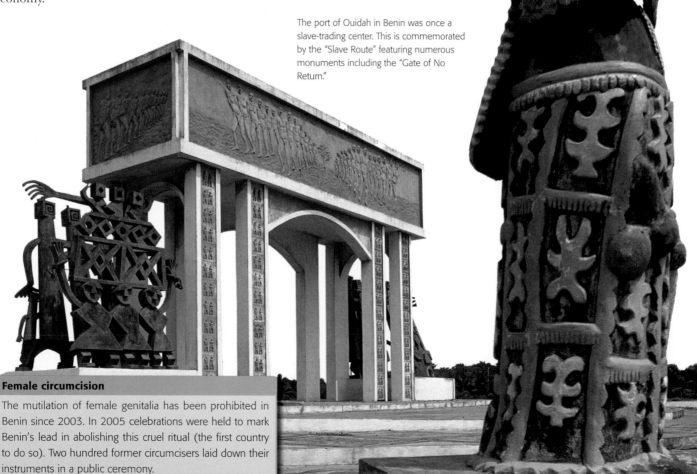

The port of Ouidah in Benin was once a
slave-trading center. This is commemorated
by the "Slave Route" featuring numerous
monuments including the "Gate of No
Return."

Female circumcision
The mutilation of female genitalia has been prohibited in
Benin since 2003. In 2005 celebrations were held to mark
Benin's lead in abolishing this cruel ritual (the first country
to do so). Two hundred former circumcisers laid down their
instruments in a public ceremony.

NIGERIA

Flag

Currency
1 naira (NGN) = 100 kobo

System of government
Presidential federal republic since
1979 (Commonwealth member)

Capital
Abuja

Languages
English (official language), Yoruba, Kwa
languages (including a colloquial form
of Hausa)

Surface area
356,669 sq miles (923,768 sq km)

Population 140 million

Religion
50% Muslim, 40% Christian, 10%
traditional religions

In Makoko, near Lagos, women sell their wares from canoes.

Is there ethnic conflict in Nigeria?

Nigeria was a British colony for nearly 100 years, from 1861 until independence in 1960. Since then there have been regular armed clashes between the Muslim north and the Christian south. Nigeria is home to some 280 different ethnic groups, the largest of which are the Ibo, making up 30 per cent of the population, and the Yoruba, making up 20 per cent. Due to the permanently simmering violence, the country has not been able to exploit its petroleum resources enough to drag itself out of poverty.

What was Biafra?

Biafra was a small state in eastern Nigeria that existed for barely three years (between 1967 and 1970). It owed its existence to a military coup and was never recognized by any other nations. The state took its name from the Bight of Biafra, a bay in the Gulf of Guinea. During the entire period of its existence as an independent state, Biafra was at war with Nigeria and the conflict ended up costing over two million lives. Children were among the main victims of the three-year famine caused by the war.

Which type of crime is causing major social problems in Nigeria?

Organized gangs regularly tap into the petroleum pipelines that cross the country and sell the stolen petroleum on the black market. The authorities are doing nothing to stop these activities, which often result in powerful explosions caused by sparks or carelessness with fire. Hundreds of people have lost their lives in this way.

Interesting facts
- Nigeria is Africa's most populous country.
- Since the 1970s Nigeria has been the continent's biggest petroleum exporter.

What kind of environmental damage does Nigeria suffer from?

In the Niger Delta and along the pipelines that run—with no consideration for the population—through the middle of villages and across pasturage and arable land, the environment has suffered from almost irreparable damage over the last 40 years.

Does Nigeria have compulsory school attendance?

Yes. But because of a shortage of teachers—due to unpaid salaries—and inadequate infrastructure, almost 50 per cent of children do not attend school at all. In the northern states many schools have closed completely. Only Qur'an schools remain active, but in addition to contributing to the education of children, they often serve to aggravate the smoldering religious and ethnic hostility.

Polio

In 2004 Muslim clerics started a rumor that the polio vaccine caused infertility. In large parts of the country the whispering campaign bore fruit and the local authorities suspended vaccinations. As a result, Nigeria had more cases of polio that year than anywhere else in the world—more than 800 of the 1,250 cases. Not only did Nigeria suffer from the consequences of this prejudice, the disease also spread to the neighboring countries.

Does Nigeria have a film industry of any substance?

Nigeria's film industry, nicknamed Nollywood, is extremely vibrant and provides the whole of Africa with TV soap operas. A number of scriptwriters have even succeeded in selling their screenplays in the United States as much of their work is highly dramatic. In terms of the number of films produced within its borders (estimated at between 1,000 and 2,000 per year), Nigeria is the third-largest film nation in the world.

Oshodi Road is one of the main arteries in Lagos.

Nigerian musician Fela Kuti (1938–1997) was an active campaigner for the rights of the poor.

CAMEROON

Flag

Currency
1 Communauté Financière Africaine
CFA franc (XAF) = 100 centimes

System of government
Presidential republic since 1972
(Commonwealth member)

Capital Yaoundé

Languages
French, English (official languages),
200 languages and dialects

Surface area
183,553 sq miles (475,400 sq km)

Population 16.4 million

Religion
53% Christian, 25% traditional
religions, 22% Muslim

Notable features
Bioko Island is only 25 miles (40 km)
off the coast of Cameroon but belongs
to Cameroon's southern neighbor
Equatorial Guinea.

What is Cameroon's highest mountain called?
At 13,435 ft (4,095 m) Mount Cameroon is
not only Cameroon's highest mountain, it is also the
highest point in the whole of Central Africa. It is
an active volcano located in the west of the country
close to the Atlantic coast. Cameroon's entire
northwest coast is dominated by a volcanic mountain
range that gradually drops down on the east towards
the inland plateau.

Which country was the colonial power in Cameroon?
Cameroon remained independent of European
control until 1884, when it became a German
Protectorate following a period of growing German
influence. After the First World War France and
the United Kingdom were awarded the League of
Nations mandate. The larger French part achieved
independence in 1960 and the British part a year
later. The two halves united in 1961 to form the
Republic of Cameroon.

Are there gorillas in Cameroon?
Yes. There are two main species of gorilla, the
western lowland and the eastern lowland, which
inhabit different parts of Central Africa. Cameroon is
the home of the western lowland gorilla, a subspecies
of which (the Cross River gorilla) is facing extinction.
Only 200 or so animals remain in its habitat in the
border region between Nigeria and Cameroon.

What does Cameroon export?
Petroleum, timber, cocoa, and coffee. Agriculture, in
which 60 per cent of the workforce are employed,
accounts for most of the country's economic output.
One of the main problems standing in the way of
Cameroon's economic development is corruption,
which is widespread.

Douala

Cameroon's largest city is Douala, on the Atlantic coast. Douala
was the national capital until 1920, when Yaoundé, which is
located further inland, took over the role. Douala possesses the
country's largest harbor and remains Cameroon's economic
and cultural center.

*A village
in Cameroon
with typical
straw-roofed
round huts
constructed of
clay bricks.*

Who are the inhabitants of the Central African Republic?

The original inhabitants of the Central African Republic were pygmies but, other than a small number of surviving tribes, they have all died out. Other ethnic groups include the Bantu, Sara, Runga, and Azande peoples. A few thousand Europeans, mainly French, live in the cities.

Which animals live in the Central African Republic?

The dense rainforest in the south is the last refuge of lowland gorillas and forest elephants in the country. Antelope, apes, buffalo, rare birds, monitor lizards, and hippopotamus live in the savannas.

What mineral resources does the country possess?

The country's most important minerals are diamonds but the Central African Republic nevertheless remains one of the poorest nations in the world. In 2003 roughly 67 per cent of the population lived on less than one US dollar per day.

Why did France support the Bokassa regime?

France supported Bokassa (see box) in exchange for uranium for its nuclear weapons program. President Valéry Giscard d'Estaing (born 1926) fostered particularly close contacts with the dictator.

CENTRAL AFRICAN REPUBLIC

Flag

Currency
1 Communauté Financière Africaine
CFA franc (XAF) = 100 centimes

System of government
Presidential republic since 1986

Capital Bangui

Languages
French, Sango (official languages), Banda, Fulfulde

Surface area
240,535 sq miles (622,984 sq km)

Population 3.8 million

Religion
55% tribal religions, 30% Christian, approximately 15% Muslim

Jean-Bédel Bokassa

Jean-Bédel Bokassa (1921–1996) came to power in a military coup in 1966 and had himself crowned emperor ten years later in a ceremony costing 30 million US dollars. Torture and executions in which he is believed to have participated himself made him widely feared and allegations of cannibalism were even made, though disproven during his trial in 1987. When Bokassa died at the age of 75 in 1996, he left 17 wives and at least 50 children.

African forest elephants are shown here digging in the mineral-rich mud of Dzanga-Ndoki National Park.

SÃO TOMÉ AND PRÍNCIPE

Flag

Currency
1 dobra (STD) = 100 centimos

System of government
Presidential republic since 1975

Capital
São Tomé

Languages
Portuguese (official language), Crioulo
(Portuguese Creole)

Surface area
386 sq miles (1,001 sq km)

Population 187,000

Religion
80% Catholic, 10% Protestant

Notable features
The United States wanted to establish
a military base here in order to help
it pursue its interest in the nation's
petroleum deposits.

Supporters of the center-right ADI (Independent Democratic Action)
party at a demonstration in São Tomé concerning use of the recently
discovered petroleum fields.

When were the islands discovered?

Portuguese seafarer João Santarém (dates
unknown) discovered the island of São Tomé in
1471 and the island of Príncipe, which he initially
named Santo António (it was renamed in 1502),
a year later. In 1469 King Alfonso V of Portugal
had sold exploration rights under which individuals
undertook to explore Africa's coastline at their
own expense but in the name and to the glory of
Portugal. Santarém was acting in the service of
merchant Fernão Gomes.

Are there volcanoes on the islands?

Both islands are volcanic in origin but there are no
active volcanoes on the islands any more.

Which products form the basis of the island nation's economy?

During its time as a Portuguese colony São Tomé
and Príncipe was a monoculture plantation economy
based initially on sugar cane. This was replaced
by coffee and later by cocoa. At the beginning of
the 20th century São Tomé was the world's biggest
producer of cocoa, which still makes up over 90 per
cent of its exports.

What raw materials do the islands possess?

São Tomé and Príncipe possesses rich petroleum and
natural gas fields. This is true not only of the islands
but also of the entire West African coast. A race to
secure the offshore prospecting and drilling rights is
already developing between the People's Republic of
China and the United States.

Creole

Creole is the term used to describe a pidgin or hybrid
language that has become the accepted native tongue of a
particular district or region (see Solomon Islands on p.280).
This has occurred in areas where there has been intensive
contact between the language spoken by the indigenous
people on the one hand and a European language—usually
French, Portuguese, or English—on the other.

Many old colonial-era plantation buildings, such as those of Roca
Bombaim shown here, have been abandoned and left to decay.

Is Equatorial Guinea on the Equator?

Despite its name, Equatorial Guinea on the west coast of Africa lies not on the Equator but slightly north of it. Nearly 90 per cent of the country is on the mainland, the remainder being split between several islands. The capital Malabo, which is home to roughly 20 per cent of the national population, is located on Bioko, the largest of the islands.

Who is Fernão Pó?

The Portuguese explorer Fernão Pó discovered the island of Bioko in the Gulf of Guinea in 1472. The Portuguese were at that time searching for a southern sea route to India. The island was named after the explorer until 1973. Five years before this it had become independent and merged with the mainland region of Mbini (still called Rio Muni at that time) to form Equatorial Guinea.

Does Equatorial Guinea depend on development aid?

Since 1991, when petroleum was discovered off the coast of Bioko and the mainland, the country's economy has grown significantly. Since then, oil companies have been responsible for 90 per cent of the GDP. This revenue means that Equatorial Guinea no longer needs development aid.

Why is Spanish spoken in Equatorial Guinea?

Equatorial Guinea is the only Spanish-speaking country in Africa. Portugal ceded Fernão Pó

Island to Spain in 1778 and the new colonial ruler established a plantation economy on the island. In 1926 Spain began to colonize the mainland, Rio Muni, and Spanish has remained the official language to this day.

EQUATORIAL GUINEA

Flag

Currency
1 Communauté Financière Africaine
CFA franc (XAF) = 100 centimes

System of government
Presidential republic since 1962

Capital Malabo

Languages
Spanish (official language), French (administrative language), Bantu languages Fang and Bubi

Surface area
10,831 sq miles (28,051 sq km)

Population 536,000

Religion
94% Catholic

Eric Moussambani

Swimmer Eric Moussambani from Equatorial Guinea (born 1978) achieved international fame at the 2000 Olympic Games in Sydney. Nicknamed "Eric the Eel" by the press, he took over a minute longer than the top international swimmers to complete the 100-m freestyle. Before arriving in Sydney he had never swum 50 m before, and had only trained in a 20-m hotel pool. Unfortunately, visa difficulties meant he was unable to compete at the 2004 Olympics.

Many citizens of Equatorial Guinea live illegally in neighboring Gabon. Shown here is an illegal immigrant loading his belongings onto a boat as he has to leave Gabon.

GABON

Flag

Currency
1 Communauté Financière Africaine
CFA franc (XAF) = 100 centimes

System of government
Presidential republic since 1961

Capital Libreville

Languages
French (official language), Bantu
languages (e.g. Fang)

Surface area
103,347 sq miles (267,667 sq km)

Population 1.4 million

Religion
60% Christian, 30% traditional
religions, 5% Muslim

What are Gabon's main topographical features?
Gabon's coastal plain is approximately
125 miles (200 km) wide and 550 miles (885 km)
long. Behind this is a mountainous region that rises
to some 3,300 ft (1,000 m). The country's main river
is the Ogowe (Ogoué in French), which flows for
750 miles (1,200 km) and, along with its numerous
tributaries, forms Gabon's central axis.

The rainforests of Petit Loango National Park extend all the way to the
Atlantic coast. With a degree of luck, visitors are able to observe gorillas
in the nature reserve.

Why is French spoken in Gabon?
French settlers started to arrive in Gabon in the
middle of the 19th century. In 1888 Gabon became
part of French Congo and later French Equatorial
Africa. Gabon achieved independence from France
in 1960 but retained French as its official language.

Is Gabon a poor country?
No. The country is one of the most prosperous
in sub-Saharan Africa. Its wealth derives from its
mineral resources, which include offshore petroleum
and manganese, and gold and uranium in the
interior. Crude oil and petroleum products account
for 80 per cent of export earnings.

How did the capital get its name?
The city was founded as a settlement for freed slaves
in 1849. Based on the model of Freetown, the capital
of Sierra Leone, it was named Libreville. With a
population of 580,000, it is Gabon's largest city
by far.

Albert Schweitzer and Lambaréné
Albert Schweitzer (1875–1965) founded his famous jungle
hospital in Lambaréné, Gabon, in 1913. Having already
gained doctorates in philosophy, theology, and medicine,
the multi-talented German doctor was awarded the Nobel
Peace Prize for his work in 1952. From 1952 to his death,
he worked against nuclear tests and nuclear weapons. The
Albert Schweitzer Hospital still exists today. It has a range of
specialist departments and also conducts research into, and
treats, malaria.

REPUBLIC OF CONGO

Flag

Currency
1 Communauté Financière Africaine
CFA franc (XAF) = 100 centimes

System of government
Presidential republic since 2002

Capital Brazzaville

Languages
French (official language),
Monokutuba, Kikongo, Lingala, others

Surface area
212,509 sq miles (342,000 sq km)

Population 3.9 million

Religion
50% Christian,
48% traditional religions

What are Kinshasa and Brazzaville?

Kinshasa is the capital of the Democratic Republic of Congo, formerly Zaire, and Brazzaville is the capital of the Republic of Congo. The two cities face each other across Pool Malebo, a lake-like expansion of the Congo River.

What is the Republic of Congo's main industrial sector?

The country's main economic activity is forestry. Around 60 per cent of the country is covered by tropical rainforest, much of which is made into veneers prior to export. Other important sectors are textiles, cement, and chemicals. The country also has extensive oil reserves that have not yet been exploited on a large scale due to inadequate infrastructure and the three civil wars that have taken place between 1997 and 2003.

Why is there no livestock farming to speak of?

Animal husbandry is relatively uncommon because of the tsetse fly (*Glossina* species). These biting flies cause the much-feared sleeping sickness in humans and nagana disease, which is fatal, in animals.

Lefini Nature Reserve is about 90 miles (140 km) from Brazzaville. On September 21, 2006 the first gorilla to be born in freedom here in over 50 years was spotted.

Pygmies

The Republic of Congo's population is made up mainly of Bantu peoples (98 per cent) while pygmies, Africans of small stature (in this case belonging to the Baka tribe), account for just one per cent of the total. The word "pygmy" is a widespread but politically incorrect term used to describe a number of unusually short indigenous peoples in Central Africa (totaling around 150,000). The word is derived from the Ancient Greek *pygmaios* (literally "as short as a fist"), an antique measurement of length corresponding to around 14 in (35 cm). Members of these ethnic groups are usually no more than 4 ft 9 in (145 cm) tall.

The city of Brazzaville owes its name to Frenchman Count Pierre Savorgnan de Brazza, who established the first expedition station here in 1883.

Flag		Surface area

Flag

Currency
1 Congolese franc (CDF)
= 100 centimes

System of government
Presidential republic since 1978

Capital Kinshasa

Languages
French (official language), Lingala, Kikongo, Swahili, around 200 other languages

Surface area
0.90 million sq miles (2.34 million sq km)

Population 65.75 million

Religion
50% Catholic, 20% Protestant, 10% Kimbanguist, 10% Muslim

Notable features
The province of Katanga was independent for a short period.

What was the country called previously?

From 1908 the then Belgian colony was known as the Belgian Congo. The Belgians left the country in 1959 and it gained independence the following year under its present name. Its name was changed to Zaire in 1971 after the fall of the first prime minister Patrice Lumumba (1925–1961). Until 1997 the nation was ruled in a highly authoritarian fashion by Mobutu Sese Seko (1930–1997). Since then the country has changed its name back to the Democratic Republic of Congo.

Near Mbandaka, in the north, the Congo River flows through extensive marshlands.

What is the Congo Basin?

The extensive Congo Basin is the drainage area of the Congo River, Africa's second-longest river but the one with the biggest flow. The approximately 1,300-ft-high (400-m) Congo Basin covers some 60 per cent of the Democratic Republic of Congo. Bordered by hills, it accommodates the second-largest rainforest in the world (after the Amazon Basin).

Is Katanga still part of Congo?

Congo's southernmost province is now called Katanga once more. Between 1971 and 1997 it was called Shaba and repeatedly made the headlines because of numerous outbreaks of armed violence there. The region is rich in copper, cobalt, and uranium, which kindled the acquisitiveness of the neighboring countries and also gave rise to independence movements. Katanga was only properly independent from 1960 to 1963, however.

Stanley and Leopold II of Belgium

Explorer Henry Morton Stanley (1841–1904) was the first European to visit the Congo region. Great Britain, however, was not interested in colonizing the area. King Leopold II of Belgium (1835–1909), on the other hand, was. As the Belgian government and people did not share his enthusiasm, Leopold appropriated the region without further ado as his private property. Thus in 1885 the Congo Free State and all its inhabitants became the personal possessions of one man. The subsequent economic exploitation of the land was carried out with such cruelty that in 1908 the king was forced to hand over the administration of the Congo to the Belgian Parliament.

ANGOLA

Flag

Currency
1 kwanza (AOA) = 100 centimos

System of government
Republic since 1975

Capital
Luanda

Languages
Portuguese (official language), Bantu

languages (Umbundu, Kimbundu, Kikongo, and others)

Surface area 0.48 million sq miles (1.24 million sq km)

Population 11.2 million

Religion
47% traditional religions, 38% Catholic, 15% Protestant

Notable features
The exclave of Cabinda (see box) also forms part of Angolan territory.

What was the Angola Treaty?

At the end of the 19th century Portugal was in poor economic shape. In the Angola Treaty of 1898 the two colonial powers of Germany and Great Britain agreed to lend Portugal money, using its colonial possessions as security. Were it to default, Angola and northern Mozambique would fall to Germany and southern Mozambique to Britain. In the end the treaty was never signed.

When did Angola gain its independence?

The first uprising of nationalist forces against the Portuguese (who had been the region's colonial rulers since the 15th century) took place in 1959. However, independence was not achieved until after the Carnation Revolution put an end to the dictatorship in Portugal (see p.58) in 1974.

Why did independence fail to bring peace to Angola?

After independence the liberation movement MPLA, backed by the Soviet Union, tried to gain exclusive control of the new nation. The rival group UNITA was immediately given military support by the United States and South Africa. Agreement was finally reached by the two sides in 1991.

Why is the infant mortality rate so high in Angola?

A child under five years of age dies in Angola every three minutes. Medical provision is completely inadequate and only 40 per cent of the population have access to clean drinking water. Nearly 75 per cent of the people live below the poverty line and more than half are unemployed. Almost the entire working population is employed in agriculture and the biggest agricultural export is coffee. As a result of the decades of war, landmines still litter large parts of the countryside and many people refuse to work in the fields. A third of the population are dependent on overseas food aid.

As a result of the civil war, many people had to live under the most basic conditions, as here in the refugee village of Camacupa.

Giraffes have become rare in Angola. Other animals, including lions and elephants, are also endangered by poaching.

The exclave of Cabinda

Also part of Angolan national territory is a tiny region (2,812 sq miles/7,283 sq km) north of the Congo estuary that is completely surrounded by other countries. Petroleum has been pumped there since 1968 and now accounts for 80 per cent of Angola's national budget. All moves towards independence have been suppressed militarily by Angola. The Organization of African Unity (OAU) regards Cabinda as an independent state.

ZAMBIA

Flag

Currency
1 kwacha (ZMK) = 100 ngwee

System of government
Presidential republic since 1964
(Commonwealth member)

Capital
Lusaka

Languages
English (official language), Bantu languages

Surface area
290,586 sq miles (752,614 sq km)

Population 11.3 million

Religion 28% Catholic,
26% Protestant, traditional religions

Notable features
In terms of height and breadth Victoria Falls is the largest waterfall in the world.

A tailor at a market in Lusaka, Zambia, making clothes from traditionally patterned fabrics.

What is meant by the term "cool tropics"?

High-altitude tropical regions near the Equator such as Zambia—almost all of which lies at between 3,300 and 4,600 ft (1,000 and 1,400 m)—benefit from relatively low temperatures and are sometimes referred to as the "cool tropics."

Who discovered the Victoria Falls?

Scottish missionary and explorer David Livingstone (1813–1873) had heard of the falls on the Zambezi as early as 1851. In November 1855 he became the first European to set eyes on them and named them after his queen. The falls lie on the frontier between Zimbabwe and Zambia—the Zambezi River forms

After coming across the Victoria Falls on November 16, 1855, David Livingstone wrote of what he had witnessed: "...scenes so lovely must have been gazed upon by angels in their flight."

Copper Belt

The Copper Belt extends from northwestern Zambia into the Democratic Republic of Congo, where lead and zinc are also mined. Zambia is one of the largest producers of copper in the world although it is predicted that its deposits will be exhausted before long.

the actual border. In 1989 they were designated a UNESCO World Heritage site.

What were the falls called by the local indigenous people?

The Kololo tribe, which moved to the area north of the Victoria Falls after the Zulu wars at the beginning of the 19th century, calls this wonder of nature Mosi-oa-Tunya (meaning "smoke that thunders"). This name stems from the fine mist—up to 1,000 ft (300 m) high and visible from a distance of over 20 miles (30 km)—that rises from the water as it crashes into the depths.

Is good use made of the Zambezi River's water power?

Yes. The Cahora Bassa and Kariba dams have already been completed and there are plans to build a third at Batoka Gorge. Conservationists are warning that this project will destroy the flora and fauna of the unspoiled gorge and there is also the danger that it will damage tourism.

Does Djibouti possess raw materials?

Does Djibouti possess raw materials? No. Djibouti possesses no mineral resources or industry to speak of, and only nine per cent of the land can be used for agriculture. Most of the population is crammed into the capital Djibouti, whose port is the economic center of the country.

How do the people earn their livelihoods?

Sixty per cent of the population are unemployed. The main source of work is the port in the capital. A harbor worker has to work for ten days in order to earn enough to pay one month's rent for a bed in a hostel. Most of the population depends on United Nations food aid.

What is French Somaliland?

Djibouti was acquired from the ruling sultan by France in 1862 and declared French Somaliland in 1896. The people voted against independence on two occasions, in 1958 and 1967, choosing instead to remain under French control. Independence eventually came in 1977.

DJIBOUTI

Flag

Currency
1 Djibouti franc (DJF) = 100 centimes

System of government
Presidential republic since 1977

Capital
Djibouti

Languages
Arabic, French (official languages), Somali, Afar

Surface area
8,958 sq miles (23,200 sq km)

Population 477,000

Religion 95% Sunni Muslim

Notable features
Lake Assal is 509 ft (155 m) below sea level.

Does tourism offer opportunities for the future?

Yes, although work has only just begun on the development of the necessary infrastructure. Not only does the Gulf of Tadjoura offer wonderful sandy beaches, its coral reefs also make the region an inside tip among divers.

Lake Abbe is a salt lake on the Ethiopia-Djibouti border famous for its flamingo colonies.

Operation Enduring Freedom

Operation Enduring Freedom is a military response to the terrorist attacks of September 11, 2001 on New York and Washington DC. Designed to combat international terrorism, one component of the operation involves military surveillance of the Horn of Africa. A number of countries in the region, such as Afghanistan, Algeria, and Mauritania, are regarded as politically unstable and as possible supply bases or places of retreat for terrorists.

SOMALIA

Flag

Currency
1 Somali shilling (SOS)
= 100 centesimi

System of government
Presidential republic up to 1991
(no state structures since then)

Capital
Mogadishu

Languages
Somali (official language), Maay, others

Surface area
246,201 sq miles (637,657 sq km)

Population Over 8 million

Religion
9% Sunni Muslim

Why are there no de facto state structures in Somalia?

Since the overthrow of the government of Mohamed Siad Barre (1919–1995) in 1991, Somalia has been in a state of civil war and until the creation of the Transitional Federal Government in 2004, which still conducts state business although it controls only the region of Somalia, it was without leadership at national level.

Why is it difficult to give an accurate population figure?

Sixty per cent of all Somalis lead a nomadic existence. Furthermore, the country has been torn apart by civil war leading to high levels of emigration. As a result, estimates of the size of the population range from 8 million to 12 million.

What are the main features of Somalia's social structure?

Somalia is dominated by a highly ramified clan system that plays a major part in the political situation. Each clan is divided into subclan and lineage. Individuals are afforded protection within this system, but because blood feuds exist between many of the clans, those same individuals become embroiled in disputes over water or pasturage rights or, in recent years, political power.

How important are the nomads to Somalia's economy?

Agriculture and livestock herding still form the backbone of the Somali economy. The extensive animal herding explains why over half of the people still lead a nomadic or semi-nomadic existence while only a third live in towns and cities. Mainly cattle are raised in the south while sheep, goats, and, above all, camels are herded in the dryer northern regions. All these animals are driven from place to place in search of food. Together with the country's oral poetry tradition, nomadism is the main defining feature of Somali culture.

An artfully laden Somali truck parked on the edge of a road in Mogadishu.

The Horn of Africa

The Horn is the easternmost part of Africa, a peninsula that juts into the Arabian Sea. It rests on its own tectonic plate, which could separate from the continent and form a new island in the Indian Ocean—as Madagascar did 160 million years ago. In addition to Somalia the region also includes eastern Ethiopia.

The traditional clothing of the Masai is extremely colorful. Handmade jewelry is worn by both men and women.

KENYA

Flag

Currency
1 Kenyan shilling (KES) = 100 cents

System of government
Presidential republic since 1963 (Commonwealth member)

Capital Nairobi

Languages
English, Swahili (official languages), Kikuyu, Luhya, other tribal languages

Surface area
224,962 sq miles (582,650 sq km)

Population 3.8 million

Religion
70% Christian, 20% Muslim, 10% traditional religions

Notable features
The Ilemi Triangle in the north of the country is administered by Kenya but claimed by Ethiopia and Sudan.

Who are the Masai?

The Masai are a nomadic tribe of animal herders who inhabit the Serengeti, an expanse of almost treeless savanna. They are widespread throughout southern Kenya and northern Tanzania and are proud of their traditions and reputation as both warriors and herders. Due to the international fame of the Serengeti National Park, the Masai have become the best-known indigenous ethnic group in East Africa.

The giraffe's main habitat is the savannas of eastern and southern Africa, as here at the foot of Mount Kilimanjaro. It is the tallest land-dwelling animal in the world.

What is the Rift Valley?

The Kenyan Rift Valley is a section of the African Eastern Rift Valley, a geological feature that occurs at the point where a number of plates of the Earth's crust meet. It is up to 60 miles (100 km) wide and runs in a north-south direction through eastern Kenya. The valley's plains are extremely fertile in places. The Rift Valley is famous for fossil and bone finds that have shed significant light on the history of the planet.

Which ethnic groups live in Kenya?

Around 40 different ethnic groups live in Kenya, most of them Bantu peoples. The Kikuyu represent the biggest single ethnic group, making up 22 per cent of the population. The east coast is also home to Arabs, Indians, and Chinese, who originally came to the country as traders.

Is Kenya a poor country?

No. Kenya's economy is developing successfully. Although the country has only modest mineral resources, it is a major exporter of coffee, tea, and flowers. It also earns significant amounts of foreign currency from tourism. Tourists from all over the world are attracted to Kenya not only by its broad, sandy beaches but also by its nature reserves such as the Amboseli and Lake Nakuru national parks.

Out of Africa

The internationally successful film *Out of Africa* (1985) depicts the life of European settlers in Kenya at the beginning of the 20th century. Based on an autobiographical novel by Danish author Karen Blixen (1885–1962), it stars Meryl Streep, Robert Redford, and Klaus Maria Brandauer and has won seven Oscars.

UGANDA

Currency
1 Ugandan shilling (UGX) = 100 cents

System of government
Presidential republic since 1967
(Commonwealth member)

Capital
Kampala

Languages
English (official language), Swahili, Ganda

Surface area
93,262 sq miles (241,548 sq km)

Population 27.3 million

Religion
33% Catholic, 33% Protestant,
18% traditional religions, 16% Muslim

What was Operation Entebbe?

On June 27, 1976 an Air France flight from Athens to Paris was hijacked and diverted via Benghazi (Libya) to Entebbe in Uganda. The hijackers were eight terrorists including members of the Popular Front for the Liberation of Palestine (PFLP) and German Revolutionary Cells (RZ). Supported by the pro-Palestinian regime of Idi Amin, they demanded five million US dollars plus the release of 53 prisoners. Operation Entebbe (known in Israel as Operation Jonathan after the commander of the rescue mission, Colonel Jonathan Netanyahu, who lost his life in Entebbe) took place during the night of July 3. Three of the 103 hostages died during the operation.

At 100 sq miles (260 sq km) Lake Mburo National Park is Uganda's smallest nature reserve but has an extremely varied landscape and a great diversity of flora and fauna.

In what sense is Uganda part of the "cradle of mankind"?

Two million years ago an early form of *Homo sapiens* (modern man) emerged in East Africa. Around 120,000 years ago *Homo sapiens* left Africa and migrated to India and the Middle East, from where they eventually spread throughout the world.

Who are the original inhabitants of Uganda?

The Twa people, also known as Batwa (commonly referred to as pygmies), have lived in Uganda longer than any other ethnic group. Semi-nomadic hunter-gatherers, they are thought to number around 50,000 to 80,000 today. Because they are regarded as the true indigenous people of the region, they have traditionally considered themselves to be the "owners of the land."

What are Uganda's main raw materials?

Copper, cobalt, limestone, and rock salt. The good soil quality and plentiful supply of water favors the cultivation of coffee, tea, and tobacco. Winston Churchill once called Uganda the "Pearl of Africa" but today the country is among the poorest in the world. In 2003, 82 per cent of the population lived on just one US dollar a day.

Who were Milton Obote and Idi Amin?

Milton Obote (1924–2005) was Uganda's first prime minister after independence in 1962. Before long, his administration degenerated into a reign of terror as he eliminated the ancient kingdoms in a series of bloody massacres. Idi Amin Dada (1925–2003) came to power in a military coup in 1971 and instituted an even bloodier dictatorship that lasted until 1979. Over 300,000 people were killed or expelled.

RWANDA

Flag		**Languages**
		English, French, Kinyarwanda (official languages), Kisuaheli
Currency		**Surface area**
1 Rwandan franc (RWF) = 100 centimes		10,169 sq miles (26,338 sq km)
		Population 8.6 million
System of government		**Religion**
Presidential republic since 1962		48% Catholic, 44% Protestant, 5% Muslim
Capital		
Kigali		

Who were the colonial powers in Rwanda?

Rwanda was a German colony between 1884 and 1916. During the First World War it was conquered by Belgium and eventually achieved independence in 1962.

Which rare species live in Rwanda?

A few mountain gorillas still live on the slopes of the Virunga range of volcanic mountains on the borders with the Democratic Republic of the Congo and Uganda. The region and its endangered animals came to international attention through the work of US zoologist Dian Fossey (1932–1985).

Why does famine still occur in Rwanda?

One of the main reasons is the uneven rainfall pattern in Rwanda, with 40 per cent of annual rainfall occurring between March and May. The parched, often sloping ground is unable to soak up the volume of water produced by sudden, heavy downpours of this kind. The soil erodes and the harvest is ruined.

Hutu and Tutsi

In Rwanda the Tutsis (Watussi) constituted the ruling class and the Hutus (Bahutu) the commoners, even though they originated from the same ethnic group. The country's colonial rulers bolstered the Tutsis' position as a cattle-raising elite while treating the Hutus as simple farmers. This unequal treatment led to tensions between the two groups that resulted in outbreaks of violence in the 1950s when the country's first free elections were also held, and won by the Hutus. This led to further unrest and massacres and thousands of people sought refuge in the neighboring countries. The country remained in turmoil for many years, and in 1994 alone, genocide cost the lives of between 800,000 and one million people. The peace process was not regarded as formally concluded until 2003.

Mountain gorillas live in family-like groups. They communicate by means of a language of howls, roars, coughs, and growls.

Workers in the Mulindi tea plantations are paid just over one US dollar per day—during which they pick approximately 175 lb (80 kg) of tea leaves.

BURUNDI

Flag

Currency
1 Burundian franc (BIF)
= 100 centimes

System of government
Presidential republic since 1966

Capital
Bujumbura

Languages French, Kirundi (official languages), Swahili

Surface area
10,747 sq miles (27,834 sq km)

Population 7.8 million

Religion
65% Catholic, 13% Protestant, 20% traditional religions

Notable features
Burundi is very densely populated.

What are the main features of Burundi's topography?

Although technically landlocked, Burundi has 60 miles (100 km) of coastline along Lake Tanganyika, one of Africa's biggest lakes. The country is dominated by a high plateau that drops down steeply towards the lake. Burundi has a tropical climate with two rainy seasons.

A troupe of drummers from Gitega in Burundi. Drumming once formed part of the royal courtly tradition and is cherished today as an important aspect of Burundi's cultural heritage.

Why is French the official language?

Although the region was part of German East Africa at the beginning of the 20th century, following the First World War it was awarded by the League of Nations to Belgium as part of the Rwanda-Urundi mandate and French was adopted as the official language.

Why have there been so many civil wars in Burundi?

Ever since the 1960s there have been repeated conflicts between the Hutus and Tutsis. The Hutus are the biggest population group (85 per cent) and are simple farmers while the animal-herding Tutsis make up just 14 per cent of the population but have been the ruling class for centuries. During the civil war that lasted from 1993 to 2003, ten per cent of the population fled to the neighboring countries.

Is Burundi poor?

Following decades of armed struggle and expulsions, it is no longer possible to speak of functioning economy and Burundi is one of the poorest countries in the world as a result – 68 per cent of the population lived below the line of poverty in 2002. Although there is a relatively large livestock herd, productivity is very low. Burundi's only exports are coffee and tea.

The king of Burundi

Prior to colonial rule the region covered by present-day Burundi had been a kingdom, and so when the time came, Burundi was given its independence as a constitutional monarchy in 1962. However, just four years later the last king, Ntare V Ndizeye, was toppled and the monarchy abolished.

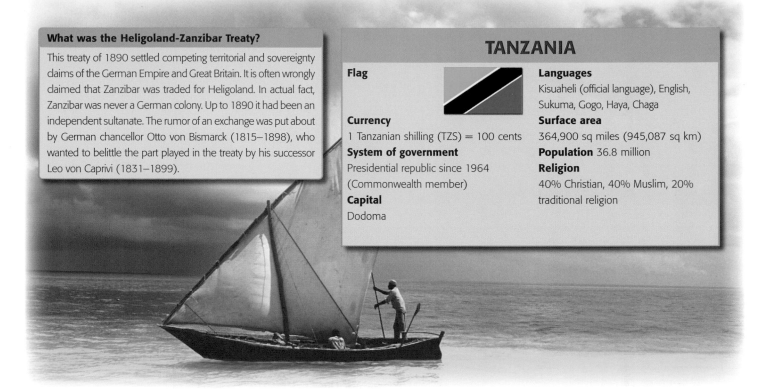

TANZANIA

Flag

Currency
1 Tanzanian shilling (TZS) = 100 cents

System of government
Presidential republic since 1964
(Commonwealth member)

Capital
Dodoma

Languages
Kisuaheli (official language), English, Sukuma, Gogo, Haya, Chaga

Surface area
364,900 sq miles (945,087 sq km)

Population 36.8 million

Religion
40% Christian, 40% Muslim, 20% traditional religion

What places of natural beauty are there in Tanzania?

Bordering Tanzania are three of Africa's largest and most beautiful lakes: Lake Tanganyika, Lake Malawi, and the famous Lake Victoria. In the north is the Serengeti National Park, one of the country's most famous nature reserves, and on the border with Kenya in the northeast is the 19,341-ft-high (5,895-m) Mount Kilimanjaro.

How did the country get its name?

After Zanzibar achieved independence in 1963, Tanganyika (Tan) and Zanzibar (Zan) merged to form the United Republic of Tanzania. There is a separatist movement on the island of Zanzibar but so far only Turkey has recognized the island as an independent state.

Was there slavery in this region?

Slavery has existed along Africa's Indian Ocean coast since time immemorial. From the 18th century onwards the islands as well as the mainland coasts were controlled by the Arabs and in the early 19th century slavery-trading became the main activity. Up to 10,000 slaves exchanged hands every year. It is thought that 75 per cent of the current population are descended from slaves.

How long did the "shortest war in history" last?

The British-Zanzibar war of 1896 lasted for precisely 38 minutes. The second son of the deceased sultan of Zanzibar forced his way onto the throne in the belief that he had the support of the German Empire. The British immediately declared war and bombarded the sultan's palace until accepting the surrender 38 minutes later.

Why is Zanzibar known as the "Isle of Spice"?

In the 19th century Zanzibar was the world's largest producer of cloves and its economy is still based on the export of spices such as nutmeg, cinnamon, vanilla, and pepper.

Who was Farrokh Bulsara?

Farrokh Bulsara was the real name of British musician Freddie Mercury (born 1946 on the island of Zanzibar, died 1991).

A fisherman in a traditional dhow sets sail off the coast of Zanzibar.

Watching lions is the climax of any visit to the famous Serengeti National Park in northern Tanzania.

SEYCHELLES

Flag

Currency
1 Seychelles rupee (SCR) = 100 cents

System of government
Presidential republic since 1976
(Commonwealth member)

Capital
Victoria

Languages
Creole (Seselwa), English, French (official
languages)

Surface area
176 sq miles (455 sq km)

Population 82,000

Religion 90% Catholic, 8% Protestant

Notable features
Conservation areas cover 49% of
the country.

Tourism is the main economic factor in the Seychelles, which were hardly affected by the 2004 tsunami.

How big is the maritime area across which the Seychelles are scattered?

The 115 islands of the Republic of the Seychelles, of which only 32 belong to the actual island group known as the Seychelles, are scattered across a total area of 154,441 sq miles (400,000 sq km). The islands are divided into the Outer Islands and the Inner Islands, the latter of which include the most densely populated islands Mahé, Praslin, and La Digue.

Who discovered and first colonized the islands?

The first Europeans to mention the islands were Portuguese explorers in around 1505, although they had already been visited by Arab traders. They were not settled, however, until the end of the 17th century (by the French). After being contested by France and Great Britain from 1794 until 1811, they eventually came under British control and were made a dependency of Mauritius. In 1903 they became a colony in their own right. They achieved independence in 1970.

What is the Seychelles' main economic sector?

Thirty per cent of the working population are employed in tourism, which also accounts for over 70 per cent of national revenue. These earnings are reinvested in hotel complexes of the highest category, leading to concerns that in the long term mid-market tourists could stay away. The tourist sector is not immune to international crises, however, as demonstrated by a collapse in visitor numbers after September 11, 2001.

Why are the Seychelles sometimes referred to as "ocean oases"?

The islands have remained unchanged for thousands of years. They have been spared from natural catastrophes such as whirlwinds and have never hosted tropical diseases or poisonous creatures. The predominant flora and fauna are largely unique to the islands. The natural environment of these "ocean oases" is therefore looked after with the utmost care.

Interesting facts

- The Seychelles are home to various species of giant tortoise. Around 150,000 Aldabra tortoises live on Aldabra Atoll alone.

- Another of Aldabra's inhabitants is the white-throated rail, the Indian Ocean's last surviving flightless bird.

- The national constitution guarantees the citizens of the Seychelles the right to a clean, healthy, and ecologically balanced environment.

MALAWI

Flag

Currency
1 Malawi kwacha (MWK) = 100 tambala

System of government
Presidential republic since 1966
(Commonwealth member)

Capital
Lilongwe

Languages
English, Chichewa (official languages)

Surface area
45,747 sq miles (118,484 sq km)

Population 12.7 million

Religion
70% Christian, 20% Muslim,
10% traditional religions

Notable features
The islands of Likoma and Chizumulu
in Lake Malawi also belong to Malawi
despite lying in Mozambique's
territorial waters.

What was Nyasaland?

Between 1891 and 1964 the region that is
now Malawi was administered by the British as the
Protectorate of Nyasaland. Lake Malawi was known
at that time as Lake Nyasa after the Bantu name
for it (*nyassa* means "lake"). The first European to
reach the lake was the great explorer of Africa David
Livingstone (1813–1873) in 1859.

What are the problems facing the country?

Malawi is one of the poorest countries in the
world. Life expectancy is just 33 years and it has
been estimated that 50 per cent of the population
are HIV positive. As this condition affects mainly
economically active age groups, there is little hope at
present for strong economic development.

What does Malawi export?

Malawi has only modest mineral resources. Small
quantities of bauxite are produced but not exported.
The economy is almost entirely agriculture-based
but yields barely satisfy the nation's own
requirements. Hopes for the near future rest on
the cultivation of tobacco, which already accounts
for 50 per cent of Malawi's export earnings.

This Malawian
family has bought
a fishing boat with
a microloan from a
British organization.

An aerial view of
heavily developed
Monkey Bay
in Malawi Lake
National Park.

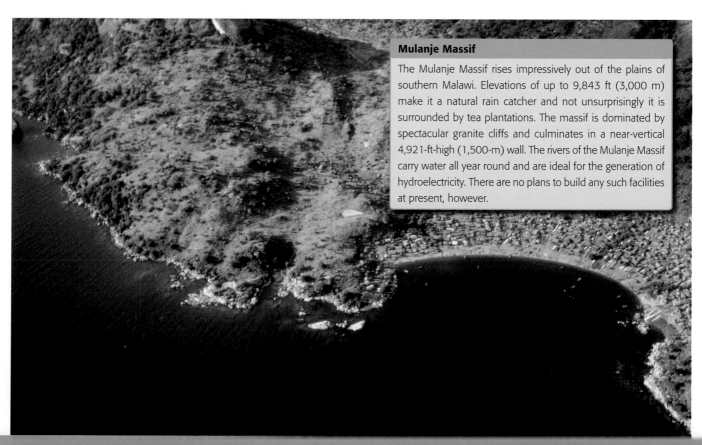

Mulanje Massif

The Mulanje Massif rises impressively out of the plains of
southern Malawi. Elevations of up to 9,843 ft (3,000 m)
make it a natural rain catcher and not unsurprisingly it is
surrounded by tea plantations. The massif is dominated by
spectacular granite cliffs and culminates in a near-vertical
4,921-ft-high (1,500-m) wall. The rivers of the Mulanje Massif
carry water all year round and are ideal for the generation of
hydroelectricity. There are no plans to build any such facilities
at present, however.

MOZAMBIQUE

Flag

Currency
1 metical (MZN) = 100 centavos

System of government
Presidential republic since 1990
(Commonwealth member)

Capital Maputo

Languages Portuguese (official

language), Makua, Swahili, other
Bantu languages

Surface area
308,642 sq miles (799,380 sq km)

Population 19.4 million

Religion
50% traditional religions, 27%
Christian, 21% Muslim

Notable features Conservation areas
cover 49% of the country.

Large rats (*Cricetomys gambianus*) are trained to associate the smell of explosives with food and are then used to clear mines, as here in Vilancoulos, 280 miles (450 km) from Maputo.

Who discovered and first colonized Mozambique?

Although Portuguese explorer Vasco da Gama (1469–1524) was the first European to reach Mozambique in 1498, Arab traders had already been living there for many years, trading gold, ivory, and slaves with India. The Portuguese took over the trading center and slave trade and subjugated the people of the region through to the 20th century.

What is Lake Nyasa?

Lake Nyasa is better known as Lake Malawi. At 11,430 sq miles (29,604 sq km) it is Africa's third-largest lake. It is 342 miles (550 km) long, an average of 31 miles (50 km) wide (up to 50 miles/80 km in places), and lies at 1,549 ft (472 m) above sea level. With a depth of up to 2,280 ft (695 m), it is also one of the deepest lakes in the world. Lake Nyasa was discovered by Scottish explorer David Livingstone (1813–1873) in 1859.

When did Mozambique achieve independence?

After nearly 500 years of Portuguese rule, Mozambique achieved independence on June 25, 1975 following the Carnation Revolution and the fall of the dictatorship in Portugal. The first president was Samora Machel (1933–1986).

The Zambezi is Africa's fourth-longest river. Around 80 per cent of those who live along the river valley earn their livelihoods by farming the fertile soil of the floodplain.

FRELIMO and RENAMO

FRELIMO stands for Frente da Libertação de Moçambique (Liberation Front of Mozambique). It emerged in the 1960s as an anti-colonial socialist organization.

RENAMO stands for Resistência Nacional Moçambicana (Mozambican National Resistance). It is an anti-communist organization founded in 1975 to fight FRELIMO both militarily and ideologically.

In 1976 the two groups plunged the country into a 16-year civil war in which advisers from East Germany, the Soviet Union, and Cuba played a part. Stability did not return to the country until 1992, by which time 900,000 people had lost their lives, 1.3 million had fled their homes, and the national economy had been almost completely ruined.

Where is Comoros?

Comoros is an island nation located between the northern tip of Madagascar and the African mainland. It consists of three large islands—Grande Comore, Anjouan, and Mohéli—and a number of small coral islands.

What political claim is symbolized by the new national flag?

The new national flag introduced in 2003 includes four colored stripes of equal width and four white stars. The number four signifies that Comoros sees itself as a nation comprising four islands. The fourth island is Mayotte, which is part of the Comoros Archipelago but currently belongs to France.

Is Comoros politically stable?

No. Since it achieved independence from France in 1975 there have been nearly 20 coups and attempted coups against the government. Several of these involved the French mercenary Bob Denard, who exerted a substantial influence over the presidents he helped to install. After 1997 the islands each had their own presidents for a period and were calling for independence but are currently still in a loose union.

Mohéli, one of the three larger islands of the Comoros. The lush vegetation is due to fertile volcanic soil which also lends itself to agricultural use.

COMOROS

Flag

Currency
1 Comoros franc (KMF) = 100 centimes

System of government
Federal republic

Capital
Moroni

Languages
French, Comorian (official languages), Arabic

Surface area
719 sq miles (1,862 sq km)

Population 671,000

Religion
95% Muslim

Notable features
Comoros is claiming the French overseas territory of Mayotte.

Mount Karthala

At 7,746 ft (2,361 m) Mount Karthala, situated not far from the capital Moroni on the island of Grande Comore, is the highest volcano in the world. It has been active over recent years and 40,000 people had to be evacuated when it erupted in 2005.

MADAGASCAR

Flag

Currency
1 ariary (MGA) = 100 iraimbilanja

System of government
Presidential republic since 1992

Capital
Antananarivo

Languages
Malagasy, French (official languages)

Surface area
226,657 sq miles (587,040 sq km)

Population 18.1 million

Religion
52% traditional religions,
41% Christian, 7% Muslim

Notable features
Madagascar is the second-largest island nation in the world after Indonesia.

Right: Lemurs have been able to survive naturally only in the particular ecological conditions that prevail on Madagascar, where they are represented by 72 species.

Seagrass farmers harvesting their crop in shallow water. Seagrass can be used as an upholstery and insulation material.

Why is Madagascar sometimes referred to as the eighth continent?

The island of Madagascar broke away from continental Africa 150 million years ago and from Asia 90 million years ago. Since that time the island's flora and fauna have developed independently of those on the mainland, resulting in unique plant and animal life. Lemurs, for example, are not found anywhere else in the world. Conversely, Madagascar lacks other creatures that are indigenous to Africa and Asia, such as poisonous snakes and apes.

What was the Kingdom of Madagascar?

At the beginning of the 19th century the Merina people, who had previously controlled areas of the highlands, gradually extended their kingdom until by 1824 the whole of Madagascar was under the rule of King Radama I. The kingdom existed until 1896, when the island was conquered by France. Reigning queen Ranavalona III went into exile in Algeria and Madagascar remained a French colony until 1960.

Is Madagascar a prosperous country?

No. On the contrary, Madagascar is one of the poorest countries in the world and is reliant upon development aid. The main foodstuff grown on the island is rice while many others have to be imported. Coffee, vanilla, cloves, and sugar are exported.

Elephant bird

Until a few hundred years ago one of the more remarkable representatives of Madagascar's unique fauna was the massive elephant bird, which could attain a height of 11 ft (3.5 m) and weighed up to 1,100 lb (500 kg). A larger relative of the African ostrich, the elephant bird died out around 1700 because, it is believed, of the destruction of its habitat by slash-and-burn.

Who were the original inhabitants of Mauritius?
There were no original inhabitants. Until the arrival of the Europeans the island was uninhabited. Today almost 70 per cent of the population are descended from Indian immigrants who arrived on the island as plantation workers in the 19th century. The remainder consists mainly of Creoles of African and European descent.

Of which country was Mauritius a colony?
Almost every European colonial power controlled Mauritius at one time or another. The first to arrive were the Portuguese, who used Mauritius as a simple base. They were followed by the Dutch, who were in turn replaced by the French. The French established the sugar plantations that were subsequently taken over by the British (1810–1968).

Is Mauritius a poor nation?
No. Mauritius has moved from being completely dependent upon sugar cane (a colonial legacy) to a more mixed economy. The stable political situation has encouraged foreign investors to pour money into the development of the country's industrial and tourist infrastructure. The per capita income of this island nation is now among the highest in Africa.

MAURITIUS

Flag

Currency
1 Mauritian rupee (MUR) = 100 cents

System of government
Republic since 1968
(Commonwealth member)

Capital Port Louis

Languages
English (official language), Mauritian (French Creole), Bhojpuri

Surface area
788 sq miles (2,040 sq km)

Population 1.2 million

Religion
50% Hindu, 26% Catholic, 17% Muslim

Notable features
Mauritius, like the French overseas territory of La Réunion, is part of the Mascarene group of islands.

The Blue Penny

The Blue Penny is one of the best-known and most valuable stamps in the world. It was issued on Mauritius in 1847 and bears an image of Queen Victoria. Today only eight used and four unused examples survive and most of the owners prefer to remain anonymous. In 1993 an unused Blue Penny sold at auction for 1.607 million US dollars. They are so highly valued because they were the first stamps issued outside of the UK.

The Île aux Cerfs is a tiny island off the coast of Mauritius. It is popular with day-trippers for its white sandy beaches and crystal-clear water.

NAMIBIA

Flag

Currency
1 Namibian dollar (NAD) = 100 cents

System of government
Republic since 1990
(Commonwealth member)

Capital Windhoek

Languages English (official language),
Ovambo, Afrikaans, Herero, German

Surface area
318,261 sq miles (824,292 sq km)

Population
2 million

Religion
62% Protestant, 17% Catholic,
13% traditional religions

Notable features
Namibia's diamond deposits are
among the biggest in the world.

Above: Young girls of the Himba tribe wear their hair in two braids that fall forward over the forehead. After they reach puberty their hair is worn in small braids coated with mud (as shown here).

Why is the country called Namibia?
The country was named after the Namib Desert that borders the country's (South Atlantic) coastline. This was chosen as a neutral name in order to avoid favoring one or other of the region's tribes.

What is Namibia's main industry?
Fifty per cent of the country's exports derive from the mining sector. Namibia has rich deposits of diamonds and uranium ore plus extensive natural gas reserves.

Why is Namibia a multiracial state?
In this region, as elsewhere, the colonial powers drew up borders without paying any consideration

Background: The Namib-Naukluft National Park covers some 19,300 sq miles (50,000 sq km) and is Namibia's largest nature reserve. It offers a magnificent variety of landscapes from steep mountains to sand dunes that stretch as far as the eye can see.

to tribal areas. As a result of this, and partly because of migrations that took place around the turn of the 20th century, Namibia became a multiracial state.

What languages are spoken in Namibia?
Namibia became a German colony (German Southwest Africa) in 1884 and many of its citizens, both Black and Caucasian, still speak German today. Until independence (from South Africa) in 1990 the official languages were Afrikaans, English, and German. Over 30 tribal languages (including Nama, San, Herero, Himba, Ovambo and Dara) and many dialects are also spoken. For reasons of neutrality English was chosen as the official language after independence but is only spoken by seven per cent of the population.

The Herero and Nama uprising

Between 1904 and 1908 these two tribes (also known as Hottentots) rebelled against the region's German rulers. The settlers considered themselves superior to the Africans but the subservience they expected of all indigenous peoples was alien to the Herero and the Nama. Furthermore, the land had been granted to the settlers without any consideration of tribal or grazing rights. The German settlers and their facilities were attacked by an extremely well-organized force numbering thousands of men under the leadership of Samuel Maharero (1856–1923). However, they had not counted on the German Empire being able quickly to get 15,000 soldiers into the country. The uprising was bloodily quelled and thousands of Africans lost their lives.

Was Botswana ever a colony?

No. It was a British Protectorate (under the name Bechuanaland) for over 100 years, however, during which time it was represented by Britain in matters of defense and foreign policy but retained a degree of autonomy over its internal affairs. It achieved independence and adopted its current name in 1966.

Why is Botswana sometimes described as a "model African country"?

Shortly after independence in 1966, diamond deposits were discovered in Botswana. This has resulted in steady economic growth which has been further boosted by the reinvestment in the development of the country of a substantial proportion of the export earnings (which account for 70 per cent of Botswana's total exports).

What is the biggest problem facing Botswana?

Botswana has one of the highest rates of HIV infection in the world—40 per cent of the population are HIV positive. The AIDS epidemic therefore threatens to undermine the entire economy. Average life expectancy dropped from 63 years of age in 1991 to an alarming 31 years of age in 2004. Since 2002 the state has been providing those affected with free medication.

BOTSWANA

Flag

Currency
1 pula (BWP) = 100 thebe

System of government
Presidential republic since 1966
(Commonwealth member)

Capital
Gabarone

Languages
English (official language), Bantu languages (including Setswana)

Surface area
224,607 sq miles (581,730 sq km)

Population 1.6 million

Religion
50% Christian, 50% traditional religions

Notable features
The Kalahari Desert covers large parts of the country.

Hippopotamus

The hippopotamus was once common throughout Africa and in biblical times it even inhabited the Jordan Valley. Although it has now died out across many of its former habitats, it still thrives in Botswana. Hippopotamus are the third-largest land mammal and are by no means placid creatures: they inflict more injuries in Africa than either the crocodile or the lion.

Today the hippopotamus is only found south of the Sahara, such as here in Botswana's Moremi Game Reserve.

ZIMBABWE

Flag

Currency
1 Zimbabwe dollar (ZWD) = 100 cents

System of government
Presidential republic since 1980

Capital
Harare

Languages
English (official language), Shona,
Ndebele (main spoken languages)

Surface area
150,804 sq miles (390,580 sq km)

Population 12.8 million

Religion
75% Christian, 24% traditional religions

Notable features
The Victoria Falls on the Zambezi River
were discovered by David Livingstone
in 1855. The breadth of the falls is over
1 mile (1.6 km) and the drop is around
400 ft (120 m).

35 years in under a decade. Between 24 and 35 per
cent of the population are now HIV positive, which
means that Zimbabwe has one of the highest rates
of infection in the world.

Which government does Robert Mugabe lead?
Robert Gabriel Mugabe (born 1924) is the leader
of the ZANU Party and has been the head of state
since independence in 1980. Having extended
government control to the judiciary and media, he
stands accused of conducting a dictatorial style of
leadership. Zimbabwe has been expelled from the
Commonwealth for massive human rights violations.

What was Zimbabwe called previously?
In the Shona language the country was called
"dzimba dza mabwe" (meaning "great houses of
stone," see box). From 1895 until independence in
1980 Zimbabwe was known as Rhodesia after the
country's colonizer Cecil Rhodes (1853–1902).

Antelope horns
are used as wind
instruments.
Members of the
Church of Zion in
Mbare are shown
here making music
in a district
of Harare.

What is the current life expectancy in Zimbabwe?
Nowhere in the world has life expectancy fallen as
dramatically and in such a short space of time as
in Zimbabwe, where it has plummeted from 55 to

Great Zimbabwe

In the 16th century the Portuguese came across the ruins of
a vast stone city between the Zambezi and Orange rivers and
spread the legend that this was the home of the legendary
Queen of Sheba. In 1871 the German explorer Karl Gottlieb
Mauch (1837–1875) succeeded in rediscovering Great
Zimbabwe. Ceramic finds at the site point to the existence of
trading links with Persia and China between the 13th and 15th
centuries. Despite intensive research, however, it has not been
possible to discover all the secrets of the ancient site, such as
who built it or what function it served.

REPUBLIC OF SOUTH AFRICA

Flag	Setswana, Swati, Venda, Tsonga (all official languages)
Currency	**Surface area** 0.47 million sq miles (1.22 million sq km)
1 rand (ZAR) = 100 cents	**Population** 44.3 million
System of government	**Religion**
Presidential republic since 1961 (Commonwealth member)	32% independent African churches, 8% Pentecostal, 7% Methodist, 7% Catholic
Capital Pretoria	**Notable features**
Languages	South Africa is the sixth-largest diamond producer in the world.
English, Afrikaans, Ndebele, Xhosa, Zulu, Northern Sotho, Southern Sotho,	

Why is South Africa nicknamed the Rainbow Nation?

South Africa has been given this nickname because it is home to people of all skin colors and a multitude of ethnic groups and countries of origin.

Why is the tip of South Africa called the Cape of Good Hope?

In 1488 the Portuguese explorer Bartholomeu Diaz discovered the cape and named it Cabo das Tormentas ("Cape of Storms"). This was changed by King João II of Portugal to its present name (Cabo da Boa Esperança in Portuguese) as an expression of the hope that the sea route to India had been discovered. The cape is not, however, the southernmost point of South Africa (that is Cape Agulhas) but its southwesternmost.

What is the Cape Floristic Region?

The Cape Floristic Region is the smallest of a total of seven floristic regions on the planet but contains the highest density of plant species. There are over 20,000 different species in South Africa, most of which are indigenous to the Cape Region. This represents ten per cent of all the plant species in the world.

What kind of economy does South Africa have?

South Africa's economy is the biggest and most developed in Africa, benefiting from an efficient, modern infrastructure. In terms of mineral resources South Africa is one of the best endowed nations in the world. In addition to producing 10.8 million carats of diamonds per year it possesses platinum, gold, vanadium, titanium, uranium, chromium, manganese, and asbestos.

Top: Contrary to popular belief, the Cape of Good Hope is not the southernmost but the southwesternmost point of South Africa.

Cape Town, which combines all the vibrancy of a big city with an enchanting ocean setting, a fascinating history, and a beautiful hinterland, attracts 7.3 million tourists a year.

Winegrowing has a long history in South Africa, having arrived in the 17th century with Huguenot settlers. Pictured here are vineyards in the Stellenbosch region.

Rocky coastline north of the Cape of Good Hope.

Apartheid

Apartheid, meaning separation or segregation, refers to the policy of racial segregation reviled throughout the world which was introduced in South Africa as a way of guaranteeing the superiority of the white Boer minority over the Black majority. It was an extreme form of racial discrimination and deprivation of rights and extended even into the private sphere. It was introduced after the victory in elections of the National Party in 1948 and was only abolished in 1990 as the result of many years of struggle. Nelson Mandela (see box) was elected South Africa's first Black president in 1994.

What was the Cullinan?

The Cullinan was a 3,106-carat rough diamond—the largest ever—found in 1906. It was cut into 105 stones, of which the nine largest were incorporated into the British crown jewels. The very first diamonds to be mined in South Africa were found in Kimberley, the capital of the Northern Cape province, in 1869. As deposits in Indonesia and Brazil were starting to be exhausted, South Africa became the world's biggest supplier.

How many different languages are spoken in South Africa?

South Africa has 11 different official languages (see country description), the highest number of any country in the world. Afrikaans is the mother tongue of 59 per cent of the Caucasian population but only 0.7 per cent of the Black population and, although English is the most widely used language in South African public life, it is spoken at home by just 40 per cent of Caucasians and a mere 0.5 per cent of Blacks.

What is Afrikaans?

Afrikaans, also known as Cape Dutch, developed from 17th-century Dutch dialects and is the language of the Boers. It has been a written language as well as a spoken one since 1861. In many respects it is simpler than Dutch but the two are mutually comprehensible.

Nelson Mandela

Along with Americans Malcolm X (1925–1965) and Martin Luther King (1929–1968), Nelson Mandela (born 1918) was one of the leading figures in the fight for Black rights. He prepared the way for a peaceful transition from Apartheid South Africa to a democratic state in which members of all races have equal rights and obligations. Mandela was a lawyer who spent 28 years of his life in jail as a political prisoner for anti-Apartheid activities. He was released in 1990 under President Frederik Willem de Klerk (born 1936) and Apartheid collapsed. In a speech to 120,000 people in a stadium in Soweto, Mandela urged all those who had renounced Apartheid to work for a non-racist, unified, and democratic South Africa with free elections in which everyone has a vote. Mandela and De Klerk were both awarded the Nobel Peace Prize in 1993. South Africa's first democratic elections were held on April 27, 1994. Mandela was inaugurated as the country's first black president and during his term (1994–1999) he presided over the transition from apartheid.

Who are the Boers?

Boer is the Dutch word for "farmer" and came to denote the South Africans who were descendants of the first Dutch to disembark in Table Bay in 1647 having been shipwrecked close to the site of present-day Cape Town. From 1652 Cape Town was systematically developed as a fortified supply station of the Dutch East India Company. Over the following years employees of the company settled in Cape Town and were joined by others from France and the Rhineland. By the mid-18th century there were already 4,000 Boer settlers (who were also known as Afrikaaners, Cape Dutch, and White Africans) living in the region.

When did wine start being made in South Africa?

In 1688 a Dutch ship arrived in Cape Town carrying French Huguenot families fleeing the religious persecution initiated by Louis XIV. These families introduced winegrowing to South Africa.

A Zulu woman in ceremonial headdress in a village in the KwaZulu-Natal province on the east coast of South Africa.

LESOTHO

Flag

Currency
1 loti (LSL) = 100 lisente

System of government
Constitutional monarchy since 1993
(Commonwealth member)

Capital
Maseru

Languages
Sesotho, English (official languages)

Surface area
11,720 sq miles (30,355 sq km)

Population 1.8 million

Religion
90% Christian (44% Catholic)

Notable features
Lesotho is completely surrounded by
South Africa.

Right: Two Basotho women carrying their burdens on their heads.

What is unusual about the geography of Lesotho?

The whole of Lesotho lies above 3,300 ft (1,000 m) and most of it above 5,900 ft (1,800 m). Most of the population live in the west of the country on a high plateau ranging in elevation from 4,600 ft (1,400 m) to 5,600 ft (1,700 m). In the east the mountains rise to heights of over 10,000 ft (3,000 m).

How is Lesotho's population made up?

Ninety-nine per cent of Lesotho's population belong to a single Bantu ethnic group, the Basotho, and therefore share the same culture and traditions and a strong sense of belonging. Unusually for Africa, Lesotho is not a country in which a wide variety of languages is spoken.

The Basotho are one of the few African people groups who had to learn to survive in the mountains.

The Lesotho Promise

Letseng diamond mine is unusual in that it has the largest percentage of large diamonds, i.e. larger than ten carats, in the world. It reopened in 2004 after nearly 40 years. In 2006 one of the biggest diamonds in the world, the Lesotho Promise, was found there. It was sold to a South African diamond corporation the same year for 12 million US dollars.

Who is the king of Lesotho?

The king of Lesotho is Letsie III, who studied law in Lesotho and England and acceded the throne in 1990 after his father was forced into exile. His reign was interrupted for a year in 1995, when he abdicated in favor of his father Moshoeshoe II who had returned to the country. Letsie III became king again after his father died in an automobile accident the following year.

Is Lesotho poor?

Yes. The land is suitable for only one form of agriculture and self-sufficiency is therefore impossible. Food is imported from neighboring South Africa and many of Lesotho's citizens are forced to earn their living there as migrant workers. The country receives aid from the United States, the European Union, and the World Bank.

What is the main ethnic group?

The Swazi, a Bantu people, make up around 90 per cent of Swaziland's population. Zulus, Tongas, Sothos, Whites, and so-called *coloreds* (mixed-race citizens with one white parent or parents from different tribes) represent the remainder.

What are Swaziland's main industries?

Mainly agriculture and forestry. In addition to subsistence farming, some produce is exported (pineapples, corn, millet, cotton, potatoes, and sugar cane) but most of the plantations are owned by a small number of White farmers and international corporations. Stockbreeding (cattle, sheep, and goats) is also a significant economic factor. In terms of natural resources, diamonds, asbestos and coal are produced, although sales of asbestos, are declining because of the health concerns. Another important source of revenue is tourism. Swaziland's main attractions are the casino outside Mbabane and the

HIV/AIDS in Swaziland

Around 44 per cent of the population are HIV positive, the highest rate in the world. Moreover, studies suggest that HIV prevalence rates continue to increase. Children and the elderly are also badly affected. Swaziland now has one of the lowest life expectancies in the world (33) and no substantial population growth. A collapse of the population structure therefore looks almost inevitable.

SWAZILAND

Flag

Currency
1 lilangeni (SZL) (plural: emalangeni) = 100 cents

System of government
Absolute monarchy since 1973 (Commonwealth member)

Capital
Mbabane

Languages
Siswati, English (official languages)

Surface area
6,704 sq miles (17,363 sq km)

Population 1.2 million

Religion
40% Church of Zion, 20% Catholic

nature reserves. The economy as a whole is heavily dependent upon South Africa.

Is the monarchy popular with the people?

No. In this country with extreme poverty there is growing dissatisfaction with the king. In 1996 this expressed itself in violent demonstrations against the monarchy. King Mswati III, who has been the most powerful man in the country since 1986, is Africa's last absolute monarch and head of state, with both executive and legislative powers. Political parties have been banned in Swaziland since 1973. Infamous for his dissolute lifestyle, to mark his 37th birthday the king had 37 Mercedes automobiles with gold-plated license plates flown in from Germany.

In rural areas schoolchildren are taught how to grow vegetables. Older pupils are placed in charge of their own patches.

▲ Palau   Micronesia   New Zealand

Australia

AUSTRALIA

Australia is the world's flattest continent: only 5% of its terrain is more than 2,000 ft (600 m) above sea level. It is also the driest continent after Antarctica: a third of it is desert and another third is steppe. Australia and Oceania comprise over 7,500 islands, a land surface area of approximately 3.5 million sq miles (9 million sq km), and an ocean surface area of 27 million sq miles (70 million sq km). The 2,100 or so islands that are inhabited are home to some 35.9 million people. Only one of the states of Australia and Oceania, Papua New Guinea, possesses a land border: all the others are surrounded by water.

Fiji   Solomon Islands   Samoa

PHYSICAL MAP

120° E

Luzon · 9,606 ft Pulog

Manila

Palawan

Sulu Sea

Mindanao

· 13,432 ft Kinabalu

Celebes Sea

Molucca Sea

Sulawesi

Buru

Seram

Banda Sea

Flores Sea

Flores

Sawu Sea

Sumba

Timor

Dili

Timor Sea

140° E

Northern Mariana Islands

Guam

Yap

Koror · Babeldaob

Pacific Ocean

Caroline Islands

Maloelap Atoll

Equator

Nauru

160° E

180°

Gilbert Islands

0°

Ellice Islands

Halmahera

16,503 ft Central Range Sepik
Puncak Jaya New Guinea
Aru Islands

Tanimbar Islands

Arafura Sea

14,793 ft Mount Wilhelm

New Britain

Bismarck Sea

New Ireland

Solomon Sea

Solomon Islands

Honiara

Santa Cruz Islands

Rotuma

13,363 ft

Port Moresby

Coral Sea

New Hebrides

Vanua Levu

Port Vila

Viti Levu Suva

20° S

Arnhem Land

Gulf of Carpentaria

Mount Lush · 2,579 ft Lake Argyle
Fitzroy

Barkly Tableland

Cape York Peninsula

Mitchell

5,289 ft

Great Dividing Range

New Caledonia

Nouméa

180° 170° W 160° W 0°

150° W

Tanami Desert

Flinders

Apia

Samoa Islands

Cook Islands

Pacific Ocean

Society Islands

Great Sandy Desert

Macdonnell Ranges

Mount Bruce · 4,052 ft
Ashburton

Mount Zeil · 4,954 ft
Ayers Rock · 2,844 ft
4,724 ft ·
Mount Woodroffe

Georgina

Simpson Desert

Finke

Diamantina

Cooper Creek

Warrego

20° S

Friendly Islands

Niue

Nuku'alofa

Papeete

170° W 160° W 20° S 150° W

Gibson Desert

Murchison

Great Victoria Desert

Lake Eyre

Darling

Lachlan

Bluff Knoll
3,648 ft ·

Nullarbor Plain

Great Australian Bight

Murray

Murray Canberra

Mount · 7,316 ft Kosciusko

North Island

Tasman Sea

Ruapehu · 9,175 ft

40° S

Tasmania

Wellington

1:40 000 000

Indian Ocean

12,316 ft · South Island
Mount Cook

40° S

100° E 120° E 140° E 160° E 180°

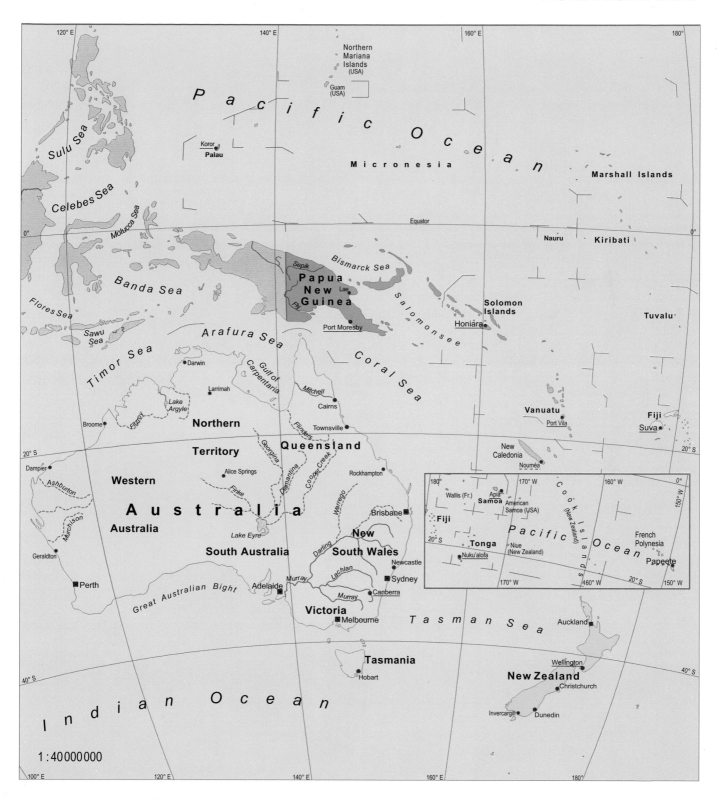

P a c i f i c   O c e a n

Northern
Mariana
Islands
(USA)

Guam
(USA)

Sulu Sea

Koror
Palau

M i c r o n e s i a

Marshall Islands

Celebes Sea

Molucca Sea

Equator

0°

Nauru
Kiribati

0°

Banda Sea

Sepik
**Papua
New
Guinea**
Lae
FN

Bismarck Sea

Salomonsee

**Solomon
Islands**
Honiara

Tuvalu

Flores Sea

*Sawu
Sea*

Port Moresby

Arafura Sea

Coral Sea

Timor Sea

Darwin

Larrimah

Mitchell
Cairns

*Gulf of
Carpentaria*

Townsville

Vanuatu
Port Vila

Fiji
Suva

*Lake
Argyle*

Fitzroy

Northern

Flinders

Broome

20° S

Territory

Georgina

Queensland

New
Caledonia
Nouméa

20° S

Dampier

Ashburton

Alice Springs

Western

Finke

Diamantina

Cooper Creek

Rockhampton

180°
170° W
160° W
0°

Geraldton

Murchison

Australia

A u s t r a l i a

Australia

Warrego

Brisbane

Wallis (Fr.)
Samoa
Apia

American
Samoa (USA)

C o o k   I s l a n d s
(New Zealand)

150° W

Perth

Great Australian Bight

Lake Eyre

South Australia

Darling

Adelaide

Murray

Lachlan

Murray

**New
South Wales**

Newcastle

Canberra

Sydney

Fiji

20° S

Tonga
Nuku'alofa

Niue
(New Zealand)

P a c i f i c   O c e a n

French
Polynesia
Papeete

20° S

170° W
160° W
150° W

Victoria
Melbourne

T a s m a n   S e a

Auckland

Tasmania
Hobart

40° S

Wellington

New Zealand

40° S

I n d i a n   O c e a n

Christchurch

Invercargill
Dunedin

1 : 40 000 000

Introduction

Do Australia and Oceania form a single continent in a geographical sense?

The term "continent" is tectonically and geographically incorrect here as the different countries do not all rest on the same continental plate but are split between the Indo-Australian Plate, the Pacific Plate, and a number of smaller plates. East of Tonga, for example, is the 36,000-ft-deep (11,000-m) Tonga Trench, where the heavy Pacific Plate slides under the Indo-Australian Plate forming a so-called subduction zone (which explains why these areas are so earthquake prone).

What is Oceania?

Oceania is the name of the island world scattered across the "South Seas." It is a geographical, often geopolitical, region consisting of numerous lands. From west to east this region is in turn subdivided into Melanesia, Micronesia and Polynesia. Hawaii is also in Polynesia but as it politically belongs to the United States, it is deemed to be part of North America rather than Oceania.

What are the origins of the term "South Seas"?

When explorer Vasco Nuñez de Balboa (1475–1517) crossed the Isthmus of Panama in 1513, he named the ocean that lay before him the "Mar del Sur" ("South Sea"). Geographically speaking this covers all areas south of Panama but in practice the term "South Seas" refers to Oceania alone.

Where is Tasmania?

Tasmania lies around 125 miles (200 km) off the southeast coast of Australia. Just 12,000 years ago it was still part of the Australian mainland, but at the end of the last Ice Age the Bass Strait was created by rising water levels, making Tasmania an island. Much of Tasmania is covered by unspoiled rainforest including the highest and oldest deciduous forests on the planet. The island was discovered and colonized

---

Rarotonga Treaty

On August 2, 1986 the 13 members of the Pacific Island Forum met on Rarotonga, one of the Cook Islands, to sign a treaty banning the testing, stationing, possession or manufacture of nuclear weapons or the storage of nuclear waste in the South Pacific. Not only does the treaty prohibit the five nuclear powers from detonating nuclear devices, it also prohibits them from threatening to do so. The signatories were Australia, New Zealand, the Cook Islands, Kiribati, Nauru, Vanuatu, Tuvalu, Fiji, Papua New Guinea, Samoa, Niue, and the Solomon Islands. China and the USSR signed the agreement in 1989 (neither possesses any territories in the South Pacific). The United States and the United Kingdom only signed on March 23, 1996, and France on September 10 of that year, after completing their nuclear weapons testing programs in the region.

Many South Sea Islands, including New Britain shown here, have mangrove forests that grow right up to the edge of the sea.

Background: An interesting feature of Tonga's main island Tongatapu is its blowholes (connected by underground conduits to the sea) through which water shoots into the air in high fountains.

at the beginning of the 19th century, the start of a period of British influence over the island that ended in genocide. The indigenous population in 1803 has been estimated at between 5,000 and 10,000 people. Just a century after the discovery of Tasmania, all of them had been wiped out by the British.

What are the consequences of global warming for the region?

The greenhouse effect is causing devastating drought, bush fires, and floods in Australia. The cost of this damage is already in the billions of dollars. Thousands of creatures have died and many people have come to harm. In Oceania numerous islands and entire nations are at risk of being submerged by ever-rising sea levels.

Who were the original inhabitants of Oceania and where did they come from?

Oceania's original inhabitants were descended from the Austronesian peoples—the Aborigines, the Maori, and the Polynesians. The Maori and Polynesians are believed to have arrived in wooden boats and rafts from the north and the Aborigines from the southeast. The Norwegian zoologist Thor Heyerdahl (1914–2002) tried to prove that Polynesia could have been settled from the east (South America). He set off from Peru in the *Kon-Tiki*, a raft made of balsa wood and reeds, in 1949 and allowed the trade winds and powerful Humboldt Current to drive him west to Polynesia.

Lalomanu Beach on the southeast coast of Upolu Island, Samoa, is one of the longest and most beautiful in the country.

What are *waka*?

Waka is a Maori word for richly decorated outrigger canoes used by the Polynesians. For longer journeys on the high seas, double-hull canoes up to 130 ft (40 m) long are used. These are paddled by up to 80 men but are also equipped with a sail. Smaller *waka* are made from a hollowed-out tree trunk while the larger vessels are made from separate sections joined together. The specific construction method is largely dependent on the available vegetation. On the Chatham Islands, for example, the boats are made of reeds because no big trees grow there.

What is a *didgeridoo*?

A *didgeridoo* is an Aboriginal musical instrument. It belongs to the aerophone class of musical instrument in which sounds are generated by vibrating air. The musician produces a range of sounds by varying his or her mouth movements and employing a special breathing technique and vocal effects while the pipe of the instrument acts as an amplifier. The result is a dark, rather monotone sound. *Didgeridoos* are made from eucalyptus boughs and are usually brightly painted. They are often used to provide a rhythmic accompaniment to singing and dancing.

Steam rising from one of the many geothermal pools (the so-called Champagne Pool at Wai-o-Tapu) in the district of Rotorua on the North Island of New Zealand.

Who are the Aborigines?

The Aborigines are a nomadic people who arrived in Australia 50,000 years ago. The name was first used in 1770 by European sailors under the command of James Cook (1728–1779). It is derived from the Latin *ab origine* meaning "from the beginning." Aborigines live in Australia, Tasmania, and a number of neighboring islands. They make up about 2.4 per cent of Australia's modern population.

Snow-covered mountains in Cardrona Valley on New Zealand's South Island.

disks were carved comes from the island of Palau 250 miles (400 km) away and the danger inherent in its transportation increased and guaranteed the currency's value. When the journey became easier, faster, and safer at the beginning of the 20th century, the system was hit by inflation. Rai is used today exclusively by men and mainly for symbolic transactions.

A man carving a boomerang in Uluru National Park using the traditional Australian Aboriginal technique.

How important was art to the continent's indigenous peoples?

Although writing was unknown to the region's original inhabitants, art played an important part in the transmission of history and the story of origins. As indigenous peoples died out, knowledge of the meaning of much of their art was lost with them, which is why information about the period before the 16th century is lacking. Western-style written history has only existed since the discovery and colonization of the region by Europeans.

Tattoos

The word "tattoo" derives from the Tahitian *tatan*, meaning "to draw." The origins of this Tahitian word are thought to be onomatopoeic—an imitation of the noise made by the traditional Polynesian tattooing comb. Tattooing involves decorating the skin with abstract or figurative designs, either by applying pigment to the deeper skin layers or by cutting the skin in order to cause scarring. In Polynesian society, tattoos were not only for decoration but were also an indication of status and occupation.

A traditional men's longhouse (*bai*) in a village on the island of Babeldaob, Palau.

What was the attitude of the Church towards voyages of discovery to the South Seas in the 17th century?

By the 17th century most of the South Pacific had been explored and mapped. Many blanks remained, however, and hopes of the discovery of fabulous riches had not yet been fulfilled. It was at this point that the Catholic Church started to consider the consequences of possible interbreeding between Christians and "heathens." On the one hand, "sexual license" had to be discouraged while on the other, the local people needed to be guided onto the "rightful path." Sexual relations with "savages" were denounced and missionaries accompanied the voyages of discovery in order to spread the Christian faith by "fire and sword."

What is Rai?

Rai is the name of a form of stone currency used on the island of Ulithi in Yap, one of the federal states of Micronesia. Rai is still valid as a means of payment or exchange even though no new stones (which measure up to 13 ft/4 m) have been manufactured since 1931. The stone from which the

AUSTRALIA

Flag

Currency
1 Australian dollar (AUD) = 100 cents

System of government
Constitutional monarchy since 1901
(Commonwealth member)

Capital
Canberra

Languages
English (official language), Aboriginal
languages

Surface area
2.97 million sq miles
(7.69 million sq km)

Population 20.1 million

Religion
26% Catholic, 21% Anglican,
2% other Christian religions,
5% other religions

Notable features
Australia is claiming an Antarctic
territory but this has not been
recognized internationally.

When was Australia discovered and colonized?

When was Australia discovered and colonized?
Dutch merchant ships repeatedly visited individual sections of the Australian coastline from 1606 onwards. As the land looked barren, however, the Dutch made no attempt to colonize it. In 1770 Captain James Cook (1728–1779) reached the fertile east coast and claimed the country for Great Britain, naming it New South Wales.

Sydney's two main landmarks, the Opera House and Sydney Harbor Bridge. The 1,650-ft-long (503-m) bridge is known to locals as the "Coathanger."

How did Australia become a penal colony?

After Britain's defeat in the American War of Independence, the British government looked for other ways of transporting prisoners out of the country. Australia, claimed for the British crown shortly before as the colony of New South Wales, offered a good opportunity. The first fleet of ships containing British settlers and convicted criminals arrived in remote Australia in 1788. By 1868 160,000 offenders had been transported there. In addition to the mainland, the island of Tasmania (still known at that time as Van Diemen's Land) to the south was also used as a penal colony. It was used mainly for the more dangerous criminals because its smaller size made it easier to keep watch over.

What is so remarkable about Sydney Opera House?

Sydney Opera House, located by the harbor, is probably the best-known building on the continent. Its fascinating architecture has earned the structure universal praise and recognition. Its special charm stems from its fan-like roof that resembles seven ship's sails. Designed by Danish architect Jorn Utzon (born 1918), the building finally opened in 1973 after many long, difficult, and above all expensive years of planning and construction.

Is Australia still a destination for emigrants?

Along with the United States and Canada, Australia has traditionally been one of the main destinations for European emigrants. More than 90 per cent of Australia's population are of European (mainly British or Irish) descent. Immigration from Europe was particularly strongly promoted after the Second World War, partly because many Europeans were prepared to emigrate in order to escape the aftermath of war and partly because the immigration of Europeans corresponded to the "White Australia" policy of the day. Since the 1960s increasing numbers of immigrants have arrived from Asia, which has led to occasional outbreaks of ethnic conflict.

How important is stockbreeding to Australia's economy?

Stockbreeding is very important as it is one of the country's biggest economic sectors. There are around 100 million sheep, 25 million cattle, and correspondingly extensive pasturelands in Australia. The country is responsible for 29 per cent of world wool production. In most regions the cultivation of cereals is only possible with the help of artificial irrigation.

Interesting facts

- Australia is the sixth-largest country in the world.

- The country's name derives from the Latin expression *Terra australis*, meaning "Southern Land."

- Australia is often referred to as "down under" because it is traditionally positioned at the bottom of maps with Europe and North America towards the top.

- There are 400 public and private airports and airstrips in Australia and the country has one of the densest networks of air routes in the world.

- In addition to a number of smaller islands, Tasmania (which is almost as large as Ireland) is also part of Australia.

Aborigines with one of their traditional musical instruments, the *didgeridoo*, which is known to go back at least 2,500 years.

A kangaroo with a joey. The young animal remains in the safety of its mother's pouch for the first six months of its life.

The Great Barrier Reef, which has been called "one of the seven natural wonders of the world." It is visited by more than eight million tourists each year.

Christmas Island

Two different islands are known by this name. One is part of the Pacific republic of Kiribati and was discovered by James Cook (1728–1779) on December 24, 1777. The other is part of Australia and was discovered by William Mynors on December 25, 1643. Both owe their name to the date on which they were discovered. The Australian Christmas Island measures just 52 sq miles (135 sq km), and although phosphate was once mined here, two thirds of its surface area is now covered by a conservation area. Flying Fish Cove, its capital, is home to around 500 people, a third of its population.

Is the kangaroo an Australian animal?

Like the koala, the kangaroo is a peculiarly Australian animal and features alongside the emu on the Australian coat of arms. The only other place to which members of the kangaroo family are endemic is New Guinea. The kangaroo was once an important source of meat to indigenous Australians.

What is the Great Barrier Reef?

Located off Australia's northeast coast, the Great Barrier Reef is the world's largest coral reef, extending for more than 1,250 miles (2,000 km). One of Australia's biggest tourist attractions, it was designated a UNESCO World Heritage site in 1981.

What and where is Ayers Rock?

Ayers Rock is a large rock formation in central Australia 210 miles (340 km) west of Alice Springs. Today it is known as Uluru, not only by indigenous Australians but officially too. It towers some 1,150 ft (350 m) above the surrounding desert landscape. Although visitors are allowed to climb Ayers Rock, the Aborigines are not happy about it as Uluru is regarded by them as a holy site.

Is the boomerang a peculiarly Australian hunting weapon?

No. The latest discoveries indicate that the boomerang was used as a hunting weapon all over the world long before the birth of Christ, although it is now only used as such by the indigenous Australians and a few Native American peoples. Over recent years it has achieved popularity as a piece of sporting equipment.

Tasmanian devil

The Tasmanian devil is a beast of prey that now survives only in Tasmania. It was once hunted intensively in order to protect herds of grazing animals and almost died out as a result. It has been a protected species since 1941. The Tasmanian devil has a dark coat and an unpleasant smell and is curious and highly aggressive. It is not dangerous to humans, however, as it grows to a length of just 24 in (60 cm) and weighs a mere 18 lb (8 kg). Since 1999 the creature's survival has been further threatened by the outbreak of a cancer-like disease.

Why is Canberra, the country's eighth-largest city, the national capital?

After Australia achieved independence from Great Britain in 1907, a competition developed between Sydney and Melbourne for the distinction of being chosen as capital of the new nation. In 1908 the conflict was settled by a decision to build a new capital from scratch. Five years later, after an international urban planning competition had been held, work began on the construction of the new city in the southeast of the country. Canberra is located 220 miles (300 km) southwest of Sydney and 400 miles (650 km) northeast of Melbourne.

Uluru (Ayers Rock), an enormous sandstone outcrop in the Central Australian Desert. It has a circumference of around 6 miles (10 km).

MICRONESIA

Flag

Currency
1 US dollar (USD) = 100 cents

System of government
Federal republic since 1980

Capital
Kolonia (seat of government: Palikir)

Languages English (official language),
Micronesian languages (including
Chuukese and Pohnpeian)

Surface area
271 sq miles (702 sq km)

Population 108,000

Religion
50% Catholic, 47% Protestant

Notable features
Micronesia comprises more than
700 islands.

Which nations have occupied the islands over the centuries?

Although the islands were discovered in the 16th century by the Portuguese, they were not occupied until 1696 (by Spain). Following the Spanish-American War they were sold in 1899 to the German Empire, which incorporated them into its colony of German New Guinea. Just a few years later, at the outbreak of the First World War, Japan occupied the islands and was subsequently awarded the League of Nations mandate in 1920. After the Japanese surrender in the Second World War they passed to the United States in 1947 and finally achieved independence in 1991 as the Federated States of Micronesia.

Background:
Bechiyal is the
northernmost
point of the island
of Yap.

How long have the islands been inhabited?

How long have the islands been inhabited? Archaeological finds on the islands, particularly on the island of Yap in the West Carolines, have shown that a civilization lived here as long ago as the 4th millennium BC.

Which languages are spoken in Micronesia?

The official language is English and is spoken in at least rudimentary fashion by most of the population. In addition there are six local official languages (Yapese, Pohnpeian, Kosraean, Chuukese, Ulithian, and Woleaian) and over ten minority languages, mostly versions of Creole spoken on the different islands. Fluent Japanese is still spoken by many older people.

What is the geological structure of the islands?

Most of the islands are coral islands that rise just a few feet above sea level. The main islands such as Yap, Ponape, and the Chuuk islands are the summits of volcanoes that rise up from great depths and reach heights of up to 2,625 ft (800 m) above sea level. These volcanic islands are extremely rugged and are surrounded by reefs.

Fishermen of
Ifaluk Atoll in the
Caroline Islands
returning to shore
with a good
tuna catch.

Health problems

As throughout the Pacific region, the inhabitants of Micronesia have major weight problems. The highest proportion of overweight people in the world live in Micronesia and on Nauru. Over three quarters of all women are overweight. This is not seen as an aesthetic problem, however, as fatness corresponds to the Pacific ideal of beauty.

What measures have been introduced in Palau to prevent pollution of the ocean by plastic bags?

In order to ensure that plastic bags are not blown into the sea by the strong local winds, visitors who bring plastic bags to the islands are fined one US dollar. Any storekeepers caught handing them out are fined 100 US dollars per offending item.

What was the German-Spanish Treaty?

After the Spanish defeat in the Spanish-American War of 1898 (often referred to as the first war for the redivision of the world), the German Empire exerted pressure on Spain and on February 12, 1899 acquired the Caroline, Mariana, and Palau islands for 17 million gold marks.

When did the Battle of Peleliu take place?

Japan had occupied the Palau islands at the beginning of the First World War and maintained a garrison there. During the Battle of the Pacific in the Second World War, heavy fighting took place between US and Japanese forces for the islands of Angaur (September 17–30, 1944) and Peleliu (September 15–November 30, 1944).

Who was Ibedul Gibbons?

In 1978 the people of Palau voted against joining the Federated States of Micronesia and for independence. Over the next few years their leader Ibedul Gibbons campaigned for the right of the people to refuse to allow the United States (provider of the nation's defense) to station nuclear weapons anywhere on the islands. Palau was declared a nuclear-free zone in 1983 and Gibbons and his people were awarded an "Alternative Nobel Prize."

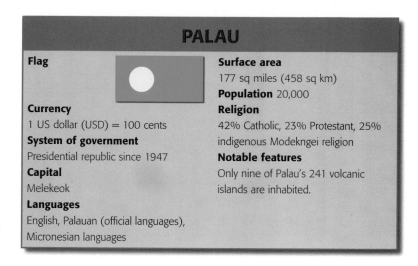

PALAU

Flag

Currency
1 US dollar (USD) = 100 cents

System of government
Presidential republic since 1947

Capital
Melekeok

Languages
English, Palauan (official languages), Micronesian languages

Surface area
177 sq miles (458 sq km)

Population 20,000

Religion
42% Catholic, 23% Protestant, 25% indigenous Modekngei religion

Notable features
Only nine of Palau's 241 volcanic islands are inhabited.

What is Jellyfish Lake?

Jellyfish Lake is a saltwater lake on Mercherchar Island. This divers' paradise is home to millions of non-stinging jellyfish, which give the lake its name. They move through the water in a circular motion in response to the movement of the sun. They are completely harmless and so divers need not fear coming into physical contact with them.

The Rock Islands, 22 miles (35 km) south of the capital Melekeok, are a chain of over 70 small islands covered by dense vegetation.

Dugong

The dugong (sometimes called a "sea pig") is a large marine mammal that feeds on seagrass and lives in the shallow coastal waters around the islands of Palau. Covered with tactile hairs, it weighs between 510 and 1,985 lb (230 and 900 kg) and measures between 5 and 13 ft (1.5 and 4 m), occasionally more. The females are slightly bigger than the males and the highest recorded weight is 2,002 lb (908 kg). Dugongs are hunted for their meat, which tastes like veal, although their fat, skin (for leather), bones, and tusks (for ivory sculptures) are also prized. A number of Asian countries use parts of the dugong for medicinal purposes.

MARSHALL ISLANDS

Flag

Currency
1 US dollar (USD) = 100 cents

System of government
Republic since 1990

Capital
Majuro

Languages
English, Marshallese (official languages)

Surface area
70 sq miles (181 sq km)

Population 59,000

Religion 90% Protestant, 9% Catholic

Notable features
Due to their nutrient-poor soil and the great distance that separates them from the continent of Asia, the vegetation of the Marshall Islands is characterized by a relative paucity of species.

Right: An atomic mushroom above Bikini Atoll in 1946. The bomb was detonated under water.

Is the population distributed evenly across the Marshall Islands?

No. Although the Marshall Islands, which are part of the island world of Micronesia, consist of more than 1,150 islands and atolls, almost 70 per cent of the population live on Majuro Atoll.

What is the name of the capital?

The Marshall Islands are hoping to develop tourism to its idyllic South Sea islands.

The official national capital is Majuro, which is located on one of the 64 islands comprising the circular coral reef Majuro Atoll. Most of the population, however, are concentrated on three other islands in the atoll, which is why the Dalap, Uliga, and Darrit group is often referred to as the capital.

Is the country's economy in good shape?

No. In 2006 direct financial assistance from the United States accounted for 50 per cent of the national budget. It is hoped that the economy will be boosted in the near future by tourism and the extraction of manganese from the ocean floor.

Bikini

Bikini Atoll is part of the Marshall Islands. It became a household name throughout the world as a result of the nuclear testing conducted here by the United States between 1946 and 1958. The population had been evacuated beforehand and was only able to return at the end of the 1960s. In 1978 the inhabitants had to leave the atoll again, however, because the radiation levels were discovered to be too high still. The most outspoken critics of atomic testing do not believe that Bikini Atoll will become inhabitable again until 2040.

Incidentally, the two-piece swimsuit of the same name was launched within days of the first nuclear test, and owes its name to its "explosive" effect.

How did Nauru acquire its phosphate deposits?
The island is covered by beds of soluble limestone in which deep craters have been eroded. Over thousands of years, millions upon millions of seabirds nested in these crevices and their excrement formed deposits many feet deep. The influence of the weather gradually turned this guano into the purest calcium phosphate in the world (90 per cent).

What has been the significance of this phosphate for Nauru?

For a number of years these enormous phosphate deposits made Nauru the country with the highest per capita income in the world. Now that the phosphate is exhausted, Nauru is becoming impoverished and is facing imminent economic collapse.

NAURU

Flag	Surface area
	8 sq miles (21 sq km)
	Population 13,000
Currency	**Religion**
1 Australian dollar (AUD) = 100 cents	67% Protestant, 33% Catholic
System of government	**Notable features**
Republic since 1968 (Commonwealth member)	Nauru is an atoll formed by the summit of an extinct volcano whose sides
Capital Yaren	fall away steeply. Less than ½ mile
Languages	(1.1 km) from the coast, the water is
English, Nauruan (official languages)	already 3,280 ft (1,000 m) deep.

Interesting facts

- Nauru is the smallest republic and third-smallest independent state in the world but has one of the highest population densities at 1,616 people per sq mile (624 people per sq km).

- There is hardly any crime on the island. The only offenses committed are traffic offenses, trespass, and bicycle theft.

- During the island's period of prosperity each Nauruan possessed two or three automobiles (for 18 miles/29 km of constructed roads) and a powerboat.

- Drinking water is in extremely short supply because although it rains a lot, the water seeps away through the porous limestone and phosphate bedrock. Water is therefore imported from Australia.

Which countries have sought to share in Nauru's wealth?

Germany annexed Nauru in 1888 and became involved in the exploitation of phosphate in 1900. Between the end of the First World War and 1968 the phosphate was mined and sold by Australia. Today the Nauruan government is demanding compensation on the basis that it was cheated by the Australians.

Why does Nauru have such a high incidence of diabetes?

Almost one in three adults on Nauru suffers from diabetes—the highest incidence in the world. The probable reason is that the local diet is extremely fatty and, in common with the rest of the Pacific region, fatness is regarded not as a problem but as aesthetically pleasing and desirable. Statistically speaking, the island nation is home to the fattest people in the world.

For a long time large parts of Nauru were covered with phosphate, though deposits have now been exhausted.

FIJI

Flag	**Languages** English, Fijian (official languages), Fiji Bat
Currency	**Surface area**
1 Fijian dollar (FJD) = 100 cents	7,093 sq miles (18,370 sq km)
System of government	**Population** 848,000
Republic since 1987	**Religion** 53% Christian, 38% Hindu,
(Commonwealth member)	8% Muslim
Capital	**Notable features**
Suva	Only 106 of Fiji's 330 islands are inhabited.

Indigenous Fijians at a typical *kava* ceremony. *Kava* is the national drink of Polynesia.

Where is Fiji and how many islands does it comprise?

Fiji is a group of 330 islands in the southwest Pacific. The two main islands Viti Levu and Vanua Levu account for 90 per cent of the surface area. The island nation is located 1,550 miles (2,500 km) east of Australia and 1,250 miles (2,000 km) north of New Zealand.

Why are there so many Hindus on Fiji?

During British colonial rule a sizable labor force was imported from India to work the sugar-cane plantations. Their descendants have at times represented a majority of the population although the indigenous Melanesian population is now the largest single ethnic group at 50 per cent.

Wakaya, one of more than 300 Fijian islands, has 32 magnificent beaches.

Is Fiji affected by hurricanes?

Yes. The hurricane season lasts between November and April and causes varying degrees of damage to parts of the island nation each year. One of the worst of recent years was Hurricane Ami in 2003.

How big a role does tourism play in the islands?

Fiji is one of the main tourist destinations in the South Pacific region, attracting visitors mainly from Australia (33 per cent) but also from New Zealand, the United Kingdom, and Japan. In addition to tourism, other important economic sectors include the sugar and textile industries.

"Fiji Water"

One of the world's most exclusive mineral waters comes from the Fiji Islands. "Fiji Water" is famous for its softness and has become the most popular spring water in the US. The company was formed in 1996 and the first bottles were exported in 1997. The advertising strategy is based around the idea that there is no environmental pollution in Fiji and the water has become a major export success for the island nation.

How many languages are spoken in Papua New Guinea?

The particular geographical conditions prevailing on the several larger and over 600 smaller islands have resulted in over 770 languages being spoken. The pidgin languages Tok Pisin and Hiri Moto, which are gradually developing into creoles (see São Tomé and Príncipe), therefore play an extremely important role as lingua francas and more and more people are learning them as mother tongues.

What is the most important mode of transport in Papua New Guinea?

Because of the ruggedness of the terrain and the vast undeveloped areas, there are no railways and hardly any proper roads. The airplane is the most important mode of transport.

What is Tolai, and where can one get hold of it?

Tolai is the name of an ethnic group to which two thirds of those living on the island of New Britain belong. It is also the name of their shell money. Tolai has been legal tender in Papua New Guinea since 2002, when the first shell money bank in the world (the Tolai Exchange Bank) opened in Rabaul. The bank changes the national currency kina into strings of shells known as "fathoms." The exchange rate is 4 kina for one fathom. It is estimated that there are 8 million kina of fathoms in circulation.

What was Kaiser-Wilhelmsland?

Germany had shown considerable interest in the islands to the north of Australia as early as the beginning of the 19th century. In 1885 the German Empire and Great Britain divided the territory between them. Northeast New Guinea became Kaiser-Wilhelmsland, a protectorate of the German New Guinea Company. Other German territories in the region included the Mariana and Caroline islands, Palau, the Marshall Islands, and Nauru. Australian forces occupied the German colonies at the beginning of the First World War.

PAPUA NEW GUINEA

Flag

Currency
1 kina (PGK) = 100 toea
1 fathom = 4 kina

System of government
Constitutional monarchy since 1975 (Commonwealth member)

Capital
Port Moresby

Languages
English, Tok Pisin, Hiri Motu (official languages), 742 Papuan languages

Surface area
178,704 sq miles (462,840 sq km)

Population 5.5 million

Religion
66% Christian, 34% traditional religions

Notable features
Papua New Guinea is the only nation in the world in which shell money is legal tender (since 2002).

Pidgin

Unlike creole languages, pidgin languages are not as a rule learned as a mother tongue. They are characterized by a limited vocabulary and simple sentence structures. Pidgin English developed in Chinese ports in the 19th century as a lingua franca for communication between the British and the Chinese and combined elements of English vocabulary with Chinese pronunciation and grammatical rules. The term "pidgin" itself is a Chinese corruption of the English word "business." In 1977 two pidgin languages became the youngest languages in the world when they were awarded official status in Papua New Guinea.

Sago is obtained through a process of washing, filtering, and drying the pith of the sago palm. It is used in Papua New Guinea as a flour for cooking and baking.

SOLOMON ISLANDS

Flag	(Neo-Solomonic or pidgin English), Kwara'ae, over 80 regional languages
Currency	**Surface area**
1 Solomon Islands dollar (SBD)	10,985 sq miles (28,450 sq km)
= 100 cents	**Population** 466,000
System of government	**Religion**
Constitutional monarchy since 1978	33% Anglican, 19% Catholic,
(Commonwealth member)	17% South Sea Evangelical Church,
Capital Honiara	21% other Protestant
Languages	**Notable features**
English (official language), Pijin	This group of volcanic islands comprises 998 islands and atolls.

Uepi Island, which belongs to the New Georgia Archipelago, encloses Marovo Lagoon, the largest saltwater lagoon in the world.

Which languages are spoken on the Solomon Islands?

In addition to the lingua franca English, around 70 languages belonging to the Oceanic and Papuan language groups are spoken by the indigenous population. In addition there are various immigrant groups (mainly Chinese and Indian) that speak their own tongues. A second lingua franca is Pijin (also known as Solomons pidgin), which is related to the creole (see São Tomé and Príncipe) languages Tok Pisin (see Papua New Guinea) and Bislama (see Vanuatu) spoken in the Micronesian region.

What shape is the Solomon Islands' economy in?

In addition to agriculture and fishing, the islands have large deposits of gold, copper, bauxite, zinc, phosphate, lead, silver, and cobalt. Tourism was an important economic sector too—until 1998, when ethnic conflict paralyzed the entire economic infrastructure and foreign investment dried up. The hostilities lasted until 2003 and the Solomon Islands is now one of Oceania's poorest countries.

What form of birth control used to be practiced on the Solomon Islands?

The small island of Tikopa covers no more than 2 sq miles (5 sq km) and its population was maintained at a more or less constant 1,000 people for hundreds of years. The reason for this is that the island would not have been able to sustain a larger number of people. In order to stay within this level, only the eldest sons were permitted to have children and any unwanted offspring were killed.

Interesting facts: Media

There are no television transmitters on the Solomon Islands because the islanders believe that television will destroy their culture. The only radio station broadcasts in English and Pijin.

What are the main geological features of the islands of Vanuatu?

The Vanuatu Archipelago consists of over 80 mostly volcanic islands and island groups that stretch for a distance of more than 800 miles (1,300 km). The two largest islands are Espiritu Santo and Makalula. The islands of Tanna and Aoba have active volcanoes (Mount Yasur and Manaro respectively).

How long have the islands been inhabited?

The oldest archaeological indications of human life on the island date from around 2000 BC.

What are the origins of bungee jumping?

According to legend, this extreme sport (jumping from a great height attached only to a rubber cord, which causes the jumper to rebound several times before resting just above the ground) originated in Vanuatu. A young woman is said to have fled her jealous husband by climbing a tree and then jumping into the void. The man jumped too but his wife had employed a trick, escaping death by tying a liana around her legs before leaping. Her husband, meanwhile, fell to the ground and died. Throughout the Pacific region liana jumping has been used for hundreds of years as a test of courage for young men and is also supposed to guarantee a bountiful harvest.

Who were the archipelago's colonial rulers?

On May 3, 1606 the Portuguese sailor Pedro Fernandez de Quirós (1565–1614) claimed the island of Espiritu Santo for the Spanish crown and the Catholic Church, thinking he had found the fabled southern continent. James Cook (1728–1779) visited the islands twice and European settlers started to arrive in 1839. In 1906 France and Britain agreed to rule the archipelago jointly and established a condominium (from the Latin *con-dominium*, meaning "common ownership") that eventually came to an end with Vanuatu's independence in 1980.

The happiness factor

Vanuatu has no natural resources to speak of. Its economy is based simply on agriculture, fishing, and a steadily developing tourist industry. Furthermore it is prone to natural disasters. Nevertheless, in a study by the British NEF (New Economics Foundation) to find the happiest people on the planet (the criteria being general contentedness, life expectancy, and environmental impact), the people of Vanuatu came out on top.

VANUATU

Flag

Currency
1 vatu (VUV) = 100 cents

System of government
Parliamentary republic since 1980 (Commonwealth member)

Capital
Port Vila

Languages
English, French, Bislama (Vanuatu pidgin) (official languages)

Surface area
4,710 sq miles (12,200 sq km)

Population 206,000

Religion
35% Presbyterian, 15% Anglican, 15% Catholic, folk religions and cargo cults (a minority)

Notable features
Until 1980 the archipelago was called the New Hebrides.

What is the economic significance of the Internet for Vanuatu?

Vanuatu rose to international Internet prominence with its free ".vu" domain. Numerous network operators and software manufacturers switched their operations to Vanuatu in order to benefit from the tax advantages. The island nation eventually started charging for use of the ".vu" domain and has raised over 42 million euros from sales.

An inhabitant of Vanuatu in the traditional garb of the ni-Vanuatu warrior.

KIRIBATI

Flag

Currency
1 Australian/Kiribati dollar (AUD)
= 100 cents

System of government
Presidential republic since 1979
(Commonwealth member)

Capital
Bairiki

Languages English, I-Kiribati
(Gilbertese) (official languages)

Surface area
313 sq miles (811 sq km)

Population 103,000

Religion
55% Catholic, 39% Protestant

Notable features
Kiribati comprises 32 islands. Some
are in Micronesia while the rest are
in Polynesia.

Below: A boy climbing a coconut palm.
Harvesting coconuts in this way is still
common.

Right: Kiribati's population and culture are still
largely indigenous. Nearly 99 per cent of the
people are Micronesian.

How many islands are there in Kiribati?

Kiribati is an island nation in the Pacific
consisting of 32 widely dispersed atolls (ring-shaped
coral reefs). There are three main groups of atolls:
the Gilbert Islands, the Phoenix Islands, and the
Line Islands. The island nation extends for
nearly 3,100 miles (5,000 km) east-west and nearly
1,250 miles (2,000 km) north-south.

What are the country's main sources of revenue?

Kiribati's phosphate deposits were more or less
exhausted by the time it achieved independence.
Fishing and the cultivation of coconuts are now the
main sources of income. Because of the islands'
remoteness from world markets, an export-oriented
economy would stand little chance of success. Aid
from Australia and Japan plays an important part in
the national finances.

Is the country at risk from climate change?

Yes. Because much of the land lies less than
7 ft (2 m) above sea level, Kiribati is at risk of sinking
below the surface of the ocean. Climate change is
causing the Pacific to rise and Kiribati is expected
to be one of the first nations to be submerged in the
21st century. The water in a number of freshwater
reservoirs has already been rendered unusable by
rising sea levels and the islanders have become
dependent on rainfall for drinking water.

Millennium Island

The International Date Line (180 degrees longitude) passes
through the island nation. This used to mean that in one
part of the country it was one day and in the rest of the
country it was another. On December 1, 1995 the Date
Line was moved so that the whole island group lay to the
west of it. Kiribati's easternmost island—an uninhabited atoll
named Caroline Island—therefore became the first place
in the world to enter the third millennium. Its name was
changed to Millennium Island to mark the occasion.

Why is New Zealand sometimes called the "green island?"

New Zealand is nicknamed the "green island" because of its low population density, its unspoiled nature, its unique fauna, and the high level of environmental awareness of its people.

What is the Bay of Plenty?

The Bay of Plenty is a region of New Zealand's North Island. The Earth's crust is so thin here that abundant geothermal activity in the form of geysers can be observed. The bay forms the northern limit of the region of the same name, covering an area of 4,633 sq miles (12,000 sq km). The area is known for its agricultural productivity. As well as being New Zealand's biggest kiwifruit-growing area, large quantities of avocados and apples are grown here. The Bay of Plenty is also one of New Zealand's most important tourist regions. It was named by Captain James Cook (1728–1779), who discovered it onboard his ship *Endeavour* and was struck by its rich flora and fauna.

How productive is New Zealand's agriculture?

Unlike many other countries, New Zealand's soils are extremely productive and agricultural produce accounts for 50 per cent of all the nation's export earnings. Sheep farming has been an important economic factor ever since the first European settlers arrived. In the early days it was only the wool that was exported (New Zealand is the world's

NEW ZEALAND

Flag

Currency
1 New Zealand dollar (NZD)
= 100 cents

System of government
Constitutional monarchy since 1907
(Commonwealth member)

Capital Wellington

Languages
English, Maori, New Zealand
Sign Language (official languages)

Surface area
104,454 sq miles (270,534 sq km)

Population 4.2 million

Religion
16% Anglican, 13% Catholic,
12% Presbyterian

Notable features
86% of New Zealanders (the highest proportion in the world) are town and city dwellers. Auckland alone is home to 32% of the population.

The *Rainbow Warrior*

After the Second World War, New Zealand, Australia, and the United States signed a security treaty. Differences soon developed with the United States because of its aggressive nuclear policy. In 1984 New Zealand withdrew from the treaty and declared itself a nuclear-free zone three years later. In 1985 the ship *Rainbow Warrior*, which was used as a support vessel for many protest activities against seal hunting, whaling, and nuclear testing, supported Greenpeace's attempts to frustrate French nuclear testing in Polynesia. It was sunk by French secret service agents in Auckland's harbor.

Mitre Peak in Milford Sound (Fjordland National Park), southwest New Zealand, is one of the country's most photographed mountains.

third-largest producer) but since the 1880s and the introduction of refrigerator ships, New Zealand became a major exporter of meat and butter too—above all to Asia and Africa, which it opened up as new markets.

What are kiwis?

As well as the nickname of the people of New Zealand, the Maori word "kiwi" denotes both a fruit and a bird. The kiwifruit (also known as the Chinese gooseberry) is a vitamin C-rich fruit of the *Actinidia* family measuring 2–4 in (5–10 cm) in diameter. Although regarded as New Zealand's national fruit, the world's biggest producer is surprisingly not New Zealand but Italy.

The kiwi bird (of the *Apterygidae* family) is a ratite (flightless bird) with degenerate wings and soft, fur-like feathers. The forests of New Zealand are the bird's sole natural habitat. Kiwis dig nesting burrows in the ground and feed at night on small creatures which they locate using their keen sense of smell. Kiwis retain the same mate throughout their lives. The females weigh around 5.5 lb (2.5 kg) and the male just 3.3 lb (1.5 kg). Kiwis lay a single egg (weighing around 1 lb/500 g) that is incubated by the male for 80 days without feeding. The kiwi is New Zealand's national animal and national emblem.

Interesting facts: Land and environment

- There are no snakes in New Zealand.
- Approximately 85 per cent of New Zealand's plant species are found nowhere else on the planet.
- Italy, not New Zealand, is the world's biggest producer of kiwifruit.
- More than 15 per cent of New Zealand's energy requirements are met from renewable sources (water, wind, and sun).

What was German Samoa?

WIn 1855 a German company established a trading post in Samoa and a consul was sent out shortly afterwards. Following a lengthy dispute among the colonial powers, the islands were divided into Eastern Samoa (later American Samoa) and Western Samoa, a German Protectorate. At the beginning of the First World War, New Zealand occupied the German colony. Some years before, however, in 1903, a Samoan independence movement (the Mau) had emerged and been suppressed by the Germans. Under New Zealand rule the (non-violent) resistance intensified.

What were the "Three Powers"?

The Three Powers were the three countries that wanted to exercise control over the region: the United States, Great Britain, and Germany. The Samoa Act signed in Berlin in 1889 defined Samoa as a formally independent kingdom under the "protection" of the Three Powers, but after the death of Samoan king Malietoa Laupepa that same year, hostilities between the three countries resumed.

How did Spanish flu arrive in Samoa?

In 1918 the New Zealand military authorities allowed a quarantine ship on which Spanish flu victims were being treated to dock in Apia. The disease was thus introduced to Samoa and wiped out a third of the population.

What are the country's main economic sectors?

Although most Samoans work in agriculture, the sector contributes a mere 14 per cent to the country's GDP. The main industries are the manufacture of automobile parts, wood processing, and the production of cigarettes from imported tobacco. The economy is given a significant boost by remittances from Samoans who work overseas.

SAMOA

Flag

Currency
1 tala (WST) = 100 sene

System of government
Constitutional monarchy since 1962
(Commonwealth member)

Capital
Apia

Languages
Samoan, English (official languages)

Surface area
1,093 sq miles (2,831 sq km)

Population 184,000

Religion
70% Protestant, 20% Catholic

Notable features
Samoa consists of ten islands, of which only the four larger ones are inhabited.

What are blowholes?

Along the coast of Savaii Island some 22 miles (35 km) from Saleloga, the sea has sculpted the volcanic rock into bizarre shapes. In some places it has carved channels underneath the rock and created blowholes through which water shoots up to 200 ft (60 m) into the air. So powerful are these fountains that objects thrown into the holes are also flung high into the air by the water.

Mangroves and coconut palms line the idyllic beaches of the Samoan islands.

Interesting facts: Population

- There is a striking lack of middle-aged women in Samoa (1.66 men to every woman). The main reason for this is thought to be the high level of emigration of women of this age group.

- Samoa does not have any armed forces of its own due to the absence of threats from abroad. The country is not involved in any international disputes and since 1962 New Zealand has undertaken to provide it with any military assistance it might need.

TONGA

Flag

Currency
1 pa'anga (TOP) = 100 seniti

System of government
Constitutional monarchy since 1875
(Commonwealth member)

Capital
Naku'alofa

Languages
Tongan, English (official languages)

Surface area
289 sq miles (748 sq km)

Population 113,000

Religion 36% Methodist,
15% Catholic, 15% Mormon

Notable features
Of the kingdom's 200-plus islands, only
36 are inhabited.

How long have the islands of Tonga been inhabited?
Ceramic artifacts found on the islands have been dated to 800–750 BC. The Fiji, Samoa, and Tonga island groups have been described as the "cradle of Polynesian culture."

Was Tonga ever ruled by a colonial power?
The islands were discovered in 1616 by the two Dutchmen Willem Schouten (circa 1567–1625) and Jacob Le Maire (1585–1616). Although Tonga became a British protectorate in 1900 and its foreign affairs were looked after by the United Kingdom until 1965, Tonga is the only nation in the South Pacific never to have been colonized. It achieved full independence in 1970.

What status does the king of Tonga have?
The king is accorded absolute respect by his people and is granted greater powers by the constitution than are enjoyed, for example, by the British monarchy. Criticism of the monarchy is considered "un-Tongan" and impolite. In return the people enjoy good social conditions, medical care is free, there is no illiteracy, and the population comprises a relatively high proportion of graduates.

What is the state doing to combat obesity?

Nationwide competitions are held in Tonga in which citizens who lose the most weight win a monetary prize. As throughout the Pacific region, fatness is regarded as attractive in Tonga and consequently 58 per cent of men and 75 per cent of women are overweight. In the 1990s King Taufa'ahau Tupou IV (reigned 1965–2006) set a good example by dropping from 463 lb (210 kg) to around 310 lb (140 kg).

One of Tonga's typical indigenous villages.

Right: The islands of the Vava'u group are formed of coral limestone and rise just a few feet above sea level.

Do the archipelago's islands share the same geological structure?
In terms of geology Tonga's 200 islands fall into two groups. The first consists of volcanic islands such as Kao, Late, and Tofua, which are covered with tropical rainforest and rise to 3,300 ft (1,000 m) and more. The second consists of islands such as Tongatapu, the main island, formed of coral limestone. This process of formation was possible because the average water depth around these islands is just 1,650 ft (500 m).

What type of government does Tuvalu have?

What type of government does Tuvalu have? The archipelago that used to be known as Ellice Islands achieved independence on October 1, 1978. It is now a constitutional monarchy and a Commonwealth Realm, in other words a sovereign state that recognizes the British monarch as its head of state. Queen Elizabeth II is represented by Governor General Filoimeia Telito. Since 2006 the head of government has been Apisei Ielemia. (For a list of all Commonwealth Realms see United Kingdom.)

What are the origins of the name?

Tuvalu means "eight islands." In reality there are nine although originally just eight were inhabited. The ninth and southernmost island, Niulakita, remained uninhabited until 1949 and was not taken account of in the name for that reason.

What is the basis of Tuvalu's economy?

Traditionally the economy is based on copra (see box below) and fishing. Because the soil is largely unsuitable for agriculture and hardly any crops are grown, most of the necessary food is imported. There is no industry other than small-scale copra processing. The main sources of foreign currency earnings are postage stamps and the sale of fishing rights within the archipelago's 200-mile (320-km) zone.

TUVALU

Flag

Currency
1 Australian dollar (AUD) = 100 cents

System of government
Constitutional monarchy since 1978 (Commonwealth member)

Capital
Funafuti

Languages
Tuvaluan, English (official languages)

Surface area
10 sq miles (26 sq km)

Population 12,000

Religion
97% Protestant

Notable features
The islands of Tuvalu are slowly sinking below the surface of the ocean. Flooding occurs on a daily basis.

Is the archipelago's nature still intact?

The beaches of the atolls are sinking as a result of erosion and rising sea levels caused by global warming. The population has to contend with floods almost continually and soil salination is making it increasingly difficult to obtain drinking water and grow food. The government is making plans to evacuate the entire population to the Fijian island of Kioa as it believes the islands will be completely submerged during the course of the 21st century. It is envisaged that the costs will be borne by the industrial nations that are responsible for climate change.

The island of Fongafale is part of Funafuti Atoll and is Tuvalu's main island. Tuvalu is the world's fourth-smallest nation.

What is copra?

Copra is dried coconut flesh from which coconut oil is extracted in oil mills by grating copra then boiling it in water. The word derives from Malayalam, a language spoken in India that is related to Tamil. It means "dried coconut."

▲ Seal with pup　　　　　Lofoten, Norway　　　　　　　　　　　　　Beluga whale

Iceberg, Antarctica

THE ARCTIC AND ANTARCTICA

Captain James Cook circumnavigated Antarctica without ever stepping ashore. After him came other explorers who mapped its coasts and mountains. Robert Falcon Scott, who reached the South Pole in 1912 shortly after Roald Amundsen, wrote of Antarctica: "Great God, this is an awful place." Like many later explorers, Scott died in his attempt to uncover its secrets. Unlike the Antarctic, which can be regarded as a continent in its own right, the Arctic is split between North America, Asia, and Europe.

Fishing village, Norway

Springtime in Alaska

Polar bear

MAP OF THE ARCTIC

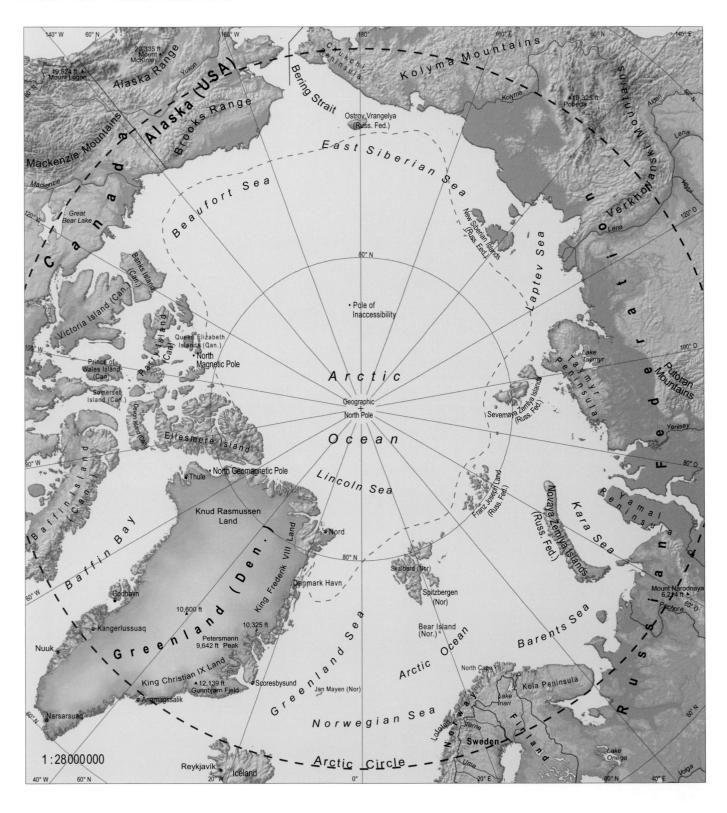

140° W   60° N   160° W   180   160° E   60° N   140° E

20,335 ft
Mount
McKinley

19,524 ft
Mount Logan

Alaska Range

Yukon

Mackenzie Mountains

Brooks Range

Alaska (USA)

Chukchi Peninsula

Kolyma Mountains

Kolyma

10,325 ft
Pobeda

Verkhoyansk Mountains

Aldan

Lena

Canada

Mackenzie

Great Bear Lake

Bering Strait

Ostrov Vrangelya
(Russ. Fed.)

East Siberian Sea

Lena

120° W

120° O

Banks Island (Can.)

Beaufort Sea

New Siberian Islands
(Russ. Fed.)

Laptev Sea

Victoria Island (Can.)

80° N

Pole of
Inaccessibility

Parry Islands (Can.)

Lake Taymyr

Prince of Wales Island (Can.)

Queen Elizabeth
Islands (Qan.)

North
Magnetic Pole

Arctic

Taymyr Peninsula

Putoran Mountains

100° W

100° O

Somerset Island (Can.)

Devon Island (Can.)

Geographic
North Pole

Severnaya Zemlya Islands
(Russ. Fed.)

Yenisey

Ellesmere Island

Ocean

80° W

80° O

Baffin Island (Can.)

North Geomagnetic Pole

Lincoln Sea

Franz Joseph Land
(Russ. Fed.)

Kara Sea

Yamal Peninsula

Russian Federation

Thule

Knud Rasmussen
Land

Baffin Bay

Novaya Zemlya Islands
(Russ. Fed.)

Nord

Mount Narodnaya
6,214 ft

60° W

60° O

Baffin Bay

King Frederik VIII Land

80° N

Pechora

Godhavn

Greenland (Den.)

Denmark Havn

Swalbard (Nor)

Spitzbergen
(Nor)

Barents Sea

Kangerlussuaq

10,600 ft

10,325 ft

Nuuk

Petersmann
9,642 ft Peak

Bear Island
(Nor.)

Arctic Ocean

North Cape

Kola Peninsula

King Christian IX Land

12,139 ft
Gunnbjørn Fjeld

Scoresbysund

Jan Mayen (Nor)

Lake Inari

Angmagssalik

Greenland Sea

Lofoten

Torne

Norway

Lake Onega

Narsarsuaq

60° N

Norwegian Sea

Sweden

Finland

Ume

Volga

1 : 28 000 000

Reykjavik   Iceland

Arctic Circle

40° W   60° N   20° W   0°   20° E   60° N   40° E

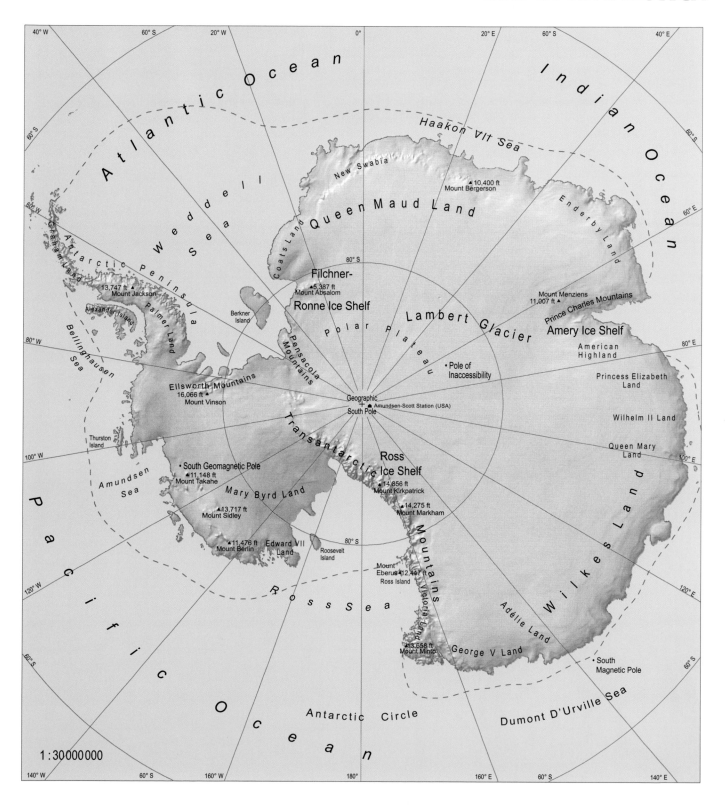

Atlantic Ocean

Indian Ocean

Haakon VII Sea

New Swabia

Queen Maud Land

▲10,400 ft
Mount Bergerson

Enderby Land

Weddell Sea

Coats Land

Filchner-

▲5,387 ft
Mount Absalom

Ronne Ice Shelf

Berkner Island

Lambert Glacier

Mount Menziens
11,007 ft ▲

Prince Charles Mountains

Amery Ice Shelf

13,747 ft ▲
Mount Jackson

Antarctic Peninsula

Palmer Land

Alexander Island

Polar Plateau

Graham Land

Bellinghausen Sea

80° W

Pensacola Mountains

American Highland

Princess Elizabeth Land

80° E

Ellsworth Mountains
16,066 ft ▲
Mount Vinson

• Pole of
Inaccessibility

Wilhelm II Land

Thurston Island

Geographic
South Pole

▲ Amundsen-Scott Station (USA)

Queen Mary Land

100° W

Transantarctic

100° E

• South Geomagnetic Pole
▲11,148 ft
Mount Takahe

Mary Byrd Land

Ross
Ice Shelf

▲14,856 ft
Mount Kirkpatrick

Wilkes Land

Amundsen Sea

▲13,717 ft
Mount Sidley

▲14,275 ft
Mount Markham

Mountains

▲11,476 ft
Mount Berlin

Edward VII
Land

Roosevelt
Island

Mount
Eberus ▲12,447 ft
Ross Island

Victoria Land

Adélie Land

120° W

Ross Sea

120° E

▲13,658 ft
Mount Minto

George V Land

• South
Magnetic Pole

Pacific

Ocean

Antarctic   Circle

Dumont D'Urville Sea

1 : 30 000 000

40° W   60° S   20° W   0°   20° E   60° S   40° E

60° S   60° E

80° W   80° E

100° W   100° E

120° W   120° E

140° W   60° S   160° W   180°   160° E   60° S   140° E

60° S   60° S

What is the Arctic?

The Arctic is the region (consisting of both land and sea) around the North Pole. Its boundaries are based on a range of factors including climate and vegetation (northern tree line). At the center of the region is the frozen Arctic Ocean and its marginal seas. Territory belonging to the United States, Canada, Russia, Denmark, Iceland, Norway, Sweden, and Finland lies within the Arctic Circle.

What does the word "Arctic" mean?

The word "Arctic" derives from the Ancient Greek *árktos* ("bear") and means something like "the land under the constellation of the Great Bear." The rear portion of the Great Bear is the Big Dipper and is depicted on the flag of the US federal state of Alaska along with the North Star.

How is the population of the Arctic made up?

Until a few decades ago the population of the Arctic was made up mainly of polar peoples including Inuits, Lapps, Yakuts, Nenets, and Evenks. While the number of indigenous inhabitants is steadily decreasing, the number of outsiders moving into the region is steadily increasing. At the moment around two million people live in the Arctic Circle, most of whom are from areas outside it, including North America, Scandinavia, and Russia.

Climate change in the Arctic

Global warming is causing the Arctic ice to melt. Different studies have calculated that by 2100 between 10 and 50 per cent of the ice could have melted. Some scientists are even predicting that at some point between 2040 and 2080 the Arctic will become completely ice-free during the summer months, which would mean that low-lying coastal areas such as Florida could be flooded.

Is there only one North Pole?

No. In general usage the term "North Pole" designates the northernmost place on Earth. The technical term for this is the "Geographic North Pole." This is used in order to avoid confusion with the North Magnetic Pole, the North Geomagnetic Pole, and the Pole of Inaccessibility. All four lie within the Arctic Ocean.

What is the Pole of Inaccessibility?

The Pole of Inaccessibility is the point furthest away from any coastline. It is located at 83° 03' north and 174° 51' west, around 410 miles (660 km) away from the Geographic North Pole. The Arctic Ocean is some 8,850 ft (3,000 m) deep at this point.

Are there insects in the Arctic?

It is estimated that there are approximately 1,000 species of insect in the Arctic, mainly midges, bees,

The Lapps, also known as the Sami, are semi-nomadic reindeer herders of Finnish-Ugric origin.

and butterflies. There are also many different types of spider living in the tundra.

Has the Arctic always been covered with ice?

No. Borehole evidence including fossil finds (e.g. forests buried in the ice) indicates that the Arctic had a subtropical climate 40 to 50 million years ago. It is thought that the temperature of the Arctic Ocean was also higher. One theory even goes so far as to suggest that the Arctic Ocean could once have been an enormous, isolated freshwater lake.

What is the Antarctic?

The Antarctic is the region around the South Pole, again comprising both land and sea. Unlike the North Pole, however, which is located in the middle of a deep sea covered with drift ice, the South Pole lies at the center of an enormous landmass measuring some 4.78 million sq miles (12.39 million sq km). This land mass is a continent in its own right named Antarctica. Most of it is covered by an ice shelf 6,600–13,200 ft (2,000–4,000 m) thick. Only 110,000 sq miles (280,000 sq km) of its surface area are ice-free.

What is Mount Erebus?

Mount Erebus is the world's most southerly active volcano. It is located on Ross Island in the Antarctic and is 12,447 ft (3,794 m) high.

Aerial view of Glacier National Park, Alaska, showing numerous glaciers and mountain ranges.

What is the world's biggest glacier called?

The highest glacier in the world is the Lambert Glacier in the Antarctic. It is over 25 miles (40 km) wide, approximately 250 miles (400 km) long and around 8,200 ft (2,500 m) thick. It flows into the sea at velocities of up to 3,300 ft (1,000 m) per year.

What creatures live in the Antarctic?

The Antarctic is home to the polar bear, which feeds off seals, and to 19 species of birds including the

Background: The seas around the towering cliffs of Illulissat Iceberg in Greenland are rich fishing grounds.

The phenomenon of *aurora borealis* (northern lights) is caused by solar winds colliding with the Earth's magnetic field. More than one million MW of power light up the night sky.

What is meant by the term "iceberg calving"?

Ice appears static but in fact is constantly moving, reforming, melting, and refreezing. Calving is the process whereby new icebergs are born when ice masses become detached from an iceberg or glacier.

How much ice is there in Antarctica?

Around 98 per cent of Antarctica is covered by ice while just two per cent is ice-free. The volume of Antarctica's ice has been estimated at 8.26 million cu miles (34.42 million cu km). This represents 90 per cent of all the ice in the world and approximately 70 per cent of the world's drinking water. The volume of ice that comes and goes each year is around 480 cu miles (2,000 cu km).

An igloo is a domed shelter constructed by the Inuit out of blocks of ice.

southern royal albatross and the snow petrel. Each summer around 100 million migratory birds arrive here to breed, sharing the ice-free land and pack ice with penguins, seals, and sea lions. The seas around Antarctica are teeming with swarms of krill that are consumed by whales and the region's plentiful squid.

Quotation from Captain James Cook (circa 1770)

"The risk incurred by anyone who would explore this coast in these unknown and frozen seas is so great that I can confidently assert no man will ever risk more than I, and that the southern lands will remain unexplored perhaps forever."

When did hunting begin in the Antarctic?

Captain James Cook (1728–1779) ended his circumnavigation of the Antarctic in 1775. Lured to the region by his reports, the first hunters and whalers started to arrive in 1820. They found an unspoiled paradise full of whales, sea lions, seals, and penguins. Hundreds of whales were killed and in the 1821/22 season, hunters slew 320,000 seals.

> **Antarctic Treaty**
>
> The Antarctic Treaty, a multilateral agreement defining the region's political status, promoting scientific research at the South Pole, guaranteeing use of the territory for exclusively peaceful purposes, and undertaking to maintain Antarctica's ecological balance of the region, was signed by 45 nations on December 1, 1959. In practical terms, however, the treaty has done nothing to prevent interested states constructing around 35 new research stations (with scant regard for the natural environment) in order to support subsequent territorial claims. In 1991 the treaty was supplemented with a Protocol on Environmental Protection that was ratified in 1998 by all the signatories.

Left: There are 18 species of penguin, of which the king penguin, at 4 ft (1.2 m), is the tallest and the little penguin, at 1 ft 2 in–1 ft 4 in (35–40 cm), the smallest. Penguins are flightless birds of the *Spheniscidae* family that live by the cold seas of the southern hemisphere.

What is an ice shelf?

An ice shelf is an enormous platform of ice 7–700 ft (2–200 m) thick that floats on the sea but is connected to the land by a glacier. The seaward edges of ice shelves tend to break off (calve), forming drifting icebergs. Around a third of Antarctic coastlines are covered by ice shelves. The largest of these are the Ross (188,032 sq miles/487,000 sq km) and Filchner-Ronne (173,360 sq miles/449,000 sq km) ice shelves in the Antarctic.

What is ozone depletion?

In the 1980s scientists discovered a hole in the ozone layer above Antarctica. The ozone layer protects the earth's atmosphere from harmful ultraviolet rays. The hole was caused by CFC (chlorofluorocarbon) compounds that rise to the upper atmosphere, where they attack and destroy the ozone layer.

A fishing boat on Vestvagoy in the Lofoten group of islands.

▲ Population   Religions   Climatic zones

THE COUNTRIES OF THE WORLD

This chapter compares the countries of the world from a range of perspectives and categorizes them according to various criteria. Which countries are exceptionally large or small, rich or poor? How are the different religious communities or climatic zones distributed throughout the world? Which countries share similar geographical properties or political situations? To these and many more questions this chapter gives the answers. Informative tables provide the reader with rapid access to facts and data that are supplemented with detailed information on the individual countries and continents concerned.

Island nations   Geography   Politics

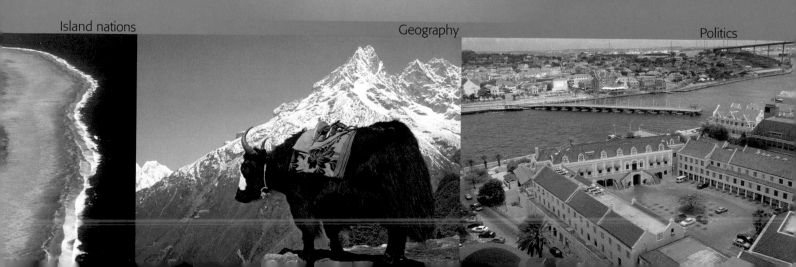

Countries and population

Was the United States always such a big country?
No. When the United States of America declared itself independent in 1776, the nation consisted of just the first 13 states along its eastern coast. During the course of the 19th century the country extended further west, increasing in economic and political power as it did so.

Was the Vatican always such a small country?
No. During the Middle Ages the Vatican was considerably bigger. It controlled large parts of central Italy and reached its largest territorial extent under Pope Julius II (1443–1513). Its current boundaries were established by the Lateran Accords of 1929.

Below: China is currently the most populous country in the world and it is predicted that by 2030 its population will have grown to 1.5 billion.

Will China always be the world's most populous country?
No. India's population growth is currently twice as high as China's. The UN estimates that India will overtake China in the population table in or around 2045.

What is Monaco's statistical claim to fame?
As well as being one of the world's smallest countries, in absolute terms the Principality of Monaco in Western Europe has one of the lowest populations in the world. Nevertheless, there are still enough Monegasques to give it an extremely high population density. The same principle applies to the two other countries with the highest population densities: Singapore and the Vatican City. As city-states these three countries cannot really be compared to territorial states in this respect.

Background: Tarawa is the main atoll of the Republic of Kiribati. It consists of 24 islands, of which eight are inhabited.

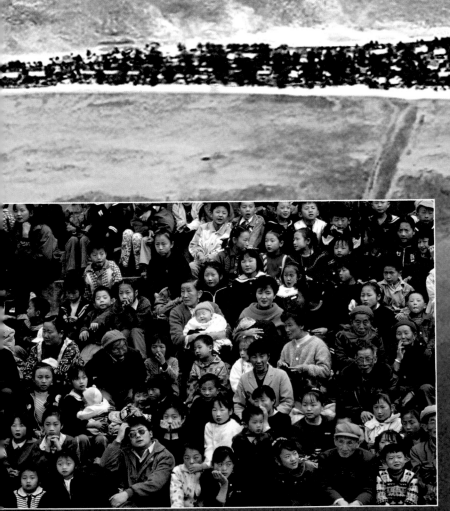

The ten largest countries in the world

	Name	Area (sq m)
1	Russian Federation	6.59 million
2	Canada	3.85 million
3	United States of America	3.72 million
4	People's Republic of China	3.69 million
5	Brazil	3.29 million
6	Australia	2.97 million
7	India	1.27 million
8	Argentina	1.07 million
9	Kazakhstan	1.05 million
10	Sudan	0.97 million

The ten smallest countries in the world

	Name	Area (sq m)
1	Vatican City	0.17
2	Monaco	0.75
3	Nauru	8
4	Tuvalu	10
5	San Marino	23
6	Liechtenstein	62
7	Marshall Islands	70
8	St Kitts and Nevis	104
9	Maldives	115
10	Malta	122

Why are so many countries so sparsely populated?
Low population densities are generally due to unpropitious natural conditions. Very hot regions are often covered by deserts (e.g. Niger) that are unsuitable for habitation. In countries like Suriname and Guyana, tropical rainforest prevents the population from spreading.

Why does Greenland not appear in the list of largest countries?
Were Greenland an independent state, it would be the 13th-largest country in the world. However, its political status is somewhat unusual. It is an autonomous region of Denmark and is fully independent in terms of domestic policy but its foreign affairs are looked after by Denmark. Because of this rather ambiguous status, Greenland is regarded neither as an independent state nor as part of Danish national territory.

Lake Balkhash in the steppes of eastern Kazakhstan, the world's largest landlocked country.

The ten most populous countries in the world

	Name	Population
1	People's Republic of China	1.3 billion
2	India	1.1 billion
3	United States of America	300.9 million
4	Indonesia	242.0 million
5	Brazil	186.4 million
6	Pakistan	162.8 million
7	Bangladesh	144.3 million
8	Russian Federation	142.4 million
9	Nigeria	140.0 million
10	Japan	127.4 million

The ten highest population density in the world

	Name	Population per sq m
1	Monaco	43,831
2	Singapore	16,783
3	Vatican City	5,486
4	Malta	3,266
5	Maldives	3,033
6	Bangladesh	2,533
7	Bahrain	2,507
8	Barbados	1,681
9	Taiwan	1,634
10	Nauru	1,608

The ten least populous countries in the world

	Name	Population
1	Vatican City	870
2	Tuvalu	12,000
3	Nauru	13,000
4	Palau	20,000
5	San Marino	30,000
6	Monaco	33,000
7	Liechtenstein	34,000
8	St Kitts and Nevis	39,000
9	Marshall Islands	59,000
10	Antigua and Barbuda	69,000

The ten lowest population density in the world

	Name	Population per sq m
1	Mongolia	5
2	Namibia	5
3	Australia	8
4	Suriname	8
5	Botswana	8
6	Iceland	8
7	Mauritania	8
8	Libya	8
9	Canada	8
10	Guyana	10

Wealth is often demonstrated through expensive status symbols such as this restored vintage Jaguar sports car.

Economic circumstances

What is gross national product (GNP)?
In national accounting, gross national product is the sum of all income generated by the citizens of a nation during a specific period, usually a year, including earnings from work and income from investments. GNP is calculated at market prices, in other words it includes sales taxes but excludes subsidies.

What is gross domestic product (GDP)?
Gross domestic product measures the value of the goods and services produced by a country within a specific period, for example a calendar year. As GDP is a way of measuring the size of a domestic economy, it does not take into account income earned abroad by the citizens of the country in question.

What is gross national income (GNI)?
Gross national income is the total value of the goods and services produced within a specific country

The 20 richest countries in the world		
Rank	Country	GDP
1	United States of America	12,455,825
2	Japan	4,567,441
3	Germany	2,791,737
4	China	2,234,133
5	United Kingdom	2,229,472
6	France	2,126,719
7	Italy	1,765,537
8	Canada	1,132,436
9	Spain	1,126,565
10	Brazil	795,666
11	South Korea	787,567
12	India	771,951
13	Mexico	768,437
14	Russian Federation	763,287
15	Australia	708,519
16	Netherlands	629,911
17	Belgium	371,695
18	Switzerland	367,571
19	Turkey	362,461
20	Sweden	358,810

Values in million US dollars per year.
Source: International Monetary Fund 2006 (figures for 2005).

The 20 poorest countries in the world		
Rank	Country	GDP
1	Kiribati	63
2	São Tomé and Príncipe	70
3	Tonga	215
4	Dominica	283
5	Solomon Islands	294
6	Guinea-Bissau	302
7	East Timor	331
8	Vanuatu	332
9	Samoa	336
10	Comoros	369
11	St Vincent and the Grenadines	421
12	St Kitts and Nevis	453
13	Gambia	461
14	Grenada	490
15	Liberia	530
16	Seychelles	695
17	Djibouti	709
18	Guyana	786
19	Maldives	787
20	Burundi	799

Values in million US dollars per year.
Source: International Monetary Fund 2006 (figures for 2005).

(GDP) plus earnings and investment income from abroad less similar income repatriated to other countries. It is an international statistical standard that is actually the same measure as GNP.

Where are the world's richest countries?

The world's richest countries are in Europe. Of the 20 countries with the highest GDP, ten are European. Europe's dominant economic position becomes even clearer when one looks at per capita income. Here, 15 of the top 20 are European, whereby the world's largest countries by surface area are pushed down the table by a handful of small European states. Thus, the US, the richest country in the world when you look at its total GDP, falls down to the 8th position when it comes to GDP per capita.

Where are the world's poorest countries?

The world's poorest countries are in Africa. While Africa does not dominate the list of poorest countries by GDP (the picture painted by this table is that the poorest countries are the tiny states whose economic power is limited by their size alone), the table of per capita income reveals that 16 of the 20 poorest countries are African.

The citizens of poorer countries, such as Mali shown here, have to work the unproductive soil using the simplest of tools.

Background: Two thirds of the African state of Niger is desert. Unfavorable natural conditions are one of the main reasons for poverty in Africa.

Highest income per capita		
Rank	Country	GDP
1	Luxembourg	80,288
2	Norway	64,193
3	Iceland	52,764
4	Switzerland	50,532
5	Ireland	48,604
6	Denmark	47,984
7	Qatar	43,110
8	United States of America	42,000
9	Sweden	39,694
10	Netherlands	38,618
11	Finland	37,504
12	Austria	37,117
13	United Kingdom	37,023
14	Japan	35,757
15	Belgium	35,712
16	Canada	35,133
17	Australia	34,740
18	France	33,918
19	Germany	33,854
20	Italy	30,200

Values in million US dollars per year.
Source: International Monetary Fund 2006 (figures for 2005).

Lowest income per capita		
Rank	Country	GDP
1	Burundi	107
2	Ethiopia	153
3	Liberia	161
4	Malawi	161
5	Guinea-Bissau	190
6	Eritrea	209
7	Myanmar	219
8	Sierra Leone	223
9	Rwanda	242
10	Niger	274
11	Madagascar	282
12	Afghanistan	300
13	Uganda	303
14	Gambia	306
15	Nepal	322
16	Mozambique	331
17	Central African Republic	335
18	Tanzania	336
19	East Timor	352
20	Guinea	355

Values in million US dollars per year.
Source: International Monetary Fund 2006 (figures for 2005).

Religion

What is a world religion?

There is no universally accepted definition of the term "world religion." The expression is commonly used to refer to religions with an especially large number of adherents, religions that are widely dispersed throughout the world, or those that have a particularly long tradition. Only Christianity, Islam, and Buddhism satisfy all three conditions although Hinduism and Judaism are often counted as world religions too.

How old are the world religions?

The oldest world religion is Judaism, which originated around 1500 BC. Hinduism and Buddhism emerged around 1,000 years later, followed by Christianity and Islam, which both developed out of the Jewish tradition. The Christian calendar begins with the birth of Christ and the Islamic calendar with the arrival of Prophet Muhammad in Medina on July 16, 622. Islam is therefore the youngest of the five world religions.

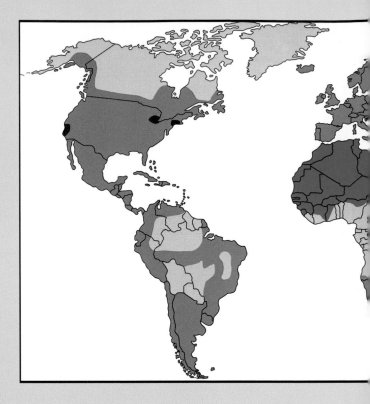

Mass being celebrated in the Basilica of St Theresa in Lisieux, France.

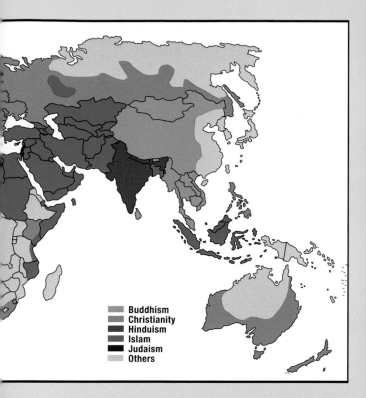

Buddhism
Christianity
Hinduism
Islam
Judaism
Others

In which areas is Christianity the dominant religion?

Christianity was originally a European religion. Missionaries spread this religion to other continents during the colonial age, and the emigration of Europeans to North America and Australia also played an important role. Today Europe, North and South America, Australia, and the southern half of Africa are predominantly Christian.

When did the spread of Islam occur?

Until the death of Prophet Muhammad, Islam was confined mainly to the Arabian Peninsula. Over the subsequent period the Arab Empire—and with it Islam—spread far in both an easterly and westerly direction. To the east large parts of Central Asia and to the west the whole of North Africa fell under the Arab influence. The expansion of the Arab Empire only came to a halt in the 9th century.

Why do most Hindus live in India?

Unlike Christianity and Islam, the other three world religions have never actively sought to convert people of other faiths. Another reason is that they were never associated with large empires that extended their sphere of influence militarily. Hinduism is therefore confined mainly to the Indian subcontinent where it originated. It has spread to other continents only to a minor extent and only through emigration.

Is Judaism a world religion?

Although there are followers of the Jewish faith all over the world, outside Israel they only represent a small minority in any given country. Neither does Judaism compare with the other faiths in terms of total number of believers as there are more Sikhs in the world than Jews. The importance of Judaism stems more from the influence exerted by a number of its fundamental principles on the development of Christianity and Islam.

What major religious wars have there been?

The Thirty Years' War (1618–1648), a conflict about the balance of power in Europe, was at least superficially a religious war between different Christian groups: the Protestants and the Catholics. The Crusades gave rise to an extended period of military conflict in the Middle East between 1096 and 1444.

Mecca is the religious center of Islam and a place of pilgrimage for millions of Muslims. Each Muslim is expected to make the pilgrimage to Mecca once in his or her lifetime.

The distribution of world religions

Rank	Religion	Main areas	Believers
1	Christianity	Europe, Australia, North and South America	2.1 billion
2	Islam	Middle East, North Africa, Indonesia	1.3 billion
3	Hinduism	India, Nepal, Bangladesh, Sri Lanka, Bali	900 million
4	Buddhism	Japan, China, Taiwan, Sri Lanka	400 million
5	Judaism	Israel, USA, Russian Federation, Europe	15 million

Climate

What is the difference between weather and climate?

The term "weather" is used to describe the condition of the Earth's atmosphere in a particular place at a particular time with respect to precipitation, temperature, and air circulation. Studying the weather over an extended period of time allows conclusions to be drawn about recurrent weather patterns across large geographical areas and for different seasons. These recurring patterns, which are subject to a limited degree of fluctuation and relate to a specific region, are known as the "climate."

Below: A moose in the tundra of the Denali National Park in central Alaska.

What is a climate zone?

There are large areas of the planet that share roughly the same climate and whose natural habitats have been subject to similar meteorological forces producing similar results (the creation of deserts, for example). These areas can be banded together as climate zones. Over the course of the scientific examination of this subject, various different ways of dividing up the planet have developed depending on which differences are considered important: temperature, precipitation, or the effect of the climate on flora and fauna.

What are the different climate zones?

A rough division can be undertaken based primarily on average temperature (which depends in turn on how long the sun shines in that particular zone). The coldest regions on Earth are the two poles, hence the coldest climate zone is known as the polar zone. At the opposite extreme is the region immediately north and south of the Equator, the tropical zone. Between these

The Earth's climate zones		
Climate zone	**Boundaries**	**Average temperature**
Polar	Pole to polar circle	−13°F to 30°F (−25°C to −1°C)
Temperate	Polar circle to 40° latitude	41°F to 59°F (5°C to 15°C)
Subtropical	40° latitude to tropics (23.5°)	54°F to 77°F (12°C to 25°C)
Tropical	Tropics to Equator	73°F to 79°F (23°C to 26°C)

two extremes is the temperate zone. The different climate bands between the poles and the Equator can therefore be described as follows: polar zone, cool zone or subpolar zone, temperate zone, subtropics, and tropics.

What type of landscapes are found in the tropics?
In the tropics there are no strongly delineated seasons and the climate remains very even throughout the year. The difference in temperature between day and night is greater than the difference between the warmest and coldest months of the year. Typical landscapes are rainforest in areas close to the equator (the Amazon Basin, for example) and savannas such as the Serengeti in Africa in the adjoining regions to the north and south.

Which climate zone is Europe in?
Most of Europe is in the temperate zone. Typical of this zone are strongly differentiated seasons with days of different lengths and a wide range of temperatures. A common feature of the vegetation is coniferous and deciduous forest. The prevailing winds are westerly, which is why this zone is also called the west wind zone.

What are cold deserts?
The Arctic and Antarctic are in the polar zone and are sometimes referred to as cold deserts. Temperatures remain below 32°F (0°C) all year round and there is 40 per cent less sunshine that in the tropics and hardly any precipitation. Under these conditions it is almost impossible for any plant life to thrive.

Background: The tropical rainforest plays a key role in regulating the Earth's climate. Deforestation is destroying vast swathes of this important ecosystem each year.

The Sossusvlei is a region of enormous sand dunes in the Namib Desert on the west coast of Africa. Rising to heights of over 980 ft (300 m), these orange dunes are among the highest in the world.

Maritime and continental climates
There can also be marked climatic differences within the same climate zone as proximity to the ocean has a decisive influence on weather. Water is very good at storing warmth. Although cold water takes a long time to heat up, once warm, it cools down again only very slowly. As the temperature of coastal regions is heavily influenced by the temperature of the water, the ocean can be seen as having a balancing effect on climatic fluctuations. A maritime climate (i.e. the meteorological conditions that prevail in coastal regions) is therefore less prone to sharp fluctuations than a continental climate in the interior of a continent and maritime areas generally experience cool summers and mild winters.

Island nations

What is an island nation?
An island nation is a state located on one or more islands rather than on the continental mainland.

How many island nations are there?
There are 47 island nations—around 25 per cent of all the countries in the world.

Which island nation is made up of the biggest number of islands?
Indonesia has the most islands—17,508 in total, of which 6,000 are inhabited. In terms of both surface area and population Indonesia is the world's largest island nation and in terms of population alone it is the fourth-largest nation in the world.

The Federated States of Micronesia is a small island nation in the western Pacific. Because of its remote location, it has barely been developed as an international tourist destination as yet.

Island nations	
Country	**Surface area in sq m**
Indonesia	0.74 million
Madagascar	226,657
Papua New Guinea	178,704
Japan	145,884
Philippines	115,831
New Zealand	104,454
United Kingdom	93,788
Cuba	42,803
Iceland	39,769
Ireland	27,135
Sri Lanka	25,332
Dominican Republic	18,696
Republic of China (Taiwan)	13,900
Solomon Islands	10,985
Haiti	10,714
Fiji	7,093
East Timor	5,794
Bahamas	5,382
Vanuatu	4,710
Jamaica	4,244
Cyprus	3,572
Brunei	2,228
Trinidad and Tobago	1,980
Cape Verde	1,558
Samoa	1,093
Mauritius	788
Comoros	719
São Tomé and Príncipe	386
Kiribati	504
Dominica	290
Tonga	289
Bahrain	275
Micronesia	271
Singapore	270
St Lucia	238
Palau	177
Seychelles	176
Antigua and Barbuda	171
Barbados	166
Grenada	133
St Vincent and the Grenadines	131
Malta	122
Maldives	115
St Kitts and Nevis	104
Marshall Islands	70
Tuvalu	10
Nauru	8

Are there any islands that are split between more than one country?

Most islands belong to a single country. However, a small percentage have one or more national boundaries running through them. This division of islands was far more common in the past than it is today (see box on right).

Are there islands with borders that are not internationally recognized?

There is an unrecognized frontier between the Republic of Cuba and Guantánamo Bay, which has been under United States sovereignty since 1903. Since 1983 an unofficial border has also divided Cyprus, separating the Turkish Republic of Northern Cyprus from the Republic of Cyprus. Tiny Hans Island (0.5 sq miles/1.3 sq km) in the Kennedy Channel of the Nares Strait is claimed by both Greenland and Canada. Since 2005 it has been administered jointly by the two countries.

Background: The Kuril Islands are a chain of islands that link the island nation of Japan with the Russian mainland. After the Second World War they fell to the Soviet Union.

Islands split between two or more countries

Island	Countries	Dates
Borneo	Brunei, Indonesia, Malaya	since 1963
Tierra del Fuego	Argentina, Chile	since 1881
Hispaniola	Dominican Republic, Haiti	since 1808
Rebirth Island	Kazakhstan, Uzbekistan	1991–2002
King Fahd Causeway Island	Bahrain, Saudi Arabia	since 1986
Ireland	United Kingdom, Ireland	since 1921
Kataja	Finland, Sweden	since 1809
Märket	Finland, Sweden	since 1809
New Guinea	Indonesia, Papua New Guinea	since 1949
Sakhalin	Russia, Japan	1905–1945
Saint-Martin	France, Netherlands Antilles	since 1648
Sebatik	Indonesia, Malaya	since 1891
Timor	Indonesia, East Timor	since 2002
Usedom	Germany, Poland	since 1945
Cyprus	Republic of Cyprus, Turkish Republic of Northern Cyprus	since 1983

Interesting facts

- The border between Sweden and Finland once ran between Kataja and the then Russian island of Inkari. Due to a drop in the sea level, the islands have become joined and so the border now runs overland.

- The King Fahd Causeway is a combined bridge and dike between Bahrain and Saudi Arabia built in 1982. Halfway across there is an artificial (and nameless) island where the border formalities are carried out. This is Bahrain's only land border.

- The Republic of China was originally founded on the mainland (in 1911). Since the end of the civil war, however, it has consisted only of Taiwan, Penghu, Matsu, and a few other islands. Mainland China is now the People's Republic and the Republic of China (Taiwan) has effectively become an island nation.

- As a consequence of the Aral Sea drying up, Rebirth Island (Vozrozhdeniye) has become a peninsula.

- While the islands of Samoa constitute the state of Samoa, American Samoa, to the east, is US territory.

Special physical conditions

What problems are faced by mountainous countries?
The main problem is the lack of agricultural land. This is compounded by unfavorable climatic conditions such as the drop in temperature with increasing altitude. Another frequent problem is aridity as there are very few water storage opportunities. Finally, steep mountainsides are not conducive to infrastructure expansion and it is often only possible to build transportation routes in the valleys.

The yak is an ox indigenous to Central Asia. Its long coat protects it against even Nepal's harsh mountain climate.

Which nations are considered to be mountainous countries?
There is no fixed definition of a mountainous country. As a rule the term is used to describe countries whose terrain lies mostly at elevations above 5,000 ft (1,500 m). Typical examples would be Nepal in the Himalayas and Andorra in the Pyrenees.

Which areas of the Earth are barely populated?
Because of the extreme conditions that prevail there, deserts, the poles, and high mountains are barely populated. Such regions are to be found, among other places, in Northern Canada, Greenland, Siberia, the interior of Australia, and North Africa.

Which countries are particularly vulnerable to climate change?
The highest point of many of Oceania's island nations is just a few feet above sea level. The rise in sea level expected as a result of the melting of the glaciers and icebergs raises the fear that many such islands could literally sink into the sea. A typical

Countries on two continents
While the continents of Africa, America, and Australia are clearly circumscribed by the oceans that surround them, the border between Europe and Asia is predominantly a land border (the Ural Mountains). For this reason, Europe and Asia are often regarded as the single continent Eurasia forming the largest land mass on the planet. South of the Urals the border is generally accepted as running through the Black Sea and the Bosporus. The location of the border means that two states that are generally regarded as part of Europe lie mostly within Asia: Russia and Turkey.

example is the island nation of Tuvalu, whose government has signed an agreement with New Zealand under which all Tuvaluans will be permitted to emigrate to New Zealand in the long term.

Which is the world's highest capital?

While it may not be Bolivia's official capital (that honor falls to Sucre), La Paz is both the seat of government and the biggest city in the land and for that reason is generally regarded as the world's highest capital.

Nicknamed "the city that touches the cloud," it is situated at an elevation of between 10,500 and 13,500 ft (3,200 and 4,100 m). Within the city, the height of the various districts determines the social status of those who live there—the higher the district, the poorer the residents.

Which is the world's coldest capital?

Due to its high elevation, the world's coldest capital is Ulaanbaatar. The average annual temperature of the Mongolian capital is 28°F (−2°C), which does not, of course, mean that there is frost all year round. The low average temperature is due to the region's extremely cold winters. During the summer, daytime temperatures of 68°F (20°C) are not uncommon.

In Istanbul it is possible to look out from Europe across the Bosporus to Asia. The two continents are connected at this point by two suspension bridges.

Background: The Tanami Desert is one of Australia's six deserts. A termites' nest towers up among the sparse vegetation.

Tristan da Cunha

The most remote inhabited island group in the world, this island is located 1,990 miles (3,200 km) from South America and 1,740 miles (2,800 km) from Africa. A mere 300 or so people, split between eight families, live on the island, which has only been inhabited since 1810 and which is now a dependency of the British overseas territory of St Helena. The population of Tristan da Cunha owes its existence to a 19th-century British garrison established to prevent any attempt to free Napoleon from his place of exile on St Helena.

Special political status

What types of special political status are there?

Some regions of the Earth are not independent but nevertheless play a special role within the state to which they belong. This can be due to their geographical location, their legal status, their administrative structure, or their particular economic situation.

What is an exclave?

An exclave (Latin: "excluded portion") is a small part of national territory that is geographically separated from the rest of the nation in such a way that it can only be reached from the parent country by crossing the territory of another state. The term is not clearly defined, however. Islands are not considered exclaves while, on the other hand, Alaska is regarded as an exclave of the United States even though it can be reached from the United States by sea without the need to cross Canadian territory.

A view across the Tiber to St Peter's in the Vatican City.

Above: Willemstad, the capital of the Netherlands Antilles, is located on the Caribbean island of Curaçao but has the air of a small port in the Netherlands.

What is an enclave?

An enclave is a portion of one state that is completely surrounded by the territory of another. An exclave is not necessarily simultaneously an enclave. For example, Kaliningrad on the Baltic Sea is a Russian exclave but is not an enclave because it is surrounded

Politically dependent regions (a selection)		
Region	**Parent country**	**Political status**
Christmas Island	Australia	Australian external territory
Hong Kong	China	Special administrative region
Macau	China	Special administrative region
Faroe Islands	Denmark	Autonomous province within the Kingdom of Denmark
Greenland	Denmark	Autonomous province within the Kingdom of Denmark
French Guiana	France	French overseas department
Falkland Islands	United Kingdom	British overseas territory
Gibraltar	United Kingdom	British overseas territory
Bermuda	United Kingdom	British overseas territory
Cook Islands	New Zealand	Self-governing territory in free association with New Zealand
Netherlands Antilles	Netherlands	Autonomous region within the Kingdom of the Netherlands
Ceuta	Spain	Spanish exclave on the North African coast
Guam	United States	Unincorporated territory in American Oceania
Guantánamo Bay	United States	Region leased from Cuba
Athos	Greece	Autonomous monastic republic
Antarctic		Neutral region, territories claimed by various countries

by more than one country, namely Poland and Lithuania. An example of a real enclave would be Büsingen am Hochrhein, which belongs to Germany but is completely surrounded by Swiss territory.

Can whole states be enclaves?
Yes. The European microstate San Marino, for example, is completely surrounded by Italian territory and is therefore an enclave. Another example is Lesotho, which is surrounded by South Africa. Examples such as these are enclaves without being exclaves.

What special status do Hong Kong and Macau enjoy?
Hong Kong and Macau are special administrative regions of the People's Republic of China. Under the "One nation, two states" principle propagated by Chinese premier Deng Xiaoping (1904–1997), Hong Kong and Macau belong politically to China but are allowed to continue operating the free market economies that enabled Hong Kong in particular to become one of Asia's most important financial centers.

What is an overseas territory?
During the decolonization process, a number of overseas colonies were granted limited autonomy rather than full independence by their European rulers. Such regions are still administered by France (for example, French Polynesia), the United Kingdom (for example, the Falkland Islands), and the Netherlands (for example, the Netherlands Antilles) today.

The Panama Canal

In 1903 a zone was identified in Panama through which the canal of the same name was to be built. Thereafter this region was controlled by the United States, which financed and completed the construction of the canal over the subsequent years. After the canal was finished the United States retained control of the region—as an exclave within Panama—for nearly 100 years. The canal zone was not returned to the state of Panama until December 31, 1999. It is still a key conduit for international shipping.

The 50-mile (80-km) Panama Canal connects the Atlantic and Pacific oceans. A pilot has to be taken on board for the entire 12-hour navigation of the canal.

Colonies and colonial rulers

What is a colony?

The term "colony" is very old. In the ancient world it denoted the establishment of a new community (*colonia* means "settlement" in Latin) outside the settlers' original territory. In most cases the new settlement or colony retained economic or political links with the parent city. From the Middle Ages onwards, colonization generally meant military conquest and economic exploitation of the territories in question.

Present-day Sri Lanka was known as Ceylon until 1972. The island's colonial history goes back to 1512. The British were its last colonial rulers.

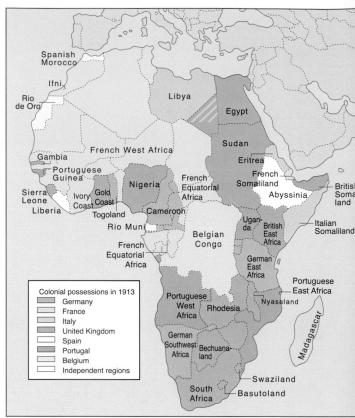

The race for Africa began in the last quarter of the 19th century. Within 50 years the entire continent had been carved up between the European powers.

Did colonial powers exist in the ancient world?

Yes. The Minoans, the Phoenicians, and the Greeks were all colonial rulers in areas outside their original sphere of influence. The biggest colonial power in antiquity was the Roman Empire, which at its zenith controlled almost the entire Mediterranean region. Furthermore, the Roman colonial model displayed all the typical features of modern colonialism: the dissemination of the colonial power's culture, frequent enslavement of the conquered peoples, and the economic exploitation of the colonies.

Did Europe's colonial history begin in the modern era?

No. Europe's leading maritime powers started to establish colonies during the Middle Ages. The republics of Genoa and Venice (both city-states) acquired numerous ports and fortresses in order to guarantee their trading routes and hegemony in the Mediterranean region. At the beginning of the 15th century the Portuguese started looking for the sea route around Africa in order to facilitate their lucrative spice trade with India. During the course of these voyages of discovery, the first Portuguese colonies were established on the west coast of Africa.

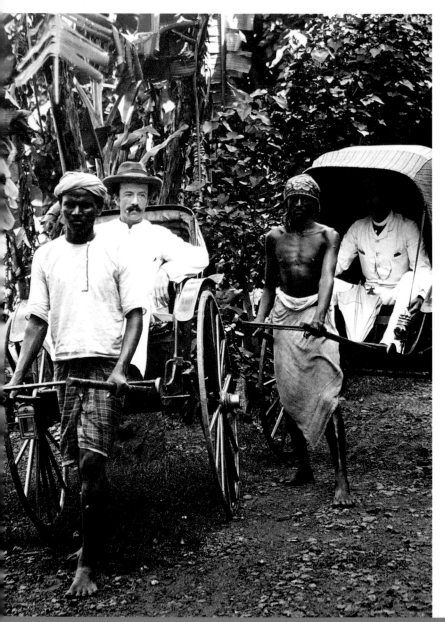

Major colonies

This table offers a mere snapshot of colonial history and is intended to illustrate the worldwide distribution of colonialism. It is by no means a comprehensive list of the territories controlled by these colonial powers.

Colony	Colonial power	Period	Present-day state
Belgian Congo	Belgium	circa 1880–1960	Democratic Republic of Congo
German New Guinea	Germany	1885–1914	various states in Oceania
German East Africa	Germany	1885–1919	Tanzania
New France	France	circa 1534–1763	Eastern Canada (Quebec)
French West Africa	France	1895–1958	West African states including Senegal, Niger, and Mali
Madagascar	France	1896–1960	Madagascar
French Indochina	France	1863–1954	Cambodia, Laos, Vietnam
Corsica	Genoa	1347–1768	part of France
Libya	Italy	1911–1951	Libya
Rhodes	Italy	1912–1947	part of Greece
Manchuria	Japan	circa 1905–1946	part of China
Dutch Guiana	Netherlands	1667–1815	Suriname, Guyana
Brazil	Portugal	1500–1822	Brazil
Angola	Portugal	1576–1975	Angola
Mozambique	Portugal	circa 1500–1975	Mozambique
Alaska	Russia	1799–1867	part of the United States
New Spain	Spain	1535–1822	Southwestern United States and Central America
Viceroyalty of Peru	Spain	1542–1821	large parts of South America
Spanish Morocco	Spain	1912–1956	northern Morocco
Egypt	United Kingdom	1882–1922	Egypt
British East Africa	United Kingdom	1895–1963	Kenya
Rhodesia	United Kingdom	1891–1944	Zambia and Zimbabwe
South Africa	United Kingdom	1806–1961	South Africa
New England colonies	United Kingdom	1609–1783	East Coast of the United States
Canada	United Kingdom	1763–1867	Canada
Ceylon	United Kingdom	1796–1948	Sri Lanka
British India	United Kingdom	1858–1947	India, Pakistan, and Bangladesh

What was the scramble for Africa?

During the age of imperialism (1870–1914) many European nations sought to increase their power and economic base by establishing overseas colonies. This led to the intensive colonization of Africa, which by 1914 was almost completely split between the United Kingdom, France, Italy, Germany, Belgium, the Netherlands, Spain, and Portugal. Only Abyssinia (present-day Ethiopia) managed to escape colonization.

Slaves were generally transported under inhumane conditions. This woodcut from 1860 shows the slave deck of the *Wildfire*, which carried slaves from Africa to America.

The struggle for independence

Although the Gaza Strip is part of autonomous Palestine, it is economically dependent upon Israel.

How many independent states are there in the world?

Generally speaking the term "independent states" refers only to those states recognized as independent by the United Nations. As of 2007 there were 193, of which 192 are members of the UN. The state that is not a member of the UN is the Vatican City.

Regions striving for independence

This list of regions striving for independence is by no means comprehensive. Many other regions, such as Tibet, the Basque Country, Kosovo, and Kurdistan, have not been included. The regions listed are those that currently appear to have the best prospects of achieving recognition as states over the next few years.

Abkhazia

Abkhazia is located on the north coast of the Black Sea and is officially a part of Georgia. The former "autonomous republic" of the USSR declared its independence in 1992 but this has not yet been recognized by the UN.

South Ossetia

This region of the Caucasus on Georgia's northern border declared itself independent in 1990. The UN continues to regard the territory as part of Georgia.

Transnistria

Transnistria is located in the east of Moldova on the border with Ukraine and has regarded itself as an independent state since 1991. It has not yet achieved international recognition as such, however.

Turkish Republic of Northern Cyprus

Since 1974 the Mediterranean island of Cyprus has been divided into Greek Cypriot (southern) and Turkish Cypriot (northern) parts. The Turkish part declared itself a sovereign state in 1983 but is only recognized as such by Turkey.

Somaliland

The Republic of Somaliland is located in northern Somalia in the Horn of Africa. It unilaterally declared independence from Somalia in 1991 and is de facto independent. The UN continues to regard Somaliland as part of Somalia, however.

Sahrawi Arab Democratic Republic

When the Spanish quitted Western Sahara in 1975, Morocco immediately occupied large parts of the territory. The following year the liberation movement POLISARIO proclaimed the region the Sahrawi Arab Democratic Republic. Although this has been accepted by many states, the UN has not yet achieved a consensus on the issue.

Palestinian autonomous territories

Large parts of the Palestinian autonomous territories (the West Bank and the Gaza Strip) are still under Israeli military rule. Control of these areas is due to pass to the Palestinian Authority in order to pave the way for independence.

When is a territory considered a state?

There is no universally accepted definition of the term although the "three elements doctrine" of Austrian philosopher Georg Jellinek (1851–1911) has gained widespread currency. This contends that a nation must possess its own territory and people (who regard themselves as the legitimate population of that country), and exercise power within its national territory.

Why are so many regions not recognized as states?

If a territory that regards itself as a state is not recognized as such by the majority of nations, it fails to satisfy the criteria of the "three elements doctrine." Recognition is sometimes withheld for

political or economic reasons, however, even when all three criteria for statehood are fulfilled.

Is Taiwan a state?

The Republic of China (generally known as Taiwan) effectively meets all the conditions of statehood. However, not only does it lay claim to the island of Taiwan, it also sees itself as the legitimate representative of the whole of China, and this places it at loggerheads with the People's Republic of China. The People's Republic of China pursues a so-called "one China policy" and therefore refuses to recognize a second Chinese state. Because the People's Republic will only deal with states that do not recognize Taiwan, the Republic of China has full diplomatic relations with only 24 nations. Since the Republic of China has been operating as an independent state since 1912, however, it has been included in this book as the 194th country.

The 14th Dalai Lama, Tenzin Gyatso, is a member of the Tibetan government in exile. Officially, Tibet has been a province of the People's Republic of China since 1959.

Below: Taipei, with a population of over 2.5 million, is the biggest city in the Republic of China (Taiwan).

Index

Picture credits

Corbis: 2 Jai, 4 Arthur Thèvenart (top left), Gavin Hellier/Jai (top right), 4/5 Grand Tour Collection (Hintergrund), Paul A. Souders (top center), 5 Steven Vidler/Eurasia Press (top left), Danny Lehman (top right), 6 Onne van der Wal (top left), Paul A. Souders (top right), 6/7 Jose Fuste Raga (big), Galen Rowell (top center), 7 John and Lisa Merrill (top left), Demetrio Carrasco/Jai (top right), 8 Jon Arnold/Jai (bottom), 8/9 Jose Fuste Raga, 9 Eberhard Streichan/zefa (top), 10 John and Lisa Merrill (top), 10 Herbert Kehrer/zefa (bottom), 11 Sergio Pitamitz, 12 Atlantide Phototravel (big), Tibor Bogner (bottom right), Jai (bottom left), 12/13 Guenter Rossen-bach/zefa (bottom), 13 Bertsch/zefa (top), Steven Vidler/Eurasia Press (bottom right), 16 Joachim Pfaff/zefa (bottom), 16/17 Jai, 18 Skyscan (top), Ladis- lav Janicek/zefa (bottom), 19 Doug Pearson/Jai, 20 Arctic-Images, 21 Atlantide Phototravel, 22 Atlantide Phototravel, Jorma Jaemsen/zefa (bottom), 23 Jorma Jaemsen/zefa, 26 Steven Vidler/Eurasia Press, 27 Gavin Hellier/Jai (bottom), 28 G. Richardson/Robert Harding World Imagery, 29 Manfred Mehlig/zefa (top), Bertsch/zefa (bottom), 30 Roy Rainford/Robert Harding World Imagery (top), Eberhard Streichan/zefa (big), 31 Atlantide Phototravel, 32 Louie Psihoyos (top), Doug Pearson/Jai (bottom), 33 Tibor Bogner, 34 John Miller/Robert Harding World Imagery (top), Eberhard Streichan/zefa (bottom), 36/37 Atlantide Phototravel, 37 Karl-Heinz Haenel, 38 Eberhard Streichan/zefa (top), Karl-Heinz Haenel (bottom), 39 Manfred Mehlig/zefa, Russell Young/Jai (small), 40 Jai, 41 Jai (bottom), 42 CardinaleStephane/Corbis Sygma, 43 H.P. Merten/Robert Harding World Imagery (top), Atlantide Phototravel (bottom), 44 Upperhall Ltd./Robert Harding World Imagery, 45 Thomas Rubbert/zefa, J.Hall/photo-cuisine (small), 46 Ladislav Janicek/zefa (top), Klaus Hackenberg/zefa (bottom), 48 Herbert Spichtinger/zefa, 49 Atlantide Phototravel (top), 50 Josè Fuste Raga/zefa, 51 Gavin Hellier/Robert Harding World Imagery (top), C. Voigt/zefa (bottom), 52 Jaques Langevin/Corbis Sygma, 54 Jai (top), David Turnley (bottom), 55 Archivo Iconografico, S.A., 56 Guenter Rossenbach/zefa (top), Richard Klune (bottom), 57 Demetrio Carrasco/JAI, 58 Josè Fuste Raga/zefa (left), JAI (right), 60 Fred de Noyelle /Godong (top), John and Lisa Merrill (bottom), 62 Puku/Grand Tour, 63 Alessandra Benedetti (top), Bob Krist (bottom), 64 Jeremy Horner, 65 Macduff Everton (top), 66 Robert Landau (bottom), 67 Grand Tour, 73 Josè Fuste Raga/zefa, 75 David C Poole/Robert Harding World Imagery, 76 Michele Falzone/Jai (big), Jitendra Prakash/Stringer/Reuters (bottom left), Jeffrey L. Rotman (bottom right), 77 Atlantide Photo-travel (big), J.P .Laffont/Sygma/Corbis (bottom left), J.P. Laffont/Sygma/Corbis (bottom right), 80 Kazuyoshi Nomachi (bottom left), 80/81 Kazuyoshi Nomachi, 81 Gideon Mendel (top), 82 Pascal Deloche/Godong (top), 82 Gavin Hellier/Jai (bottom), 83 Ed Kashi (bottom), 84 David Samuel Robbins, 85 Gèrard Degeorge, 86 Janet Wishnetsky, 87 Bruno Fert (top), David Samuel Robbins (bottom), 88 Nevada Wier (top), Keren Su (bottom), 89 Sybil Sassoon/Robert Harding World Imagery, 90 Pat O'Hara, 91 Caroline Penn (top), David Mdzinarishvili/Reuters (bottom), 92 Bob Krist, 93 Kaveh Kazemi (top), Kazuyoshi Nomachi (bottom), 94 Abilio Lope, 95 Reuters, 96 Ivan Vdovin/Jai, 97 J.P. Laffont/Sygma/Corbis, 98 Alison Wright, 99 Kazuyoshi Nomachi (top), 100 Reuters, 101 Christine Osborne (top), Dave G. Houser (bottom), 102 Jon Hicks, 103 Jeremy Horner (left), Jose Fuste Raga (right), 104 Arthur Thèvenart, 105 Sergio Pitamitz/Robert Harding World Imagery, 106 Michele Falzone/Jai (top), Gideon Mendel (bottom), 108 Gavriel Jecan, 109 Fernando Bengoechea/Beateworks (right), 112 Gideon Mendel, 113 Craig Tuttle, 114 Michael Busselle/Robert Harding World Imagery (top), Gavin Hellier/Jai (bottom), 115 Hamid Sardar, 116 Reuters, 117 Nir Elias/Reuters (top), Jon Arnold/Jai (bottom), 118 Goebel/zefa, 118/119 Bruno Levy/zefa, 119 Atlantide Photo-travel, 120 Kapoor Baldev/Sygma/Corbis (bottom), 121 Atlantide Phototravel, 122 Christian Kober/Robert Harding World Imagery (small), 122/123 Demetrio Carrasco/Jai, 123 Atlantide Phototravel, 124 Pierre Perrin/Sygma/Corbis, 125 Roulier/Turiot/photo-cuisine (top), Michele Falzone/Jai (bottom), 126 Simon Kwong/Reuters, 127 Jane Sweeney/Robert Harding World Imagery, 128 Bernd Kohlhas/zefa, 129 Jane Sweeney/Robert Harding World Imagery, 130 Bruno Morandi/Robert Harding World Imagery, 131 Atlantide Phototravel, 132 Steven Vidler/Eurasia Press, 123 Murat Taner/zefa, 134 Karl Kinne/zefa (top), Josè Fuste Raga/zefa (bottom), 136 Visuals Unlimited (top), Michele Falzone/Jai (bottom), 137 Lirio da Fonseca/Reuters, 138 James Randklev (big), Ellen Rooney/Robert Harding World Imagery (bottom left), Atlantide Phototravel (bottom right), 138/139 Tom Bean (bottom center), 139 Onne van der Wal (big), Barry Lewis (bottom left), Pearl Bucknall/Robert Harding World Imagery (bottom right), 142 Jose Fuste Raga (bottom), 142/143 Roger Ressmeyer, 143 Danny Lehman (top), 144 Andy Clark/Reuters (top), Jose Fuste Raga (bottom), 145 E. & P. Bauer/zefa (top), Jenny E. Ross (bottom), 146 Pearl Bucknall/Robert Harding World Imagery, 147 Rob Howard (top), Bettmann (bottom), 148/149 James Randklev, 149 Michael T. Sedam (top), 150 Joseph Sohm/Visions of America (top left), Keith Bedford/Reuters (bottom left), 151 Onne van der Wal, 152 Macduff Everton, 153 Keith Dannemiller/D70s (top), Atlantide Phototravel (bottom), 154 Reuters (top), Atlantide Phototravel (bottom), 155 W. Perry Conway, 156 Carl & Ann Purcell, 157 Alex Pena/Reuters (top), Galen Rowell (bottom), 158 Barry Lewis, 159 Atlantide Phototravel, 160 Danny Lehman, 161 Ellen Rooney/Robert Harding World Imagery (top), Patrick Robert/Sygma/Corbis (bottom), 162 Grafton Marshall Smith, 163 Lynn Goldsmith (top), Denis Anthony Valentine (bottom), 164 Philip Gould, 165 Tom Bean, 166 Nik Wheeler, 167 Bob Krist, 168 Earl & Nazima Kowall (top), Reinhard Eisele (bottom), 169 Dallas and John Heaton/Free Agents Limited, 170 Catherine Karnow (top), Fridmar Damm (bottom), 171 John Miller/Robert Harding World Imagery, 172 Nik Wheeler, 173 Blaine Harrington III, 174 Peter Adams/Jai (big), Robert Caputo/Kontributor (bottom left), Richard T. Nowitz (bottom right), 174/175 Philippe Giraud (bottom center), 175 Stuart Westmorland (big), Paolo Ragazzini (bottom left), Jon Hicks (bottom right), 178 Atlantide Phototravel (bottom), 178/179 Galen Rowell (big), 179 John and Lisa Merrill (top), 180 Peter Adams/Jai (top), Jay Dickman (bottom), 181 Peter Adams/Jai, 182 Enzo & Paolo Ragazzini (big), Jeremy Horner (small), 183 Robert Caputo/Kontributor, 184 Philippe Giraud, 185 Robert Caputo/Kontributor, 186 Arthur Morris (top), Paul Souders (bottom), 187 Fridmar Damm/zefa, 188 Alain Keler/Sygma/Corbis (top), Peter Adams/Jai (bottom), 189 Paulo Fridman, 190 Stuart Westmorland (top), Danny Lehman (bottom), 192 Richard T. Nowitz (big), Guido Cozzi/Atlantide Phototravel (small), 193 Dennis Degnan, 194 Paul Almasy (top), James Davis/Eye Ubiquitous (bottom), 195 Dave G. Houser, 196 Walter Bibikow/Jai (bottom left), Caroline Penn (bottom right), Martin Harvey (big), 196/197 James Sparshatt (bottom center), 197 Hoberman Collection (big), Roger de la Harpe (bottom left), Winfred Wisniewski/Frank Lane Picture Agency (bottom right), 200 Andrew Holbrooke (bottom), 200/201 Kazuyoshi Nomachi (big), 201 Torleif Svensson (top), 202 Eye Ubiquitous (top), Remi Benali 8u.), 203 Paul A. Souders, 204 Walter Bibikow/Jai, 205 Frans Lemmens/zefa, 206 Alessandro Saffo/Grand Tour (top), Riccardo Spila/Grand Tour (bottom), 207 Wolfgang Kaehler, 208 - 209 Jose Fuste Raga, 210 Jose Fuste Raga (top), Frans Lemmens/zefa (bottom), 211 Lynsey Addario, 212 Chris Hellier, 213 Gavin Hellier/Jai (top), Caroline Penn (bottom), 214 Atlantide Phototravel, 215 Gavin Hellier/Jai, 216 Olivier Martel, 217 Radu Sigheti/Reuters (top), Atlantide Phototravel (bottom), 218 Riccardo Spila/Grand Tour, 219 Nik Wheeler (top), Robert van der Hilst (bottom), 220 Christine Osborne (top), Theo Allofs (bottom), 221 Dave G. Houser, 222 Anthony Bannister, 223 Charles & Josette Lenars (top), Patrick Robert/Sygma/Corbis (bottom), 224 Reuters, 225 Sophie Elbaz/Sygma/Corbis (top), Martin Harvey (bottom), 226 Michel Gounot /Godong, 227 David C Poole/Robert Harding World Imagery (top), 228 Lucille Reyboz/Sygma (bottom), Atlantide Phototravel (top), 229 Atlantide Phototravel, 230 George Esiri/Reuters, 231 Reuters (top), Sophie Elbaz/Sygma/Corbis (bottom), 233 Martin Harvey, 234 James Sparshatt (top), 238 Paul Almasy, 239 Louise Gubb (top), Winfred Wisniewski/Frank Lane Picture Agency (bottom), 240 Caroline Penn (top), Annie Belt (bottom), 241 Tony Waltham/Robert Harding World Imagery, 242 Antony Njuguna/Reuters, 243 Martin Harvey/Gallo Images (top), Sharna Balfour/Gallo Images (bottom), 244 Ivan Vdovin/Jai, 245 Gallo Images (top), Finbarr O'Reilly/Reuters (bottom), 246 Kennan Ward, 247 Martin Harvey (top), Joe McDonald (bottom), 248 Aron Frankental/Gallo Images, 249 Pieter Hugo (top), Anthony Bannister/Gallo Images (bottom), 250 Howard Burditt/Reuters (top), Atlantide Phototravel (bottom), 251 Robert van der Hilst, 252 Stuart Westmorland (top), Chris Hellier (bottom), 253 Roger de la Harpe, 254 Michele Westmorland (big), Frans Lemmens/zefa (small), 255 Paul Souders, 256 Gideon Mendel, 257 Charles O'Rear (top), Hoberman Collection (bottom), 258 Jon Hicks (top), Steve & Ann Toon/Robert Harding World Imagery (bottom), 259 Hoberman Collection, 260 Earl & Nazima Kowall, 261 Gideon Mendel for The Global Fund, 262 Anders Ryman (bottom left), John Turner (bottom right), Bob Krist (big), 262/263 Charles & Josette Lenars (bottom center), 263 Sergio Pitamitz (top), Grand Tour Collection (bottom left), Grand Tour Collection (bottom right), 266 Grand Tour Collection (bottom), 266/267 Franz-Marc Frei (big), 267 Grand Tour Collection (top), 268 Paul Souders (top), © Neil Farrin/Jai (bottom), 269 Richard T. Nowitz (top), Bob Krist (bottom), 270/271 © Michele Falzone/Jai, 271 Claire Leimbach/Robert Harding (top), 272 Charles Philip Cangialosi (top), Theo Allofs/zefa (bottom), 273 Patrick Ward, 274 Bob Krist (big), Anders Ryman (small), 275 Bob Krist, 276 Bettmann (top), Doug Wilson (bottom), 278 Larry Dale Gordon/zefa (big), Charles & Josette Lenars (small), 279 Rob Howard, 280 Grand Tour Collection, 281 Neil Farrin/Jai, 282 Charles & Josette Lenars (top), Caroline Penn (bottom), 283 Wilfried Krecichwost/zefa, 284 John Turner (big), Richard Cummins (small), 285 Grand Tour Collection, 286 Ted Streshinsky (top), Neil Rabinowitz (bottom), 287 Matthieu Paley, 288 Tom Brakefield/zefa (big), Atlantide Phototravel (bottom left), Art Wolfe (bottom right), 288/289 Barry Lewis (bottom center), 289 Charles Mauzy (bottom left), 289 Paul A. Souders (big), 292 Hans Reinhard/zefa (bottom), 292/293 Fridmar Damm/zefa (big), 293 Harvey Lloyd (top), 294 Daniel J. Cox (top), Beat Glanzmann (bottom), 295 Winfried Wisniewski/zefa (left), Atlantide Phototravel (right), 296 Ann Johansson (big), Frans Lemmens/zefa (bottom left), Galen Rowell (bottom right), 297 Walter Bibikow/Jai (top), Bob Sacha (bottom right),298 Atlantide Phototravel (bottom), 299 (top), 300 Car Culture (top), 300/301 Ann Johansson, 301 Karen Kasmauski (top), 302 Phillippe Lissac/Godong, 303 Reuters, 304 Paul A. Souders, 304/305 Galen Rowell, 305 Stuart Westmorland, 310 John and Lisa Merrill (bottom), Bob Sacha (top), 311 Danny Lehman, 312 Michael Maslan, 313 Bettmann, 314 Peter Turnley (top)

Getty Images: 13 Altrendo Travel (bottom left), 17 Altrendo Panoramic (top), 23 altrendo nature (small), 24 Holger Leue/Lonely Planet Images, 25 Altrendo Travel, 27 Michael Rosenfeld (top), 35 Richard Passmore/Stone, 41 Rosemary Calvert (top), 47 DEA/C.Sappa, 49 Jonathan Smith (bottom), 53 De Agostini, 59 Rolf Richardson, 61 Atlantide Phototravel, 65 Antonio M. Rosario (bottom), 66 Daryl Benson/The Image Bank (top), 68 Gary John Norman (top), Martin Ruegner/The Image Bank (bottom), 69 Robert Everts, 70 Graham Lawrence, 71 Greg Elms/Lonely Planet Images (top), Peter Essick/Aurora (bottom), 72 Raul Touzon (top), G.R. Richardson (bottom), 74 DeAgostini (top), James L. Stanfield (bottom), 76/77 Hans Christian Heap (bottom), 83 Raveendran (top), 99 Hans Christian Heap (bottom), 107 Dorling Kindersley, 109 DAJ (left), 110 Steve Allen/Image Bank (top), Panoramic Images (bottom), 111 Steve Allen/Image Bank, 120 Tony Wheeler (top), 135 Robin Smith, 148 Sylvain Grandadam/Image Bank (bottom), 191 Antonio Scorza, 227 Issouf Sanogo (bottom), 232 Sylvain Grandadam, 234 Martin Van Der Belen/AFP (top), 235 Christophe Simon/AFP, 236 Michael Nichols/National Geographic, 237 Jean Pierre Kepseu/Panapress (top), Desirey Minkoh/AFP (bottom), 277 Tim Graham, Harvey Lloyd (bottom left), Berndt-Joel Gunnarsson (bottom right), 296/297 John Elk III (bottom center), 297 Steve Satushek (bottom left), 298/299 Torsten Blackwood, 306 John Elk III, 306/307 Astromujoff (big), 308 Steve Satushek (small), 308/309 Theo Allofs, 309 Hugh Sitton (top), 314/315 Jeremy Woodhouse, 315 P. Deliss/Godong

This is a Parragon Publishing Book
This edition published in 2008

Parragon Publishing
Queen Street House
4 Queen Street
Bath BA1 1HE, UK

ISBN: 978-1-4075-2528-0

Printed in Indonesia

German edition created and produced by: ditter.projektagentur GmbH; Editor: Ulrike Kraus; Picture editor: Claudia Bettray; Design: Sabine Vonderstein; Cartography: geo3, Martin Fimiarz 2007; Burga Fillery; Topography: SRTM 2000; Lithography: Fischer Graphische Produktionen GmbH

English-language edition produced by Cambridge Publishing Management Ltd; Project editor: Diane Teillol; Translator: Richard Elliot; Copyeditor: Anne McGregor; Layout: Julie Crane; Proofreader: Jan McCann; Indexer: Marie Lorimer